The Labor Supply for Lower-Level Occupations

Harold Wool
assisted by
Bruce Dana Phillips

The Praeger Special Studies program—utilizing the most modern and efficient book production techniques and a selective worldwide distribution network—makes available to the academic, government, and business communities significant. timely research in U.S. and international economic, social, and political development.

The Labor Supply for Lower-Level Occupations

PRAEGER SPECIAL STUDIES IN U.S. ECONOMIC, SOCIAL, AND POLITICAL ISSUES

Praeger Publishers   New York   Washington   London

Library of Congress Cataloging in Publication Data

Wool, Harold.
      The labor supply for lower-level occupations.

      (Praeger special studies in U.S. economic, social, and
political issues)
      Bibliography: p.
      1. Labor supply—United States.   2. Unskilled labor—
United States.   3. Labor supply—United States—History.
4. Employment forecasting—United States.   I. Phillips,
Bruce Dalton, joint author.   II. Title.
HD5724.W627   331.1'1   76-23378
ISBN 0-275-23160-7

PRAEGER PUBLISHERS
111 Fourth Avenue, New York, N.Y. 10003, U.S.A.

Published in the United States of America in 1976
by Praeger Publishers, Inc.

Printed in the United States of America

Much of the voluminous literature on occupations in the American labor force has focused on the higher-status occupations, particularly those involving the professionals, the managers, the technicians, and the highly skilled. This emphasis is understandable, since many of these occupations have been the growth occupations in our society: they are the ones which most young people aspire to and which call for the greatest investment in terms of formal education and specialized training. Conversely, research interest in low-status or low-wage occupations has been addressed mainly to the plight of workers engaged in these occupations—the high incidence of poverty among them, the apparent entrapment of many nonwhite workers and other minorities in these occupations, and their high turnover and unemployment rates. In this context, statistical indicators of the declining long-range trend in some of these occupations and of a movement of nonwhite workers out of them have been viewed as positive measures of social progress.

Yet, any realistic assessment of the structure of jobs in the contemporary American economy indicates that many millions of American workers still occupy jobs which do not fit into the preferred categories. The least desirable of these jobs have many of the following characteristics: low skill requirements, low status, limited training or advancement opportunities, boring or menial duties, poor working conditions, and—typically—low pay. Conceptually, these occupations tend to be the jobs of last resort for those workers who have no other viable choices in the labor market. Nevertheless, despite the march of technological progress, there is no evidence that these jobs will disappear, or wither away, in the near future.

Until now, these jobs have been disproportionately filled by disadvantaged population groups, particularly the blacks, the immigrants, the poor whites moving into our cities from farms or depressed rural areas, and the least educated. The point of departure for the present study is a premise that a confluence of social and demographic forces has contributed to a sharp reduction in these earlier sources of supply of low-level manpower. These include the continued increase in the educational attainment of the labor force; increased legal constraints on the number and types of immigrants; a slowdown in the volumes of rural outmigration; and evidence of a significant exodus of black workers from many of the least desirable occupations. Rising levels of family income, including social security and welfare payments, have also given many potential workers an effective choice of abstaining from conventional work activity entirely, in preference to accepting low-status, demeaning types of jobs.

Our second assumption is essentially optimistic: that, under assumed conditions of full or near-full employment, this same set of factors will continue to operate to further reduce the supply of workers for low-level jobs—at least, as these jobs are at present constituted and reimbursed. Particularly, we assume that there will be continued momentum in providing equality of opportunity to all segments of the population, in terms of both access to education and training and access to the better jobs. In addition, the predictable reduction in the number of new young entrants into the labor force in the decade of the 1980s will further deplete the potential labor supply for these jobs.

Based on these premises, our research design has provided for (1) the development of labor supply-relevent criteria for ranking and grouping of occupations, to systematically identify these lower-level occupations; (2) an analysis of past sources of labor supply for these occupations, with particular emphasis on trends in the 1960-70 decade; (3) an analysis of the relationship between labor supply variables and relative wages in these occupations; (4) projections of occupational labor supply and demand to 1985; and (5) an assessment of the nature of probable future labor market adjustments, as well as of possible policy implications.

Chapter 1 reviews a number of theoretical and empirical criteria for ranking of occupations and describes the methods followed in arriving at a status grouping of occupations for the present study.

Chapter 2 includes a broad historical review of the earlier sources of manpower for lower-level jobs, identifying the successive contributions of black workers, immigrants, farm-to-city migrants, and of other disadvantaged groups, in relation to the changing occupational needs of the economy.

Chapter 3 presents the results of a detailed analysis of 1960-70 trends in occupational labor supply, by such characteristics as age, sex, race, educational level, and nativity.

Chapter 4 analyzes the relationship between labor supply and relative wages in lower-level occupations, based on examination of aggregate 1960-70 trends and on a cross-sectional analysis of inter-area wage differences based on 1970 census data.

Chapter 5 presents projections of the expected labor force by broad occupational groups in 1980 and 1985, and compares these with projected trends in employment (or labor requirements) to identify potential surpluses or deficits under full-employment conditions.

Chapter 6 includes a more detailed analysis of labor force, employment, and wage trends in four low-level occupations—household maids, construction laborers, apparel operatives, and hospital attendants—to provide insights as to factors affecting past and prospective labor market adjustments in these occupations.

Chapter 7 summarizes our major findings and discusses their policy implications. The Appendix describes the procedures followed in adjustment of 1960-70 census occupational statistics for our trends analysis.

This study was conducted over a three-year period from July 1972 to June 1975, under a research grant to the National Planning Association by the Manpower Administration of the U.S. Department of Labor. An interim (phase 1) report, including Chapters 1-3 and a preliminary version of the manpower projections appearing in Chapter 5, was completed in October 1973. The second phase included the materials in Chapters 4, 6, and 7, as well as a revision and extension to 1985 of the manpower projections appearing in Chapter 5.

In the preparation of this study, the undersigned received invaluable support from his associate, Bruce D. Phillips, in the planning and design of the statistical analyses and projections, in the case study of construction laborers, and in the initial drafts of the Appendix and portions of Chapters 4-6. Chapter 6 also incorporates in summary form the results of separate case studies of domestic maids, by J. Peter Mattila, and of hospital attendants, by Neal Rosenthal and Dixie Sommers, both of which were prepared for this study.

We are particularly indebted to our colleague, Mark Kendall of the National Planning Association (NPA), for technical advice on the econometric cross-sectional analyses of occupational wage differentials, in Chapter 4, and on the occupational labor force projections, in Chapter 5.

We are indebted, too, to Margaret Takenaka, who served outstandingly as administrative assistant in the project, and to Y.J. Tien, Albert Gillespie, and Sally Wagley, who provided statistical support.

It would be difficult to identify all of the individuals who provided information or advice on various aspects of the study. The following individuals were particularly helpful: Stanley Greene, John Priebe, and Larry Suter of the Bureau of the Census; John Bregger, Denis Johnston, John Lukasiewiez, and John Stinson of the Bureau of Labor Statistics; Dr. Lazare Teper, research director of the International Ladies Garment Workers Union; Carl Pressland, economic consultant to the American Apparel Manufacturers Association; Marion Parsons, training director for the Laborers' International Union of North America; Alan Fechter of the Urban Institute; Robert Kahn, director of the Survey Research Center, University of Michigan; Otis Dudley Duncan, University of Michigan; and Ann Miller, University of Pennsylvania.

Stuart Garfinkel and Ellen Sehgal of the Office of Research and Development, Manpower Administration, U.S. Department of Labor, served successively as monitors of this study, and provided many helpful comments and suggestions.

Finally, our discussion of major policy issues, in Chapter 7, relied—in good measure—upon insights obtained from the concurrent assessment of policy implications conducted by the NPA Joint Committee on Lower-Level Jobs, chaired by Dr. William Bowen.

Since grantees conducting research and development projects under government sponsorship are encouraged to express their own judgment freely, this study does not necessarily represent the official opinion or policy of the Department of Labor. The author is solely responsible for the contents of this study.

CONTENTS

LIST OF TABLES AND FIGURE

xiv

The Labor Supply for Lower-Level Occupations

THE DIMENSIONS
OF LOW-STATUS WORK:
THEORY AND
MEASUREMENT

The existence of a broad hierarchy of occupations, closely linked to both social status and material rewards, has been a basic characteristic of human societies. Historically, the most unpleasant tasks in this hierarchy were assigned to an underclass, sharply defined in terms of caste or status. In preindustrial societies, the heavy unskilled labor of the most onerous type, as well as the menial housekeeping duties, were often performed by slaves or bondmen or by forced labor levies upon the peasant population.

In modern industrial societies, the substitution of mechanical power and machinery has reduced, but not eliminated, the requirement for heavy physical labor and has altered the nature of many of the other unpleasant duties previously performed by forced labor. Technological advance has also been accompanied by a great proliferation of occupational specialties. The immense variety of goods and services and the high degree of division of labor characteristic of modern industry have resulted in multifold increases in the number of occupational designations. The most comprehensive cataloguing of these occupations, the U.S. Labor Department's Dictionary of Occupational Titles (DOT), includes definitions of more than 35,500 occupational titles in its third edition.[1]

This process of occupational specialization has complicated the task of defining occupational strata or ladders, and, hence, of identifying the characteristics of the social groups performing these activities. It has, in fact, led some scholars to question the validity of any single vertical scaling of occupations, in terms of status or relative desirability. Nevertheless, faced with overwhelming evidence that occupations do vary widely in monetary rewards, in social status, and in the inherent pleasantness or unpleasantness of the work and its surroundings, social scientists from diverse disciplines have devoted considerable effort to studies of the factors contributing to occupational differentiation in our society.

The systems of occupational classification and ranking developed by various investigators have varied widely depending upon the criteria employed and the intended uses. It is possible to group these broadly into two categories: (1) systems based on analysis of occupational duties and qualifications, and (2) systems based on occupational rewards, whether the latter are defined in monetary or nonmonetary terms. These alternative systems are discussed in the following sections, to assess their relevance and utility for the purposes of this study. Later in the chapter, an alternative system for occupational stratification is presented.

RANKINGS BASED ON OCCUPATIONAL DUTIES AND QUALIFICATIONS

A central task of occupational analysis and classification has been to identify and group together, as single occupations, those jobs which are substantially similar in terms of work performed and in the qualifications needed to perform this work. The degree of specification of occupations in various occupational classification systems has varied widely, depending upon the uses intended and other considerations. For example, the DOT has been designed for operational use by the public employment service and other labor market agencies, in matching individuals and jobs. This has dictated a very detailed cataloguing of occupations and job titles. Comprehensive statistical data on the distribution of the labor force based on this classification are however not available.

The Census Bureau, on the other hand, has employed a much more abbreviated list of detailed occupations, for use in decennial censuses and in its monthly sample labor force surveys, notably, 297 occupations in the 1960 census and 441 in the 1970 census. In the census occupational scheme, for example, many thousands of titles for specific semiskilled operative jobs, which are unique to a given industry or function, have been broadly categorized as "operatives, not elsewhere classified," although tabulated separately by industry group. This coarse-grained approach to occupational classification, characteristic of most national population censuses, has been necessitated in large part by practical data-gathering considerations. Information on an individual's occupation obtained from household surveys is too imprecise to permit use of a very detailed occupational classification scheme, particularly if derived from responses of persons other than the individual worker. Moreover, the past uses

made of the census occupational data, typically for broad economic
and sociological studies, have placed greater emphasis on analysis
of broader occupational groupings rather than on the detail for specific
occupations.

Inherent in the job content approach to occupational analysis,
under either the DOT or census classification systems, has been an
effort to group and rank the various occupations in broader classes
based on certain common functional characteristics, and on their
relative complexity. Until 1940, the principal criterion followed in
the grouping of occupations for the decennial U.S. censuses had been
industrial affinity rather than skill level. With the notable exception
of certain white-collar occupations, such as professionals and clerical
workers, the detailed census occupations had been grouped by broad
industry categories. Under this approach, for example, managers,
as well as laborers, employed in manufacturing industries were
classified separately from those performing similar duties in transportation or trade.

With the 1940 census, a revised scheme of occupational grouping
was introduced by the Census Bureau, based in large part on the work
of Alba M. Edwards—for many years the census expert on occupational statistics. The rationale for these new occupational groupings,
as originally developed by Edwards, was "to bring together into an
occupationally homogeneous group all of the workers belonging to the
same socio-economic class, with but minor regard to the particular
occupations they pursue or to the particular part of the industrial
field in which they work."[2] The original Edwards socioeconomic
groups consisted of the following six broad classes:

1. professional persons
2. proprietors, managers, and officials (farmers; wholesale
   and retail dealers; other)
3. clerks and kindred workers
4. skilled workers and foremen
5. semiskilled workers
6. unskilled laborers (farm laborers; laborers, except farm;
   servant classes).

The grouping, it will be evident, made a broad distinction between the white-collar and blue-collar occupations, and in accordance
with conventional wisdom placed the former at the top of the occupational hierarchy. The grouping, as a whole, was recognized by
Edwards to be a hybrid, which gave weight to both social status and
economic criteria. Empirically, educational attainment (years of
school completed) was cited by Edwards as a guide to social status,
and annual income, as a measure of economic status. Thus, Edwards

justified the ranking of clerical workers above skilled craftsmen on
the ground that the social factor, as reflected in higher educational
attainment of clerical workers, outweighed the economic factor, as
reflected in the higher median earnings of the craftsmen.

One of the features of the Edwards classification that has special
interest for our present study was an attempt to group manual workers
into three broad skill-level categories, based on such considerations
as length of training, degree of judgment and of manual dexterity,
ability to work with limited supervision, and degree of responsibility
for valuable product and equipment. The skilled workers encompassed
most of the conventional craft occupations, mechanics and foremen,
as well as policemen and firemen. Included among the semiskilled
group, in addition to the bulk of the operative occupations, were certain intermediate-level service workers, such as barbers, guards,
housekeepers, practical nurses, and hospital attendants. At the bottom
of the occupational ladder, based on these criteria, was the broad
class of unskilled workers, including farm laborers, nonfarm laborers
(including miners) and the servant classes—the latter including such
workers as domestics, waiters, cooks, charwomen, janitors, and
porters.

The classification of occupations by major occupational groups
adopted by the Census Bureau in 1940, although largely retained since
then, has deviated in a number of respects from that formulated by
Edwards. The census groupings have continued to reflect the distinction between white-collar and blue-collar occupations. However,
within the latter category, the Census Bureau has departed from
Edwards's original attempt to broadly distinguish among occupations
on the basis of a formal skill-level hierarchy—notably in the treat-
ment of workers in service-type occupations. These occupations,
rather, have been treated functionally and consolidated into two
separate service worker groups—one for private household workers,
the other for all other nonprofessional service workers, irrespective
of skill level. Manual workers, other than service workers, have
moreover been grouped under occupationally descriptive titles—
"craftsmen, foremen, and kindred workers"; "operatives and kindred
workers"; "laborers and kindred workers"—rather than in terms of
an explicit statement of skill level.

Since these census groups were developed pragmatically to serve
a wide range of possible interests, it was inevitable that they would
not prove ideal for any specific research or analytical design—whether
for economic analysis of wage structures or for studies of class structures in our society. Both economists and sociologists have been
particularly critical of the heterogeneous nature of certain of the major
occupational groupings. For example, the census group identified as
"managers and officials, except farm" combines, in one category, the

highest-ranking governmental and corporate officials with operators
of hot dog stands. Similarly, the census group for "service workers,
excluding household workers" ranges from police detectives, marshals,
and sheriffs to charwomen and bootblacks.

The decision by the government statisticians to avoid an explicit
occupational ranking by skill level was probably influenced by a number of considerations, not least of which were the obvious limitations
of the occupational information obtainable under mass census procedures. In part, too, it was undoubtedly influenced by the inherent
difficulties of any rank ordering of occupations, based on available
job content criteria. Increasingly, occupational analysts had become
aware of the multidimensional character of occupational duties. Different occupations entailed exercise of different types of human abilities (mental, physical, mechanical), as well as different orders of
difficulty. Any attempt to convert these into a single ordinal scale in
ascending order of skill was likely to be based in part on subjective
judgment factors and therefore was rendered vulnerable to criticism.

These same considerations have influenced the structuring of
occupations under the <u>Dictionary of Occupational Titles</u>. The first
edition of the DOT, published in 1939, included groupings of occupations analogous to the major census groups, and were based generally
on similarity of work performed or on technical job content. These
jobs were in turn arranged within each functional category in order
of skill level, that is, skilled, semiskilled, or unskilled. The third
edition, issued in 1965, replaced this skill-level grouping with new
six-digit code numbers which classified jobs, not only in accordance
with earlier functional job content criteria, but in terms of the worker
traits or characteristics associated with each job. This supplemental
code is designed to reflect the complexity of each job as it relates to
three broad dimensions, data, people, and things. Thus the fourth
digit of the code number (relating to data) ranks each job in order of
difficulty in handling of data, from "comparing" and "copying," at
the lowest levels, to "synthesizing" and "coordinating," at the highest.
Similarly, the order of difficulty under the sixth digit (relating to
things) ranges from "handling," at the bottom, to "setting up" and
"precision working," at the top.

In addition to this coding system, worker trait profiles have been
developed for some 14,000 defined job titles, in which groups of jobs
are described under a series of more specific worker traits, including
the general educational development (GED), specific vocational preparation (SVP), and physical demands required of the worker.[3]

It will be evident that this multidimensional classification scheme
complicates any simple hierarchical approach to occupational groupings. The rationalization for this departure is provided by Sidney

Fine, an occupational psychologist who played a major role in the revision of the DOT:

> Although the skilled, semi-skilled and unskilled break-
> down may have been useful and may have had some
> meaning up until about the turn of the century before
> modern technology began to dominate the job picture,
> it is inaccurate and irrelevant today. To replace it,
> there is the concept that people function on a continuum
> of difficulty from the simple to the complex and that the
> patterns of functioning are diverse. For example, a
> worker may function on a simple level in relation to
> Things, on a complex level with regard to Data, and on
> an intermediate level with regard to People. In an
> analysis of 4,000 jobs, 72 possible and 45 actual com-
> binations were found. [4]

Despite these reservations, several investigators have attempted to use the body of occupational analysis data incorporated in the third edition of the Dictionary of Occupational Titles for analysis of occupational structures. Thus, James Scoville undertook a comprehensive restructuring of the census list of detailed occupations, based on DOT job content criteria, on the premise that the existing census socioeconomic grouping of occupations was poorly adapted to economic analysis of wage structures and labor mobility and for related studies of labor supply and demand. For this purpose, Scoville defined 18 job families, based on broad functional groupings, and arranged each of the census occupations in five skill-level groups within the appropriate job families. To develop the latter ranking, Scoville used—as a point of departure—a worker traits analysis of a sample of 4,000 DOT job titles developed by staff of the U.S. Employment Service (USES), which included estimates of educational and vocational training time requirements for each job. Scoville regrouped the DOT occupations into about 200 census occupations and derived average values, or rankings, for the latter based on these criteria. The results obtained from this procedure were admittedly crude in a number of respects. The element of subjective judgment entailed in the initial USES staff assignment of values to jobs, in terms of educational aptitude requirements, was further compounded by the task of assigning each of 4,000 DOT occupations to about 200 census occupational categories. As a result, Scoville was compelled on a judgmental basis to reassign a number of occupations to more appropriate skill levels than those derived by his use of the worker traits data. [5]

In order to forge a more reliable statistical bridge between the DOT and the census occupational classifications, the Office of

Management and Budget initiated a pilot study under which the occupational returns from a one-month sample of the Census Bureau's Current Population Survey, for October 1966, were recoded on the basis of the DOT. An initial analysis of these data, by Ann Miller, has included a distribution of GED requirements of occupations of men and women in the experienced civilian labor force for each of the DOT major occupational groups and for selected subgroups.[6]

Unfortunately, similar tabulations expressed in terms of the census occupational classifications have not been derived from this study, thus precluding any direct linkage between this possible scaling criterion and the variety of other characteristics which are available only in terms of the census occupational classifications. Inspection of the derived GED requirements for various occupational groups also raises serious questions as to the usefulness of the GED criterion as shown in the DOT. To illustrate, the median GED requirement computed for the protective service occupations group, including such jobs as policeman, fireman, and guard, is shown as 3, equivalent to an eighth-grade educational level. This is about the same as that computed for female domestic service workers and lower than that shown for men in farming and allied occupations. It is difficult to reconcile these scalings with other information concerning the relative educational demands of these occupations.

More fundamentally, our examination of efforts to derive a skill-level ranking of occupations based on job content analysis and on estimates of the length of formal education or training required has illustrated certain inherent difficulties in this approach. The available data suggest that although the education and training requirements criterion can readily differentiate between the most skilled and the least skilled occupations, they have limited explanatory power in differentiating among many middle-level and lower-level occupations which do, in fact, appear to differ significantly in relative attractiveness and in the rewards provided. It is evident that many other variables related to the intrinsic nature of the work and the work environment and not directly correlated to training time criteria are relevant to determination of occupational status.

For this reason, most studies of occupational stratification have relied on use of reward criteria rather than on functional job content analyses.

RANKINGS BASED ON OCCUPATIONAL REWARDS

The occupational reward criteria followed by various investigators in assessing relative job value or desirability have, understandably, varied depending upon their respective disciplines and research objectives. Thus, from Adam Smith on, most economists—while recognizing that occupations differ in both pecuniary and nonpecuniary rewards—have tended to rank occupations in terms of the value assigned to these occupations by the marketplace, as reflected in differential wage rates or income streams.

The focus of sociologists in their studies of occupational hierarchies has been primarily related to their interest in social class structure and social mobility. Social status or prestige rankings of occupations have been developed for this purpose.

Finally, social psychologists and those in allied behavioral science fields have had a primary research interest in identifying those aspects of work and of the working environment which contribute to personal job satisfaction or dissatisfaction, that is, in meeting human wants, broadly defined. We shall briefly discuss below the contributions—both theoretical and empirical—stemming from this diverse body of literature.

The Theory of Occupational Wage Differentials

The cause of inequality of wages among different classes of workers has long been a focal point of interest for economists and has in turn directed their attention to the factors influencing supply, as well as demand, for workers in the various occupations. In a classic chapter devoted to this theme in The Wealth of Nations, Adam Smith attributed the wide observed differentials in earnings from different occupations to two sets of circumstances: first, those inherent in the nature of the occupation itself and, secondly, those attributable to constraints upon a fully competitive market. Occupations differed inherently in the investment of time and cost required to qualify in them, as well as in many other respects. Among the latter, Smith identified such factors as the physical ease or hardship of the work, its "cleanliness or dirtiness," the social respect or "honorableness" accorded the occupation, the degree of responsibility entailed, the regularity of employment, and the probability of success or failure. The normal structure of occupational wage differentials, under conditions of competitive equilibrium, thus reflected "the whole of the advantages and disadvantages" of different occupations. These were modified, however, by various institutional constraints on the free movement of labor, such as apprenticeship or licensing regulations, as well as by short-term fluctuations in demand for specific occupations or industries.[7]

As in so many other aspects of economic thought, this initial formulation by Smith served as a point of departure for the work of succeeding generations of economists. In principle, Smith's formulation implied a continuum, in which each occupation could be matched with all other occupations based on its respective advantages and disadvantages and where the interaction of supply and demand would tend to equalize the whole of the advantages and disadvantages of the different types of work in a particular labor market. This analysis could not however be fully reconciled with the realities of the nineteenth century wage structure; it was apparent that many of the most undesirable occupations—those involving heavy and dirty work and commanding little social respect—received the lowest wages, while many of the professions which commanded high prestige and high intrinsic interest appeared to receive a higher wage differential than would appear to be justified by their additional training investment.

To explain this phenomenon, John Stuart Mill advanced an explanation based on the existence of rigid class boundaries which served to restrict access to the more desirable occupations. This concept of an occupational hierarchy was further developed by J.E. Cairnes in his theory of noncompeting groups, in which he described the broad occupational strata as follows:

> What we find, in effect, is, not a whole population competing indiscriminately for all occupations, but a series of industrial layers, superimposed on one another, within each of which the various candidates for employment possess a real and effective power of selection; while those occupying the several strata are, for all purposes of effective competition, practically isolated from each other. We may perhaps venture to arrange them in some such order as this: first, at the bottom of the scale there would be the large group of unskilled or nearly unskilled labourers, comprising agricultural labourers, labourers engaged in miscellaneous occupations in towns; or acting in attendance on skilled labour. Secondly, there would be the artisan groups. . . . The third layer would contain producers and dealers of a higher order . . . engineers, chemists, opticians, watchmakers, and others of the same industrial grade . . . above them would be a fourth, comprising persons still more favourably circumstanced . . . learned professions, etc . . . [8]

Alfred Marshall, in commenting on the occupational structure of British industry towards the close of the nineteenth century, suggested

that the earlier formulations by Mill and Cairnes, based on a rigid
class stratification, had been undermined by the process of job breakdown and specialization: "We cannot any longer regard different occupations as distributed among four great planes; but we may perhaps
think of them as resembling a long flight of steps of unequal breadth,
some of them being so broad as to act as landing stages. Or even
better still we might picture to ourselves two flights of stairs, one
representing the 'hard handed industries' and the other 'the soft handed
industries,' because the vertical division between these two is in fact
as broad and as clearly marked as the horizontal division between
any grades. "9

Under Marshallian theory, the net marginal product of each class
of labor, resulting from the interaction of both supply and demand
factors, determined its wages. The fact that work of a disagreeable,
or dirty, nature was often also the lowest-paid work was attributed
by Marshall to the relatively large supply of labor for this type of
work which, in turn, reduced the incentive for employers to ration-
alize such jobs. "Hence arises the paradoxical result that the dirtiness of some occupations is a cause of the lowness of the wages earned
in them. Few employers find that this dirtiness adds much to the
wages they would have to pay to get the work done by skilled men of
high character working with improved appliances; and so they often
adhere to old methods which require only unskilled workers of but
indifferent character and who can be hired for low (time-) wages, because they are not worth much to any employer. "10

From this brief discussion, the theoretical model of the occupational wage structure developed by the nineteenth-century economists,
may be summarized as follows. The dependent variable of interest
to the economist was relative wages. Under competitive equilibrium
conditions, the supply of labor for different classes of occupations
determined the normal (long-run) structure of occupational wage differentials. The major occupational supply factors (or independent
variables) were (1) training and educational investment, and (2) nonpecuniary factors affecting preference or tastes for different occupations (working conditions, inherent job interest, social status, and
so on). To varying degrees, all of these theories also recognized
imperfections in the market for workers in various skill categories
due to a combination of supply constraints; that is, (1) the existence
of noncompeting groups based on class structure and/or on unequal
access to education and training opportunities, and (2) various other
institutional constraints limiting the free access of labor to various
occupations, whether stemming from governmental regulations, from
the operation of guilds or unions, or other factors. Further, since
labor supply tended to be relatively inelastic in the short term, fluctuations of wages in particular occupations were largely determined

by fluctuations in demand for the various classes of workers, as reflected in their net marginal product.

While not completely abandoning the major elements of the classical theory, contemporary economists, relying upon a wide range of empirical studies, have increasingly questioned the relevance of classical theory in explaining observed patterns of wage differentials, as well as other aspects of labor market behavior. They have noted that the emergence of large-scale collective bargaining and of internal labor markets, as well as increased governmental intervention in the wage setting process, have all tended to institutionalize wage structures to a degree not anticipated by the classical economist—as evidenced, for example, by the persistence of wide interindustry disparities in rates of pay for given occupations in the same labor market. Moreover, mobility of workers in response to differential wages has been restricted by such factors as seniority and pension rights, by various constraints on free entry into occupations, and by the workers' lack of full labor market information.

The concept of noncompeting labor markets, originally developed by Mill and Cairnes in the nineteenth century, has also been applied, in more modern form, to explain the operation of the labor market in urban ghetto areas. A neo-Cairnesian concept of the segmented labor market, advanced by Francis Edgeworth in the 1920s, was further developed during the 1960s by Peter Doeringer, Michael Piore, Barbara Bergmann, Bennett Harrison, and by a number of other economists. This theory postulates that, as a result of pervasive discrimination, certain categories of workers in the labor force, such as black ghetto residents, have been mainly confined to a secondary labor market, consisting of the least desirable jobs—jobs with such characteristics as low wages, low status, unpleasant working conditions, little or no promotion opportunities, and unstable employment patterns. The de facto exclusion of most black workers from mainstream jobs under this theory has resulted in an overcrowding of workers into the less desirable jobs and has served to depress wage rates in these jobs. Moreover, among those whose options are confined to this category of jobs, exclusion has induced a lifestyle antagonistic to stable employment. Similar reasoning has also been used to explain observed adverse wage differentials for other groups subject to systematic labor market discrimination, such as women.[11]

However, despite a considerable volume of literature on the dual or segmented labor market, this concept has not yet been adequately subjected to rigorous empirical analysis. Studies by economists which have attempted to distinguish between good and bad jobs have usually tended to treat low-wage jobs as synonymous with bad jobs, in the absence of other readily quantifiable occupational characteristics. Alternatively, use has at times been made of classification schemes

developed by sociologists and social statisticians for somewhat different purposes, as discussed below.

Occupations and Social Status

Sociological interest in the study of occupational stratification
has stemmed in part from the theories of Karl Marx and his nineteenth-century followers, who focused on the emerging class of industrial workers as the vehicle of social revolution. The unique feature
of the new industrial system, for Marx, was the separation of the
worker from ownership of the means of production and from control
over the productive process. Analysis of the impact of industrialization and of the accompanying division of labor upon the occupational/
social class structure thus became a central theme in early Marxist
writings. Other non-Marxist sociologists, including Max Weber and
Emile Durkheim, also contributed to the study of work roles and of
occupations, particularly in relation to emerging concepts of social
classes and social prestige strata. Contemporary sociologists, while
recognizing that other variables also affect social stratification, have
continued to rely heavily upon occupational position as the prime de-
terminant of social status.[12] The central role of occupational position
for sociological analysis has, in turn, prompted a search for suitable
criteria for a social status ranking of occupations.
    The strong influence of sociological theory upon occupational
classification practices is illustrated by the efforts by Edwards, as
well as earlier government statisticians, to establish a socioeconomic
grouping of occupations as a frame of reference for analysis of broad
occupational trends in the United States. This scheme was, as discussed above, only partially adopted in the official structuring of
census occupations by major occupational groups which has been in
effect since 1940.
    In the face of the obvious limitations of the official census occupa-
tional groupings, sociologists began experimenting with more objective approaches to ranking occupations by social status, based on the
use of occupational prestige surveys. The unique feature of the prestige yardstick is the effort to obtain a single ranking or hierarchy of
occupations based not on an analysis of specific attributes of these
occupations, but rather on the composite judgment of a population
cross section in which each respondent compares the relative standing
or social desirability of each of a particular list of occupations or job
titles with that of the other occupations on the list. Experimentation
with this survey technique in the United States began with a pioneering
inquiry by George S. Counts in 1925, followed by a series of such

surveys which differed considerably in sample size and design, in occupational coverage, and in the questions used to elicit prestige ranking. Despite these differences in methodology, the resulting overall rankings have been found by some observers to be remarkably close to invariant over a period of several decades, and—to a considerable extent—independent of variation in the composition of the particular respondent groups. Moreover, comparisons of similar surveys in other countries indicated substantial consistency of rankings in a wide range of countries.[13]

One of the major limitations of the prestige survey method, however, is that this technique cannot readily be applied to the full spectrum of occupations in the labor force. It has not been practicable to include in any survey the full list of 300 or more separate occupational designations included in the censuses of population nor—obviously—the many thousands of more specific job titles by which these occupations are commonly known. To illustrate, one of the most comprehensive prestige surveys conducted in the United States was that conducted by the National Opinion Research Center (NORC) in 1947. This survey covered a total of 90 titles of which only 45 could be reasonably matched with detailed occupations as reported in the 1950 census. Efforts have been made to fill this gap by linkage of results of successive surveys. Paul Siegel thus developed consolidated prestige ratings, expressed in a standard metric, for all of the detailed 1960 census occupations. He was, however, careful to note that, because of variations in occupational titles, only a "poor" match could be achieved for nearly one-half of the census occupations.[14] Moreover, careful reviews of prestige survey rankings have indicated that the high overall correlations achieved are due mainly to consistency in the placing of occupations at the higher and lower extremes of the scale, with much larger deviations in ranking of the broad middle-level group of occupations.[15]

To meet the need for a social class ranking system or index which could readily be applied to all occupations in the labor force, Otis Duncan developed an index of socioeconomic status (SES) in the early 1960s. The index, derived from 1950 census data on male workers, is based on a weighting of two variables: education and income. Education is measured on the basis of the percentage of male workers in each occupation with four years of high school or more; income, based on the percentage of males in each occupation with incomes of $3,000 or more in 1949. A multiple regression between NORC prestige ratings for 45 occupations, comparable to census occupations in their titles, and these two variables (standardized for age differentials) had produced a correlation coefficient of .91. Based on this empirical finding, the two variables, weighted by their respective coefficients of regression, were then used to derive an SES scale for each detailed 1950 census occupation.[16] A similar method was also developed by Census Bureau staff to derive socioeconomic status scores for each occupation.[17]

The Duncan index, when combined for major census occupational groups, has tended to confirm the broad ranking implicit in the aforementioned Edwards occupational groupings: professional, technical, and kindred workers receive the highest SES score, followed by nonfarm managers, while nonfarm laborers and domestics receive the lowest scores. At the same time, the Duncan scores, as well as similar prestige or social status rankings have all indicated a wide variation of ratings for individual occupations within these broad occupational groups. For this reason, extensive use has been made of the Duncan ratings, or similar scales, in lieu of the standard census groupings, in studies designed to measure status of individuals, where information on their specific occupation is available.

Despite its wide use, some limitations of the Duncan index should be noted. First, since occupational prestige has been normally measured for men, the census statistics used by Duncan in deriving SES ranks related to male workers only. Such data are not necessarily representative of occupational status for those occupations predominately staffed by women. Secondly, the income data used by Duncan in his formula refer to money income of men in 1949. These census data have many limitations as a measure of differential occupational earnings because they included part-year, as well as full-year, workers and because of the importance of income in kind in certain occupations, such as farming. Finally, the numerous revisions in detailed census occupational classifications since 1950 have complicated any direct application of the Duncan scale to the later (1970) census data.

More fundamentally, the prestige measure—as well as the SES index—suffer from some conceptual difficulties when applied to studies of labor market behavior. On the one hand, the partial correlation between prestige and earnings conforms to expectations, derived from economic theory, that those occupations which are most highly valued in market terms also tend to command greater prestige—both because they reflect possession of a relatively scarce skill with high demand in society and because the resulting high pay makes such occupations more attractive. On the other hand, the partial correlation of prestige or status with education—holding income constant—is subject to varying interpretations, not clearly developed in the sociological literature. Edwards, in his rationale for use of both of these criteria, formulated the relationship as follows: "Education is a very large factor in the social status of workers, and wage or salary income is a very large factor in their economic status."[18]

Other explanations of this observed relationship are, however, equally plausible. For example, given the fact that relative income, alone, provides an admittedly imperfect measure of the true market value of different occupations (because of the many nonmarket factors influencing the wage structure and because of the technical limitations of available income and wage statistics), it is possible that the education variable mainly reflects some of the nonmonetary factors which make some occupations inherently more desirable than others, such as differences in fringe benefits and job security, long-term income opportunities, physical working conditions, social work environment, and the intrinsic nature of the work itself. These work values have been explored, in depth, by a number of behavioral scientists, as described in the following section.

Occupational Differentials in Job Satisfaction

In contrast to the studies of economists and sociologists, who have attempted to differentiate among occupations based on some measure of social rewards—whether defined in terms of money wages or of social status or prestige—a number of behavioral scientists have attempted to assess the relative desirability of employment in different occupations based on its psychological impacts upon the individual worker. They have, in fact, attempted—mainly through job satisfaction survey techniques—to develop a latter-day felicific calculus, to measure the full stream of satisfactions and dissatisfactions associated with the work experience, in all its dimensions. In the process, a large body of theoretical literature has also emerged, which may be broadly defined as work motivation and job satisfaction research.

As in the study of social status of occupations, some of the theoretical origins of job satisfaction research can be found in Marxian theory which postulated that the objective separation of industrial workers from control over the means of production would have as its subjective counterpart a deep-seated alienation of wage workers from the industrial system in which they were entrapped. Although this theoretical framework has been reflected in some of the later literature on worker alienation, much of the empirically-based research on job satisfaction since the 1920s has in fact been fostered by management itself, with the aim of development of personnel policies conducive to improved morale, reduced turnover, increased productivity, and related management objectives. The scope of interest in worker satisfaction issues is suggested by the fact that some 2,000 empirical studies of job satisfaction have been catalogued in the United States

since the 1920s. These have ranged from studies of workers in particular establishments or occupations to surveys of national cross-
sections of the working population.[19] The methodology generally used
has been to query workers on the degree of their overall satisfaction
or dissatisfaction with their job, as well as to probe on specific aspects of their work or work environment which they found either satis-
fying or dissatisfying. These studies have often correlated the job
satisfaction responses with related information on worker and job
characteristics, job changing plans, work interests, generalized psychological attitudes, and—to a much more limited extent—with certain
work behavior patterns, for example, turnover, absenteeism, productivity.

A central premise in much of the research literature on job
satisfaction is that, quite apart from the economic rewards for work,
the intrinsic nature of the work has a great influence upon the degree
of satisfaction derived from different types of jobs. When viewed from
this perspective, work is valued by the individual not merely or ex-
clusively as a source of income, but in terms of its contribution to an
individual's self-esteem, social status, and sense of fulfillment. One
formulation, by Frederick Herzberg, distinguishes between extrinsic
and intrinsic job factors. Extrinsic factors, such as inadequate pay,
poor supervision, or bad physical working conditions, may lead to
dissatisfaction. But positive job satisfaction depends on the provision
of intrinsic factors, such as a feeling of achievement, responsibility,
and challenging work. Proponents of this theory further contend that
with rising education and affluence, a growing proportion of American
workers are placing greater emphasis on intrinsic job content in their
occupational choices, as against material rewards, such as higher
pay or improved working conditions: "What workers want most, as
more than 100 studies in the past 20 years show, is to become masters
of their immediate environments and to feel that their work and themselves are important—the ingredients of self-esteem."[20]

The emphasis upon work content as a prime source of job satisfaction has inevitably led to comparative analyses of job satisfaction
in different types of occupations or work situations. Robert Blauner,
in a study of the pertinent survey literature available in the late 1950s,
summarized his findings as follows: "Work satisfaction varies greatly
by occupation. Highest percentages of satisfied workers are usually
found among professionals and businessmen. In a given plant, the
proportion satisfied is higher among clerical workers than among
factory workers, just as in general labor force samples it is higher
among middle-class than among manual working-class occupations.
Within the manual working class, job satisfaction is highest among
skilled workers, lowest among unskilled laborers and workers on
assembly lines."[21] Blauner and other observers have also noted that

these rankings tend to correspond closely to other measures of occupational status or prestige, such as the Edwards socioeconomic
groupings.

In contrast to approaches designed to develop a single generalized
index of job satisfaction, later research has emphasized that job satisfaction has many dimensions and must be interpreted as the product
of an interaction between the individual worker with his work environment. The degree of variability in satisfaction with various aspects
of work, within any occupation, as well as the general ordering of
satisfaction ratings among various occupations is suggested by a
summary analysis by Robert L. Kahn, based on a survey of 1,244
adults in urban areas of the United States. This analysis summarizes
worker ratings of seven different job aspects in a total of 28 occupations.[22] Inspection of these data indicates that the overall pattern of
ratings by occupational group conforms to that indicated by earlier job
satisfaction and prestige surveys. Thus, professional occupations and
other higher-status white-collar jobs tend to receive above-average
ratings on all of the seven job characteristics. Notable exceptions are
artists and musicians, who understandably give low ratings to the pay
and security aspect of their professions. Conversely, low-skilled
manual workers report an above-average amount of dissatisfaction
with most aspects of their work. Thus laborers rate their jobs poorly
in terms of all seven job aspects and operatives rate their jobs poorly
in all aspects other than pay. Household workers rate their jobs
poorly with respect to all aspects other than freedom to plan, while
other personal service workers and sales clerks also rate their jobs
below average on a majority of the job aspects shown. The skilled
crafts, as well as most clerical and sales jobs, generally fall into
an intermediate position in these ratings.

This summary serves to illustrate some of the strengths and
limitations of the job attitude survey methodology for analysis of
occupational preferences or occupational studies. On the one hand,
the surveys—although varying widely in scope and methodology—do
serve to differentiate between financial rewards of work and other
significant work characteristics, such as physical working conditions,
social interactions, degree of autonomy exercised, the opportunity
to use skills, and other intrinsic job aspects. To the extent that occupational choices are influenced by both measurable financial rewards
and by a variety of less-measurable qualitative factors, the large
volume of attitudinal research emphasizing the latter variables has
contributed to our understanding of their relative importance. For
example, initial findings from the Ohio State University longitudinal
study of labor market behavior indicate that young men who place
greater emphasis on intrinsic job factors, that is, the kind of work
they are doing, are more likely to have a higher attachment to their

current job than those emphasizing pay, thus tending to corroborate Herzberg's thesis that intrinsic factors are generally the source of positive job satisfaction. [23]

Nevertheless, any effort to use the available results of job satisfaction research in an empirical scaling of occupations is fraught with many difficulties. The most apparent is the lack of occupational detail. The great majority of the job satisfaction surveys have been limited to particular, small segments of the labor force. Differences in methodology, timing, and coverage have handicapped any attempts at systematic comparisons. Those surveys which have sampled all, or most, of the labor force such as surveys conducted by the University of Michigan's Survey Research Center, have been based upon samples too small to permit a disaggregation of the data much below the level of major occupational groups. Moreover, interpretation of the survey findings has been rendered difficult by the fact that, over a period of years, only a small percentage of workers surveyed have in fact expressed dissatisfaction with their jobs: "Few people call themselves extremely satisfied with their jobs, but still fewer report extreme dissatisfaction. The modal response is on the positive side of neutrality—'pretty satisfied.'"[24]

Although there have been many hypotheses concerning these response patterns, the result has been a tendency to discount findings based on responses to generalized questions, such as "How satisfied are you with your job?" and to rely on alternative approaches, such as analysis of specific job aspects, or on responses to questions of the following type: "If you had to decide all over again whether to take the job you now have, what would you decide?" Responses to the latter type of questions tend to provide much sharper differentiation among occupations, but—as noted by Robert Kahn and others—may represent no more than another measure of the status or prestige ranking of various occupations, thus yielding little additional information to our understanding of the process of occupational choice.

COMPARISON OF AVAILABLE OCCUPATIONAL RANKING CRITERIA

Our examination of the major approaches taken by social scientists in development of occupational rankings has revealed a wide divergence in criteria and methodology as well as common handicaps imposed by limitations of available source data. Despite these differences, the resulting ordering of occupations has been quite consistent in the delineation of both extremes of the occupational spectrum. This is illustrated by the average rank ordering of major census occupational groups in Table 1.1 under three separate set of criteria: Duncan's socioeconomic status index, Siegel's composite prestige ranking data, and Scoville's analysis of job content. It must be emphasized that these rankings are composites representing our weighted averages of the specific rankings for 200 or more detailed census occupations within these major groups and that there is wide divergence of rankings, among many of the specific occupations, from the group averages. Nevertheless, under all of these ranking systems, professional and technical workers and nonfarm managers and proprietors appear at the head of the list, whereas laborers and domestic servants are assigned the lowest ranks. Operatives and service workers, other than protective service, are generally at the next lowest rungs of the occupational ladder, above the laborers and domestics.*

There is somewhat less consistency, however, in ranking of occupations in the intermediate range of status. For example, sales workers receive a higher average ranking under Duncan's index than they do in the other two studies cited, probably because Duncan's data reflect the status of male sales workers who are concentrated in the more technical and better-paying sales activities. Conversely, craftsmen and protective service workers are ranked above the sales workers group by both Siegel and Scoville, whereas Duncan assigns these groups lower average ranks. Other marked divergences among these three approaches are found in the ranking of farmers and of protective service workers.

Our own assessment suggests that both the correspondence in broad ordering of occupations as high- or low-level occupations, and the ambiguities in ordering of the large middle-level range of occupations can be explained by the basic criteria and methodologies followed in the various systems of occupational ranking. On the one hand, all of these systems have had at least one common denominator: they have, directly or indirectly, assigned major weight to the relative difficulty of entry into occupations, as reflected in the length and cost of the training required. Measures of the socioeconomic status of occupations, such as Duncan's index, give direct weight to educational attainment. Scoville's analysis of job content is heavily weighted by a factor designed to measure relative educational demands of different

---

*Our inspection of available summaries of job satisfaction survey findings by occupational groups indicates that these, too, generally conform to the rank orderings outlined above. However, disparities in occupational classification and other methodological problems have precluded a simple rank ordering of these findings by census occupational groups.

TABLE 1.1

Rankings of Major Census Occupational Groups
under Alternative Criteria

Occupational Group	Socioeconomic Status[a]	Prestige[b]	Job Content
Professional and technical	1	1	1
Managers, officials, and proprietors, excluding farm	2	2	2
Clerical and kindred workers	3	4.5	5
Sales workers	4	7	6
Craftsmen, foremen, and kindred workers	5	4.5	3.5
Protective service workers	6	6	3.5
Operatives and kindred workers	7	8	8.5
Farmers and farm managers	8	3	7
Other service workers	9	9	8.5
Private household workers	10	10	10.5
Laborers (farm and nonfarm)	11	11	10.5

[a]Rankings based on weighted indices of income and educational attainment of workers for specific 1960 census occupations.

[b]Rankings based on integrated results of several prestige surveys conducted by the National Opinion Research Center, University of Chicago.

Sources: Socioeconomic status rankings are adapted from Otis Dudley Duncan, "Socioeconomic Status Scores for Detailed Occupations," mimeographed (Chicago: University of Chicago, Population Research and Training Center, October 1961). Prestige rankings are adapted from Paul M. Siegel, "Prestige in the American Occupational Structure" (Ph.D. diss., University of Chicago, March 1971). Job content rankings are adapted from James G. Scoville, The Job Content of the U.S. Economy (New York: McGraw-Hill, 1969), app. 1.

occupations, as were earlier attempts to differentiate occupations by skill level. And prestige surveys, too, appear to be heavily influenced by this factor. [25]

The extent of formal education and training required for entry into the various occupations is however most clearly defined at both extremes of the occupational spectrum and least adequately, for the broad middle range. At the upper extreme, nearly all professional and salaried management occupations now require, as a minimum standard, completion of a four-year college program and/or a first professional degree; at the lower extreme, most unskilled labor jobs still have few, if any, requirements for either formal education or specific occupational training. Understandably, therefore, virtually every approach to occupational rankings has placed the first group at ·the top and the latter at the bottom of the job hierarchy.

Between these two extremes, it is far more difficult to differentiate among occupations in terms of the amount of formal educational or training preparation needed. The previously noted data on general educational demands of occupations in the U.S. labor force compiled by Miller, based on DOT worker traits analyses, suggest that these formal educational demands are in fact quite limited; that is, about one-half of all jobs in the contemporary labor force require no more than an elementary school-level of education while an additional one-third require only the equivalent of a high school diploma. [26] Of course, many of the latter occupations—such as skilled mechanics and other craftsmen—also impose requirements of substantial periods of specific vocational preparation, either in formal courses or through on-the-job training and work experience. Nevertheless, it is apparent that the criterion of length of education or training can do little to differentiate among a large and diverse array of less-skilled jobs, whether white-collar or blue-collar.

As suggested by our above discussion, a host of additional variables do, in fact, make some of these jobs much more desirable for the average worker than other jobs. The effect of these other work-related variables is reflected in varying degrees and forms by the available indices. Thus Duncan, in assigning about equal weight to occupational earnings in his index of social-economic status, implicitly supports the contention of classical economists that, despite some market imperfection, occupational wage differentials do tend to reflect the whole of the advantages and disadvantages of different occupations. The occupational prestige surveys, as well as the job satisfaction research, represent alternative (although related) approaches towards measuring the full range of qualitative variables at work. In view of the many difficult methodological and conceptual problems it is scarcely surprising that these approaches have produced somewhat different occupational scalings.

AN ALTERNATIVE APPROACH TO IDENTIFICATION
OF LOW-LEVEL JOBS

In comparing the above methods for measuring occupational
stratification, an averaging out of several of the available criteria
could have been expected to produce generally credible results and
this was, in fact, computed at an early stage of the present study.
There were two sets of considerations which impelled us, nevertheless, to develop an alternative method of ranking occupations. The
first consisted of technical problems stemming from a major revision
in occupational classifications and enumeration procedures introduced
in the 1970 census. The second stemmed from our interest, in the
present study, in developing a labor supply-relevant ranking of occupations which would serve to group together those occupations which,
based on empirical labor market criteria, were most likely to experience a reduction in potential labor supply under existing relative
wages and working conditions in the event of a continuation of trends
towards a better-educated and more homogeneous labor force.

From a technical standpoint, a number of major procedural
changes in the 1970 census had, at least in part, rendered obsolete
the occupational rankings developed by investigators such as Duncan,
Siegel, and Scoville, on the basis of occupational data from the 1950
or 1960 censuses. The changes introduced in the 1970 census—the
most far-reaching in their effect since 1940—had, as major objectives:
(1) an improvement in the definition and coding of specific occupations
and a corresponding reduction in the large number of respondents
previously reported in such catchall categories as "operatives, not
elsewhere classified" or "laborers, not elsewhere classified," and
(2) an improvement in the accuracy of enumeration procedures for
reporting of occupational information.

The revisions in occupational definition and classification resulted
in an increase in the number of specified occupations from 297 in 1960
to 441 in 1970, as well as in substantial revision in coverage of many
occupations of the original 1960 list. In an effort to increase the
number of respondents assigned to specific occupations, rather than
to the "not elsewhere classified" categories, extensive use was made
of computer coding and editing, as a supplement to manual coding.
In order to improve the accuracy of responses concerning occupation,
two additional questions were inserted in the 1970 enumeration schedule, one requesting a description of major duties performed, and the
second, the individual's formal job title. (Further details are found
in the Appendix.) The combined effect of these revisions was to result in a major break in comparability of census data for large numbers of specific occupations between 1960 and 1970. As a result, it

proved impracticable to analyze trends in composition of many specific
lower-level occupations between 1960 and 1970, particularly in the
operatives and nonfarm laborer groups. Most of the operative occupations, other than transport operatives, as well as the nonfarm laborers,
were grouped by us into large occupational categories. These were
however disaggregated for our study, by broad industry groups (for
example, operatives in the textile, apparel, and leather products
industries), drawn from information included in the census public
use sample tapes, based on the 1960 census of population. However,
since these special occupation-industry combinations did not correspond to published census data for 1960 or earlier years, no rankings
for these groups were available in the existing occupational stratification literature.

     More fundamentally, none of the available indices, as we have
noted, were originally designed to provide what we have termed a
labor supply-relevant ranking of occupations. Two of these scales—
Duncan's and Siegel's—are both designed to provide a measure of an
individual's social or prestige status based on his occupation. There
is no assurance that the criteria relevant to a general societal evaluation of occupations necessarily correspond to those motivating individual workers to enter or remain in these jobs. The third index,
Scoville's rankings by job content, is designed to measure relative
skill level or complexity as determined, mainly, by the estimated
general educational development required. This index, therefore,
does not purport to reflect the full range of factors (monetary or
nonmonetary) which are likely to influence occupational preference.

     As an alternative to these approaches, our point of departure is
the premise that different groups of workers in the labor force, as
defined by such characteristics as race, age, educational level, and
sex, have widely differing ranges of job options in the contemporary
labor market. Thus, under labor market conditions existing in the
1960s and earlier, there is abundant evidence from the extensive
literature on employment discrimination that—other factors being
equal—employers generally tended to favor whites over nonwhites,
adults over youth, and those with at least a high school diploma over
those with less education. In many occupations and industries, employers also gave systematic recruitment preference to men over
women. The many factors contributing to these patterns of labor
market discrimination have been subject to intensive study from a
number of perspectives. These need not concern us directly here;
it is sufficient that these patterns have existed on a pervasive scale
throughout our economy. They can be readily illustrated by the observed differentials in unemployment rates, for March 1970, by age,
sex, color, and educational attainment, as shown in Table 1.2.
In each of the separate comparisons shown, the preferred labor force

TABLE 1.2

Unemployment Rates, by Selected Sociodemographic
Characteristics, March 1970

Sociodemographic Characteristic	Percent of Labor Force Unemployed
Age	
18–24	8.3
25 and over	3.3
Race	
White	3.9
Nonwhite*	6.7
Educational level	
Less than high school graduate	5.6
High school graduate or more	3.4
Sex	
Men	3.7
Women	4.9
Total civilian labor force, 18 years and over	4.2

*The term "nonwhites" as used here and in subsequent tables in
this study normally refers to blacks and other races.

Source: Adapted from Educational Attainment of Workers,
March 1969, 1970, Special Labor Force Report 125, U.S. Depart-
ment of Labor, Bureau of Labor Statistics (Washington, D.C.: U.S.
Government Printing Office, 1971), tables B, K, L.

group has experienced unemployment rates substantially below the
less preferred group. The unemployment rate differentials, when
these separate groups are cross-classified, are of course far wider.
For example, the unemployment rate in March 1970 for black youths,
aged 18-24 years, who were high school dropouts was 21 percent, or
more than ten times as great as the rate of 2 percent for adult white
workers, aged 25 years and over, who had completed one or more
years of college.

A second premise underlying our method is that workers do, in
fact, have a collective occupational preference schedule in which

alternative jobs are compared in terms of relative desirability based on their perception of such attributes as pay, job content, working conditions, and other characteristics, and on the relative importance they assign to each of these factors in their job choice. This is supported by the extensive survey literature on occupational prestige, career goals, and job satisfaction. For example, numerous occupational prestige surveys have indicated high degrees of consistency in ranking of occupations, in terms of desirability, by individuals from widely varying occupational and socioeconomic backgrounds. Similarly, surveys of career goals of high school youth show a disproportionate concentration (in terms of available jobs) of aspirants for the more elite professional, managerial, and skilled occupations, and very low proportions who look forward to entering the lower-status occupational groups.[27]

If these premises are valid, the actual differential occupational distribution of those labor force groups who have a preferred status in the labor market, that is, the broadest job options, provides a sensitive measure of relative occupational preferences of American workers. Such a measure, based on observed compositional characteristics of the various occupations, has the obvious advantage of eliminating the need for subjective judgment factors on such imponderables as the relative importance of financial versus psychic rewards in occupational choice or of attempting to estimate the relative costs or difficulties of qualification in different occupations.

The specific occupational index used for the present study was based on the percentage of white workers, with 12 or more years of education, in the age group 25-34 years, as computed for each of 57 occupations or occupational clusters, from the census public use sample for 1960. These values, expressed as percentiles based on the size of the experienced civilian labor force, in each occupation in 1960, are shown in Table 1.3. This index therefore directly reflects the combined effect of two major factors affecting occupational opportunity in the contemporary labor market: education and race. The selection of a single age group of young adult workers is designed to more accurately reflect occupational choices made by such workers in the years immediately preceding 1960, thus eliminating possible biases from inclusion of older groups of workers, who entered and often remained in occupations based on labor market conditions in earlier periods, or from inclusion of youth, whose occupational choices as a group are much more constrained (particularly in the case of those engaged in part-time employment).

The index was computed for both sexes, combined, partly because sample size limitations did not permit a further disaggregation of the 1960 data by sex. However, in order to test the extent to which a sex-standardized index would have affected the resulting rankings,

TABLE 1.3

Selected Occupational Status Indices

Status Group and Occupation	Experienced Civilian Labor Force, 1960 (000)	Occupational Status Indices (percentile ranks)			Mean Earnings, Full Time, 1959
		Labor Force Composition	Socioeconomic Status	Prestige	
Group 1					
Engineers	870	97.8	96	95	8,478
All other professional and technical workers[a]	3,448	90.3	91	90	6,448
Teachers, excluding college	1,682	87.0	92	92	5,240
Medical personnel[b]	1,325	84.6	86	95	5,082
Group 2					
Bookkeepers	940	83.1	79	81	3,685
Secretaries, typists, stenos	2,312	79.6	86	71	3,801
All other sales workers, excluding retail clerks	2,088	75.6	83	57	6,554
Nonfarm managers, total	5,489	69.0	86	83	8,087
All other clerical and kindred workers[c]	2,437	61.8	82	52*	—
Office machine operators	315	61.1	74	75	4,112
Telephone operators	369	60.4	74	67	3,695
Policemen, firemen[d]	426	59.3	63	75	5,383
Sales clerks—retail trade	2,720	56.9	67	34*	3,283
Cashiers	495	56.3	73	36	3,171
Postal clerks, mail carriers	423	55.6	77	66	5,306

Group 3

Foremen, not elsewhere classified	1,198	54.1	77	75*	6,679
All other craftsmen^e	1,879	51.1	63	52*	5,771
Mechanics, excluding auto	1,594	48.3	56	46	5,243
Deliverymen, routemen	441	47.5	57	30	4,190
Metalworking, crafts, excluding mechanics, machinists	607	46.6	61	56	5,932
Farmers, farm managers, unpaid farm workers	2,812	43.9	31	58	3,023
Electricians, brickmasons, excavating machine operators^f	1,239	41.7	62	58	5,604
Machinists	516	40.9	58	82	5,696
Checkers, examiners	518	40.2	37	48	4,614
Operatives—nondurable goods manufacturing, including chemical, petroleum industries^g	832	38.5	45	23	—
Barbers, bartenders, practical nurses^h	1,431	36.9	49	31	3,558
Operatives—transport equipment manufacturing	538	35.8	50	53	5,520
Carpenters	924	34.4	44	60	5,008

(continued)

27

(Table 1.3 continued)

Status Group and Occupation	Experienced Civilian Labor Force, 1960 (000)	Occupational Status Indices (percentile ranks)			Mean Earnings, Full Time, 1959
		Labor Force Composition	Socioeconomic Status	Prestige	
Group 4					
Taxi drivers, bus drivers[i]	442	33.8	37	31	—
Auto mechanics	705	32.4	44	57	4,229
Operatives—nonmanufacturing industries, total	1,776	29.4	46	18	4,548
Auto service and parking attendants	379	28.8	44	17*	3,185
Operatives—metalworking industries[j]	2,028	25.4	52	55*	4,786
Guards and watchmen, crossing guards, and bridge tenders	281	25.2	40	17*	4,412
Housekeepers and babysitters	506	24.8	20	28	1,096
Housekeepers	152	—	(44)	(46)	—
Babysitters	354	—	(10)	(20)*	—
Waiters and counter and fountain workers	1,063	23.2	31	13	2,118
Shipping and receiving clerks, messengers, and office boys	357	22.0	52	27	4,419

Laborers—metalworking industries[k]	399	21.8	n.a.	n.a.	4,582
Operatives—food and tobacco industries	555	20.9	33	21*	—
Construction painters, plasterers, cement and concrete finishers, roofers, paperhangers	589	20.0	35	36*	4,686
Hospital attendants	408	19.3	20	41*	2,661
Truck and tractor drivers	1,663	15.4	30	38*	4,696
Operatives—textiles, apparel, leather industries	1,826	12.8	17	25	3,119
Packers	497	12.0	41	10	3,674
Welders, flamecutters	390	11.3	53	60	5,460
Operatives—lumber, furniture, stone, clay, and glass industries	578	10.4	30	23*	4,096

Group 5

Laborers—nonmanufacturing industries, excluding construction	1,407	8.6	n.a.	n.a.	3,478
Janitors, sextons	624	8.1	15	7*	3,184
Cooks	599	7.4	15	24	2,916

(continued)

(Table 1.3 continued)

Status Group and Occupation	Experienced Civilian Labor Force, 1960 (000)	Occupational Status Indices (percentile ranks)			Mean Earnings, Full Time, 1959
		Labor Force Composition	Socioeconomic Status	Prestige	
(Group 5 continued)					
Construction laborers	776	6.1	n.a.	n.a.	3,805
Laborers—lumber, furniture, stone, clay, and glass industries	373	5.6	n.a.	n.a.	4,077
Laborers—nondurable goods[1]	346	5.1	n.a.	n.a.	4,062*
Farm laborers—paid	1,241	3.3	09	13*	2,163
Kitchen workers	332	3.0	18	17	2,302
Laundry and dry cleaning operators	410	2.5	30	10	2,248
Cleaners and charwomen, porters, chambermaids, elevator operators	610	1.8	09	07	2,425
Private household workers, not elsewhere classified	1,310	0.3	10	10	1,116

Notes to Table 1.3

[a]Includes all other professional and technical workers not elsewhere classified.
[b]Includes physicians, dentists, medical and dental technicians, and all other health personnel classified as professional.
[c]Includes all other clerical and kindred workers not elsewhere classified.
[d]Includes marshals and constables; sheriffs and bailiffs.
[e]Includes all other craft workers not elsewhere classified.
[f]Includes grading and road machinery operators, plumbers and pipefitters, and structural metal workers.
[g]Includes operatives not elsewhere classified in the following nondurable goods industries: paper and allied products; printing and publishing; chemicals and allied products; petroleum and coal products; rubber and plastic products; not specified nondurable manufacturing.

hIncludes hospital attendants, recreation and amusement workers, ushers, and all other service workers not elsewhere classified.

iIncludes rail conductors, subway motormen, mine motormen, railroad brakemen, railroad switchmen, and boatmen and canalmen.

jIncludes operatives, not elsewhere classified, in the following industries: metal industries; machinery, except electrical; electrical machinery; professional and photographic equipment; miscellaneous manufacturing.

kSame industrial distribution as for operatives in note j.

lIncludes laborers in all nondurable goods industries.

Notes: Labor force composition is based on percentage of white workers, with 12 or more years of education, in the experienced civilian labor force of each occupation, for the age group 25–34 years, in 1960; mean earnings are wage and salary income of workers employed 35 hours or more in census survey week, and who were employed 48 weeks or more in 1959. Occupation/industry coverage is not precisely comparable in socioeconomic status scores; in prestige scores asterisked data had a poor match between the census occupational title and the actual title related in the prestige survey.

Entries with a (–) in this and subsequent tables signify either that a reliable estimate could not be derived from the source data or that its frequency was very low, that is, less than 0.05 percent; n.a. signifies that data were not available.

Sources: The experienced labor force and labor force composition were computed from the recoded 1/1,000 sample of the census public use tape released in July 1971 by the Bureau of the Census, U.S. Department of Commerce. The socioeconomic status percentile scores were derived from Otis Dudley Duncan, "Socioeconomic Status Scores for Detailed Occupations," mimeographed (Chicago: University of Chicago, Population Research and Training Center, October 1961). The prestige percentile scores are from Paul M. Siegel, "Prestige in the American Occupational Structure" (Ph.D. diss., University of Chicago, March 1971).

31

we subsequently computed such an index for 1970 based on the somewhat larger public use sample for that year. The procedure followed
was to compute separate occupational indices for each sex and to
weight the indices by the respective proportions of men and women
in the labor force of each occupation as of 1970. Thus, in effect, the
relative standing of female-type occupations, such as secretaries or
domestic servants, was determined largely by the comparative proportion of white female high school graduates in such occupations.
Comparison of the resulting rankings with those derived from the
percentiles for both sexes combined revealed no significant difference,
however, as indicated by a correlation coefficient (R) of .993 between
the two rankings.

The limited impact of sex differentiation upon occupational status
may appear surprising, in view of the massive evidence concerning
job and pay discrimination against women generally in the labor market. It is probably explained by the fact that the de facto segregation
of large numbers of working women in certain occupations has, in
part, taken the form of relatively high concentrations of women in
white-collar-type jobs, such as office and sales work. Such occupations, although generally offering lower pay than that available to
male counterparts with similar qualifications, tend to command higher
status than many of the more onerous but higher-paying industrial and
laborer jobs, which are predominantly staffed by men.

In addition, the need to rely upon relatively broad census occupational subgroupings in the present study has necessarily blurred the
differentiation by sex which exists among the more specific occupations within these subgroups. To illustrate, all professional and
technical occupations were combined, for our purposes, into only
four occupational subgroups: engineers, medical personnel, teachers,
and all other professional and kindred workers. The medical personnel
subgroup includes a broad range of professional and technical occupations in the health field, from physicians and dentists to medical and
dental technicians. The former high-status occupations include a very
small percentage of women; the lower-status technician occupations,
a very high percentage. Predictably, a more refined occupational
classification scheme would have revealed more status differentiation
by sex than suggested by our comparisons, particularly among occupations within the white-collar group. However, further disaggregation within the latter category was not considered relevant in view of
our primary focus upon lower-level occupations, and—in most instances—was not practicable, because of technical constraints of
intercensal comparability and sample size.

Based on this index, the 57 occupational clusters used for this
analysis have been grouped into five broad occupational status groups
in lieu of the conventional census occupational categories. In

establishing these status groups, an effort was made to delineate group boundaries in a way to assure maximum correspondence with matching census occupational groupings, consistent with the percentile ranking scores of the occupations. Group 1 thus corresponds to the census group comprising professional, technical, and kindred workers. Group 2 includes most remaining white-collar occupations, with the exception of one subgroup including shipping and receiving clerks, messengers, and office boys. It also includes policemen, firemen, and allied protective service workers. Group 3 includes foremen; most of the skilled craftsmen, mechanics, and repairmen; operatives in certain high-wage industries (for example, transportation equipment, chemicals, petroleum); and certain of the more skilled service occupations (for example, barbers and beauticians, bartenders, practical nurses). Group 4 includes most of the operative occupations (exclusive of those in Group 3 and of laundry workers); certain low-level clerical workers such as shipping clerks; automobile mechanics, construction painters, plasterers, roofers, and cement and concrete workers; certain intermediate-level service personnel, such as waiters, hospital attendants, and housekeepers; and laborers in metalworking industries. Group 5 in turn includes both farm and nonfarm laborers (exclusive of those in metalworking industries); domestic servants; other personal service workers (cooks and kitchen workers, janitors, charwomen, and cleaners) and laundry and dry cleaning operatives.

The percentile rankings derived from this status index have been compared by us with percentile rankings adapted from the Duncan SES index and from Siegel's prestige index, and with the mean 1959 earnings of full-time workers employed in these occupations in 1960. These comparisons produced correlations (R) of .923 with the Duncan index and of .843 with Siegel's composite prestige ratings for the approximately 50 occupations for which comparisons could be made. The simple correlation between this index and median full-time wage and salary earnings was relatively low (.604). However, when allowance was made for the differential proportion of males in the various occupations, the partial correlation between earnings and our status index, holding sex constant, increased to .735.

A relatively high correlation with the Duncan index was to be expected in view of the fact that the percentage of high school graduates is a common component of both indices although based on different rationales. (Duncan had however computed his index based on 1950 data for men only and had given nearly equal weight to occupational income.) The correlation with the Siegel prestige index appears quite reasonable when allowance is made for the differences in purpose of the two measures and for the inherent limitations of the occupational prestige survey technique, as noted earlier in this chapter. Finally, a lower correlation of our occupational status scale with earnings than with status or prestige is also consistent with our understanding of the many nonpay factors which enter into occupational preferences, and of the large role played by institutional factors in influencing the pattern of occupational wage differentials.

Although the above comparisons, as well as other checks on the reasonableness of our criteria, have tended to support the usefulness of this index for our specific purposes, some of its limitations should be clearly noted.

First, our primary objective, in developing the above index, was to arrive at a means for ranking of occupations, based on occupational preferences of workers, in order to (1) differentiate among high-level, middle-level, and lower-level occupations, broadly grouped, and (2) to differentiate, particularly, among more specific occupations within the lower and lower-middle levels of this preference scale. This emphasis resulted, as noted above, in our use of relatively broad aggregations of higher-level occupations, that is, in the professional and managerial categories, since the latter were of secondary interest in the present context.

Second, this broader occupational clustering has produced some apparent anomalies. For example, nonfarm managers and officials are ranked below bookkeepers, secretaries, and sales workers other than retail clerks. This, we believe, is at least partially due to the heterogeneous nature of the broad managerial group, which includes large numbers of proprietors of small retail stores and similar establishments, as well as smaller numbers of top executives in government and business.

Third, and more generally, it has been apparent that further refinements based on larger samples than the census 1/1,000 public use sample and on additional standardization (for example, by region or size of community) could further improve the usefulness of this approach for a broader range of occupational studies. Thus, small differences in occupational position, based on the present method, cannot be considered as significant.

Finally, to the extent that our methodology is based on the premise of pervasive labor market discrimination on such grounds as race and educational level, any major change in the degree or nature of such discrimination, would either invalidate this approach or require its modification for future years. In fact, to the extent that some categories of employers, such as the federal government, were less discriminatory in the hiring of nonwhite workers than other employers, prior to 1960, our index does tend to lower the relative ranking of those occupations, such as postal clerks, whose employment was concentrated in the less discriminatory sectors. Unfortunately, there is little indication that this factor produced any appreciable distortion in our occupational rankings as of 1960.

NOTES

1. U.S. Department of Labor, Manpower Administration, Dictionary of Occupational Titles, vol. 1, 3d ed. (Washington, D.C.: U.S. Government Printing Office, 1965), p. xv.

2. Alba M. Edwards, Comparative Occupational Statistics for the United States, 1870 to 1940 (Washington, D.C.: U.S. Government Printing Office, 1943), p. 175.

3. Dictionary of Occupational Titles, op. cit., p. xviii.

4. Sidney A. Fine, The 1965 Third Edition of the Dictionary of Occupational Titles—Contents, Contrasts, and Critique (Kalamazoo: W.E. Upjohn Institute for Employment Research, December 1968), p. 6.

5. James G. Scoville, The Job Content of the American Economy, 1940-1970 (New York: McGraw-Hill, 1969), chap. 2.

6. Ann R. Miller, Occupations of the Labor Force According to the Dictionary of Occupational Titles, Statistical Evaluation Report no. 9, Office of Management and Budget (Washington, D.C.: U.S. Government Printing Office, February 1971), tables 11, 12.

7. Adam Smith, The Wealth of Nations (New York: Random House, 1937), bk. 1, chap. 10.

8. J.E. Cairnes, Some Leading Principles of Political Economy, Newly Expounded (New York: Hargward Brothers, 1874), pp. 66-67.

9. Alfred Marshall, Principles of Economics (London: Macmillan and Co., 1961), p. 181.

10. Ibid., p. 464.

11. A review of this literature appears in David M. Gordon, Theories of Poverty and Underemployment (Lexington, Mass.: Lexington Books, 1972).

12. See for example, Peter M. Blau and Otis Dudley Duncan, The American Occupational Structure (New York: John Wiley and Sons, 1967), chap. 1.

13. Ibid., p. 119. See also Paul M. Siegel, "Prestige in the American Occupational Structure" (Ph.D. diss., University of Chicago, March 1971), chap. 1.

14. Siegel, op. cit., table 5.

15. A.F. Davies, "Prestige of Occupations," in Man, Work and Society, ed. Sigmund Nosow and William H. Form (New York: Basic Books, 1962), p. 263.

16. Blau and Duncan, op. cit., chap. 4.

17. U.S. Department of Commerce, Bureau of the Census, Methodology and Scores of Socioeconomic Status, Working Paper no. 15 (Washington, D.C.: U.S. Government Printing Office, 1963).

18. Edwards, op. cit.

19. Results of these surveys have been periodically summarized since 1946 by Robert Hoppock in the Personnel and Guidance Journal. See also, Robert Blauner, "Work Satisfaction and Industrial Trends in Modern Society," in Labor and Trade Unionism, ed. Walter Galenson and Seymour Martin (New York: John Wiley and Sons, 1960), pp. 339-60, and Robert Kahn, "The Meaning of Work: Interpretation and Proposals for Measurement," in The Human Meaning of Social Change, ed. Angus Campbell and Philip E. Converse (New York: Russell Sage Foundation, 1972) pp. 173-74.

20. Work in America, Report of a Special Task Force to the Secretary of Health, Education and Welfare (Cambridge, Mass.: MIT Press, 1973).

21. Blauner, op. cit., p. 341.

22. Robert L. Kahn, "The Meaning of Work: Interpretation and Proposals for Measurement," in Campbell and Converse, op. cit., pp. 186-87.

23. Herbert S. Parnes et al., Career Thresholds: A Longitudinal Study of the Educational and Labor Market Experience of Male Youth, vol. 1, Manpower Research Monograph no. 16, 1970, U.S. Department of Labor (Washington, D.C.: U.S. Government Printing Office, 1971), pp. 149, 155. This report notes, however, that a similar relationship was not evident in a comparable analysis of a cohort of older male workers.

24. Robert Kahn, "The Meaning of Work and Proposals for Measurement," in The Human Meaning of Social Change, op. cit., p. 169.

25. See Paul K. Hatt and C.C. North, "Prestige Ratings of Occupations, in Man, Work and Society, op. cit., p. 277.

26. Miller, op. cit., p. 39.

27. Parnes et al., op. cit., p. 172.

2

CHANGING SOURCES
OF LOW-LEVEL MANPOWER:
A HISTORICAL PERSPECTIVE

In examining several criteria for identifying the occupations which historically ranked lowest in desirability in the labor market, we noted, in the preceding chapter, a broad consensus that these jobs consisted, predominantly, of low-skilled laborer, service, and operative occupations, and that these shared certain characteristics: limited skill or educational requirements, heavy physical and/or socially demeaning work, unpleasant working conditions, and—typically—low pay.

Despite their wide differences in job content, these occupations shared one other common characteristic: the duties they entailed had in fact become specialized functions, performed by particular categories or classes of workers, under the prevailing division of labor. The emergence of large-scale requirements for lower-level manpower therefore coincided historically with the evolution of forms of economic organization which differentiated between a laborer, wage earner, or servant class, on the one hand, and an ownership or managerial class on the other.

THE PRE-CIVIL WAR ERA

Such differentiations had long been traditional in the caste- and class-dominated societies of the Old World. However, one of the unique features of the American experience was the limited and uneven development of a distinctive laboring class of free wage earners in the first two centuries following the settlement of the American colonies. The ready availability of land and the opportunities to follow one's own calling as an independent farmer, artisan, or merchant,

were the chief lodestones attracting the early European immigrants
here, from colonial days to the early decades of the nineteenth century.
In 1820, over 90 percent of the population was still rural, and of a
total estimated labor force of 3.1 million, 2.5 million or nearly 80
percent was engaged in farming activities.[1] In the North, as well as
in the Piedmont region of the South, the dominant pattern was that of
the small independent farmer, cultivating his own land with the aid of
his family and occasional hired help, and performing the myriad tasks
associated with survival in a frontier agrarian society. Newly arrived
immigrants, as well as the sons and daughters of farmers, provided
a limited source of hired labor both in the towns and in rural areas,
but this was usually transitory until they moved on to their own farms
or established their own nonfarm households.

In contrast, a large-scale plantation economy had emerged in the
tidewater region of the South and in the newly opening lands of the
delta region, centered on production of basic export staples, such as
tobacco, cotton, rice, and sugar, and whose very structure became
linked to availability of imported slave labor. Some indication of the
relative importance of slave manpower during this period is provided
by Stanley Lebergott, based on his analysis of early census data and
other historical source materials. Of a total gainfully occupied population of 2,470,000 in agriculture as of 1820, he estimates that
1,040,000 were farmers (owners or tenants), 515,000 were free
farm laborers including family workers, and 915,000 were slaves
(see Table 2.1). Lebergott further estimates that a total of only
665,000 were engaged in nonagricultural occupations in 1820. Even
if we assume that as many as two-thirds of the latter were performing
unskilled labor or service activities, slave labor still accounted for
at least one-half of the supply of low-level manpower at that time.

The decades between 1820 and the outbreak of the Civil War
witnessed a rapid upsurge of industry and trade, with the introduction
of the factory system, the rapid growth of urban centers, and the
establishment of a growing transportation network of turnpikes,
canals, and the first railroads. By 1860, the U.S. labor force had
grown nearly fourfold, to more than 11 million and, of this total,
nearly one-half, 5.2 million workers, were engaged in nonagricultural
activities. Although comprehensive occupational statistics are not
available for this period, it is clear that the expansion of industry,
construction, and trade entailed a greatly increased requirement for
unskilled and semiskilled wage workers and for allied service occupations.

In large part, this need was met from the swelling stream of free
immigrants drawn to our shores both by the pull of economic opportunity and by the push of grinding poverty, famine, or political turmoil
in their homelands. The annual rate of immigration mounted, in

TABLE 2.1

Estimated Distribution of U.S. Labor Force, Ages 10 and Over,
by Industry and Class of Worker: 1800, 1820, 1840, 1860

(in thousands)

Year	Total Labor Force	Agriculture				Nonagriculture			
		Total	Farmers	Free Farm Laborers	Slave Laborers	Total	Manufacturing	Other, Excluding Domestics	Domestic Service
1800	1,900	1,400	600	310	490	500	n.a.	n.a.	40
1820	3,135	2,470	1,040	515	915	665	n.a.	n.a.	110
1840	5,660	3,570	1,440	720	1,410	2,090	500	1,350	240
1860	11,110	5,880	2,540	1,120	2,220	5,230	1,530	3,100	600

Source: Adapted from Stanley Lebergott, Manpower in Economic Growth: The American Record Since 1800 (New York: McGraw-Hill, 1964), pp. 510-11.

almost geometric progression, from an average of less than 10,000 per year in the early 1820s to a pre-Civil War peak of nearly 400,000 per year in the early 1850s.[2]

These mid-nineteenth-century immigrants were drawn almost entirely from the countries of Northern and Western Europe. Two nationality groups predominated, the Irish and the Germans, with immigrants from Great Britain, other Northwest European countries, and Canada accounting for all but a small percentage of the remainder.[3] The pattern of geographical and occupational distribution of these earlier immigrant groups—as was true of those to follow—appears to have been largely influenced by two sets of variables: (1) the capital stock which they brought with them, in the form of prior occupational skills, education, and financial resources; and (2) the specific economic opportunities available to them at the time of their arrival, which in turn were a function of the differential rates of growth in the various industries and trades, as well as of the ability of various nationality groups to gain entry into the more desirable occupations, based on their social acceptance (or nonacceptance) by ethnic groups already established in these occupations here.

Among the major immigrant groups of this period, the Germans and Irish offer the most obvious contrasts in terms of social and economic status. The German immigrants, who arrived in particularly large numbers in the late 1840s and 1850s, following the 1848 revolution, included a large proportion of political refugees and intellectuals, as well as of individuals who had been either independent farmers or skilled workmen in Germany. Many of them moved westward to the farm areas and the emerging urban centers of the Ohio Valley and Great Lakes regions. These German immigrants, according to one authority, were in greater demand than those of other nationalities: "They were considered to have sturdy characters, law abiding instincts, habits of industry, painstaking zeal, honesty and intelligence."[4]

The Irish, on the other hand, probably ranked lowest in social status among the principal immigrant nationality groups of this period. Their handicaps were succinctly summarized by John R. Commons, as follows: "They were ignorant, poor and held to the Roman Catholic faith."[5] The Irish early established concentrations in the large eastern seaboard cities of Boston, New York, and Philadelphia, as well as in smaller New England cities and towns. To a greater degree than any other nationality group in this period, the men provided the unskilled labor for construction of canals and our early railroads and for similar heavy manual work in cities such as that of dock or stable hands. Their wives and daughters took work in large numbers as domestic servants, as well as in textile, shoe, and other light manufacturing industries.

In the process, these newly arrived immigrants displaced earlier
native American sources of labor supply for some of these occupations.
Initially, the early New England textile mill owners had recruited
young female operatives from local farm families as in the case of
the Lowell Mills which first opened in 1821; provision was made for
boarding and close supervision of these girls (under circumstances
vividly depicted in the musical Carousel). But by the mid-1840s,
growing unrest among these girl textile workers, resulting from low
wages and excessively long working hours, stimulated the beginning
of union organization and contributed to a shift in labor supply to more
tractable Irish immigrant labor. [6]

This process of displacement of native-born Americans by immigrants in low-level occupations is further described by Commons,
who cites an editorial on this issue in a New England newspaper in
1847:

> The Harbinger protested against the aristocratic and
> class feeling that had come into New England with the
> immigration of Irish and Canadian girls. Formerly the
> "sons and daughters of farmers deemed it no disgrace
> to labor for wages on a neighbor's farm or in his domes-
> tic employment." Now they "compromise their social
> standing." . . . "Would employers give $12 per month
> and $1 per week, for their neighbors' sons and daughters,
> when they could get far more compliant and servile ones
> for half the money, and with a little instruction equally
> skillful."[7]

The New England farm girls were, moreover, not the only group
of low-level American workers who felt the sharp bite of immigrant
competition during this period. By the mid-1800s, sizable colonies
of free black workers already existed in the larger northeastern
cities, such as New York, Philadelphia, and Baltimore, where they
were typically engaged in a variety of personal service or unskilled
labor occupations. In advocating the need for vocational training for
his fellow black man, Frederick Douglass, an outstanding black leader
and journalist of this period, described the plight of these urban
northern blacks as follows:

> The old avocations, by which colored men obtained a
> livelihood, are rapidly, unceasingly and inevitably
> passing into other hands; every hour sees the black
> man elbowed out of employment by some newly arrived
> emigrant, whose hunger and whose color are thought to
> give him a better title to the place . . .

> White men are becoming house-servants, cooks and
> stewards on vessels—at hotels. They are becoming
> porters, stevedores, wood-sawyers, hod-carriers,
> brick-makers, white-washers and barbers . . .
> formerly blacks were almost the exclusive coachmen
> in wealthy families; this is so no longer; white men are
> now employed, and for aught we see, they fill their
> servile station with an obsequiousness as profound as
> that of the blacks. [8]

From this brief discussion, the principal sources of low-level manpower supply in the antebellum era have been identified. In the agricultural South, such labor continued to be performed predominantly by black slaves. In the more industrial North, the limited indigenous labor resources, typically farm youth, were supplemented by a growing supply of newly arrived immigrants, with the Irish providing the largest single ethnic group among nonfarm laborers and service workers.

THE CIVIL WAR TO WORLD WAR I

Major Occupational Trends

The period between the end of the Civil War and World War I was one of very rapid industrialization, concurrent with continued agricultural expansion in the prairie and West Coast states. Although agricultural employment continued to grow, reaching a peak of nearly 12 million in 1910—about twice its 1860 level—its proportion of the total labor force declined from more than one-half in 1860 to less than one-third in 1910, reflecting in large part the increased productivity made possible by introduction of harvesters and other farm machinery and of scientific farming methods. Employment growth in the nonagricultural sector of the economy was paced by manufacturing, which mushroomed from about 2 million in 1860 to over 11 million in 1910. Employment in construction, trade, and service activities experienced similar sharp rates of growth. [9]

As a result of the researches of Alba Edwards, David Kaplan, and other census statisticians, we have available, beginning with 1900, decennial statistics on the distribution of the labor force by major occupational groups, broadly comparable in classification to those used in the censuses of population since 1940. From these data, it is evident that the economy which had emerged by the beginning of the twentieth century relied heavily on large masses of unskilled and semiskilled wage workers. Thus, of the total labor force of more than 37 million in 1910, over one-fourth were hired laborers (farm and nonfarm); nearly 15 percent were in the semiskilled operatives group and an additional 10 percent were engaged as domestics or in various service occupations (see Table 2.2). Of the nearly 10 million laborers, the largest proportion, about 60 percent, was still in agricultural work. The 4.5 million nonfarm laborers were in turn concentrated in construction work, in the railroads, in local transport (as draymen, teamsters, stable hands) and in a number of heavy manufacturing industries, such as iron and steel, metalworking, lumber, and saw-mills. Among the operative occupations, the largest number of male operatives in 1910 were found in coal mining, in iron and steel, and in allied metalworking industries, while female industrial workers were concentrated in the textile industry, in the emerging factory apparel industry, and in other light manufacturing industries. Women, in addition, composed all but a small proportion of the nearly two million domestic servants.[10]

The New Immigration

The rapid rate of growth of the U.S. labor force in the era between the end of the Civil War and the outbreak of World War I, and our emergence as a major industrial power, were made possible in large part by an unprecedented wave of immigration to our borders, supple-menting a high rate of natural population increase. The annual inflow of immigrants, which had slowed down during the Civil War and the reconstruction period, rose to an average of over 500,000 per year during the decade of the 1880s, dropped temporarily during the 1893-98 depression, and then mounted to record levels averaging more than one million immigrants per year between 1905 and 1914.[11]

During this period, the immigrant flow also changed dramatically in its ethnic composition. Until the decade of the 1890s, a large pro-portion of the immigrants continued to be drawn from the countries of Northern and Western Europe. In 1900, this region was still the homeland for about 70 percent of the foreign-born white population of the United States. However, beginning with the decade of the 1890s, the major portion of the new immigrants came from Southern and Eastern Europe including heavy concentrations of Slavs, Poles, Italians, and Russian and Polish Jews. Thus, in the decade of peak immigration, 1900-10, these newer nationality groups comprised 70 percent of the total number of immigrants, as contrasted to only 18 percent in the decade of the 1880s.[12]

TABLE 2.2

Percent Distribution of the Labor Force by Major Occupational Group, 1900–70

Occupational Group	1900	1910	1920	1930	1940	1950	1960	1970
Total workers (000)	29,030	37,291	42,206	48,686	51,742	58,999	68,006	81,336
Farm, total	37.6	30.8	27.1	21.2	17.4	11.8	6.3	3.6
Farmers and farm managers	19.9	16.4	15.4	12.4	10.4	7.4	3.9	2.1
Farm laborers and foremen	17.7	14.4	11.7	8.8	7.0	4.4	2.4	1.5
Nonfarm, total	62.4	69.2	72.9	78.8	82.6	88.2	93.7	96.4
Professional, technical, and kindred workers	4.3	4.7	5.4	6.8	7.5	8.6	11.4	14.1
Managers, officials, proprietors, excluding farm	5.8	6.6	6.6	7.4	7.3	8.7	8.5	10.3
Clerical and kindred workers	3.0	5.3	8.0	8.9	9.6	12.3	14.9	17.6
Sales workers	4.5	4.7	4.9	6.3	6.7	7.0	7.4	6.0
Craftsmen, foremen, and kindred workers	10.5	11.8	13.0	12.8	12.0	14.2	14.3	12.8
Operatives and kindred workers	12.8	14.5	15.6	15.8	18.3	20.3	20.0	18.3
Private household workers	5.4	5.0	3.3	4.1	4.7	2.6	2.8	2.1
Service workers, excluding private household	3.6	4.6	4.5	5.7	7.1	7.9	8.9	10.5
Laborers, excluding farm and mine	12.5	12.0	11.6	11.0	9.4	6.6	5.5	4.7
Total farm and nonfarm	100.0	100.0	100.0	100.0	100.0	100.0	100.0	100.0

Note: Data for 1900–40 refer to gainful workers, ages 10 and over; for 1940–60, data are for the experienced civilian labor force, ages 14 and over; for 1970, data are for the experienced civilian labor force, ages 16 and over.

Sources: Data for 1900–50: David L. Kaplan and M. Claire Casey, Occupational Trends in the United States: 1900 to 1950, Census Working Paper no. 5 (Washington, D. C.: U.S. Government Printing Office, 1958), table 2. Data for 1960: U.S. Department of Commerce, Bureau of the Census, Occupational Characteristics, U.S. census of population, PC(2)7A, (Washington, D. C.: U.S. Government Printing Office, 1963), table 1. Data for 1970: Current Population Survey, March 1970, table 24; "Employed and Unemployed Persons by Detailed Occupation Group and Sex" (unpublished table, Bureau of Labor Statistics).

Despite obvious differences among themselves in ethnic and cultural backgrounds, most of these later immigrants shared common handicaps: limited literacy, both in English and, often, in their native tongues; a lack of relevant vocational skills; and significant religious and cultural barriers between themselves and the predominant Northern and Western European stocks who had preceded them. Moreover, with the closing of the frontier, they entered in a period when employment opportunities were largely concentrated in the growing urban, industrial centers and in mining rather than in agriculture. Since the more desirable of the jobs in these industries had been preempted by the native populations, these newcomers, like their more disadvantaged predecessors were relegated, disproportionately, to the less desirable unskilled and semiskilled laborer jobs.

Racial and Ethnic Composition of the Labor Force

Throughout this period of mass immigration, the black worker, although now a freedman, maintained his unenviable status at the bottom of the occupational ladder. In 1910, black workers, 10 years and over, totaled more than 5 million, or nearly 14 percent of the U.S. labor force. About 90 percent of the black workers were still in the South and nearly three-fourths were confined to the two traditional black occupations, farming and menial service activities. In southern agriculture, their economic status as either sharecroppers or hired laborers was scarcely improved over that of the slave era. In southern as well as northern industry, they were predominantly employed in service-type or laborer jobs. In fact, to the extent that some southern black workers—slaves and freedmen—had previously been given an opportunity to enter certain skilled crafts or industrial trades, increased competition from the almost equally impoverished southern poor white population had forced them out of the more desirable of the latter occupations.

There were, however, some limited exceptions to this pattern, both in the South and the North. In the South, the pattern of segregation of the races had generated a requirement for a small black professional and middle class to provide the teachers, doctors and ministers to service the black population. Also, certain of the least desirable crafts, such as the masonry trades, were identified as black trades and predominantly staffed by blacks. In the North, where the small black population was clustered in some of the larger East Coast and midwestern cities, competition from the incoming white immigrant groups had effectively excluded all but a few blacks from mainstream economic activities, reinforced in many cases by

TABLE 2.3

Percent Distribution of Labor Force in Each Major Occupational Group, by Race and Nativity: 1910, 1950

Major Occupational Group	1910				1950			
			Percent				Percent	
	Number (000)	Native White	Foreign-Born White	Nonwhite	Number (000)	Native White	Foreign-Born White	Nonwhite
Total	37,291	65.5	20.9	13.6	58,999	81.4	8.2	10.4
Farm, occupations, total	11,533	68.5	8.5	23.0	6,953	79.3	4.5	16.2
Farmers and farm managers	6,163	74.2	11.0	14.8	4,375	83.6	4.0	12.4
Farm laborers and foremen	5,370	61.9	5.7	32.4	2,578	71.9	5.5	22.6
Nonfarm, total	25,758	64.2	26.4	9.4	52,046	81.7	8.8	9.5
Professional, technical, and kindred workers	1,758	82.7	13.1	4.2	5,081	89.9	6.2	3.9
Managers, officials, proprietors	2,462	71.7	26.0	2.3	5,155	85.5	12.2	2.3
Clerical and kindred workers	1,987	87.9	10.8	1.3	7,232	93.0	4.0	3.0
Sales workers	1,755	84.9	14.1	1.0	4,133	91.5	6.6	1.9
Craftsmen, foremen, and kindred workers	4,315	68.6	28.7	2.7	8,350	85.2	10.8	4.0
Operatives and kindred workers	5,441	63.2	31.6	5.2	12,030	80.7	9.5	9.8
Service and kindred workers	3,562	44.7	23.9	31.4	6,180	59.5	10.7	29.8
Private household workers	1,851	41.9	22.4	35.7	1,538	34.1	7.8	58.1
Policemen, firemen	113	81.8	16.9	1.3	335	94.0	4.1	1.9
Other service workers	1,598	45.2	26.2	28.6	4,307	65.9	12.2	21.9
Laborers excluding farm and mine	4,478	45.7	37.1	17.2	3,885	64.6	9.6	25.8
Male	29,847	66.9	21.9	11.2	42,554	81.6	8.9	9.5
Farm, total	10,358	72.9	9.4	17.7	6,352	80.8	4.6	14.6
Farmers and farm managers	5,883	74.8	11.1	14.1	4,255	84.2	3.9	11.9
Farm laborers and foremen	4,475	70.7	7.0	22.3	2,097	74.0	5.9	20.1
Nonfarm occupations, total	19,488	65.7	27.0	7.3	36,202	81.8	9.7	8.5
Professional, technical, and kindred workers	1,032	80.7	15.1	4.2	3,074	89.9	7.3	2.8
Managers, officials, proprietors, excluding farm	2,312	72.0	25.9	2.1	4,456	85.4	12.6	2.0
Clerical and kindred workers	1,300	85.5	12.9	1.6	2,729	90.1	5.3	4.6

Sales workers	1,376	84.0	15.0	1.0	2,715	91.2	6.9	1.9
Craftsmen, foremen, and kindred workers	4,208	68.5	28.8	2.7	8,098	85.2	10.8	4.0
Operatives and kindred workers	3,739	59.3	35.2	5.5	8,743	81.2	9.1	9.7
Service and kindred workers	1,149	48.1	27.5	24.4	2,647	63.3	14.5	22.2
Private household workers	67	32.4	22.8	44.8	80	33.4	11.8	54.8
Policemen, firemen	113	81.8	16.9	1.3	329	94.0	4.1	1.9
Other service workers	969	45.3	29.1	25.6	2,238	59.9	16.1	24.0
Laborers, excluding farm and mine	4,372	45.4	37.4	17.2	3,740	64.4	9.7	25.9
Female	7,444	59.7	15.1	25.2	16,445	80.8	6.5	12.7
Farm, total	1,174	40.5	3.9	55.6	601	63.6	4.1	32.3
Farmers and farm managers	279	60.2	10.5	29.3	120	65.8	5.6	28.6
Farm laborers and foremen	895	34.4	1.9	63.7	481	63.0	3.7	33.3
Nonfarm, total	6,270	66.7	17.8	15.5	15,844	81.4	6.7	11.9
Professional, technical, and kindred workers	726	84.8	10.9	4.3	2,007	90.0	4.5	5.5
Managers, officials, proprietors, excluding farm	150	67.4	27.3	5.3	700	86.3	9.6	4.1
Clerical and kindred workers	688	92.9	6.5	0.6	4,502	94.7	3.2	2.1
Sales workers	379	88.4	10.8	0.8	1,418	91.9	6.0	2.1
Craftsmen, foremen, and kindred workers	106	73.6	25.4	1.0	253	84.9	9.5	5.6
Operatives and kindred workers	1,702	72.7	23.0	4.3	3,287	79.4	10.8	9.8
Service and kindred workers	2,413	43.1	22.2	34.7	3,532	56.7	7.9	35.4
Private household workers	1,784	42.6	22.4	35.0	1,459	34.1	7.6	58.3
Policemen, firemen	—	—	—	—	5	91.9	3.8	4.3
Other service workers	630	44.5	21.4	34.1	2,068	72.6	8.1	19.3
Laborers, excluding farm and mine	106	61.2	23.2	15.6	145	67.7	8.1	24.2

Note: Male and female subtotals may not add to the totals for both sexes due to rounding.

Source: Data on nonwhites adapted from Alba M. Edwards, Comparative Occupational Statistics for the United States: 1870–1940 (Washington, D.C.: U.S. Government Printing Office, 1943), tables 14 and 15, and U.S. Department of Commerce, Bureau of the Census, Occupational Characteristics, PC(2)7A (Washington, D.C.: U.S. Government Printing Office, 1963), table 3. Data on foreign born for 1910 adapted from Edwards, op. cit., and, for 1950, from Edward P. Hutchinson, Immigrants and Their Children (New York: John Wiley and sons, 1956). Occupational totals are from David L. Kaplan and M. Claire Casey, Occupational Trends in the United States, Census Working Paper no. 5 (Washington, D.C.: U.S. Government Printing Office, 1958).

systematic exclusionary practices of the craft unions. Some small
proportion of blacks did, however, achieve a toehold in middle- or
upper-level occupations. For example, a survey conducted in Philadelphia in 1913 identified a total of 1,028 black businesses in that city—
mainly small marginal retail or service establishments catering to the
black population. [13] Blacks were also employed in modest numbers in
some of the less desirable operative or craft jobs, typically those
falling into the hot or heavy category, and provided a convenient source
of strikebreakers in industries such as steel and coal during some of
the turbulent strikes of the period.

The extent to which each of the two major disadvantaged social
classes of the pre-World War I era—the immigrants and black Americans—contributed to the labor supply in each major occupational group,
as compared to native white workers, is indicated by the summary
statistics for 1910 appearing in Table 2.3. This table, as well as
several succeeding tables in this chapter, provides historical comparisons of the broad racial and nativity composition of the U.S. labor
force, by occupation, based on occupational groupings comparable to
those currently followed in the census statistics. The statistics compiled here are for 1910—when the tide of European immigration was
at its peak—and for 1950, based on a special census tabulation of the
foreign born for that year. (Comparable statistics for nonwhites have
also been compiled for 1960; however, detailed occupational statistics
for the foreign born were not published in the 1960 census.)

From these summary statistics, it is evident that the proportion
of native white workers in each occupational group as of 1910 was
closely correlated with that occupational group's social and economic
ranking. Native-born white workers comprised nearly two-thirds
(65.5 percent) of the total gainfully occupied population in 1910. However, they comprised more than 80 percent of the professional, clerical, and sales occupations, and of the policemen and firemen; they
accounted for more than 70 percent of the managerial and proprietor
groups (farm and nonfarm) and 68.6 percent of the skilled craftsmen
group. Conversely, the foreign born and nonwhite workers, combined,
provided a greater-than-proportionate share of the manpower in each
of the lower-level occupational groups. Although they accounted for
less than 35 percent of the total 1910 labor force, they represented a
majority of the workers in three occupational groups: private household workers (58 percent), other service workers (55 percent), and
nonfarm laborers (54 percent). They also accounted for a somewhat
greater-than-average share of the labor force in the two other lower-
level occupational groups: operatives and farm laborers. (These relationships have been expressed in the form of relative concentration
indices in Table 2.4)

TABLE 2.4

Relative Concentration Indices for Native White, Foreign-Born White, and Nonwhite Workers, by Major Occupational Group: 1910, 1950

Major Occupational Group	1910				1950			
	Number (000)	Percent			Number (000)	Percent		
		Native White	Foreign-Born White	Nonwhite		Native White	Foreign-Born White	Nonwhite
Total	37,291	100	100	100	58,999	100	100	100
Farm, total	11,533	105	41	169	6,953	97	55	156
Farmers and farm managers	6,163	113	53	109	4,375	103	49	119
Farm laborers and foremen	5,370	94	27	238	2,578	88	67	217
Nonfarm, total	25,758	98	126	69	52,046	100	107	91
Professional, technical, and kindred workers	1,758	126	63	31	5,081	110	76	37
Managers, officials, proprietors	2,462	109	124	17	5,155	105	149	22
Clerical and kindred workers	1,987	134	52	10	7,232	114	49	28
Sales workers	1,755	130	67	7	4,133	112	80	18
Craftsmen, foremen, and kindred workers	4,315	105	137	20	8,350	105	132	38
Operatives and kindred workers	5,441	96	151	38	12,030	99	116	94
Service and kindred workers	3,562	68	114	231	6,180	73	130	298
Private household workers	1,851	64	107	262	1,538	42	95	559
Policemen, firemen	113	125	81	10	335	115	50	18
Other service workers	1,598	69	125	210	4,307	81	149	211
Laborers, excluding farm and mine	4,478	70	177	126	3,885	79	117	248

Note: The relative concentration index for a particular population group is the ratio of the percentage of workers in a specific occupational group to the corresponding percentage for the population group in the labor force as a whole.

Source: Compiled by the author from data in Table 2.3.

Although the immigrants, as a group, shared certain common
handicaps with the native black population, these handicaps differed
in degree and were reflected in marked contrasts in their respective
occupational distributions. The foreign-born white population contributed only a small proportion (8.5 percent) of the farm labor force.
The blacks, on the other hand, had continued to be heavily concentrated
in southern agriculture, where they were locked in by the limited employment opportunities available to them elsewhere, as well as by the
sharecropper system, which had imposed a condition of financial ser-
vitude upon them.

In the nonfarm sector, both the foreign-born and black workers
were underrepresented in white-collar occupations, such as professional, clerical, and sales jobs, as a result of their limited educational and communication skills, and because of discrimination in
favor of the established native white population. At the bottom of the
occupational hierarchy, both foreign-born and black men were heavily
represented among unskilled laborers, among domestic servants, and
in other personal service occupations. However, whereas foreign-
born workers contributed a relatively large proportion of the labor
supply for the operative and craftsmen occupational groups and in
certain lines of small business—and in fact dominated certain of these
industries or trades—relatively few of the blacks had gained entry to
such occupations as of 1910, except where they entailed particularly
onerous working conditions.

The extent to which the black worker was differentially concentrated in the lowest rungs of the occupational status ladder is clearly
indicated, in Table 2.5, in a more detailed occupational distribution
of nonwhite workers as of 1910, grouped in accordance with our five
previously described broad occupational status groups. The occupations included in each of these groups correspond—except as noted
below—with the occupational status rankings shown in Table 1.3. The
major departure from this grouping was our assignment of black
farmers to group 4 rather than the group 3 category, in view of the
fact that the black farmer, as of 1910, was characteristically a sharecropper whose subordination to his white landlord was so complete as
to place him, precariously, only one step higher on the status ladder
than the hired farm laborer. By the same token, black farm family
workers (who had been combined with farmers in our original status
groupings as of 1960 because of their low frequency) have been included with paid farm laborers in group 5, for our historical comparisons. Other smaller departures in status grouping were necessitated by changes in census occupational classification over the years,
which prevented a precise matching of occupations, by status category,
with those based on our analyses of the 1960-70 census data. For
example, since it was not possible to distinguish between the lowest

TABLE 2.5

Percentage Distribution of Nonwhite Workers, by Occupational Status Groups and Subgroups: 1910, 1950, 1960

Occupational Status Group	Both Sexes			Male			Female		
	1910	1950	1960	1910	1950	1960	1910	1950	1960
Total	100.0	100.0	100.0	100.0	100.0	100.0	100.0	100.0	100.0
Group 1—professional, technical, kindred workers, total	1.5	3.2	5.5	1.3	2.2	4.0	1.6	5.2	7.7
Engineers	—	—	0.2	—	0.1	0.3			—
Medical personnel	0.6	0.5	1.1	0.2	0.3	0.6	1.3	1.0	1.8
Teachers, excluding college	0.2	1.5	2.2	0.2	0.5	0.9	0.1	3.3	4.1
All other	0.7	1.2	2.0	0.9	1.3	2.2	0.2	0.9	1.8
Group 2	1.8	6.9	10.8	2.5	6.9	9.9	0.9	7.3	12.4
Managers, officials, proprietors, excluding farm	1.1	1.9	1.9	1.5	2.3	2.4	0.5	1.4	1.2
Clerical and kindred workers, total	0.5	3.6	6.9	0.6	3.1	5.4	0.2	4.5	9.2
Secretaries, stenographers, typists	0.1	0.5	1.2	—	0.1	0.1	0.1	1.4	2.7
All other clerical workers	0.4	3.1	5.7	0.6	3.0	5.3	0.1	3.1	6.5
Sales workers	0.2	1.3	1.8	0.4	1.3	1.7	0.2	1.4	2.0
Policemen, firemen[a]	—	0.1	0.2	—	0.2	0.4	—	—	—
Group 3	3.7	11.1	13.0	5.2	11.1	14.7	1.5	10.3	10.7
Craftsmen, foremen, and kindred workers									
Foremen, not elsewhere classified	0.1	0.2	0.4	0.1	0.3	0.5	—	0.1	0.1
Mechanics and metal craftsmen	0.4	1.9	2.8	0.6	3.0	4.5	—	0.1	0.1
Carpenters	0.6	0.7	0.8	1.0	1.1	1.2	—	—	—
Brickmasons, electricians[b]	0.3	0.8	0.9	0.5	1.1	1.5	—	—	—
Craftsmen, not elsewhere classified	0.5	1.1	1.6	0.8	1.4	2.6	0.1	0.4	0.5
Barbers, bartenders, miscellaneous services[c]	1.6	5.4	5.4	1.9	3.0	3.0	1.3	9.0	9.2
Operatives—printing, petroleum, and related	0.2	1.0	1.1	0.3	1.2	1.4	0.1	0.7	0.8

(continued)

(Table 2.5 continued)

	Both Sexes			Male			Female		
Occupational Status Group	1910	1950	1960	1910	1950	1960	1910	1950	1960
Group 4	25.6	29.2	27.2	32.6	36.8	33.1	10.5	15.5	17.9
Farmers and farm managers, total	18.0	8.8	3.0	25.6	12.6	4.5	4.6	1.6	0.7
Construction painters, plasterers, roofers	0.3	0.8	0.5	0.4	1.1	0.8	—	—	—
Transport operatives	0.9	4.1	5.2	1.1	6.7	8.7	—	0.2	0.1
Operatives, durable goods manufacturing									
Metalworking industries	0.2	2.6	4.0	0.2	3.4	5.2	—	1.5	2.0
All other durables	0.3	1.1	1.0	0.4	1.6	1.3	0.1	0.4	0.4
Operatives, nondurable goods manufacturing									
Food and tobacco	0.4	1.6	1.9	0.4	1.6	1.9	0.6	1.8	1.8
Textile, apparel, leather	0.3	1.7	1.9	0.2	0.8	0.8	0.4	3.8	3.5
Operatives, nonmanufacturing									
Mining, not elsewhere classified	1.0	0.7	0.3	1.3	1.2	0.4	—	—	—
All other nonmanufacturing including not specified operatives	0.9	3.3	3.6	0.5	3.3	4.8	2.5	1.8	1.8
Service occupations									
Guards, watchmen	0.1	0.2	0.3	0.1	0.3	0.4	—	—	0.1
Waiters, waitresses	0.9	1.5	1.6	1.3	1.1	1.0	0.6	2.3	2.6
Hospital attendants, practical nurses, midwives	1.6	1.0	2.5	—	0.5	1.0	1.7	1.9	4.8
Laborers, metalworking industries	0.7	1.8	1.4	1.1	2.6	2.3	—	0.2	0.1
Group 5	67.4	49.6	43.5	58.4	43.0	38.3	85.5	61.7	51.3
Farm laborers and foremen, total	33.9	9.5	6.0	30.7	10.5	7.6	35.4	7.7	3.5
Paid workers	17.4	6.1	5.4	18.0	7.3	7.1	15.8	3.9	2.9
Unpaid workers	16.5	3.4	0.6	12.7	3.2	0.5	19.6	3.8	0.6

52

Laborers, excluding farm and mine	2.8	1.3	0.8	3.8	2.0	1.4	0.1	0.2	0.1
Durables, excluding metals									
Nondurable goods manufacturing									
Food and tobacco	0.5	0.6	0.6	0.6	0.9	0.9	0.2	0.2	0.2
Textile, apparel, leather	0.3	0.2	0.2	0.5	0.4	0.3	0.1	0.2	—
Other nondurable	0.5	0.8	0.6	0.7	1.1	1.0	—	0.2	—
Nonmanufacturing									
Construction	1.0	3.4	3.3	3.1	5.0	5.3	—	0.2	0.1
All other nonmanufacturing (including not specified)	9.9	8.4	6.9	13.5	12.1	10.9	0.5	0.5	0.7
Personal services									
Cooks	1.8	2.1	2.3	1.3	1.5	1.5	3.1	3.2	3.4
Janitors and sextons	0.5	2.4	2.7	0.7	3.3	3.9	0.1	0.7	0.7
Other cleaning and building services[e]	2.1	3.3	2.9	2.1	3.7	3.6	2.1	1.8	1.9
Private household workers	13.6	15.0	14.8	1.0	1.1	0.8	43.1	41.5	36.4
Laundry and dry cleaning operatives	0.5	2.6	2.4	0.4	1.4	1.1	0.8	5.3	4.3

Notes to Table 2.5

[a]Includes marshals and constables; sheriffs and bailiffs.

[b]Includes plumbers; excavating, grading, and machinery operators; and structural metal craftsmen.

[c]Includes boardinghouse and lodginghouse workers, miscellaneous personal attendants, ushers, and recreation and amusement workers.

[d]Includes crossing watchmen and bridge tenders.

[e]Includes porters, elevator operators, cleaners, and charwomen.

Source: Compiled by the author from census data (see Table 2.3).

level of clerical occupations, such as shipping clerks (included in group 4) and the remaining clerical jobs, all clerical workers were included in group 2. The latter adjustments have had only a minor impact upon the overall comparability of these data for broad trend analysis.

To illustrate the degree of concentration of the 1910 nonwhite labor force in the lowest-status occupational categories (as evidenced by the data in Table 2. 5), over two-thirds of all black workers were in group 5 occupations and 93 percent were in the Group 4 and Group 5 classes combined. The black woman was even more constrained in her occupational range than the black man: over 85 percent of nonwhite women in 1910 were in group 5 occupations, mainly domestic service and other personal service jobs, and in farm labor.

Another useful measure of the degree of inequality of occupational distribution of blacks in the 1910 labor force is the index of relative concentration by occupation, which is a ratio of the percent of non-whites in a specific occupation to the percent of nonwhites in all occupations. If nonwhites were proportionately represented in all occupations, this index would have a value of 100 in each occupation. Thus, deviations from 100 indicate the degree of underrepresentation—or overrepresentation in a particular occupation. These indices (see Table 2. 6) demonstrate the very limited penetration of black workers into the whole range of middle- and upper-level occupations as well as into the more desirable of the group 4 occupations, such as manufacturing operatives. Conversely, nonwhites were heavily overrepresented in nearly all of the group 5 occupations—most heavily in the menial personal service occupations such as domestics, cooks, charwomen, cleaners, and porters.

WORLD WAR I TO 1960

Industrial and Occupational Trends

The half century which elapsed between the beginning of World War I and 1960 witnessed profound transformations in the nation's economy and in the occupational distribution of its labor force. The most dramatic of these changes were (1) the sharp decline in labor requirements for agriculture, (2) the rapid growth of service activities and of white-collar occupations, (3) major shifts in occupational composition within the industrial work force, and (4) the continued movement of many functions previously performed within the household to the nonhousehold market economy.

Although these trends resulted from a complex of economic and technological changes, an overriding influence was the vastly increased reliance on mechanical power for production of goods anJ services. Between 1910 and 1960, the total horsepower of all prime movers had multiplied eightyfold, from 139,000 to 11,008,000. Dominating the trend was the substitution of the internal combustion engine in automobiles, trucks, and airplanes, for earlier modes of land transportation, such as the steam railroad and horse-drawn vehicles. In 1910, the latter transportation methods were still predominant. By 1960, automotive vehicles (cars, trucks, and buses) had become the dominant means of land transportation; animals had become a negligible source of motive power for transportation while railroads had declined drastically in relative importance. Concurrently the mechanical power utilized in factories, farms, mines, and households had also increased manyfold.[14]

The labor force effects of the new mechanical revolution were most dramatically visible in the two sectors which, as of 1910, were still the most technologically retarded, that is, agriculture and the household economy. In agriculture, which had been a major user of unskilled manual labor in 1910, the progressive mechanization of additional farm crops and farm processes and the increased application of scientific methods of farming, combined with the curtailment of export markets, released millions of former farmers and farm laborers for employment in higher-paying nonagricultural pursuits. The result was a sharp decline in the proportion of the labor force engaged in farm occupations, from 31 percent in 1910 to 6 percent in 1960.

In the household economy, the proliferation of labor-saving household appliances and the increased reliance upon market sources for preparation of ready-made foods and for laundry and related personal services were most directly reflected in a reduction by nearly one-half in the percentage of workers in private household occupations, from 5.0 percent in 1910 to 2.8 percent in 1960, and in the growth of many of the personal service occupations performed outside the home. Of even greater significance, these developments—combined with the long-term trend towards reduction in family size—had made it possible for many millions of women to enter gainful employment. In the early 1900s, only about 20 percent of women, 14 years and over, were in the labor force; by 1960, this proportion had risen to nearly 35 percent.[15]

Within the nonfarm sector, the emergence of new mass production industries, such as automobiles, rubber, and electrical and electronics equipment, and the continued mechanization of older industries resulted in a major shift in the occupational structure of the industrial work force. Many jobs previously performed by

TABLE 2.6

Relative Concentration of Nonwhites in Each Occupation:
1910, 1950, 1960

Occupational Status Group	Both Sexes		
	1910	1950	1960
Total, experienced civilian labor force	100	100	100
Group 1—professional, technical, kindred			
workers, total	30	38	48
Engineers	4	6	14
Medical personnel	17	29	56
Teachers, excluding college	35	74	84
All other	32	31	37
Group 2	11	24	35
Managers, proprietors, officials,			
excluding farm	16	22	23
Clerical and kindred workers, total	9	29	47
Secretaries, stenos, typists	3	18	32
All other clerical workers	10	33	51
Sales workers	7	18	24
Policemen, firemen[a]	9	18	35
Group 3	25	64	73
Craftsmen, foremen, and kindred workers			
Foremen, not elsewhere classified	9	14	20
Mechanics and metal craftsmen	13	38	56
Carpenters	27	41	53
Brickmasons, electricians[b]	20	40	52
Craftsmen	17	36	44
Barbers, bartenders, miscellaneous services[c]	63	109	98
Operatives—printing, petroleum, and			
related industries	37	94	108
Group 4	70	98	105
Farmers and farm managers, total	104	119	76
Construction painters, plasterers,			
roofers	31	79	173
Transport operatives	62	103	115
Operatives—durable goods manufacturing			
Metalworking industries	14	63	80
All other durables	45	126	118
Operatives—nondurable goods manufacturing			
Food and tobacco	56	111	132
Textile, apparel, leather	9	48	65

Operatives—nonmanufacturing			
Mining, not elsewhere classified	49	66	49
All other nonmanufacturing, including			
not specified operatives	38	115	135
Service occupations			
Guards, watchmen[d]	32	44	60
Waiters, waitresses	172	107	100
Hospital attendants, practical nurses,			
midwives	109	154	240
Laborers, metalworking industries	43	218	224
Group 5	194	308	331
Farm laborers and foremen, total	228	217	249
Paid workers	210	220	275
Unpaid workers	245	213	131
Laborers, excluding farm and mine			
Durables, excluding metals	184	288	251
Nondurable goods manufacturing			
Food and tobacco	129	216	250
Textile, apparel, leather	44	129	186
Other nondurables	108	254	264
Nonmanufacturing			
Construction	136	249	278
All other nonmanufacturing (including			
not specified)	127	249	254
Personal services			
Cooks	394	257	245
Janitors and sextons	158	288	283
Other cleaning and building services[e]	318	458	441
Private household workers	251	559	527
Laundry and dry cleaning operators	170	337	419

[a]Includes marshals and constables; sheriffs and bailiffs.

[b]Includes plumbers; excavating, grading, and machinery operators; and structural metal craftsmen.

[c]Includes boarding house and lodginghouse workers, miscellaneous personal attendants, ushers, and recreation and amusement workers.

[d]Includes crossing watchmen and bridge tenders.

[e]Includes porters, elevator operators, cleaners, and charwomen.

Note: The relative concentration index is the ratio of the percent of nonwhites in a specified occupation to the percent of nonwhites in all occupations.

Source: Compiled by the author.

unskilled laborers were eliminated or converted to machine-tending or machine-operating functions, thus making possible a sharp reduction in the proportion of nonfarm laborers in the work force, from 12 percent in 1910 to 5.5 percent in 1960. Requirements for many of the traditional crafts were also greatly reduced, as their work was subdivided into more specialized, repetitive duties, or replaced entirely—as in the case of glassblowers—by highly automated equipment. In their place, there emerged an expanded work force of operatives and of mechanics and repairmen. Thus, in 1960 the operatives constituted the largest single occupational group, accounting for 20 percent of the civilian labor force, as compared to 14.5 percent in 1910. The craft occupations group also experienced a net growth, of 2 percent in its share of the labor force between 1910 and 1960 as rapid growth of the mechanic and repairman occupations, as well as in occupations associated with the construction industry, offset declines in other skilled crafts.

A concomitant of these developments was a sharp increase, too, in requirements for all categories of white-collar occupations. These included many new professional, technical, managerial, and clerical specialities needed to develop and apply the results of modern science and technology, and to service the recordkeeping, communications, and control needs of increasingly complex organizations in both the private and the expanding public sectors. The most rapid expansion in the white-collar groups was among the professional, technical, and clerical occupations, with smaller increases in the proportion of nonfarm managers, officials, and proprietors, and of sales personnel. However, whereas the managerial group in 1910 had consisted in large part of proprietors of small retail shops and similar establishments, by 1960, two-thirds of the total consisted of salaried managers and officials in business and government.

The net effect of these changes was a pronounced upgrading in the occupational distribution of the labor force. Thus, based on the summary data for the major census occupational groups, the combined proportion of workers in the laborer category (farm and nonfarm) and in private household occupations declined from about 26 percent in 1910 to less than 8 percent in 1960. Even if we further combine these occupations with the expanding operative and service worker groups, the net decline in this broader category (roughly corresponding to our status groups 4 and 5) was still very substantial, that is, from 51 percent in 1910 to 39 percent in 1960.

These trends developed unevenly over this 50-year period, punctuated—as it was—by three major wars and by alternating periods of prosperity and depression. For example, during the depression decade of the 1930s, the decline in the proportion of hired farm laborers slowed down appreciably, while the proportion of domestics actually increased. In the decade of the 1940s the World War II mobilization and the continued high levels of economic activity in the immediate postwar period were reflected in particularly sharp reductions in the proportion of workers in the laborer and domestic service groups.

It should be noted, too, that the standard census occupational statistics, which we have cited previously, refer to the civilian labor force and, therefore, exclude one labor force component which grew significantly over this period, notably, the armed forces. Until the World War II period our peacetime military establishment—staffed entirely by volunteers—had been comparatively modest in size, although it grew gradually from a level of 139,000 in 1910 to 334,000 in 1939. Following World War II, the nation's assumption of increased responsibilities for security of the non-Communist world, combined with the onset of the cold war, required the maintenance of a much larger military establishment staffed by a combination of draftees and volunteers. Thus, after the immediate post-World War II demobilization in 1948, our active-duty military strength of about 1.4 million was still fully four times as great as in 1939. It rose, moreover, to a Korean War peak of 3,550,000 in 1953. Even after substantial cutbacks in the following years, it still stood at 2,476,000 in 1960, or 3.5 percent of the total labor force. [16]

The evolution of the occupational structure of the military services in the period since World War I has, in broad outline, closely paralleled that of the civilian economy. Thus, at the peak of the World War I mobilization in 1918, about 63 percent of all military personnel were assigned to relatively low-skilled ground combat duties, to service or laborer activities, or to other unskilled activities. An additional 20 percent were working as mechanics or in other craft occupations, while only 17 percent were in white-collar activities, including officers, enlisted technicians, and clerks. By 1960, the proportion in the lower-level enlisted occupations had declined sharply to 16 percent; the percentage in mechanical and craft occupations had risen to 37 percent, while the white-collar occupational specialties now accounted for 47 percent of total military personnel. [17]

Immigration Trends

The transformations in occupational structures described above were accompanied by equally dramatic shifts in sources of labor supply. Until the 1920s, our national policy had been one of virtually unrestricted immigration. Although this policy, in part, reflected our long-standing tradition of providing asylum to the oppressed and underprivileged, it had been maintained—in spite of mounting opposition from organized labor—because it accorded with the perceived manpower needs of the nation, during an era of rapid expansion. Demands for some forms of control over the number and types of immigrants had flared at various times in the nineteenth century, notably in the 1840s, when the Know-Nothing movement was organized in part as a reaction to the large influx of Irish immigrants. The demands grew in intensity, beginning in the 1880s, when organized labor became increasingly concerned about wage competition from the new immigrant groups, particularly their utilization by employers as strikebreakers. However, with the notable exception of legislation barring importation of Chinese coolies and a gentlemen's agreement in 1907, barring Japanese immigration, no substantial legal constraint upon the inflow of immigrants was enacted until after World War I— although a series of laws beginning in the 1880s did provide for screening of certain undesirable categories.[18] A dominant consideration during the early 1900s was the continuing need of industry for a large supply of unskilled manual workers: "Employers, during the period of industrial development after 1898 wanted labor—abundant labor, cheap labor, strong backed labor, in large measure common labor, and always docile labor."[19]

With the outbreak of World War I in Europe, the mass entry of immigrants was, however, suspended. The number of alien immigrants admitted, which had averaged 1.2 million per year in the two preceding years, fell to an average of 300,000 per year in 1914-17 and to only about 100,000 per year in 1918 and 1919. Immediately after the end of the war, the flow of immigrants was temporarily resumed, reflecting the effect of extreme dislocations and war-induced hardships in Europe, and the efforts of many immigrants to rejoin members of their family who had immigrated here shortly before the war. However, the era of mass immigration was effectively terminated by legislation, enacted in 1921, which established an immigration quota system, whose effect was with certain exceptions to limit the overall number of immigrants of any nationality admitted each year, based on the percentage of foreign-born persons of that national origin residing in the United States as of a base census year. The initial legislation established a quota of 3 percent, based on the percentage of foreign born from each national group as shown in the 1910 census. A revised law, enacted in 1924, reduced the quota to 2 percent and substituted the 1890 census as the base year, thus systematically curtailing the inflows of ethnic groups from the later immigrant sources of Southern and Eastern Europe. Asiatics were generally precluded from immigration as under previous practice. However no quotas were established for residents of the Western Hemisphere.[20]

This fundamental reversal of American immigration policy was due to a combination of influences, including intensified opposition by organized labor to a resumption of large-scale immigration, widespread ethnic and religious prejudices against the newer immigrant groups, and the near hysteria concerning the dangers of imported bolshevism or anarchism. [21] Of possibly equal importance was the fact that, as a result of its experience in recruitment of labor for the World War I industrial mobilization from internal, rather than external sources (discussed below) and of the progressive displacement of unskilled labor by mechanization, American industry no longer found the unskilled immigrant essential for its post-World War I manpower needs. [22]

The 1924 act was to continue as the basic statutory framework of U.S. immigration policy for a period of more than four decades. It was subject to numerous amendments and modifications in the light of changing exigencies—notably to permit importation of contract agricultural labor, mainly from Mexico, during and immediately after World War II (the bracero program) and to facilitate immigration of war brides and of various displaced persons or refugee groups. In addition, in 1952, special preference within quota limits was provided for individuals with specialized skills or abilities.

The combined effect of these statutory constraints was to sharply curtail the volume of immigration and to significantly change the composition of the later immigrant groups. Following enactment of the 1924 law, immigration fell to a rate of about 300,000 per year in 1925-29; it remained well below 100,000 per year during the depression decade of the 1930s and the World War II period, and—despite special nonquota provisions for war brides and certain refugee groups—averaged only about 250,000 per year in the decade of the 1950s. (See Table 2.7.) As a result of the national origin quota system and other special provisions, the percentage of immigrants from the favored nationality groups, including those from Northern and Western Europe and from Canada (to whom no quota applied), rose from less than one-fourth of the total in the 1901-10 period, to 54 percent in 1921-30, and to 60 percent in 1951-60. At the same time, immigration from Mexico, the West Indies, and other Latin-American countries, which in common with that from Canada was not subject to quota limitation during this period, rose from only 2 percent of the total in 1901-10, to about one-fourth in 1951-60. [23] This was supplemented, moreover, by an increased flow of illegal immigrants mainly across the Mexican border—the so-called wetbacks. Moreover, beginning in the 1940s, there was a growing inflow of Puerto Ricans to the mainland, where they settled mainly in the New York City area. Thus, the Puerto Rican-born population in New York City, which had totaled only 70,000 in 1940, grew to 187,000 in 1950. In the following

TABLE 2.7

Alien Immigration and Net Migration from Farms,
by Decade: 1910-70
(in thousands)

Period	Immigrants	Net Migration from Farms
1901-10	8,795	n.a.
1911-20	5,736	(5,100)
1921-30	4,107	5,921
1931-40	528	4,557
1941-50	1,035	10,636
1951-60	2,515	9,597
1961-70	3,322	5,940

Note: Data on immigrants also includes effects of net reclassification of residence; estimate for 1911-20 is an approximation based
on net change in farm population between 1911 and 1920 and on
natural growth rate for farm population, based on 1920-25 experience.

Sources: Data on immigrants are from U.S. Department of
Justice, Immigration and Naturalization Service, 1971 Annual Report
(Washington, D.C.: U.S. Government Printing Office, 1972), table
1. Net migration data are from U.S. Department of Agriculture,
Rural Development Service, Farm Population Estimates, 1910-70,
Statistical Bulletin no. 523 (Washington, D.C.: U.S. Government
Printing Office, 1973), table 6.

decade, the total Puerto Rican population including the children of
those born in Puerto Rico, mushroomed to 613,000 in New York City
alone, and to a nationwide total of 893,000.[24] The latter, although
not "immigrants," represented a major component of the growing
U.S. population of Spanish language or origin.

The shift in ethnic composition of immigrants, combined with
increased selectivity in admissions and concurrent economic and
social trends in the countries of origin, was to greatly alter the occupational composition of the immigrant group. Thus, in 1907, the peak

year of the pre-World War I immigrant inflow, one-third of the nearly one million immigrants who reported an occupation upon arrival were classified as farm laborers and nearly three-fourths of the total (74 percent) were classified as either farm or nonfarm laborers, as domestics, or as other service workers. By the period 1951-60, the proportion of farm laborers had declined to 4 percent, while those in the broader group of laborer and service occupations had declined to less than one-fourth of the total (23 percent). In contrast, the percentage reported as professionals or in other white-collar occupations had increased from less than 5 percent of the total in 1907 to 37 percent in the 1950s.[25]

The extent to which these trends affected the contribution of immigrants to the labor supply of the various occupations is suggested by the statistics in Table 2.3. By 1950, the percentage of foreign-born whites in the labor force had been reduced to 8.2 percent as compared to 20.9 percent in 1910—a consequence of the post-World War I reduction in new immigration and of attrition in the labor force among the large cohorts of immigrants who had entered in earlier decades. Analysis of the proportion of foreign-born workers in each major occupational group indicates that in spite of both the higher-level occupational background of later immigrants and the occupational upgrading of many who had arrived in this country early in their working lives, the foreign-born workers continued to be underrepresented in most of the preferred white-collar occupations, that is, the professional and technical, and clerical and sales groups, and continued to be overrepresented in most of the lower-level occupational groups. There were, however, significant shifts in relative concentration of the foreign-born workers by occupational group, as indicated in Table 2.4. Among the higher-level occupations, foreign-born workers increased their relative proportions, as compared to 1910, in the nonfarm managerial and proprietor group, in professional and technical occupations, and in sales jobs. Among the lower-level occupational groups, the most significant shifts were sharp declines in the relative proportions of foreign-born workers in the nonfarm laborer and operative groups and in private household occupations, and a relative increase in the farm laborer groups—the latter reflecting the large-scale immigration of Mexican farm workers into the southwestern states.

On balance, therefore, it is evident that in 1950 the first-generation immigrant population in the labor force contributed a much smaller proportion of manpower to nearly all of the lower-level manual occupations than during the earlier era of mass immigration. Of equal significance, the sons and daughters of the first-generation immigrants had, as a group, experienced a high degree of upward occupational mobility in relation to their parents' occupations. Thus, by 1950, the native white population of foreign or mixed parentage—the population of foreign stock—held a greater-than-proportionate share of all the white-collar occupations, a roughly proportionate share of the nonfarm blue-collar and service jobs, and a much smaller relative share of the farm occupations. [26]

The Role of Internal Migration

The reversal of American immigration policy in the early 1920s was—as we have noted earlier—prompted, in part, by a number of ideological and political pressures. However, the fact that the revised policy was maintained for more than four decades can be attributed mainly to the development of alternative, internal sources of labor supply to meet the changing manpower needs of the post-World War I era. The most important of these sources was a large and growing volume of migration from the farms. The rural population, with its historically high natural growth rate, had probably always provided a significant source of manpower recruitment for industry and for other urban employment, beginning with the early decades of the nineteenth century. However, until the turn of the century, the continued substantial growth of the rural population (then mainly composed of farm residents) suggests that net migration from farm to city was of modest dimensions.

Beginning with 1910, separate statistics on the size of the rural-farm population have provided a basis for estimating the net outflows of population from farms to nonfarm areas. These estimates indicate that, for the decade 1910-20, as a whole, approximately five million persons moved from farms to nonfarm areas. During that decade, the farm population had continued to rise slightly until our entry into World War I, from 32.1 million in 1910 to a peak of 32.5 million in 1916. Between 1916 and 1919 it fell by 1.3 million, thus suggesting that a major portion of the farm-to-city migration in this decade was concentrated during the World War I period, in response to the sharp growth in urban employment opportunities created by expanding war employment and the virtual stoppage of immigration. Net migration from farms continued at a high rate in the decade of the 1920s, averaging nearly 600,000 per year; was temporarily slowed down during the depression decade of the 1930s (with some net reverse flow in 1931-32); and then reached its crescendo in the wartime decade of the 1940s, when a total of 10.6 million persons were drawn from farms to provide manpower for the World War II industrial mobilization and for the armed forces. It continued, moreover, near peak levels in the decade of the 1950s, when an additional 9.6 million

persons moved from farm to nonfarm areas. As a result, the resident
farm population had been reduced by more than one-half, from its
pre-World War I peak of 32.5 million in 1916 to 15.6 million in 1960.

The extent to which migrants from farms had replaced the foreign
immigrants as a major source of manpower for the expanding nonfarm
economy is suggested by the comparisons of these two population
flows appearing in Table 2.7. The net gains in the nonfarm population
provided by farm-to-city migrants, in the decades of the 1940s and
the 1950s, substantially exceeded, in absolute volume, the gross inflow of immigrant aliens in the decade of peak immigration, 1901-10.
The foregoing statistics on net farm outmigration exclude, moreover,
the substantial outflows of nonfarm residents from rural areas, such
as the coal mining region of Appalachia or the northern Michigan
timber cutover area, which also added substantially to the urban labor
supply during these decades.

The Black Worker

Of particular significance, for our discussion of sources of manpower for lower-level jobs, was the major role played by blacks in
this mass movement from farm to city. For five decades following
their emancipation, the black population had remained highly concentrated in the rural South. In 1860, 90 percent of blacks lived in the
South (that is, in the South Atlantic, East South Central, and South
Central states); 50 years later, in 1910, 80 percent were still in the
South. And while the small northern black population had already
formed enclaves in some of our larger cities, nearly 8 out of 10
southern blacks still resided in rural areas. The limited movement
of the black population out of the rural South during the half century
from 1860 to 1910, despite their very low level of living and restricted
economic opportunities there, was directly related to the ready availability of large masses of white immigrants to northern employers.
In short, although the push of poverty and discrimination had been
relatively constant factors in the condition of the southern black population, the pull of job opportunity for them in the North had not yet
emerged.

This situation was reversed by the stoppage of immigration
during World War I and the sharp expansion of wartime manpower
needs. Northern employers turned to the South and particularly to
the southern black to fill the void left by the suspended inflow of
Italians, Slavs, and other later immigrant groups. The World War I
period thus witnessed the first large-scale inflow into what were soon
to become the black ghettos of our northern metropolises. Particularly

difficult conditions in the cotton belt further facilitated this movement
as indicated by this description of the World War I inflow of blacks
into Chicago:

> For several years the cotton kingdom had been ravaged
> by the boll weevil surging up from Mexico. Flood and
> famine, too, had continuously harassed the cotton farmers
> of the Mississippi Valley. Prior to 1915, however, there
> had been little to encourage plantation laborers to risk
> life in the city streets. Now there were jobs to attract
> them. Recruiting agents travelled South, begging Negroes
> to come North. For the first time, Southern Negroes
> were actually being invited, even urged, to come to
> Chicago. They came in droves—50,000 of them between
> 1910 and 1920. [27]

The initial momentum of black migration from the farm achieved
during the First World War was maintained through the decade of the
1920s; it slowed down during the depression and then reached tidal
proportions in the 1940s and 1950s, concurrent with sharp reductions
in labor requirements in southern agriculture, associated with introduction of the mechanical cotton pickers and diversification of crops.
Although the most visible movement of the black population was to the
northern and western cities, large numbers moved to southern urban
centers as well. As a result, by 1960, whereas 60 percent of the
black population were still residing in the South, 73 percent were
living in urban areas, as contrasted to only 27 percent in 1910. [28]
Within the urban economy, the types of jobs available to the
black inmigrants in the decades between 1910 and 1940 were substantially the same as those previously filled by the small resident
black urban population and by the more disadvantaged of the immigrant
groups who had preceded them. By 1940, two-thirds of all black
workers were in nonfarm occupations, as compared to only one-half
of the total in 1910. (See Table 2.8.) All but a modest percentage of
these, however, continued to be engaged in the low-skilled manual
occupations: the men, predominantly, as unskilled laborers and
service workers; the women, as domestics or in similar menial
service occupations. During this period, the proportion employed
as operatives or in other semiskilled occupations had also grown
gradually, from about 5 percent to 10 percent of the total. Very
limited inroads had been made by black workers into the skilled
crafts or the white-collar occupations. In 1910, 11 percent of all
black nonfarm workers were reported in such occupations; by 1940,
this percentage had risen only slightly to 13.5 percent. In contrast,
the percentage of white nonfarm workers in these occupations had
grown from 51 percent in 1910 to 58 percent in 1940.

TABLE 2.8

Percentage Distribution of Black Labor Force,
by Occupational Field: 1910–60

Year	Total	Farm Occupations	Nonfarm Occupations				All Other Nonfarm as Percent of Nonfarm Total
			Total	Laborers and Service Workers	Semiskilled Workers and Operatives	Allb Other	
1910	100.0	50.4	49.6	38.7	5.4	5.5	11.0
1920	100.0	46.6	53.4	39.5	7.3	6.6	12.3
1930	100.0	36.1	63.9	46.7	9.4	7.8	12.2
1940	100.0a	32.8	66.6	47.3	10.3	9.0	13.5
1950	100.0a	19.0	69.5	45.5	18.3	15.7	18.0
1960	100.0	11.3	88.7	46.9	20.7	21.1	21.1

aFigures do not add to 100.0 percent because of inclusion of individuals for whom no occupation was reported.
bIncludes skilled workers and foremen and white-collar occupations.

Note: The above percentage distributions differ slightly from those shown elsewhere in this study for corresponding years because of differences in occupational classification.

Source: Adapted from decennial census statistics in Dale L. Hiestand, Economic Growth and Employment Opportunities for Minorities (New York: Columbia University Press, 1964), p. 42.

The World War II mobilization, with its attendant labor shortages, provided the first significant breakthrough of blacks into these higher-level occupational fields. The rapid expansion of defense-related employment in industry and government, combined with mobilization of millions of men into the armed forces, inevitably opened up a broader range of occupational opportunities for black workers, including both those already residing in urban areas and the large numbers of new wartime inmigrants from the rural South. Over this period, the percentage of blacks in farm occupations declined from nearly one-third to less than one-fifth of the total. The most significant growth was in the operatives group, which—by 1950—accounted for over 18 percent of all blacks in the labor force. Black men and women also increased their representation in the white-collar and skilled crafts occupations, which in combination, also accounted for 18 percent of all black non-farm workers in 1950, as compared to 13.5 percent in 1940. Following the war, the decade of the 1950s, punctuated by the partial mobilization for the Korean War, witnessed a continuation of the trends of the previous decade, as evidenced by a further reduction in the percentage of blacks in farm occupations and additional moderate gains by blacks in the operatives, crafts, and white-collar occupations.

Some further insight as to the net effect of the influences described above on the occupational distribution of the black labor force is provided by the more detailed occupational distribution, by status groups, which we have compiled for the years 1910, 1950, and 1960 (see Table 2.5). By 1960 the three highest-status occupational groups, as we have defined them, included 29 percent of the nonwhite labor force, as contrasted to only 7 percent in 1910. The overall proportion of blacks in Group 4 occupations remained relatively stable over this period, as a sharp reduction in the percentage of black farmers was offset by increases in the proportion of blacks working as transport operatives, in various other operative occupations, and in intermediate-level service occupations, as hospital attendants, waiters, or waitresses. In contrast, the percentage of blacks in the group 5 occupations declined sharply, from 67 percent in 1910 to 44 percent in 1960, mainly reflecting the very sharp reduction in the percentage of blacks in the farm labor occupations, including family workers.

Although these statistics confirm the fact that a significant upgrading in occupational status of blacks did occur, mainly during the 1940-60 period, these gains were concentrated in certain of the occupations which had experienced a particularly rapid overall growth during this period, notably in some of the lower-paid professional and clerical occupations, in mechanical repair work, in transportation operative occupations (such as truck and taxi driver), and in the more skilled service jobs. An analysis of the trends in relative concentration of blacks in various occupations (Table 2.6) therefore indicates—

as would be expected—that the relative improvement in occupational status of blacks, as compared to white workers, has been much more modest than indicated by trends in the overall occupational distribution of blacks over this period. For example:

1. From the statistics for 1950 by major census group (Table 2.4), it is apparent that—relative to white workers—blacks had made very little progress in penetration of either white-collar or the skilled crafts jobs. Among the lowest-status occupations, their movement from farm to city had resulted in a slightly reduced share of the farm laborer jobs, but in sharp increases in their relative proportion of jobs as nonfarm laborers or domestics. Blacks continued also to be disproportionately represented in other service occupations (other than protective service). Their most significant progress over this period had been in their movement into the semiskilled operatives group, where they had achieved near parity by 1950, in contrast to their very limited representation in this occupational group in 1910.

2. The extent to which blacks had effectively replaced white immigrants in some of the lower-status nonfarm occupations is indicated by the following comparison of the net change in the occupational concentration indices for each group, between 1910 and 1950. For this purpose, we have ranked the major occupational groups in order of the increase of the concentration index for nonwhites between the two years:

Occupational Group	Nonwhites	Foreign-Born Whites
Private household workers	+297	-12
Laborers, excluding farm and mine	+122	-60
Operatives and kindred workers	+ 56	-35
Craftsmen and foremen	+ 18	- 5
Clerical and kindred workers	+ 18	- 3
Farmers and farm managers	+ 10	- 4
Sales workers	+ 9	+13
Protective service workers	+ 8	-31
Professional, technical, and kindred workers	+ 6	+13
Managers, officials, and proprietors	+ 5	+25
Other service occupations	+ 1	+24
Farm laborers and foremen	- 19	+40

Thus, the three occupational groups which experienced the largest relative increase in proportions of black workers—private household workers, nonfarm laborers, and operatives—were also those in which the participation of foreign-born whites had declined significantly. Conversely, the three occupational groups in which foreign-born whites had shown the greatest relative increase over the period—farm laborers, other service workers, and the managerial group—were those in which the relative concentration of nonwhites had either declined or showed little significant change over the period.

3. The more detailed statistics for nonwhites for 1910, 1950, and 1960 (Tables 2.5 and 2.6) provide insights as to trends in their relative concentration in greater occupational detail, and also indicate a continuation of the longer-range trends, reflected in the summary statistics through 1950. Despite some further limited progress, nonwhites continued to be significantly underrepresented in nearly all of the higher-status, Group 1-3 occupations. Among the Group 4 occupations, they increased their relative share in most of the operative occupations, in the less-skilled construction crafts (painters, roofers, plasterers) and in the nontechnical health services occupations. Nonwhites, moreover, continued—as in the past—to be heavily concentrated in the Group 5 occupational category where increases in the concentration index for nonwhites in most laborer groups offset small reductions in the personal service occupations.

4. Finally as a useful summary device, Table 2.9 indicates the occupational progress made by nonwhites relative to whites, based on a comparison of the respective occupational status indices for these groups in 1910, 1950, and 1960. These comparisons indicate that the composite occupational status of nonwhite workers (based on the status ranks developed in Chapter 1) declined, relative to white workers, from 52.5 in 1910 to 49.6 by 1950, and rose only to 52.7 by 1960— much the same as it had been a half century earlier.

White Inmigrants from Farm to City

Despite the fact that blacks continued to supply a relatively large proportion of the labor for the lowest-level occupational fields, our summary statistics indicate that the percentage of native white workers in these occupations had also increased as the percentage of foreign-born workers declined. When measured in terms of relative concentration (Table 2.4), the proportionate participation of native white workers rose significantly in all of the lower-level, blue-collar and service occupations, other than domestic service, between 1910 and 1950, in contrast to declines in their relative concentration in white-collar and

TABLE 2.9

Occupational Status Indices for the Experienced
Civilian Labor Force, by Race:
1910, 1950, 1960

Year	Nonwhite	White	Nonwhite Relative to White
1910[a]	19.0	36.2	52.5
1950[b]	22.1	44.6	49.6
1960[c]	25.2	47.8	52.7

[a]1910 data are for gainful workers, 10 years and over.

[b]1950 data are for the experienced civilian labor force, 14 years and over.

[c]1960 data are for the experienced civilian labor force, 16 years and over.

Note: The status index is our percentile score for each occupation (Table 1.3), based on the percentage of white workers, with 12 or more years of education, relative to total workers, age 25-34 years, in each occupation, in 1960, weighted by the employment in each occupational group.

Source: Compiled by the author.

farm occupations. The limited amount of detail available from earlier censuses precludes a definitive analysis of the characteristics and origins of the native white labor force in these lower-level jobs. Nevertheless, an analysis of the more detailed census materials for the 1940-60 period, combined with collateral survey data, permit us to identify some of the key variables.

First, it is clear that native white inmigrants from farm to city, in common with the white immigrants and blacks, contributed disproportionately to the supply of workers for most lower-level and lower-middle-level, urban occupations. As a group, they also suffered handicaps due to limited education and lack of relevant vocational skills. This was true, particularly, of those who migrated in large numbers to the industrial Midwest or the West Coast from the deep South, from Appalachia, from the Ozarks, and from other distressed rural areas.

One of the most definitive analyses of the occupational implications of the migration process is included in a comprehensive study of inter-generational occupational changes, done by Peter Blau and Duncan, based on a special census current population survey, in March 1962. This survey included data on current occupation, first occupation, and father's occupation, together with a wide range of relevant social and demographic characteristics, including migrant status, for a sample of men aged 20-64 years at the time of the survey. Of this sample, about 8.5 percent had moved from rural areas to large cities. This group—particularly those of rural farm background—were found to hold occupations significantly lower in status than those born in cities, although they enjoyed a higher occupational status than non-migrant rural residents. In contrast to the experience of black migrants, the white migrants appear to have been handicapped only by inferior education and poor occupational preparation, rather than by any job discrimination based on their rural or southern origin. More-over, rural white inmigrants, once settled in cities, appear to have moved up the occupational ladder from low beginnings at a more rapid rate than indigenous white workers with similar qualifications. This process is explained by Blau and Duncan, in part, on the basis of the selective nature of most migrant streams: "Men with ambition and initiative born amidst the poor opportunities of rural areas must move to cities to achieve upward mobility. . . . Despite the fact that their poor qualifications force rural migrants to the bottom of the occupa-tional hierarchy of the large city, they tend to achieve upward mo-bility. "29

Additional insight as to the relative occupational concentration of farm to nonfarm migrants is available from a special analysis of this group included in the 1950 census of population. The data cover in-dividuals of both sexes who were residing in nonfarm areas in 1950 but had reported a rural farm residence one year earlier. The occu-pational distribution of this group thus provides a close approximation of the first jobs obtained by these migrants following their move from the farm. These more specific statistics support the findings of the Blau-Duncan study concerning the relatively low occupational status of inmigrants from the farm, as compared to other residents of non-farm areas. Thus, the highest relative concentration of such inmi-grants in lower-level jobs was in the nonfarm laborer group, which accounted for 12.4 percent of all employed inmigrants as compared to 6.7 percent of all nonfarm residents, resulting in an occupational concentration index of 185. (See Table 2.10.) The inmigrants were also disproportionately represented in the operatives group and—to a lesser extent—in the craftsmen group, the latter probably re-flecting the diverse mechanical and handyman skills acquired by many white farmers and farm family members.

TABLE 2.10

Relative Occupational Concentration of Migrants from Farm to Nonfarm Areas
between 1949 and 1950, Compared to Total Nonfarm Residents: 1950

Occupational Group	Percent Distribution[a]		Occupational Concentration Index for Farm-to-Nonfarm Migrants[b]
	Total, Nonfarm Residents	Farm-to-Nonfarm Migrants	
Total employed in nonfarm occupations	100.0	100.0	100
Professional and technical	10.1	9.5	94
Managers, officials, and proprietors	10.4	5.6	54
Clerical workers	14.4	7.9	55
Sales workers	8.2	5.6	68
Craftsmen and foremen	15.9	18.5	116
Operatives	22.5	29.8	132
Service workers	11.8	10.7	91
Laborers	6.7	12.4	185

aExcludes nonfarm residents employed in farm occupations, and occupations not reported.

bBased on ratio of percentage of all nonfarm migrants employed in a given occupational group to corresponding percentage of all employed nonfarm residents.

Source: Adapted from data in U.S. Department of Commerce, Bureau of the Census, Census of Population,
1950, Special Report, "Population Mobility—Farm-Nonfarm Movers" (Washington, D.C.: U.S. Government
Printing Office, 1957), table 3.

Conversely, the migrants were underrepresented in the white-collar occupations and in the heterogeneous service worker group. It is noteworthy, however, that the proportion of inmigrants in professional and technical occupations was only slightly lower than the corresponding proportion of all nonfarm workers, in contrast to much lower concentration indices in the other white-collar occupations. This probably reflects the very high geographical mobility of college graduates from farm backgrounds and the particularly sharp differential for this group between employment and income opportunities in urban areas, as compared to those available to them in rural farm areas. It should be noted that the data we have cited refer to both white and nonwhite workers; however, since white workers accounted for 81 percent of all inmigrants in the year studied, it is evident that white rural inmigrants, as well as nonwhites, had contributed a disproportionate share of the manpower for the less-skilled nonfarm occupations.

Although the findings from our analysis of 1950 census data apply to only a one-year sample of migrants, these data—when combined with the parallel findings from the Blau-Duncan longitudinal survey and with a wide range of other materials—suggest that internal migration within the United States, typically from economically backward rural regions to expanding metropolitan centers, provided a continuing replenishing source of native white, as well as black, workers to perform many of the unskilled and semiskilled manual jobs required in our growing urban economy. The fact that a disproportionate number of migrants entered these occupations appears to be due primarily, however, to their much lower level of educational achievement rather than to discrimination against white workers with a farm or southern background, per se.

The Less Educated

The above discussion of the educational attainment of rural white inmigrants leads logically to a more general exploration of the implications for manpower supply in lower-level occupations of the steady increase in the educational attainment of the U.S. labor force. The historical statistics below will serve to place this trend in perspective.

In 1900, illiteracy was still extensive among the more disadvantaged elements of the population. The overall illiteracy rate for persons 10 years and over was reported as 10.7 percent by the census; moreover, 44.5 percent of nonwhites and 12.7 percent of foreign-born whites were reported as illiterate in any language as compared to 4.6 percent of the native whites. The number of high school graduates corresponded to only 6.4 percent of all persons 17 years of age. The typical adult worker, early in the century, had an elementary school education or less.[30]

By 1940, illiteracy rates had declined sharply—to 2.9 percent for the total population, 10 years and over, to 11.5 percent for nonwhites, to 9.0 percent for the foreign born, and to 1.1 percent for native whites. The percentage of high school graduates, in relation to all persons 17 years of age, had increased to 50.8 percent. Three out of ten workers in the labor force were high school graduates. Moreover, by 1960, the percentage of new high school graduates had further increased to 65 percent, and nearly one-half of all workers (46.8 percent) were then high school graduates.

This sharp uptrend in the length of schooling for workers has been attributed to a number of concurrent social and economic influences: increased urbanization; compulsory school attendance laws and the lengthening of the mandatory period of schooling under these laws; rising standards of living and, particularly, the increasing requirements for education and training associated with the changing pattern of occupational demands in our increasingly technological society.

The rapid growth in white-collar occupations, with their higher demands for education-based skills, has been emphasized in the above context. Yet, a comparison of the rates of growth in the proportion of workers in white-collar occupations with the increase in educational attainment of the labor force, indicates that the availability of jobs which, in earlier periods, were conventionally associated with higher levels of education, has not kept pace with the growth in educational levels. Thus, in 1900 the percentage of new high school graduates (6.4 percent) was significantly lower than the percentage of workers in professional, technical, and clerical occupations, and corresponded to less than two-fifths of the total proportion of workers in all white-collar occupations. (See Table 2.11.) At that time, even illiteracy—much less the lack of a high school diploma—was not necessarily an insurmountable barrier to entry into a wide range of skilled and managerial occupations. Based on an inspection of 1890 census data, Eli Ginzberg and Douglas Bray found that—although illiterates were concentrated in farming and in the manual nonfarm occupations— some small percentages were found in managerial and other high-status occupations, as well: "Illiterates earned their livelihood as clergymen, government officials, corporation executives, bankers, merchants, building contractors, and in other occupations usually associated with a considerable degree of education."[31]

By 1940, this pattern had already been significantly altered; the percentage of new high school graduates (50.8 percent) substantially exceeded the percentage of workers in all white-collar occupational categories (32.1 percent) and as a result, significant proportions of workers in all occupational groups now consisted of persons with a high school education or better.

TABLE 2.11

Trends in Educational Attainment and in Occupational Composition
of the Labor Force: 1900-70

	Educational Attainment			Occupational Composition	
Year	Percent[a] Illiterate	Percent High School Graduates, Among Persons 17 Years Old	Percent High School Graduates in Civilian Labor Force[b]	Percent of Workers in Professional and Clerical Occupations	Percent of Workers in All White-Collar Occupations
1900	10.7	6.4	n.a.	7.3	17.6
1910	7.7	8.8	n.a.	10.0	21.3
1920	6.0	16.8	n.a.	13.4	24.9
1930	4.3	29.0	n.a.	15.7	29.4
1940	2.9	50.8	30.4	17.1	32.1
1950	3.2	59.0	39.3	20.9	36.6
1960	n.a.	65.1	46.8	26.3	41.2
1970	n.a.	76.5	64.5	31.7	48.0

[a]Data for 1910-40 are for population 10 years and over; for 1950, for population 14 years and over and therefore not strictly comparable with earlier years.

[b]Data for 1940-60 refer to the experienced civilian labor force, ages 14 and over; data for 1940 exclude public emergency workers as well as workers whose occupation was not reported; data for 1970 refer to experienced civilian labor force, 16 years and over—the comparable percentage for 1960 was 50.7 percent.

Sources: U.S. Department of Commerce, Bureau of the Census, Historical Statistics of the United States, Colonial Times to 1957 (Washington, D.C.: U.S. Government Printing Office, 1960); Bureau of the Census, Statistical Abstract of the United States, 1971 (Washington, D.C.: U.S. Government Printing Office, 1972), p. 124; Alba Edwards, Comparative Occupational Statistics for the United States, 1870 to 1940 (Washington, D.C.: U.S. Government Printing Office, 1943); Bureau of the Census, Census of Population, 1950, Special Report, "Education" (Washington, D.C.: U.S. Government Printing Office, 1953), table 11; and Bureau of the Census, 1/1,000 public use sample tape, 1970.

A further widening in the gap between the proportion of high school graduates and the proportion of white-collar workers occurred between 1940 and 1960. Thus whereas the percentage of all workers who were high school graduates in 1940 (30.4 percent) was slightly below the percentage of workers in white-collar occupations (32.1 percent), this differential was reversed by 1960, when the percentage of workers with a high school education or better (46.8 percent) significantly exceeded the percentage in white-collar occupations (41.2 percent).

The above comparisons have been based on relatively crude statistical indicators. For example, as suggested above, many white-collar jobs, including those of proprietors of small establishments as well as the more routine clerical and sales jobs, do not require a high school education. Conversely, certain of the more sophisticated skilled crafts and mechanical repair occupations do require significant educational background as well as specialized vocational training. However, for the period 1940-60 we do have available the results of a detailed analysis by James Scoville who derived estimates of the average years of education required of the labor force as a whole in 1940-60, based on the length of schooling, or general educational development, required for each census occupation, and on the changing occupational distribution of jobs over this period. Scoville's estimates indicate that an increase of a half year in schooling, from 9.99 years in 1940 to 10.37 years in 1960, was required as a result of the upgrading of the occupational structure over this 20-year period. (This did not allow for any change in required schooling associated with changes in technical job content of specific occupations over this period.) In contrast, the actual median years of school completed, by the experienced civilian labor force, rose by over two years during this period—from 9.2 years in 1940 to 11.4 years in 1960. [32]

In the face of these trends, employers have been in a position to progressively increase formal educational standards for entry into a broadening range of the more desirable occupations. For example, in a survey of apprenticeship programs for the skilled crafts conducted by F. Ray Marshall and Vernon Briggs, Jr. in the mid-1960s, the authors found that "almost all apprenticeship programs require that applicants be high school graduates, and some require, or give extra credit for, specified courses in mathematics and sciences." [33] Further evidence of extensive and often questionable use of educational credentials in a wide array of civilian jobs is provided in studies by Ivar Berg and by Hrach Bedrosian and Daniel Diamond. [34]

Critics of the increasing use of educational certification such as a high school diploma, in selection of workers, have contended that these criteria do not necessarily predict actual job performance and that they have been used, at times, as a means of screening black applicants or members of other educationally disadvantaged groups. There is substantial evidence that these criticisms are valid in many situations. Nevertheless, the extensive use of such criteria suggests that they may fulfill a valid economic function, as viewed from the perspective of the individual firm. For example, extensive research within the military services indicates that high school graduates, irrespective of their cognitive skills or educational achievement (as measured by scores on psychological qualification tests), have a much lower incidence of disciplinary problems and are much less likely to receive "unsuitable" discharges, than is the case with enlisted personnel who have not completed high school. These and similar findings suggest that the attitudinal and emotional factors associated with successful adjustment to a high school environment are much more directly relevant to successful adjustment to a military environment than is mental attainment as such.[35] As a result of these and similar findings, the armed services have placed increased emphasis upon high school graduation as a recruitment criterion.

Similar considerations—although based on less sophisticated evidence—may have influenced many employers in civilian industry in selection of workers for low-skilled jobs which may not require the cognitive knowledge associated with a high school diploma, but which do require some assurance of worker stability and reliability. The requirement of a high school diploma has the further obvious advantage to the employer of being virtually costless, as compared to alternative methods such as psychological testing, detailed reference checks, or trial and error—particularly under conditions where an adequate supply of high school graduates is available.

One of the consequences of the trend towards establishment of higher educational qualification standards by those employers and industries in a favorable labor market situation has been a progressive narrowing of the range of occupational options for workers with limited formal schooling. This trend is illustrated by our comparison of the relative occupational concentration of workers with less than 12 years of school in 1940 and in 1960. (See Table 2.12.) As would be expected, the relative proportion of such workers was lowest, in both years, in the white-collar occupations and highest in the farm occupations and among nonfarm laborers and private household workers. Between 1940 and 1960, the relative proportion of non-high school graduates declined sharply in the professional and technical group and in the nonfarm managerial group, as well as in protective service occupations; it showed relatively little net change in the clerical and sales group and in the craftsmen groups, but rose sharply in such groups as private household workers, farm and nonfarm laborers, operatives, and other service workers. In effect, therefore, lack of educational credentials—for native white as well as other racial/ethnic

TABLE 2.12

Relative Occupational Concentration of Workers in the Experienced Civilian
Labor Force with Less than 12 Years of School Completed: 1940, 1960

	1940			1960			Net Change in Concentration Indexes 1940–1960
	Percent Distribution		Concentration Index	Percent Distributions		Concentration Index	
Occupational Group	Total	Less Than 12 Years		Total	Less Than 12 Years		
White-Collar							
Professional and technical	7.2	1.4	32	11.3	1.9	17	−15
Proprietors, managers, and officials	7.8	6.3	81	8.5	5.1	60	−21
Clerical and sales	16.6	9.7	58	22.3	14.3	64	+ 6
Blue-Collar							
Craftsmen	11.6	13.4	116	14.3	17.0	119	+ 3
Operatives	18.7	22.1	118	19.9	27.5	138	+20
Laborers, nonfarm	8.0	10.1	126	5.5	8.3	151	+25
Service							
Protective	1.4	1.6	114	1.1	1.1	100	−14
Other	6.2	6.9	111	7.9	10.5	133	+22
Private household workers	4.8	5.8	121	2.8	4.4	157	+36
Farm							
Farmers and farm managers	10.6	13.7	129	3.9	5.9	151	+22
Farm laborers	6.9	10.1	130	2.4	3.9	163	+33
	100.0	100.0	100	100.0	100.0	100	—

Note: Concentration index is based on ratio of percentage of workers with less than 12 years of education in a given occupational group to corresponding percentage for all workers.

Sources: Alba Edwards, Comparative Occupational Statistics for the United States, 1970 to 1940 (Washington, D.C.: U.S. Government Printing Office, 1943), and Bureau of the Census, Census of Population, 1960, "Occupational Characteristics," PC(2)-7A (Washington, D.C.: U.S. Government Printing Office, 1963), table 9.

groups—was proving to be an increasing barrier to access to the more desirable jobs and was forcing an increased concentration of such workers in the lower-level occupations.

Young Workers

Younger workers, because of their more limited experience and skills, typically tend to begin their work careers at the lower rungs of the occupational ladder. Farm children and youth have historically been an important component of the unpaid labor force on small family farms, particularly during periods of peak seasonal activity. In non-farm activities, young workers have—depending in part upon their educational preparation—tended to be concentrated in the low-paid factory and service jobs and in the least-skilled clerical and sales occupations. With the steady lengthening of the period of schooling for workers, there have been progressive declines in the proportion of young persons (under age 25) available for regular full-time employment; but an increasing proportion of youth of high school or college age have become part of the part-time labor force, whose employment opportunities have mainly been concentrated in trade, services, and other nonmanufacturing industries.

The extent to which young workers differentially have contributed to the supply of manpower for certain occupations is indicated by the summary data for 1940 and 1960 in Table 2.13. In both of these years, workers aged 16-24 years accounted for a particularly large proportion of the farm laborer work force and were also disproportionately concentrated in nonfarm laborers, clerical and sales occupations, and—in the case of males—the operative and service groups as well. Conversely they accounted for a relatively small proportion of the labor force in the managerial, professional, and craftsmen occupations.

Between 1940 and 1960, young workers increased their relative share of jobs in most of the white-collar occupational groups, particularly in clerical and sales jobs, reflecting in part the relatively sharp expansion of employment opportunities in the professional, clerical, and sales occupations as well as the higher educational attainment of young workers in the 1960 labor force, as compared to their 1940 counterparts. At the same time, young male workers also increased their relative share in the nonfarm laborer and service occupations, probably due to the greater availability of part-time employment opportunities in these fields, as compared to semiskilled or skilled industrial jobs. Although young women continued to be overrepresented (as compared to women 25 years and over) in such occupations as nonfarm labor and private household work (including babysitters), this pattern was much less pronounced than among young

TABLE 2.13

Occupational Concentration of 16–24–Year–Old Workers,
by Major Census Occupational Group and Sex:
1940, 1960

Sex and Occupational Group	Percent, Ages 16–24, in Each Occupational Group		Concentration Indices	
	1940	1960	1940	1960
Male				
Total, experienced civilian				
labor force	17.7	14.5	100	100
Professional and technical workers	8.6	9.3	49	64
Farmers and farm managers	6.7	5.0	38	35
Managers, proprietors, officials,				
excluding farm	3.7	3.4	21	23
Clerical and sales workers	20.7	19.7	117	136
Craftsmen and foremen	9.0	8.8	51	61
Operatives	21.1	17.4	119	120
Service workers, including private				
household workers	19.3	17.5	109	121
Farm laborers and foremen	49.7	39.2	281	270
Laborers, excluding farm	23.2	25.1	131	173
Female				
Total, experienced civilian				
labor force	29.8	19.3	100	100
Professional and technical workers	21.4	15.8	72	82
Farmers and farm managers	3.1	5.0	10	26
Managers, proprietors, officials,				
excluding farm	4.8	4.2	16	22
Clerical and sales workers	34.7	25.1	116	130
Craftsmen, foremen, and operatives	30.6	12.5	103	65
Private household workers	31.0	19.6	104	102
Service workers, excluding private				
household workers	27.3	17.5	92	91
Laborers, including farm	44.0	22.5	148	117

Note: Occupational concentration index based on ratio of percentage of workers
16-24 years, in a specific occupational group, to corresponding percentage for the total
experienced civilian labor force.

Sources: U.S. Department of Commerce, Bureau of the Census, Census of Population, 1940 and Census of Population, 1960 (Washington, D.C.: U.S. Government
Printing Office, 1943, 1963).

male workers, partly due to increases, between 1940 and 1960, in
the labor force participation of women 25 years and over, many of
whom were also constrained in their occupational choices to the
less-skilled jobs and to those which offered flexible work schedules.

It will be noted that the data shown for both 1940 and 1960 have
excluded workers aged 14-15 years, in the interest of comparability
with later labor force data. Inclusion of this age group, and restric-
tion of our analysis to the teenage labor force (those aged 14-19 years)
would manifestly have resulted in even greater variation in the occupational concentration indices than that shown in Table 2.13 for the
group aged 16-24 years.

SUMMARY AND CONCLUSIONS

In this chapter we have surveyed the changing patterns of demand
and sources of manpower for lower-status jobs as the U.S. economy
was transformed over a period of more than a century from its agrarian beginnings into a highly urbanized industrial—or postindustrial—
society. Throughout this era, we found one constant in terms of low-
level manpower sources—the black worker. Imported first as slaves
to perform the back-breaking toil of the southern plantation economy,
black men and women had—for a full century after emancipation—
remained largely concentrated in the most menial, least-skilled, and
lowest-paid occupations, even during periods of rapid industrial
growth and of equally rapid shifts in occupational structure. The
nature of their occupational duties had, of course, changed over the
years, as growing numbers moved from southern farms to northern
cities; yet, between 1910 and 1960, their relative occupational status,
as compared to white workers, had shown no net improvement.

Black workers, alone, were not sufficient in numbers to fill our
total low-level manpower needs. An additional and major source of
labor supply for these jobs was provided by the mass inflow of white
immigrants, particularly during the period of rapid industrialization
between the mid-1800s and the outbreak of World War I. Each generation of these immigrants in turn produced its share of laborers, semiskilled factory workers, and low-level service workers—with disproportionate contributions from the most disadvantaged of these new
ethnic strains, that is, the Irish, then the South and East Europeans
and, later, the Latin Americans. With the termination of mass immigration after World War I, their place was taken by the increased
inflow of native white as well as black migrants from rural farm
areas, which peaked during the World War II period and the decade
of the 1950s. Handicapped by inferior education and by lack of

industrial skills—as well as by racial discrimination, in the case of
the blacks or other minority groups—these migrants from farm to
city were differentially concentrated in the lower-skilled manual and
service occupations in urban areas.

The initial educational and training handicaps of these immigrant
and internal migrant groups were shared by significant numbers of
indigenous white workers as well—whether due to lack of opportunities
or limited aptitudes. With the growing general educational level of the
labor force, our analysis suggests that those with the least education
have been increasingly relegated to the lowest rungs of the occupational
ladder. Among them, the young worker has been further handicapped
by lack of work experience and of those practical skills typically acquired on the job rather than through formal education. Therefore—
in addition to the other manpower sources identified above—each generation of young workers has probably performed a disproportionate
share of low-level work, as part of its rites of initiation into the labor
force.

Thus, our historical view has identified a number of key sociodemographic characteristics which, in combination, have distinguished
workers in lower-level occupations from those in higher-status jobs,
that is, race, nativity, rural origins, educational level, and age.
The composition of the low-level labor force has, in turn, varied
from period to period as a result of the changing proportions of workers with these characteristics in the labor force and of concurrent
changes in the occupational distribution of labor demand.

It is probable, too, that this complex interaction of supply and
demand factors has exercised an important influence upon a number
of related labor market and economic trends—notably, the changing
pattern of occupational wage differentials and the rate of mechanization, that is, substitution of capital for labor in various industries or
occupations. Thus, a number of economists have associated fluctuations in wage rate differentials for skilled versus unskilled labor and
the long-term trend towards a narrowing of occupational wage differentials with changes in the availability of cheap unskilled labor from
external (immigrant) or internal (migrant) sources of supply as well
as with the steady increase in educational attainment of the labor
force.[36] Similarly, changes in availability of labor and in differential
wage rates have been one of the factors affecting the rate of investment in labor-saving machinery in various industries.[37]

Historical analyses of occupational supply trends and of their
impacts have been handicapped, however, by inherent limitations of
data sources—notably, the lack of reasonably comparable statistics
on the composition of the labor force by occupation over a period of
decades. As noted earlier in this chapter, decennial statistics on the
labor force, by occupation, classified on a basis comparable to that

used in censuses are available only for the period since 1900, while
more detailed data on such characteristics as nativity, race, educational level, and occupation have been developed on a comparable basis
only for selected benchmark years during this period. Moreover, with
limited exceptions, the published census statistics do not permit a
systematic cross classification of these relevant characteristics so
that, for example, the separate influence upon occupational composition of such factors as educational attainment can be measured, as
against factors such as race, age, or sex. This capability has emerged
for the first time as a result of the production and dissemination by
the Census Bureau of public use sample tapes for the 1960 and 1970
censuses of population and has served as the basis for the more intensive analysis of 1960-70 occupational supply trends in the following
chapter.

NOTES

1. Population data from U.S. Department of Commerce, Bureau
of the Census, Historical Statistics of the United States, Colonial
Times to 1957 (Washington, D.C.: U.S. Government Printing Office,
1960), p. 14 (here after cited as Historical Statistics). Labor force
estimates from Stanley Lebergott, Manpower in Economic Growth:
The American Record Since 1800 (New York: McGraw-Hill, 1964),
pp. 510-11.
2. Historical Statistics, p. 61.
3. Ibid.
4. George M. Stephenson, A History of American Immigration,
1820-1924 (Boston: Ginn and Co., 1926).
5. John R. Commons and Associates, History of Labor in the
United States (New York: Macmillan and Co., 1935), p. 414.
6. Caroline T. Ware, The Early New England Cotton Manufacture: A Study in Industrial Beginnings (Boston: Houghton Mifflin,
1931), p. 234.
7. Commons, op. cit., p. 489.
8. "Frederick Douglass' Paper," March 4, 1853, quoted in
Leslie H. Fishel, Jr. and Benjamin Quarles, The Black American:
A Documentary History (New York: William Morrow and Co., 1970),
p. 143.
9. Lebergott, op. cit., p. 510.
10. Alba M. Edwards, Comparative Occupational Statistics for
the United States, 1870 to 1940 (Washington, D.C.: U.S. Government
Printing Office, 1943), table 8.
11. Historical Statistics, p. 56-57.

12. Ibid.

13. Cited in Eugene P. Foley, "The Negro Businessman,"
Daedalus 2 (Winter 1966): 117.

14. Historical Statistics, p. 506; U.S. Department of Commerce,
Bureau of the Census, Statistical Abstract of the United States, 1971
(Washington, D.C.: U.S. Government Printing Office, 1960, p. 495
(hereafter cited as Statistical Abstract).

15. The percentage of women, 14 years and over, in the labor
force is estimated at 20.0 percent in 1900 and 22.7 percent in 1920;
directly comparable statistics for 1910 are not shown because of
overenumeration of farm family workers in the census. Historical
Statistics, p. 71. The percentage of women in the labor force in 1960
is drawn from Statistical Abstract, p. 212.

16. Harold Wool, The Military Specialist: Skilled Manpower for
the Armed Forces (Baltimore: Johns Hopkins Press, 1968), pp. 2,
28.

17. Ibid., p. 52.

18. For a useful summary of immigration legislation of this
period, see Don D. Lescohier, History of Labor in the United States,
1896-1932, vol. 3, "Working Conditions," chap. 2 (New York: Macmillan, 1935).

19. Ibid., p. 25.

20. Marion T. Bennett, American Immigration Policies (Washington, D.C.: Public Affairs Press, 1963), chap. 5.

21. Lescohier, op. cit., pp. 28-30.

22. Ibid, p. 146.

23. Historical Statistics, pp. 58-59, and Statistical Abstract,
p. 89.

24. Cited in Nathan Glazer and Daniel Patrick Moynihan, Beyond
the Melting Pot: The Negroes, Puerto Ricans, Jews, Italians, and
Irish of New York City (Cambridge, Mass.: MIT Press, 1963),
pp. 93-94. U.S. total in U.S. Department of Commerce, Bureau of
the Census, Census of Population, 1950, Subject Report, "Puerto
Ricans in the United States," PC(2)-1D (Washington, D.C.: U.S.
Government Printing Office, 1963).

25. Historical Statistics, table C115-125, and Statistical Abstract, p. 91.

26. E.P. Hutchinson, Immigrants and Their Children, 1850-
1950, Census Monograph Series (New York: John Wiley and Sons,
1956), p. 202.

27. St. Clair Drake and Horace R. Cayton, Black Metropolis
(New York: Harcourt, Brace and Co., 1945), p. 58.

28. Marion Hayes, "A Century of Change: Negroes in the U.S.
Economy, 1860-1960," Monthly Labor Review, December 1962.

29. Peter M. Blau and Otis Dudley Duncan, The American Occupational Structure (New York: John Wiley and Sons, 1967), p. 270.

30. This is suggested by the fact that the median years of school completed by men 25 years and over as of 1950 was 7.9 years, in U.S. Department of Commerce, Bureau of the Census, Census of Population, 1950, Special Report, "Education" (Washington, D.C.: U.S. Government Printing Office, 1953), table 5.

31. Eli Ginzberg and Douglas W. Bray, The Uneducated (New York: Columbia University Press, 1953), p. 30.

32. Scoville, op. cit., p. 67.

33. F. Ray Marshall and Vernon M. Briggs, Jr., The Negro and Apprenticeship (Baltimore: John Hopkins Press, 1967), p. 42.

34. Ivar Berg, Education and Jobs: The Great Training Robbery (New York: Praeger, 1970), chap. 4; Hrach Bedrosian and Daniel E. Diamond, Hiring Standards and Job Performance, U.S. Department of Labor, Manpower Research Monograph no. 18 (Washington, D.C.: U.S. Government Printing Office, 1970).

35. Wool, op. cit., pp. 87-88.

36. See, for example, Paul Douglas, Real Wages in the United States 1930; reprint ed. (Clifton, N.J.: Augusta M. Kelley); Lloyd G. Reynolds and Cynthia H. Taft, The Evolution of Wage Structure (New Haven: Yale University Press, 1956); Lebergott, op. cit., p. 162.

37. John Kendrick notes, for example, that an increase in the capital-labor ratio in agriculture during the period 1937-48 resulted from the World War II farm labor shortage. John Kendrick, Productivity Trends in the United States (Princeton: Princeton University Press, 1961), p. 151. See also, ibid., p. xii, the comment by Solomon Fabricant, in which he associates the relatively rapid long-term growth in tangible capital with the differential increase in unit labor costs, relative to capital.

CHAPTER

3

TRENDS IN OCCUPATION
LABOR SUPPLY, 1960-70

SUMMARY LABOR FORCE TRENDS

The decade of the 1960s witnessed a continuation and intensification of a number of the labor force trends of preceding decades, as well as the emergence of new forces with important implications for both demand and supply in lower-level occupations. Among the major developments were—

1. the entry into the labor force of the exceptionally large generation of youth born during the post-World War II baby boom;
2. the attainment and maintenance of sustained high levels of labor demand and of low overall unemployment rates in the second half of the 1960s, as a result of the Vietnam War and accompanying expansionist fiscal policies;
3. a continued rapid expansion in the growth of white-collar and service occupations; and
4. the emergence of a national commitment toward the goal of equal employment opportunity for blacks and other minority groups which—in conjunction with favorable labor market conditions— made possible occupational upgrading of nonwhite workers, at a significantly more rapid rate than in preceding decades.

These trends are documented by the statistics appearing in Table 3.1. The more general implications of these trends are examined briefly below.

TABLE 3.1

Selected Labor Force Trends, 1950–70

Group	1950–60	1960–70	1960–65	1965–70
		Percent Change (average annual)		
Total labor force	1.3	1.9	1.4	2.3
Men	0.8	1.1	0.8	1.3
Women	2.6	3.6	2.5	4.1
Ages 16–24	0.4	5.4	4.2	5.5
Ages 25 and Over	1.5	1.1	0.8	1.4
All employed workers, total	1.0	2.0	1.6	2.1
White-collar workers	2.8	3.3	2.3	3.9
Craftsmen, operatives, and service workers (excluding household)	1.2	2.1	2.3	1.7
Nonfarm laborers, private household workers	0.02	– 0.4	0.4	– 1.3
Farmers and farm laborers	– 4.1	– 4.0	– 4.3	– 4.6
Nonwhite employed workers, total	1.8	2.2	2.1	2.1
White-collar occupations	7.5	11.2	6.8	11.6
Craftsmen, operatives, and service workers (excluding household)	2.8	3.9	3.8	3.4
Nonfarm laborers, private household workers	0.2	– 2.2	– 0.04	– 4.3
Farmers and farm laborers	– 4.8	– 6.1	– 5.8	– 9.0
		Average Unemployment Rates		
Total, 16 years and over	4.5	4.8	5.7	3.8
Ages 16–24	8.8	10.2	11.8	8.9
Nonwhites, 16 years and over	8.2	8.9	10.8	7.2
Ages 16–24	14.3	17.9	20.0	16.3

Note: Percent changes not compounded; occupational statistics for 1950-60 are based on data in decennial censuses of population, for 1950 and 1960, and refer to employed workers, 14 years and over; data for 1960–70 refer to employed workers 16 years and over; 1960-65 average unemployment rates based on 1960-64 data, inclusive, and 1965-70 average unemployment rates based on 1965-69 data, inclusive.

Source: Data adapted from Manpower Report of the President, 1971 (Washington, D.C.: U.S. Government Printing Office, 1971). statistical app.

Labor Force Growth

During the 1960s, the total labor force, aged 16 years and over, expanded from an average of 73.0 million in 1960 to 85.9 million, an increase of more than 19 percent. This rate of growth contrasted with an increase of only 11 percent in the 1950s and exceeded that for any comparable period since the pre-World War I decade, 1900-10, when mass immigration was at its peak.[1] In contrast to that earlier era, the labor force expansion of the 1960s resulted mainly from natural population growth. Although net immigration rose moderately from an average of about 300,000 per year in the 1950s to about 400,000 per year in the 1960s, its contribution was dwarfed by the large-scale inflows into the labor force of the first post-World War II generation. The number of 16-24-year-olds in the labor force increased by 54 percent between 1960 and 1970, as contrasted to an increase for that age group of only 4 percent during the 1950s, when the much smaller generation of youth born mainly during the depression decade of the 1930s had reached working age.

Another significant source of labor force growth during the 1960s was provided by the entry or reentry of large numbers of women into the work force. The proportion of women, ages 16 and over, in the labor force rose from 37.8 percent in 1960 to 43.4 percent in 1970, with particularly large increases among married women including those with school-age or pre-school-age children. This reflected a continuation of the longer trend towards increased work participation by women, resulting from expanding work opportunities for them in white-collar and service-type occupations and from a reduction of the time demands upon them for performance of household duties, as well as from the generally favorable labor market conditions in the second half of the decade. These gains were partly offset by a reduction in the overall proportion of men, aged 16 years and over, in the work force, from 84.0 percent to 80.6 percent, due mainly to reduced labor force participation by college-age youth and by older men, aged 55 years and over.

Nonwhite workers shared less than proportionately in the overall labor force growth over the 1960s. As shown in Table 3.2, the labor force participation rates for nonwhite men declined more sharply than for white men, whereas the rates for nonwhite women rose much more slowly than those for white women. This disparity in trends was widest for black male teenage youth whose labor force participation rates declined by about ten percentage points over the decade, whereas those for white male teenagers showed little net change.

TABLE 3.2

Civilian Labor Force Participation Rates by
Sex, Age, and Race: 1960, 1970
(percentages)

Sex/Age Group	White			Nonwhite		
	1960	1970	Net Change	1960	1970	Net Change
Male total						
16 years and over	83.4	80.0	-3.4	83.0	76.5	-6.5
16-17	46.0	48.9	2.9	45.6	34.8	-10.8
18-19	69.0	67.4	-1.6	71.2	61.8	-9.4
20-24	87.8	83.3	-4.5	90.4	83.5	-6.9
25-34	97.7	96.7	-1.0	96.2	93.7	-2.5
35-44	97.9	97.3	-0.6	95.5	93.2	-2.3
40-54	96.1	94.9	-1.2	92.3	88.2	-4.1
55-64	87.2	83.3	-3.9	82.5	79.2	-3.3
65 Years and Over	33.3	26.7	-6.6	31.2	27.4	-3.8
Female total,						
16 years and over	36.5	42.6	6.1	48.2	49.5	1.3
16-17	30.0	36.6	6.6	22.1	24.3	2.2
18-19	51.9	55.0	3.1	44.3	44.7	0.4
20-24	45.7	57.7	12.0	48.8	57.7	8.9
25-34	34.1	43.2	9.1	49.7	57.6	7.9
35-44	41.5	49.9	8.4	59.8	59.9	0.1
45-54	48.6	53.7	5.1	60.5	60.2	-0.3
55-64	36.2	42.6	6.4	47.3	47.1	-0.2
65 Years and Over	10.6	9.5	-1.1	12.8	12.2	-0.6

Source: Manpower Report of the President, 1971 (Washington,
D.C.: U.S. Government Printing Office, 1971), table A-4.

Employment and Unemployment

The decade of the 1960s was characterized by rapid employment
growth, which more than kept pace with the rate of labor force expansion. Total employment rose by 13.7 million, or 20 percent, between
1960 and 1970, with a relatively large share of the increase concentrated in the period 1965-70, following our large-scale military commitment in Vietnam. This increase in civilian employment, in combination with a net growth of 700,000 in the number of active-duty
military personnel, resulted in a reduction in the unemployment rate
from an average of 5.7 percent in 1960-64 to 3.8 percent in the second
half of the decade.

These gains were not, however, shared equally by all elements
of the working population. Youth generally experienced increased
difficulty in the labor market as evidenced by a growing disparity
between their unemployment rates and those of adult workers. Thus,
whereas the overall unemployment rate for workers aged 16 years
and over had dropped from an average of 4.5 percent in the decade
1950-60 to 3.8 percent in 1965-69, the corresponding rates for young
workers, aged 16-24 years, rose from 8.8 percent to 10.2 percent
between these two periods. These difficulties were accentuated,
moreover, in the case of nonwhite youth, whose unemployment rates
throughout the 1950-69 period were substantially higher than for young
white workers.

The very rapid growth in the number of young workers was a
major factor contributing to the differential growth in youth unemployment in the 1960s. A large proportion of these new entrants were
either students seeking part-time employment or school leavers who
began looking for full-time jobs with little or no specific occupational
preparation. The disparity between the number of youth available for
low-skilled entry-level jobs, and employment opportunities for them,
was most severe in the case of black teenagers residing in urban
poverty neighborhoods and was reflected in their extremely high unemployment rates (ranging between 24 percent and 36 percent in the
years 1967-70), as well as in their relatively low rates of labor force
participation. [2]

Major Occupational Groups

An initial perspective on the broad trends in employment by
occupation is also provided by the summary statistics in Table 3.1,
based on combinations of data for the major census occupational
groups. As in preceding decades, the 1960s witnessed a continued
rapid growth in white-collar employment and a continued sharp decline in farm employment. Among the other major occupational groups

the craftsmen, operatives, and service groups (other than household workers) registered moderate gains, while the unskilled laborers and private household workers experienced small net declines over the decade.

A comparison of the average annual percentage changes in employment between the first half and the second half of the decade offers some significant contrasts. The rate of increase in white-collar employment was sharply stepped up in the period 1965-70, reflecting increased demands for professional, technical, clerical, and administrative workers in the growing services sector of the economy, as well as in many defense- and space-related manufacturing activities. Concurrently, the reduction in farm employment was accelerated and employment in low-skilled nonfarm occupations (laborers, domestics) turned downward, as compared with a small net gain for the latter groups in the first half of the 1960s.

As a result of these trends, the percentage of the experienced civilian labor force in white-collar occupations rose from 42.2 percent in 1960 to 48.0 percent in 1970, while the proportion in farm occupations declined from 6.3 percent in 1960 to only 3.6 percent in 1970. The proportion of employed workers in each of the blue-collar occupational groups also declined over the decade. However, the service worker occupational group, excluding private household workers, increased their share of the total, reflecting sharp growth in such occupations as hospital attendants, food service workers, and protective service workers (see Table 2.1).

Occupational Trends for Nonwhite Workers

As noted in Chapter 2, the decade of the 1950s had provided some indication, based on our occupational status measures, of a small narrowing in the occupational status gap between nonwhite and white workers. This is reflected, too, in the summary occupational trends shown in Table 3.1, which indicate much higher annual percentage increases for nonwhite workers in white-collar occupations and for the combined group of craftsmen, operatives, and service workers in the 1950s than for all employed workers, and a more rapid withdrawal of blacks from farm employment.

This process of occupational advancement of nonwhite workers was accelerated in the decade of the 1960s, and particularly in the second half of that decade. The average annual percentage increase in employment of nonwhites in white-collar occupations rose from 7.5 percent in the 1950s to 11.2 percent in the 1960s, in contrast to corresponding increases for all employed workers of 2.8 percent and 3.3 percent respectively. Conversely, employment of blacks in farm occupations and in the least-skilled nonfarm occupations (laborers, domestics) declined much more rapidly than for all employed workers.

A more detailed analysis of the extent of this occupational up-grading will be presented later in this chapter. However, these trends generally can be attributed to a combination of factors: (1) the high level of aggregate labor demand during the Vietnam War period; (2) the rapid progress in educational attainment of nonwhites, including increased opportunities for vocational training and work experience under new federal manpower programs; and (3) the reduction in discriminatory barriers against employment of nonwhites in higher-status jobs, as a result of the climate resulting from the civil rights movement of the 1960s and from equal employment opportunity programs. It has also been suggested that, in this climate of rising expectations, nonwhites and particularly nonwhite youth, have increasingly rejected employment in low-status jobs, such as domestic service or unskilled, casual labor—and, in the absence of more suitable jobs, have contributed to the increased proportions of nonwhite youth reported as either unemployed or not in the labor force, over the decade.

Although the summary occupational statistics examined above provided important insights as to broad trends in the occupational distribution of the labor force during the 1960-70 period, they have suffered a number of limitations for purposes of this study. As discussed in Chapter 1, the standard census major occupational groups have been found to be inadequate for purposes of measuring relative occupational status. Moreover, constraints of sample size have tended to severely limit the amount of Current Population Survey (CPS) data available on the changing sociodemographic characteristics of workers by occupation.

For these reasons, a major aspect of the present research effort consisted of preparation of detailed occupational labor force matrices, based on the decennial census public use tapes for 1960 and 1970. The methods used in developing these data and the resulting findings are described in the remainder of this chapter.

THE OCCUPATIONAL LABOR FORCE MATRICES

In order to provide the data base for analysis of occupational supply trends in the decade 1960-70, our research plan provided for a series of detailed cross tabulations of the labor force in each occupation, classified by a number of relevant sociodemographic characteristics. The availability of public use sample tapes for the decennial censuses of population of 1960 and 1970 provided a unique opportunity to analyze these trends in greater detail than had been possible in the past.

This task was greatly complicated, however, by the introduction of major revisions in census occupational classifications and in related

procedures affecting the reporting and processing of occupational information for the 1970 census (as explained previously). These revisions and the adjustment procedure used to improve the comparability of census-based occupational data for 1960 and 1970 are
described in detail in the Appendix. The major steps in the adjustment
procedure are summarized below.

Occupational Grouping

An initial work step consisted of a reconciliation of the 1960 and
1970 occupational classifications to establish the maximum feasible
occupational detail for purposes of 1960-70 comparisons, with particular emphasis on lower-level and middle-level occupations. On
the basis of this analysis and of related considerations of sample size,
the lists of detailed occupations used in the 1960 and 1970 censuses,
totaling 297 and 441, respectively, were consolidated into 57 occupational clusters. Of these, 12 occupational clusters consisted of dis-
aggregations of major groups of operatives (exclusive of transport
operatives and of certain other specified groups), and of nonfarm
laborers, by broad industrial divisions. In these groupings, an effort
was made to assure homogeneity of occupations within each occupational cluster, based on such criteria as earnings, socioeconomic
status, prestige ranking, and demographic composition.
The term "occupation," as used in the analysis of the resulting
data, refers to these separate occupational clusters. The term
"occupational status group" refers to the further aggregation of these
data into five broad groups, based on the criteria developed in Chapter
1. An intermediate level of occupational detail, identified as an occupational subgroup, has been used in some tables. This consists of a
consolidation of those occupational clusters, within each occupational
status group, which are included in the same major occupational group
under current census occupational classifications, thus retaining a
capability of rearranging our data in accordance with the conventional
census major occupational groups where this proves desirable for
comparative purposes.

Tabulations of Decennial Census Data

Based on the above occupational groupings, detailed tabulations
were developed from the Census Bureau's 1/1,000 public use sample
tapes for 1960 and 1970, in which the experienced civilian labor force
in each occupation (that is, employed workers and unemployed workers with prior work experience) was classified by sex, race (white or

nonwhite), age group, and educational attainment group. The age groups used were 16-24, 25-34, 35-44, 45-54, and 55 and over. The educational attainment groups, based on years of school completed were: less than 9 years, 9-11 years, 12 years, and 13 years and over.

These tabulations thus provided the basic data for construction of labor force matrices for 1960 and 1970, in which the labor force in each of 57 occupations was distributed among the 80 sociodemographic categories, based on sex, race, age group, and educational attainment. In addition, supplementary characteristics, by occupation, such as school enrolment status, hours of work, state/country of birth, and earnings were tabulated, and—as appropriate—have been used to further disaggregate the labor force characteristics of the primary matrix.

Occupational Trend Adjustments

The 1970 revisions in the decennial census occupational statistics resulted in a break in comparability with the available data from the 1960 as well as earlier censuses. To permit some trend comparisons, the Census Bureau has published occupational statistics for the experienced civilian labor force in 1960, in which the number in each occupation has been estimated in accordance with the revised 1970 census occupational definitions, based on a recoding of a sample of 100,000 census schedules from 1960. However, these statistics are limited to totals for each occupation by sex. Moreover, no attempt was made in these estimates to allow for the effect of concurrent changes in census occupational reporting and processing procedures.

Fortunately, for purposes of this study, the Current Population Survey did not introduce any of the revisions in occupational definition or enumeration procedures for the 1970 decennial census until January 1971. The CPS occupational data for the decennial census enumeration weeks (in March 1960 and March 1970, respectively) thus provided a potentially more reliable measure of occupational trends over the decade than did the published adjusted 1960 census occupational data, within limits of CPS sample reliability and available occupational detail.

A comparison of labor force trends by occupation, over the decade, based on these alternative sources, did in fact show statistically significant deviations for a number of major census occupational groups and subgroups (see Appendix and Table 2.4). Accordingly, the statistics on the experienced civilian labor force by occupation for 1970, derived from our census tabulations of the 1970 public use tapes, were adjusted to conform to the 1960-70 trends shown for the corresponding occupation or occupational grouping by the CPS data.

Since the degree of occupational disaggregation available from the
CPS tabulations was considerably less than that adopted for the present
study, the 1970 trend adjustment ratios based on these broader occupational groupings were applied to each of the more specific occupations included within these groups, based on our classification scheme,
and to each of the sociodemographic components of the labor force in
such occupations.

Final Matrix Adjustment

Although the CPS trends for 1960-70 served as our controls in
establishing the level of the total experienced civilian labor force in
each occupation in 1970, the decennial census tabulations provided
the source data for distributing the labor force by occupation into 80
sociodemographic subgroups. The corresponding census totals for
each of these 80 subgroups, in turn, served as our controls in the
columns of the matrix. Predictably, the adjustments in the labor
force totals for specific occupations, when distributed proportionately
among the sociodemographic groups, resulted in disparities between
the sum of the adjusted values for specific sociodemographic subgroups, (for example, white males, aged 16-24, with 9-11 years of
education), and the corresponding totals for such subgroups as derived
from the census tabulations. A final ratio adjustment in the matrix
was therefore needed to force the totals to equal the census total for
each sociodemographic subgroup. This second adjustment did not
exceed 2 percent for any column in the matrix.

Summary

Although we believe that the adjustments described above have
substantially improved the usefulness of the census data for purposes
of analysis of occupational trends for 1960-70, their limitations will
be apparent. The highly desirable efforts of the government statisticians to improve the quality of census occupational statistics have
entailed a high cost in terms of loss of comparability. It is unfortu-
nate that the Census Bureau did not directly undertake—or perhaps,
was not in a position to undertake—the types of adjustments described
above particularly in view of our unique dependence upon decennial
census data for detailed analysis of occupational trends in the United
States. To illustrate, the original occupational recoding of the sample
1960 census schedules, to conform with the revised 1970 classifications, would have been of much greater value for the purposes of
this study and related research, if the sample of 1960 census

schedules, recoded in terms of 1970 occupational classifications, had been tabulated on the basis of additional personal characteristics, such as race, age, and educational attainment, rather than sex alone, and if efforts had been made to estimate the additional impact of collateral revisions in census enumeration and processing procedures upon the resulting statistics. In the absence of more definitive source data, it is our belief that the matrix estimates developed here provide a reasonably reliable picture of the basic trends under study particularly when consolidated for the broader occupational status groups or subgroups.

LABOR FORCE TRENDS BY OCCUPATION AND STATUS GROUP

As a point of departure for our more detailed analysis, Table 3.3 compares the distribution of the experienced civilian labor force in each occupation and status group in 1960 and 1970, based on our adjusted data for the latter year. This comparison confirms the pattern of occupational upgrading suggested by the preceding inspection of occupational trends based on the summary CPS statistics for the broad census occupational groups. Thus, the most rapid growth in the labor force over the decade occurred in the two highest occupational status groups. The experienced civilian labor force in group 1, which includes the professional and technical occupations, increased by nearly 44 percent, and the labor force in group 2, which includes most of the other white-collar occupations, by 25 percent. Status groups 3 and 4, which include the skilled or semiskilled blue-collar and service occupations, grew at a lower-than-average rate—about 8 percent and 9 percent respectively—while the labor force in group 5, which includes most of the laborers and the lowest-status personal service occupations, experienced the smallest net growth over the decade—less than 2 percent. As a result, the proportion of the labor force in the group 5 occupations declined from 12.7 percent in 1960 to 11.1 in 1970. (It should be noted that new workers as well as workers whose specific occupations were not reported in the censuses have been excluded from the labor force totals on which these percentages are based and from similar data in subsequent tables.)

Within each of these occupational status groups, trends for specific occupations varied considerably from the group averages. Thus, within group 2, the most rapid growth occurred among clerical office workers, such as secretaries, bookkeepers, and office machine operators, and among cashiers, while the number of retail sales clerks experienced virtually no net change over the decade. Within group 3, certain of the higher-status operative occupations as well as the service occupations in this group (such as practical nurses and cosmetologists) experienced a more rapid growth than the skilled crafts, while the number of farmers, farm managers, and family workers declined sharply. Among the group 4 occupations, service workers such as hospital attendants, waiters, and guards, and operatives in metalworking industries, grew in number at an above-average rate in contrast to declines for truck drivers and among operatives in nondurable goods manufacturing industries, such as textiles, apparel, and leather products.

The trends for the low-level occupations within group 5 indicate a particularly wide divergence. Relatively sharp increases occurred among cooks and kitchen workers, among janitors, and among nonfarm laborers in industries such as trade, services, and government. In contrast, the number of paid farm laborers and domestics declined sharply, continuing the long-term declining trends in these occupations. Laborers in both manufacturing and construction also declined significantly.

The occupational trends described above reflect the combined impacts of (1) differential rates of growth in output in the various industries and sectors of the economy, (2) differential rates of productivity growth and related technological changes affecting occupational staffing patterns in specific industries, (3) sizable changes in man-hours per worker, in some occupations and industries, and (4) shifts in relative availability of labor in the various occupations. Although a detailed analysis of these and other relevant variables is beyond the scope of the present study, certain broad patterns should be noted.

First, the sharpest relative growth occurred, generally, in those occupations related to service-producing, rather than goods-producing, industries. Thus, in group 5 occupations, increases were limited to personal service workers, other than domestics, and to laborers in the service-producing industries in contrast to declines in the laborer work force in both the farm and the nonfarm industrial sectors. These trends are associated with the long-term relative growth in the share of national output of service-producing industries, as well as with the relatively slow productivity growth in this sector.

Secondly, it appears probable that the rate of growth or decline of particular occupations was also influenced by specific labor supply conditions during the decade of the 1960s. Thus, the rapid growth of professional occupations, although reflecting a sharp growth in demand for their services (for example, education, health, research and development) would probably not have been possible if not for the large increase in the number of college graduates in the closing years of the decade. Conversely, as noted earlier, the rate of decline in

TABLE 3.3

Distribution of Experienced Civilian Labor Force, by
Status Group and Occupation: 1960, 1970

Status Group and Occupation	Number (000)		Percent Change, 1960-70	Percent Distributions	
	1960	1970		1960	1970
Total experienced civilian labor force	64,372	75,114	16.7	100.0	100.0
Group 1, total	7,398	10,641	43.8	11.5	14.2
Engineers	825	1,187	43.9	1.3	1.6
Teachers, excluding college	1,746	2,773	58.8	2.7	3.7
Medical personnel[a]	1,309	1,695	29.5	2.0	2.3
Other professional and technical workers[b]	3,518	4,986	41.7	5.5	6.6
Group 2, total	19,813	24,711	24.7	30.8	32.9
Managers, officials, and proprietors, nonfarm	5,389	6,418	19.1	8.4	8.5
Clerical, total	9,211	12,526	36.0	14.3	16.7
Bookkeepers	970	1,570	61.9	1.5	2.1
Secretaries, stenographers, and typists	2,262	3,536	56.3	3.5	4.7
Office machine operators	309	590	90.9	0.5	0.8
Telephone operators	363	418	15.2	0.6	0.6
Cashiers	482	861	78.6	0.7	1.1
Postal clerks, mail carriers	399	578	44.9	0.6	0.8
Other clerical, not elsewhere classified[c]	4,426	4,973	12.4	6.9	6.6
Sales, total	4,754	5,207	9.5	7.4	6.9
Sales clerks—retail trade	2,342	2,380	1.6	3.6	3.2
All other sales workers, excluding retail clerks	2,412	2,827	17.2	3.7	3.7
Policemen, firemen[d]	459	560	22.0	0.7	0.7
Group 3, total	14,548	15,687	7.8	22.6	20.9
Craftsmen and foremen, total	7,939	9,030	13.7	12.3	12.0
Foremen, not elsewhere classified	1,197	1,471	22.9	1.9	2.0
Mechanics, excluding auto	1,604	1,991	24.1	2.5	2.6
Machinists	489	522	6.7	0.8	0.7
Metal working crafts, excluding mechanics, machinists	604	586	-3.0	0.9	0.8
Carpenters	946	888	-6.1	1.5	1.2
Electricians, brickmasons, excavating operators[e]	1,198	1,419	18.4	1.9	1.9
All other craftsmen[f]	1,901	2,153	13.3	2.9	2.9
Farmers, farm managers, and unpaid workers, total	2,887	1,784	-38.2	4.6	2.4
Barbers, bartenders, practical nurses[g]	1,408	1,737	23.4	2.2	2.3
Operatives, total	2,314	3,136	35.5	3.6	4.2
Deliverymen, routemen	430	696	61.9	0.7	0.9
Checkers, examiners, and inspectors	517	760	47.0	0.8	1.0
Operatives—nondurables manufacturing including chemicals, petroleum[h]	831	986	18.7	1.3	1.3
Operatives—transport equipment manufacturing	536	694	29.5	0.8	0.9

(continued)

(Table 3.3 continued)

Status Group and Occupation	Number (000)		Percent Change, 1960-70	Percent Distributions	
	1960	1970		1960	1970
Group 4, total	14,454	15,758	9.0	22.5	21.0
Craftsmen, total	1,317	1,432	8.7	2.0	1.9
Auto mechanics	733	858	17.1	1.1	1.1
Construction painters, plasterers, cement and concrete finishers, roofers, paperhangers	584	574	-1.7	0.9	0.8
Transport operatives, total	2,496	2,483	-0.5	3.9	3.3
Truck and tractor drivers	1,712	1,534	-10.4	2.7	2.1
Auto service and parking attendants	378	462	22.2	0.6	0.6
Taxi drivers, bus drivers[i]	406	487	20.0	0.6	0.6
Other operatives, total	7,637	8,322	9.0	11.9	11.1
Packers	483	609	26.1	0.8	0.8
Welders, flamecutters	382	572	49.7	0.6	0.8
Operatives—metalworking industries[j]	2,029	2,651	30.6	3.2	3.5
Operatives—lumber, furniture, stone, clay, and glass industries	588	577	-1.8	0.9	0.8
Operatives—food and tobacco industries	550	494	-10.2	0.9	0.7
Operatives—textiles, apparel, and leather industries	1,827	1,690	-7.5	2.7	2.2
Operatives—nonmanufacturing Industries	1,778	1,729	-2.8	2.8	2.3
Shipping and receiving clerks, messengers, and office boys	353	420	19.0	0.6	0.6
Services, total	2,221	2,765	24.5	3.5	3.7
Guardes, watchmen, crossing guards and bridge tenders	250	322	28.8	0.4	0.4
Housekeepers and babysitters	463	387	-16.4	0.7	0.5
Waiters, counter and fountain workers	1,001	1,327	32.6	1.6	1.8
Hospital attendants	507	729	43.8	0.7	0.9
Laborers—metalworking industries[k]	430	336	-21.9	0.7	0.4
Group 5, total	8,159	8,317	1.9	12.7	11.1
Nonfarm laborers, total	3,009	3,224	7.1	4.7	4.3
Laborers—lumber, furniture, stone, clay, and glass industries	381	246	-35.4	0.6	0.3
Laborers—nondurables manufacturing	381	344	-9.7	0.6	0.5
Construction laborers	783	676	-13.7	1.2	0.9
Laborers—nonmanufacturing industries, except construction	1,464	1,958	33.7	2.3	2.6
Farm laborers—paid	1,305	985	-24.5	2.0	1.3
Personal services, total	2,558	3,621	41.6	4.0	4.4
Cooks	607	875	44.2	0.9	1.2
Kitchen workers	320	459	43.4	0.5	0.6
Janitors and sextons	634	966	52.4	1.0	1.3
Cleaners, charwomen, porters, chambermaids, and elevator operators	590	596	1.0	0.9	0.8
Laundry and dry cleaning operatives	407	365	-10.3	0.6	0.5
Private household workers, not elsewhere classified	1,287	847	-34.2	2.0	1.1

Notes to Table 3.3

[a]Includes physicians, dentists, medical and dental technicians, and all other health personnel classified as professional.

[b]Includes all other professional and technical workers, not elsewhere classified.

[c]Includes all other clerical and kindred workers, not elsewhere classified, except shipping and receiving clerks, messengers, and office boys.

[d]Includes marshals and constables; sheriffs and bailiffs.

[e]Includes grading and road machinery operators, plumbers and pipefitters, and structural metalworkers.

[f]Includes all other craftsmen and foremen, not elsewhere classified, except those in status group 4.

[g]Includes hospital attendants, recreation and amusement workers, ushers, and all other service workers not elsewhere classified.

[h]Includes operatives not elsewhere classified in the following nondurable goods industries: paper and allied products; printing and publishing; chemicals and allied products; petroleum and coal products; rubber and plastic products; and not specified nondurables manufacturing.

[i]Includes rail conductors, subway motormen, mine motormen, railroad brakemen, railroad switchmen, boatmen and canalmen, and sailors and deckhands.

[j]Includes operatives, not elsewhere classified, in the following industries: metal industries; machinery, except electrical; electrical machinery; professional and photographic equipment; miscellaneous manufacturing.

[k]Same industrial distribution as for operatives in note j.

Note: The occupational totals and status group subtotals for the experienced civilian labor force in 1960 and 1970 in this and subsequent tables exclude workers who were identified as "occupation not reported" in the 1960 census and who were allocated to a major census occupational group, but not to a specific occupation, in 1970. In 1960, the occupation-not-reported category had 3.2 million, or 4.8 percent of the experienced civilian labor force total of 67.6 million. In 1970, 4.9 million, or 6.1 percent of the experienced civilian labor force total of 80.0 million, consisted of allocated entries.

Sources: Data for 1960: Bureau of the Census, recoded 1/1,000 public use sample tape, released July 1971; for 1970, 1/1,000 public use sample tape, state version, with 5 percent sample items .

farm employment and in domestic service workers was accelerated during the second half of the decade, concurrent with the sharp expansion of alternative (and better-paying) job opportunities in the nonfarm sector and must be attributed, in part, to a reduced labor supply for these low-status, low-wage jobs.[3]

Occupational Distributions by
Sociodemographic Groups

In the preceding sections of this chapter we have discussed, first, the major changes in the sociodemographic composition of the civilian labor force, as a whole, during the 1960s and, then, the changes in occupational distribution of the labor force. The interaction of these two sets of influences, in turn, is reflected in the changes in occupational distribution for each major demographic component of the labor force over the decade. These distributions by occupational status group are shown in Tables 3.4 through 3.12 for men and women, by race, by educational attainment, and by broad age group.

Trends by Education Level

An initial comparison of the shifts in status group distribution for the total experienced civilian labor force, with the corresponding changes for each separate educational attainment group of the labor force, in Table 3.4, reveals a striking contrast. The overall proportion of experienced civilian workers in groups 1 and 2, combined, rose from 42.3 percent in 1960 to 47.0 percent in 1970, with corresponding reductions in each of the three lower-status groups. Yet, when the trend for each educational attainment group is examined separately, we find that the proportion of workers in the upper-status groups was reduced for each education-specific group, with corresponding increases in their proportions in groups 3, 4, and 5. To illustrate, among high school dropouts of both sexes (those with 9 to 11 years of school completed), the proportion of workers in groups 1 and 2, combined, declined from 28.7 percent to 25.5 percent between 1960 and 1970, while their proportion in groups 4 and 5 rose from 45.1 percent to 48.5 percent. This pattern of occupational downgrading is evident in each educational attainment group for both men and women (all races), and is mirrored in more pronounced form in the separate statistics for white workers of both sexes.

The explanation lies, of course, in the sharp increase in educational attainment of workers during the course of the decade. Between 1960 and 1970, the percentage of workers in the experienced civilian

TABLE 3.4

Percent Distribution, by Occupational Status Group, for Each Education Level, Sex, Race, and Age Group of the Experienced Civilian Labor Force: 1960 and 1970—Total, Both Sexes, 16 Years and Over

| Occupational Group | Total | | Years of School Completed | | | | | | | |
| | | | Less than 9 | | 9-11 | | 12 | | 13 and Over | |
	1960	1970	1960	1970	1960	1970	1960	1970	1960	1970
Total, all races										
Number (000)	64,372	75,114	18,219	12,195	13,541	14,479	18,752	27,275	13,860	21,165
Percent distribution										
Group 1	11.5	14.2	1.2	1.4	2.6	2.5	6.3	6.6	40.7	39.3
Group 2	30.8	32.8	13.0	11.8	26.1	23.0	44.8	41.9	39.7	40.2
Group 3	22.6	20.9	28.8	27.1	26.2	26.0	22.8	23.5	10.7	10.5
Group 4	22.5	21.0	32.2	34.6	30.7	32.2	19.0	20.2	6.3	6.4
Group 5	12.6	11.1	24.8	25.1	14.4	16.3	7.1	7.8	2.6	3.6
Total	100.0	100.0	100.0	100.0	100.0	100.0	100.0	100.0	100.0	100.0

(continued)

(Table 3.4 continued)

| Occupational Group | Total | | Years of School Completed | | | | | | | |
| | | | Less than 9 | | 9-11 | | 12 | | 13 and Over | |
	1960	1970	1960	1970	1960	1970	1960	1970	1960	1970
White total										
Number (000)	57,654	67,117	14,953	9,979	12,082	12,486	17,503	24,869	13,116	19,783
Percent distribution										
Group 1	12.2	14.8	1.3	1.4	2.7	2.6	6.5	6.8	40.9	39.3
Group 2	33.2	34.6	15.2	13.2	28.4	25.0	46.6	43.3	40.2	40.6
Group 3	23.5	21.5	31.9	29.7	27.4	27.4	23.2	23.9	10.8	10.5
Group 4	22.1	20.2	33.6	36.0	31.0	31.8	18.3	19.2	6.0	6.2
Group 5	9.0	8.9	18.0	19.7	10.5	13.2	5.4	6.8	2.1	3.4
Total	100.0	100.0	100.0	100.0	100.0	100.0	100.0	100.0	100.0	100.0

Nonwhite total

Number (000)	6,718	7,997	3,266	2,214	1,459	1,993	1,249	2,408	744	1,382
Percent distribution										
Group 1	5.6	9.1	.7	1.2	1.5	2.1	3.8	4.9	37.8	39.1
Group 2	10.1	18.2	3.2	5.4	6.9	10.2	20.1	27.5	29.8	34.3
Group 3	14.7	15.8	14.9	15.1	15.7	17.4	16.1	18.4	9.5	10.3
Group 4	25.3	27.5	25.4	29.0	29.3	34.5	28.0	30.3	12.4	10.1
Group 5	44.3	29.4	55.8	49.3	46.6	35.8	32.0	18.9	10.5	6.2
Total	100.0	100.0	100.0	100.0	100.0	100.0	100.0	100.0	100.0	100.0

Source: Bureau of the Census, public use tapes, 1960, 1970.

labor force with 12 years of education rose from 51 percent to 65 percent, and the percentage with one or more years of college (that is, 13 or more years of schooling) rose from 22 percent to 28 percent.

As had been true in preceding decades, this rapid educational upgrading of the labor force exceeded the rate of growth of the higher-status, white-collar occupations, in which most workers with these levels of education had been concentrated in earlier decades. As a result, an increasing percentage of workers with a high school diploma, or even with some college education, found employment in blue-collar or service occupations.

Whites Versus Nonwhites

The decade of the 1960s, as we have already observed from our initial examination of summary CPS data, was marked by a significant takeoff in terms of occupational upgrading of black workers. This is further verified by the shift in occupational status distribution of non-whites, as compared to that of white workers. The proportion of nonwhite workers in group 5 declined from 44.3 percent in 1960 to 29.4 percent in 1970—a reduction of fully one-third. The sharpest relative gains for nonwhites were recorded in group 1 and 2 occupations, where their proportion rose from 15.7 percent in 1960 to 27.3 percent in 1970, with much smaller gains in groups 3 and 4. The advance of nonwhites into the white-collar occupations was most pronounced for those with 12 or more years of schooling; among nonwhites with less schooling, the greatest net movement was from group 5 jobs to the semiskilled, group 4 category of occupations. Unlike the pattern for white workers, upward shifts in occupational status distribution were achieved by nonwhites within each specific educational attainment category. Thus, among nonwhites with 12 years of education, the percentage in groups 1 and 2 rose from 23.9 percent in 1960 to 32.4 percent in 1970, whereas among white workers with 12 years of education, the percentage in groups 1 and 2 fell from 53.1 percent in 1960 to 50.1 percent in 1970.

Men Versus Women

A comparison of the statistics on occupational status distribution for men and women of each race, appearing in Tables 3.5 and 3.6, reveals some expected differences in their distribution among the five broad occupational groups. Women—and particularly nonwhite women—have tended to be differentially concentrated at both extremes of the occupational spectrum. A relatively higher proportion of women workers with 12 or more years of schooling than men with similar education are found in the group 1 and 2 (white-collar) occupations,

TABLE 3.5

Percent Distribution, by Occupational Status Group, for Each Education Level, Sex, Race, and Age Group of the Experienced Civilian Labor Force, 1960 and 1970—Male Workers, 16 Years and Over

| Occupational Group | Total | | Years of School Completed | | | | | | | |
| | | | Less than 9 | | 9-11 | | 12 | | 13 and Over | |
	1960	1970	1960	1970	1960	1970	1960	1970	1960	1970
Total, all races										
Number (000)	43,406	47,010	13,509	8,566	9,217	9,241	11,326	15,451	9,354	13,752
Percent distribution										
Group 1	10.5	13.3	1.0	1.2	2.4	2.2	6.2	6.2	37.3	36.5
Group 2	25.1	25.7	11.8	10.2	21.0	17.4	32.5	28.1	39.3	38.4
Group 3	29.2	27.9	34.4	33.1	33.1	33.5	32.3	34.0	14.0	13.6
Group 4	22.8	21.5	30.7	32.7	29.7	31.0	21.3	22.4	6.5	7.0
Group 5	12.4	11.6	22.1	22.8	13.8	15.9	7.7	9.3	2.9	4.5
Total	100.0	100.0	100.0	100.0	100.0	100.0	100.0	100.0	100.0	100.0

(continued)

(Table 3.5 continued)

Occupational Group	Total		Years of School Completed							
			Less than 9		9-11		12		13 and Over	
	1960	1970	1960	1970	1960	1970	1960	1970	1960	1970
White total										
Number (000)	39,323	42,514	11,352	7,113	8,350	8,140	10,661	14,226	8,960	13,035
Percent distribution										
Group 1	11.1	14.0	1.1	1.3	2.5	2.3	6.5	6.4	37.5	36.6
Group 2	26.8	27.0	13.4	11.1	22.4	18.6	33.4	29.0	39.9	38.9
Group 3	30.2	28.5	37.2	35.8	34.5	34.9	32.9	34.7	14.0	13.6
Group 4	22.2	20.5	31.0	32.9	29.4	30.1	20.7	21.5	6.2	6.6
Group 5	9.7	10.0	17.3	18.9	11.2	14.1	6.5	8.4	2.4	4.3
Total	100.0	100.0	100.0	100.0	100.0	100.0	100.0	100.0	100.0	100.0

Nonwhite total

Number (000)	4,083	4,496	2,157	1,453	867	1,101	665	1,225	394	717
Percent distribution										
Group 1	4.2	7.4	.7	.9	1.5	1.3	2.4	3.5	32.8	36.5
Group 2	8.5	13.5	3.3	5.9	6.6	8.0	16.5	18.1	27.4	29.4
Group 3	19.2	21.3	19.0	19.5	20.2	24.3	22.0	25.6	13.2	13.2
Group 4	29.1	30.5	29.4	31.8	33.0	37.2	31.7	33.3	14.2	13.4
Group 5	39.0	27.3	47.6	41.9	38.7	29.2	27.4	19.5	12.4	7.5
Total	100.0	100.0	100.0	100.0	100.0	100.0	100.0	100.0	100.0	100.0

Source: Bureau of the Census, public use tapes, 1960, 1970.

TABLE 3.6

Percent Distribution, by Occupational Status Group, for Each Education Level, Sex, Race, and Age Group of the Experienced Civilian Labor Force, 1960 and 1970—Female Workers, 16 Years and Over

| Occupational Group | Total | | Years of School Completed | | | | | | | |
| | | | Less than 9 | | 9-11 | | 12 | | 13 and Over | |
	1960	1970	1960	1970	1960	1970	1960	1970	1960	1970
Total, all races										
Number (000)	20,966	28,104	4,710	3,627	4,324	5,238	7,426	11,826	4,506	7,413
Percent distribution										
Group 1	13.6	15.5	1.6	1.7	3.1	3.1	6.5	7.1	48.0	44.3
Group 2	42.5	44.9	16.7	15.5	37.0	32.9	63.8	59.9	40.2	43.7
Group 3	9.0	9.3	13.0	12.9	11.2	12.7	8.2	9.7	3.9	4.7
Group 4	21.7	20.2	36.2	39.3	33.0	34.3	15.3	17.3	5.9	5.4
Group 5	13.2	10.1	32.5	30.6	15.7	17.0	6.2	6.0	2.0	1.9
Total	100.0	100.0	100.0	100.0	100.0	100.0	100.0	100.0	100.0	100.0

White total

Number (000)	18,331	24,603	3,601	2,866	3,732	4,346	6,842	10,643	4,156	6,748
Percent distribution										
Group 1	14.5	16.1	1.8	1.7	3.4	3.1	6.6	7.2	48.3	44.5
Group 2	46.9	47.8	20.9	18.5	41.7	37.1	67.1	62.5	40.9	44.1
Group 3	9.1	9.4	14.8	14.5	11.5	13.4	8.1	9.5	3.8	4.5
Group 4	22.0	19.7	42.1	43.5	34.4	35.0	14.6	16.2	5.5	5.3
Group 5	7.5	7.0	20.4	21.8	9.0	11.4	3.6	4.6	1.5	1.6
Total	100.0	100.0	100.0	100.0	100.0	100.0	100.0	100.0	100.0	100.0

(continued)

111

(Table 3.6 continued)

Occupational Group	Total		Years of School Completed								
			Less than 9		9-11		12		13 and Over	
	1960	1970	1960	1970	1960	1970	1960	1970	1960	1970
Nonwhite total										
Number (000)	2,635	3,501	1,109	761	592	892	584	1,183	350	665
Percent distribution										
Group 1	7.6	11.3	.8	1.7	1.5	3.0	5.3	6.4	43.4	42.1
Group 2	12.6	24.4	3.0	4.3	7.3	12.9	24.1	37.3	32.6	39.5
Group 3	7.8	8.7	6.9	6.7	9.1	8.9	9.4	10.9	5.4	7.1
Group 4	19.4	23.4	17.5	23.5	24.0	31.1	23.8	27.2	10.3	6.5
Group 5	52.6	32.2	71.8	63.8	58.1	44.1	37.4	18.2	8.3	4.8
Total	100.0	100.0	100.0	100.0	100.0	100.0	100.0	100.0	100.0	100.0

Source: Bureau of the Census, public use tapes, 1960, 1970.

while a larger proportion of women workers with less than a high
school education are found in the group 5 occupations (typically in
personal service activities). On the other hand, a larger relative
proportion of men, at all educational levels, are found in the intermediate group 3 and group 4 occupations.

The pattern of shifts in occupational status distribution over the
decade was however generally similar for men and women of each
race. Among the nonwhites, the better-educated women workers—
those with at least 12 years of schooling—were among the most prom-
inent beneficiaries of the improved job climate of the 1960s. In 1960,
37.4 percent of nonwhite women with 12 years of schooling—nearly
two out of five—had still been attached to the lowest-status jobs,
working as domestics, cooks, and kitchen or cleaning service workers, in laundries, or in various laborer jobs. The proportion of
nonwhite women in such jobs was more than 10 times as great as
among white women with similar levels of education. By 1970, the
proportion of nonwhite female high school graduates in group 5 occupations had declined by more than one-half, to 18.2 percent, while
the corresponding percentage for white female high school graduates
had edged up from 3.6 percent in 1960 to 4.6 percent in 1970.

The above comparison also provides one initial indication of the
magnitude of the occupational status gap still remaining between black
and whites with similar periods of schooling. In 1970, the percentages
of nonwhites in group 5 occupations still exceeded the corresponding
percentages of white workers in each sex and educational attainment
group by ratios ranging from about 4 1/2:1, in the case of nonwhite
women with 12 years of schooling, to less than 2:1, for nonwhite men
with 13 or more years of education.

Age Group Comparisons

Thus far, we have examined shifts in occupational status distributions of workers for all age groups combined. It would be reasonable to expect that the rate of change in occupational distributions in
response to a changing labor market environment would be most pronounced for young workers who, because of greater mobility, tend
to be more responsive to shifts in the employment climate than do
more mature workers. The data appearing in Tables 3.7 through
3.12 generally confirm this assumption. Among nonwhite workers,
the degree of improvement in occupational status distribution over
the decade was much more rapid for young workers, aged 16–24
years, than for those 25 years and over; whereas the overall proportion of the latter in group 5 declined from 44.3 percent in 1960 to
30.7 percent in 1970, or by 13.6 percentage points, the corresponding
reduction for nonwhites aged 16–24 years was from 44.8 percent to
24.0 percent, or by 20.8 percentage points. This pattern, of a higher

TABLE 3.7

Percent Distribution by Occupational Status Group, for Each Education Level, Sex, Race, and Age Group of the Experienced Civilian Labor Force, 1960 and 1970—Total, Both Sexes, Ages 16-24

Occupational Group	Total		Years of School Completed							
			Less than 9		9-11		12		13 and Over	
	1960	1970	1960	1970	1960	1970	1960	1970	1960	1970
Total, all races										
Number (000)	9,712	14,789	995	633	2,503	2,825	4,152	6,454	2,062	4,877
Percent distribution										
Group 1	8.1	10.6	1.0	1.9	1.3	1.5	4.3	4.1	27.2	25.7
Group 2	33.4	34.7	5.5	5.2	20.2	18.1	43.9	40.4	41.2	40.3
Group 3	15.4	15.4	18.0	19.3	17.3	15.9	15.9	18.1	10.9	11.0
Group 4	26.5	23.4	37.5	40.0	36.5	35.9	24.3	24.4	13.7	12.8
Group 5	16.6	15.9	38.0	33.6	24.7	28.6	11.6	13.0	7.0	10.2
Total	100.0	100.0	100.0	100.0	100.0	100.0	100.0	100.0	100.0	100.0

White total

Number (000)	8,657	13,175	728	519	2,168	2,381	3,804	5,730	1,957	4,545

Percent distribution

Group 1	8.7	11.2	1.0	2.3	1.4	1.6	4.5	4.3	27.6	26.0
Group 2	36.0	35.3	7.0	5.4	22.5	19.4	46.4	41.0	41.6	40.2
Group 3	15.6	15.8	18.4	21.2	17.7	16.4	16.2	18.8	11.0	11.0
Group 4	26.5	22.7	41.3	40.8	38.3	35.8	23.6	23.6	13.4	12.5
Group 5	13.2	15.0	32.3	30.3	20.1	26.8	9.3	12.3	6.4	10.3
Total	100.0	100.0	100.0	100.0	100.0	100.0	100.0	100.0	100.0	100.0

(continued)

(Table 3.7 continued)

Occupational Group	Total		Years of School Completed								
			Less than 9		9–11		12		13 and Over		
	1960	1970	1960	1970	1960	1970	1960	1970	1960	1970	
Nonwhite total											
Number (000)	1,055	1,614	267	114	335	444	348	724	105	332	
Percent distribution											
Group 1	2.9	5.9	1.1	—	0.9	1.4	1.1	2.9	20.0	20.8	
Group 2	11.7	27.8	1.5	4.4	5.4	11.5	18.4	34.4	35.3	43.1	
Group 3	13.9	12.4	16.9	10.5	14.9	13.1	12.6	13.3	7.6	10.2	
Group 4	26.7	29.9	27.0	36.0	24.3	36.0	31.6	31.4	18.1	16.3	
Group 5	44.8	24.0	53.5	49.1	54.6	38.0	36.3	18.0	19.0	9.6	
Total	100.0	100.0	100.0	100.0	100.0	100.0	100.0	100.0	100.0	100.0	

Source: Bureau of the Census, public use tapes, 1960, 1970.

116

TABLE 3.8

Percent Distribution, by Occupational Status Group, for Each Education Level, Sex,
Race, and Age Group of the Experienced Civilian Labor Force,
1960 and 1970—Male Workers, Ages 16-24

| Occupational Group | Total | | Years of School Completed | | | | | | | |
| | | | Less than 9 | | 9-11 | | 12 | | 13 and Over | |
	1960	1970	1960	1970	1960	1970	1960	1970	1960	1970
Total, all races										
Number (000)	5,840	8,081	777	424	1,697	1,846	2,196	3,211	1,170	2,600
Percent distribution										
Group 1	7.0	9.3	0.8	1.2	1.3	1.1	4.3	3.9	24.6	23.0
Group 2	20.5	19.3	4.6	2.8	14.7	10.6	23.4	19.2	33.8	28.6
Group 3	21.5	20.8	21.2	20.0	21.7	19.6	24.4	25.7	16.2	15.8
Group 4	29.1	26.5	34.4	37.0	33.6	33.2	31.1	29.6	15.1	15.8
Group 5	21.9	24.1	39.0	39.0	28.7	35.5	16.8	21.6	10.3	16.8
Total	100.0	100.0	100.0	100.0	100.0	100.0	100.0	100.0	100.0	100.0

(continued)

(Table 3.8 continued)

Occupational Group	Years of School Completed									
	Total		Less than 9		9-11		12		13 and Over	
	1960	1970	1960	1970	1960	1970	1960	1970	1960	1970
White total										
Number (000)	5,191	7,231	579	350	1,480	1,573	2,012	2,850	1,120	2,458
Percent distribution										
Group 1	7.7	9.5	1.0	1.4	1.4	1.1	4.6	4.0	24.8	23.0
Group 2	22.1	19.6	5.7	3.1	16.4	11.4	24.3	19.0	34.3	28.5
Group 3	22.1	21.7	22.3	22.0	22.4	20.2	25.0	26.6	16.3	16.1
Group 4	29.2	25.9	36.8	37.8	34.8	32.5	31.1	29.1	14.9	15.5
Group 5	18.9	23.3	34.2	35.7	25.0	34.8	15.0	21.3	9.7	16.9
Total	100.0	100.0	100.0	100.0	100.0	100.0	100.0	100.0	100.0	100.0

Nonwhite total

Number (000)	649	850	198	74	217	273	184	361	50	142
Percent distribution										
Group 1	2.0	5.3	—	—	0.5	1.1	1.1	2.8	20.0	23.2
Group 2	7.4	15.5	1.5	1.4	3.2	5.5	14.1	20.8	24.0	28.2
Group 3	17.1	15.9	18.2	10.8	16.6	16.5	17.9	18.6	12.0	12.0
Group 4	27.0	34.7	27.3	33.7	25.8	36.6	29.9	34.3	20.0	21.8
Group 5	46.5	28.6	53.0	54.1	53.9	40.3	37.0	23.5	24.0	14.8
Total	100.0	100.0	100.0	100.0	100.0	100.0	100.0	100.0	100.0	100.0

Source: Bureau of the Census, public use tapes, 1960, 1970.

119

TABLE 3.9

Percent Distribution by Occupational Status Group, for Each Education Level, Sex, Race, and Age Group of the Experienced Civilian Labor Force, 1960 and 1970—Female Workers, Ages 16–24

Occupational Group	Years of School Completed									
	Total		Less than 9		9-11		12		13 and Over	
	1960	1970	1960	1970	1960	1970	1960	1970	1960	1970
Total, all races										
Number (000)	3,872	6,708	218	209	806	979	1,956	3,243	892	2,277
Percent distribution										
Group 1	9.6	12.2	1.8	3.3	1.4	2.3	4.2	4.4	30.6	28.6
Group 2	52.9	53.0	8.7	10.0	31.9	32.4	67.1	61.1	51.1	54.0
Group 3	6.2	8.8	6.4	17.7	8.1	8.9	6.3	10.7	3.9	5.4
Group 4	22.7	20.0	48.7	46.0	42.3	41.1	16.7	19.3	11.8	9.3
Group 5	8.6	6.0	34.4	23.0	16.3	15.3	5.7	4.5	2.7	2.7
Total	100.0	100.0	100.0	100.0	100.0	100.0	100.0	100.0	100.0	100.0

White total

Number (000)	3,466	5,944	149	169	688	808	1,792	2,880	837	2,087
Percent distribution										
Group 1	10.2	13.4	0.7	4.1	1.3	2.5	4.5	4.8	31.3	29.5
Group 2	57.0	54.8	12.1	10.1	35.8	34.8	71.1	62.9	51.4	54.0
Group 3	5.8	8.0	3.4	19.5	7.4	9.2	6.3	10.1	3.9	5.1
Group 4	22.3	19.6	59.0	47.4	46.1	42.2	15.1	19.0	11.5	9.0
Group 5	4.7	4.2	24.8	18.9	9.4	11.3	3.0	3.2	1.9	2.4
Total	100.0	100.0	100.0	100.0	100.0	100.0	100.0	100.0	100.0	100.0

(continued)

(Table 3.9 continued)

| Occupational Group | Total | | Years of School Completed | | | | | | | |
| | | | Less than 9 | | 9–11 | | 12 | | 13 and Over | |
	1960	1970	1960	1970	1960	1970	1960	1970	1960	1970
Nonwhite total										
Number (000)	406	764	69	40	118	171	164	363	55	190
Percent distribution										
Group 1	4.4	6.5	4.3	—	1.7	1.8	1.2	3.0	20.0	18.9
Group 2	18.5	41.7	1.4	10.0	9.3	21.1	23.2	48.2	45.5	54.3
Group 3	8.9	8.2	13.0	10.0	11.9	7.6	6.7	8.0	3.6	8.9
Group 4	26.4	17.1	26.1	40.0	21.2	35.1	33.5	28.4	16.4	12.1
Group 5	41.8	26.5	55.2	40.0	55.9	34.4	35.4	12.4	14.5	5.8
Total	100.0	100.0	100.0	100.0	100.0	100.0	100.0	100.0	100.0	100.0

Source: Bureau of the Census, public use tapes, 1960, 1970.

TABLE 3.10

Percent Distribution, by Occupational Status Group, for Each Education Level, Sex, Race, and Age Group of the Experienced Civilian Labor Force, 1960 and 1970—Total, Both Sexes, 25 Years and Over

Occupational Group	Total		Years of School Completed							
			Less than 9		9-11		12		13 and Over	
	1960	1970	1960	1970	1960	1970	1960	1970	1960	1970
Total, all races										
Number (000)	54,660	60,325	17,224	11,560	11,038	11,654	14,600	20,823	11,798	16,288
Percent distribution										
Group 1	12.1	15.0	1.2	1.3	2.9	2.7	6.9	7.4	43.1	43.4
Group 2	30.3	32.4	13.5	12.2	27.4	24.2	45.1	42.4	39.4	40.2
Group 3	23.9	22.3	29.5	27.5	28.2	28.5	24.7	25.1	10.7	10.3
Group 4	21.7	20.4	31.8	34.4	29.5	31.3	17.4	18.9	5.0	4.5
Group 5	12.0	9.9	24.0	24.6	12.0	13.3	5.9	6.2	1.8	1.6
Total	100.0	100.0	100.0	100.0	100.0	100.0	100.0	100.0	100.0	100.0

(continued)

(Table 3.10 continued)

| Occupational Group | Total | | Years of School Completed | | | | | | | |
| | | | Less than 9 | | 9-11 | | 12 | | 13 and Over | |
	1960	1970	1960	1970	1960	1970	1960	1970	1960	1970
White total										
Number (000)	48,997	53,942	14,225	9,460	9,914	10,105	13,699	19,139	11,159	15,238
Percent distribution										
Group 1	12.8	15.6	1.3	1.4	3.0	2.8	7.1	7.5	43.2	43.3
Group 2	32.8	34.4	15.6	13.7	29.7	26.4	46.7	44.0	40.0	40.8
Group 3	24.9	22.9	32.6	30.2	29.6	30.0	25.2	25.5	10.7	10.3
Group 4	21.3	19.7	33.2	35.6	29.3	30.8	16.8	17.9	4.7	4.3
Group 5	8.2	7.4	17.3	19.1	8.4	10.0	4.2	5.1	1.4	1.3
Total	100.0	100.0	100.0	100.0	100.0	100.0	100.0	100.0	100.0	100.0

Nonwhite total

Number (000)	5,663	6,383	2,999	2,100	1,124	1,549	901	1,684	639	1,050
Percent distribution										
Group 1	6.1	9.9	0.7	1.2	1.7	2.3	4.8	5.8	40.6	45.0
Group 2	9.8	15.8	3.4	5.4	7.3	9.8	20.8	24.5	29.0	31.5
Group 3	14.8	16.7	14.7	15.3	15.9	18.6	17.4	20.6	9.9	10.3
Group 4	25.0	26.9	25.2	28.6	30.9	34.0	26.6	29.9	11.4	8.1
Group 5	44.3	30.7	56.0	49.5	44.2	35.3	30.4	19.2	9.1	5.1
Total	100.0	100.0	100.0	100.0	100.0	100.0	100.0	100.0	100.0	100.0

Source: Bureau of the Census, public use tapes, 1960, 1970.

TABLE 3.11

Percent Distribution by Occupational Status Group, for Each Education Level, Sex, Race, and Age Group of the Experienced Civilian Labor Force, 1960 and 1970—Male Workers, 25 Years and Over

Occupational Group	Total 1960	Total 1970	Less than 9 1960	Less than 9 1970	9-11 1960	9-11 1970	12 1960	12 1970	13 and Over 1960	13 and Over 1970
					Years of School Completed					
Number (000)	37,566	38,929	12,731	8,142	7,520	7,395	9,131	12,240	8,184	11,152
Percent distribution										
Group 1	11.0	14.2	1.0	1.2	2.6	2.4	6.7	6.8	39.1	39.7
Group 2	25.8	27.1	12.2	10.6	22.4	19.1	34.6	30.4	40.1	40.7
Group 3	30.3	29.3	35.2	33.9	35.7	37.1	34.2	36.3	13.7	13.1
Group 4	21.9	20.4	30.5	32.4	28.9	30.4	19.0	20.5	5.3	4.9
Group 5	11.0	9.0	21.1	21.9	10.4	11.0	5.5	6.0	1.8	1.6
Total	100.0	100.0	100.0	100.0	100.0	100.0	100.0	100.0	100.0	100.0

Total, all races

White total

Number (000)	34,132	35,283	10,773	6,763	6,870	6,567	8,649	11,376	7,840	10,577
Percent distribution										
Group 1	11.7	14.9	1.1	1.3	2.7	2.6	6.9	7.0	39.3	39.7
Group 2	27.5	28.5	13.8	11.5	23.8	20.3	35.6	31.4	40.7	41.3
Group 3	31.4	30.0	38.1	36.6	37.1	38.4	34.8	36.8	13.7	13.0
Group 4	21.1	19.4	30.7	32.6	28.2	29.5	18.2	19.6	4.9	4.6
Group 5	8.3	7.2	16.3	18.0	8.2	9.2	4.5	5.2	1.4	1.4
Total	100.0	100.0	100.0	100.0	100.0	100.0	100.0	100.0	100.0	100.0

(continued)

(Table 3.11 continued)

Occupational Group	Total		Less than 9		9-11		12		13 and Over	
	1960	1970	1960	1970	1960	1970	1960	1970	1960	1970
Nonwhite total										
Number (000)	3,434	3,646	1,958	1,379	650	828	482	864	344	575
Percent distribution										
Group 1	4.7	7.8	.8	.9	1.8	1.3	2.9	3.8	34.5	39.7
Group 2	8.7	13.1	3.5	6.2	7.7	8.8	17.4	17.0	27.9	29.7
Group 3	19.5	22.5	19.1	19.9	21.4	26.8	23.4	28.6	13.4	13.6
Group 4	29.5	30.1	29.6	31.7	35.4	37.5	32.6	32.8	13.4	11.3
Group 5	37.6	26.5	47.0	41.3	33.7	25.6	23.7	17.8	10.8	5.7
Total	100.0	100.0	100.0	100.0	100.0	100.0	100.0	100.0	100.0	100.0

Years of School Completed

Source: Bureau of the Census, public use tapes, 1960, 1970.

TABLE 3.12

Percent Distribution, by Occupational Status Group, for Each Education Level, Sex, Race, and Age Group of the Experienced Civilian Labor Force, 1960 and 1970—Female Workers, 25 Years and Over

| Occupational Group | Total | | Years of School Completed | | | | | | | |
| | | | Less than 9 | | 9-11 | | 12 | | 13 and Over | |
	1960	1970	1960	1970	1960	1970	1960	1970	1960	1970
Total, all races										
Number (000)	17,094	21,396	4,493	3,418	3,518	4,259	5,469	8,583	3,614	5,136
Percent distribution										
Group 1	14.5	16.5	1.6	1.6	3.5	3.2	7.3	8.2	52.1	51.3
Group 2	40.3	42.3	17.0	15.9	38.3	33.1	62.7	59.4	37.6	39.1
Group 3	9.6	9.5	13.3	12.6	11.9	13.5	8.8	9.3	3.9	4.4
Group 4	21.4	20.3	35.7	38.9	30.8	32.8	14.8	16.6	4.5	3.6
Group 5	14.2	11.4	32.4	31.0	15.5	17.4	6.4	6.5	1.9	1.6
Total	100.0	100.0	100.0	100.0	100.0	100.0	100.0	100.0	100.0	100.0

(continued)

129

(Table 3.12 continued)

Occupational Group	Total		Years of School Completed Less than 9		9-11		12		13 and Over	
	1960	1970	1960	1970	1960	1970	1960	1970	1960	1970
White total										
Number (000)	14,865	18,659	3,452	2,697	3,044	3,538	5,050	7,763	3,319	4,661
Percent distribution										
Group 1	15.4	17.0	1.9	1.6	3.8	3.2	7.3	8.2	52.6	51.2
Group 2	44.7	45.7	21.3	19.0	43.2	37.6	65.8	62.3	38.2	39.7
Group 3	9.9	9.6	15.3	14.2	12.5	14.4	8.7	9.0	3.8	4.2
Group 4	21.9	19.9	41.3	43.2	31.7	33.3	14.4	15.5	4.0	3.6
Group 5	8.1	7.8	20.2	22.0	8.8	11.5	3.8	5.0	1.4	1.3
Total	100.0	100.0	100.0	100.0	100.0	100.0	100.0	100.0	100.0	100.0

Nonwhite total

Number (000)	2,229	2,737	1,041	721	474	721	419	820	295	475
Percent distribution										
Group 1	8.2	12.6	.6	1.8	1.5	3.3	6.9	7.9	47.7	51.4
Group 2	11.5	19.5	3.1	4.0	6.8	11.0	24.6	32.5	30.2	33.7
Group 3	7.6	8.9	6.5	6.5	8.4	9.2	10.5	12.2	5.8	6.3
Group 4	18.1	22.6	17.0	22.6	24.7	30.1	19.8	26.7	9.2	4.2
Group 5	54.6	36.4	72.8	65.1	58.6	46.4	38.2	20.7	7.1	4.4
Total	100.0	100.0	100.0	100.0	100.0	100.0	100.0	100.0	100.0	100.0

Source: Bureau of the Census, public use tapes, 1960, 1970.

131

rate of reduction in participation in group 5 jobs for young nonwhites than for nonwhite adults, is generally evident in the separate trends for each of the sex and educational attainment subgroups.

Conversely, the data for white workers indicate significantly greater increases in the percentages of young workers, aged 16-24 years, in group 5 occupations than among adult workers, aged 25 years and over. Thus, whereas the percentage of white youths with 9-11 years of school in group 5 occupations rose from 20.1 percent to 26.8 percent between 1960 and 1970, the increase for the corresponding group of adult workers, aged 25 years and over, was only from 8.4 percent to 10.0 percent. Moreover, as shown in Tables 3.7 and 3.8, the percentage point increases in participation in group 5 occupations between 1960 and 1970 were largest for white males with 13 or more years of education.

Occupational Status Indices

The occupational status index, as noted in Chapter 2, is an average of our occupational percentile (or status) scores for each occupation (as shown in Table 2.9), weighted by the number of workers in a specified population group who are attached to that occupation. This index, thus, provides a useful summary measure of the relative occupational standings of different population groups and their changes over time. Occupational status indices have been computed for all white and nonwhite workers, and for each of the major sociodemographic groups, based on the detailed distributions of workers among the full range of the 57 occupations used in this study.

White-Nonwhite Status Differential

Our analysis of trends between 1910 and 1960, in Chapter 2, indicated that nonwhites had made limited progress in improving their overall occupational status during this half century and had made no net progress at all, relative to white workers. The mass movement of black workers from farm to city and from the South to the North had, in large part, resulted in their shift from low-status and very low income jobs on the farm to similarly low-status, and only slightly better-paying, jobs in the city. Their penetration into the higher-status, white-collar and skilled craft occupations, as well as into some of the more desirable operative occupations, was still very limited, although some progress in this direction had been achieved during World War II and the decade of the 1950s. Thus, as of 1960, the occupational status index of nonwhites, based on their distribution

TABLE 3.13

Occupational Status Indices for White and Nonwhite
Workers: 1910, 1950, 1960, 1970

Year	Status Index[a] White	Nonwhite	Ratio of Non-white Index to White Index
1950-comparable occupations[b]			
1910	36.2	19.0	52.5
1950	44.6	22.1	49.6
1960	47.8	25.2	52.7
1960/70-comparable[c] occupations			
1960	49.0	25.1	51.2
1970	51.3	34.0	66.3

[a]Except as otherwise noted, the status indices for each group were derived as the average of the percentile status scores for each occupation, as shown in Table 1.3, weighted by the number of workers in each occupation.

[b]Based on occupational distributions of white and nonwhite workers among 42 occupational subgroups, comparable to 1950 census occupational classifications, as shown in Table 2.5. Occupational status percentile scores, based on the more detailed 1960/70 occupational clusters, were reweighted, where necessary, to correspond to the coverage of the 1950 occupational groups.

[c]Based on occupational distributions of white and nonwhite workers in the experienced civilian labor force, 16 years and over, classified in accordance with the 57 occupations used in the current study, comparable with 1960 and 1970.

Source: Compiled by the author.

among the 57 occupations used in our analysis of 1960-70 trends, stood at 25.1, or only slightly more than one-half of the corresponding index for white workers. Between 1960 and 1970, however, the non-white index increased by more than one-third to 34.0, as compared to an increase of only 2.3 points, to 51.3, for white workers. As a result, the relative occupational standing of the nonwhite labor force in 1970 was 66.3 percent, or nearly two-thirds that of white workers. (See Table 3.13.)

Status Trends, by Educational Level

It will be apparent from Table 3.14 that, in the case of white workers, the overall growth in employment opportunities in higher-status occupations did not keep pace with the increase in their educational attainment. Hence—with limited exceptions—the occupational status of white workers with given levels of educational attainment declined between 1960 and 1970, whereas the overall status index for white workers increased moderately.

In the case of nonwhites, on the other hand, significant improvements in occupational status were achieved by all educational attainment groups. Thus, the impressive overall gains in occupational status of the nonwhite labor force resulted from both a sharp increase in educational attainment and from upgrading of workers at each educational level. We have estimated that approximately one-half of the overall improvement in the nonwhite occupational status index between 1960 and 1970 is associated with the increase in the educational level of the nonwhite labor force, and that the balance is a result of all those factors which contributed to upgrading of nonwhite workers within the same educational attainment groups. (We should emphasize, however, that it may well be erroneous to attribute the full improvement in status associated with increased schooling to the increased productivity resulting from education, per se, since increased education may, in part, be a proxy for other personal characteristics relevant to labor market success.)

Age Group Comparisons

The separate indices for workers aged 16-24 years (Table 3.15) provide some significant contrasts with the corresponding indices for workers of all age groups (Table 3.14). A comparison of status indices for each educational level indicates that, with some exceptions, young workers have tended to start lower on the occupational ladder than the levels attained by older workers with similar educational background. In the case of white youth, the gap between their occupational status and that of adult white men appears to have widened over the decade. Thus, in 1960, the index for white men, aged 16-24 years with 12 years of schooling, was less than five points below that of the corresponding index for all white male workers, 16 years and over. In 1970, this differential had grown to about 11 points, due to a relatively sharp reduction in occupational status of young white workers between 1960 and 1970. The reverse was the case, however, for the nonwhite male youth, who began their work careers in the less discriminatory labor market climate of the 1960s. Thus, whereas the status index of nonwhite male high school graduates, aged 16-24, had

TABLE 3.14

Occupational Status Indices for the Experienced
Civilian Labor Force, by Race, Sex, and Years
of School Completed, 1960, 1970—
Total, Ages 16 and Over

Sex, Race	Years of School Completed				
	Total	Less than 9	9-11	12	13 and Over
Both sexes, total					
1960	46.5	30.1	38.3	50.8	70.1
1970	49.5	29.2	36.8	49.9	69.4
White, total					
1960	49.0	32.9	40.5	52.3	70.6
1970	51.3	31.5	38.7	51.1	69.7
Nonwhite, total					
1960	25.1	17.1	20.1	30.9	60.1
1970	34.0	19.4	24.8	37.7	64.5
Male, total					
1960	45.1	31.8	38.3	46.3	68.6
1970	47.6	30.8	35.5	45.7	67.6
White male					
1960	47.1	34.0	39.9	48.2	69.2
1970	49.3	33.1	38.0	46.6	68.0
Nonwhite male					
1960	25.9	20.0	23.0	31.0	56.1
1970	33.1	22.2	26.8	34.9	61.8
Female, total					
1960	49.2	25.3	38.3	56.4	72.8
1970	53.2	25.9	39.4	56.6	72.7
White female					
1960	52.8	29.5	41.9	58.6	73.5
1970	55.8	29.1	42.6	57.3	73.2
Nonwhite female					
1960	23.9	11.5	16.0	30.8	64.6
1970	35.2	14.1	22.3	40.5	67.4

Note: The indices of occupational status, here and in Tables
3.15 and 3.16, are averages of the occupational status scores
weighted by employment in each occupation. The derivation of the
occupational status scores is discussed in Chapter 1.

Source: Compiled by the author.

TABLE 3.15

Occupational Status Indices for the Experienced Civilian Labor Force, by Race, Sex and Years of School Completed, 1960, 1970—Total, Ages 16-24

Sex, Race	Total	Years of School Completed			
		Less than 9	9-11	12	13 and Over
Both sexes, total					
1960	43.4	21.4	30.0	48.3	59.9
1970	45.0	22.5	28.4	44.5	57.7
White, total					
1960	45.5	23.1	31.8	49.7	60.5
1970	46.1	23.9	29.3	45.3	57.8
Nonwhite, total					
1960	25.9	16.9	18.4	32.5	48.9
1970	36.4	16.3	23.4	38.5	56.3
Male, total					
1960	37.3	21.8	28.2	40.2	55.7
1970	37.3	20.9	24.7	35.4	51.3
White, male					
1960	39.3	23.6	29.6	41.6	56.2
1970	38.1	22.2	25.2	35.7	51.3
Nonwhite, male					
1960	21.6	16.6	18.4	24.5	43.8
1970	30.8	14.7	21.7	32.8	52.1
Female, total					
1960	53.5	19.8	34.0	58.3	65.4
1970	54.3	26.1	35.5	54.0	64.9
White, female					
1960	54.8	20.9	36.7	58.9	66.2
1970	55.8	27.7	37.5	55.2	65.4
Nonwhite, female					
1960	32.8	17.5	18.3	41.5	53.6
1970	42.6	19.2	26.0	44.1	59.4

Source: Compiled by the author.

TABLE 3.16

Occupational Status Indices for Workers with
12 Years of Education, by Race, Sex,
and Age Group: 1960, 1970

	Age Group				
Sex, Race	16-24 Years	25-34 Years	35-44 Years	45-54 Years	55 Years and over
Both sexes, total					
1960	46.6	49.6	52.3	53.4	55.9
1970	43.8	48.2	51.3	52.9	53.9
White, total					
1960	48.5	51.3	53.5	54.4	56.7
1970	44.5	49.5	52.6	53.9	54.8
Nonwhite, total					
1960	31.0	32.3	32.8	—	—
1970	38.1	37.8	38.0	36.4	—
Male, total					
1960	39.7	46.3	49.9	51.0	55.0
1970	35.4	44.2	48.4	50.1	51.0
White, male					
1960	41.6	47.4	50.8	51.7	55.5
1970	35.7	45.0	49.1	51.0	51.8
Nonwhite, male					
1960	24.5	32.4	32.6	—	—
1970	32.8	35.0	38.1	32.8	—
Female, total					
1960	57.1	55.5	56.3	57.0	57.5
1970	53.9	55.1	55.2	56.5	57.5
White, female					
1960	58.9	58.8	57.9	58.3	58.7
1970	55.2	57.3	57.3	57.6	58.5
Nonwhite, female					
1960	41.5	32.2	33.0	—	—
1970	44.1	40.9	37.7	40.1	—

Note: Status indices not shown for groups with base totals less than 100,000.
Source: Compiled by the author.

been 6.5 points below that for all nonwhite men 16 years and over
with similar education in 1960, it was only 2.1 points lower in 1970.

The data for nonwhite female youth are a partial exception to the
pattern described above. In 1960, the occupational status indices for
the 16-24-year-old, nonwhite girls at each educational level, other
than college women, were higher in 1960 than the corresponding
indices for nonwhite women of all ages. This is probably due to the
fact that, in 1960, disproportionately large numbers of mature black
women were still engaged in menial service work, as maids, cooks,
charwomen, whereas a much smaller proportion of young black women
had entered those occupations. Between 1960 and 1970 the status
indices increased for nonwhite women in all age groups and at all
educational levels, with the young women still retaining a higher
average occupational standing than their adult counterparts.

To provide further insights on the extent of occupational upgrading
of workers during the 1960-70 decade, we have also computed status
indices, by ten-year age groups, for one specific educational attainment category, those with 12 years of school completed. The patterns
for male workers are particularly relevant in this context since all
but a small percentage of young men who complete high school and
do not go on to college, enter the labor force in their late teens and
remain in the labor force until death or retirement. Hence—with the
partial exception of the youngest working age group in 1960, that is,
ages 16-24 years—a cohort analysis showing the change in occupational status of men in each age group, over the period 1960-70,
provides a close approximation of the net change in occupational
status for the same group of workers; these comparisons, adapted
from Table 3.16, are shown below.

Age Group		Net Change in Status Index, 1960-70		
1960	1970	Total Males	White	Nonwhite
16–24	25–34	4.5	3.4	10.5
25–34	35–44	2.1	1.7	5.7
35–44	45–54	0.2	0.2	0.2
45–54	55 and over	0.0	0.1	n.a.

It will be evident that, even with some allowance for lack of
direct comparability in coverage of the youngest age group, upward
occupational mobility of both white and nonwhite male workers who
were high school graduates was largely concentrated in their first
two decades of working life, with very little progress in status, for
the average worker, beyond his late thirties or early forties. This
cohort analysis also confirms our earlier findings concerning the

relatively sharp occupational upgrading of young nonwhite workers
over the decade. In contrast to the very significant improvements in
status of nonwhite male workers with a high school diploma, who were
in the age group 16-34 years in 1960, those who were 35 years and
over in 1960 experienced little or no net upgrading over the decade.

The status indices for white female high school graduates indicate
no similar pattern of upgrading with age, reflecting both the limited
advancement opportunities for such women (who are mainly concentrated in clerical and sales jobs) as well as the effects of less continuous labor force experience. In contrast, the data for nonwhite
female high school graduates indicate that the age group 25-34 years
and the group 35-44 years, as of 1960, were both able to improve
their status significantly over the decade, typically by moving into
white-collar jobs from lower-status service-type occupations.

Extent of Reductions in the White/Nonwhite Status Gap

The net effect of these changes in occupational distribution upon
the relative occupational position of nonwhite versus white workers
in specific age, sex, and educational achievement groups is indicated
in Table 3.17. In addition to showing the net changes in the ratios of
the respective nonwhite/white occupational status indices between
1960 and 1970 for each of these groups, we have expressed these
changes as percentages of the status gap for each group as of 1960.
Thus the 1960 occupational status index, of 25.1, for all nonwhite
workers, 16 years and over, compared to that for white workers, of
49.0, had resulted in a ratio of .512. The 1960 status gap, defined
as the complement of this ratio, was therefore .488. In 1970, the
ratio of the nonwhite-to-white occupational status indices was .663,
an increase of .151 points. This in turn corresponded to a reduction
of 31 percent in the nonwhite/white status gap, of .488, over the
decade.

Based on this criterion, an inspection of Table 3.17 indicates that
progress of nonwhites in bridging their occupational status gap relative to white workers was positively and strongly associated with
educational level. The greatest percentage reductions in the nonwhite/
white occupational status differential were achieved by college-educated nonwhites, those with 13 years or more of school completed.
For the total nonwhite experienced civilian labor force, the status
gap for college-educated workers was reduced by 50 percent over the
decade, as contrasted to reductions of 36 percent for those with 12
years of education, 29 percent for those with 9-11 years of schooling,
and only 20 percent for those with less than 9 years of school completed.

TABLE 3.17

Occupational Status Index Ratios of Nonwhite Workers,
Relative to White Workers, by Sex, Age Group,
and Educational Attainment: 1960, 1970

Sex/Age Group	Total	Years of School Completed			
		Less than 9	9–11	12	13 and Over
Total, 16 years and over					
1960	.512	.520	.496	.591	.851
1970	.663	.616	.641	.738	.921
Net change	.151	.096	.145	.147	.074
Percent reduction in					
status gap	31	20	29	36	50
Males, total					
1960	.550	.588	.576	.643	.811
1970	.671	.671	.705	.749	.909
Net change	.121	.083	.129	.106	.098
Percent reduction in					
status gap	27	20	30	30	52
Females, total					
1960	.453	.390	.382	.526	.879
1970	.631	.485	.523	.707	.921
Net change	.178	.095	.141	.181	.042
Percent reduction in					
status gap	33	16	23	38	35
Ages 16–24					
1960	.569	.732	.579	.654	.808
1970	.790	.682	.799	.850	.974
Net change	.221	−.050	.220	.196	.166
Percent reduction in					
status gap	51	−19	52	57	87
Males, 16–24					
1960	.550	.703	.622	.589	.779
1970	.808	.662	.861	.919	1.016
Net change	.258	−.041	.239	.330	.237
Percent reduction in					
status gap	57	−14	63	80	107
Females, 16–24					
1960	.599	.837	.499	.705	.810
1970	.763	.693	.693	.799	.908
Net change	.164	−.146	.194	.094	.098
Percent reduction in					
status gap	41	−90	38	32	52

Source: Compiled by the author.

Young nonwhite workers, aged 16-24 years, achieved much more rapid relative progress in status advancement than did adult nonwhites, 25 years and over. Over the decade, the former group's occupational status gap, as compared to white workers, aged 16-24 years, was reduced by 51 percent, whereas the corresponding reduction for all nonwhite age groups was 31 percent. The disparity in occupational progress by educational level was particularly wide for these young nonwhite workers. In the case of college-educated nonwhites, the occupational status gap with white youths had been virtually closed by 1970. In contrast, the gap had actually been widened between 1960 and 1970, in the case of that small proportion of nonwhite youth which had not progressed beyond the eighth grade. (The latter figures, indicating an increase in the status gap of 19 percent over the decade are, however, subject to particularly large sampling variability.)

Among the young nonwhites, male workers achieved greater gains in occupational upgrading, relative to whites, than did female workers. Nonwhite men aged 16-24 years reduced their status gap, as compared to white male youth, by 57 percent over the decade, with particularly sharp gains for those with 13 or more years of school (107 percent) and with 12 years of school (80 percent). Nonwhite women in most age/education-related categories tended to lag in their relative rate of progress as compared to nonwhite men with similar educational attainment.

The very positive advances towards occupational integration of the better-educated nonwhite workers indicated by these statistics must be balanced, however, against the evidence cited earlier in this chapter, of significant declines in labor force participation among nonwhite males, particularly youth, and against the persistence of differentially high unemployment rates for blacks throughout the decade. Labor force participation rates, moreover, were particularly low among the less-educated black youth out of school, that is, those who had not completed high school and whose job opportunities were mainly confined to low-status group 5-type jobs.

One inference which has been drawn from a juxtaposition of the two trends described above has been that increasing numbers of black youths with very limited occupational options have effectively withdrawn from conventional work or work-seeking activity, because of rejection of the low-status jobs available to them—in some cases engaging in illicit activities, in lieu of conventional employment. Another possible explanation is that many of the types of low-status jobs previously occupied by nonwhite youths or adults, such as food service jobs or construction labor, have become less accessible to nonwhites because of the more rapid growth of these jobs in the suburbs and because of increased competition from the growing number of white youths for such work.

Occupational Composition

Following up our examination above of the changes in distribution of major sociodemographic components of the labor force among occupations over the decade 1960-70, we shall now turn to an inspection of these trends in the composition of the labor force within specific occupations or occupational status groups, based on such characteristics as sex, race, age, and educational attainment. We shall examine the differential impact of the overall changes in labor force composition during the 1960s, upon the work force of the various occupations—and particularly of the low-status occupations—in terms of their respective age composition, racial composition, the proportion of women in each occupation, and shifts in educational attainment. Collateral data on trends in part-time employment, and in participation of foreign-born workers in various occupations, will also be examined.

Status Group Summaries

An initial overview of these shifts in occupational composition is provided in Table 3.18, which shows the 1960 and 1970 distributions of the labor force within each occupational status group, by broad age group and race. The decade of the 1960s had been marked, as noted earlier in the chapter, by a large-scale inflow of youth and young adults into the civilian labor force. Young workers, in previous decades, tended to be disproportionately concentrated in the least-skilled, entry-type occupations, and particularly in those jobs which have been most amenable to utilization of a part-time casual labor force, such as laborers, personal service occupations, and retail sales (see Chapter 2). The summary statistics indicate that this trend was accentuated for white youth in the decade of the 1960s. Thus, although the total labor force in group 5 occupations grew by only 160,000, or 28 percent, over the decade, this was the net result of a large inflow of young white workers offsetting sharp reductions in the number of nonwhites in this occupational class. As a result, the proportion of young white workers in group 5 occupations rose from 14 percent in 1960 to nearly 24 percent in 1970, with corresponding reductions among nonwhites (youth and adults), as well as among white adult workers, 25 years and over.

The separate summaries for men and women (Tables 3.19 and 3.20) indicate that the increased concentration of youth in group 5 occupations consisted almost entirely of white males. Between 1960 and 1970, the percentage of white male workers, aged 16-24 years, in group 5 occupations, rose from 18.1 percent to 31.0 percent—

a much greater increase than in any other occupational status group. In contrast, young female workers, aged 16-24 years, have accounted for a much smaller proportion of the total female labor force in group 5 occupations than has been the case for young male workers. Moreover, the percentage of 16-24-year-olds among women in group 5 occupations rose only marginally from 12.0 percent in 1960 to 13.4 percent in 1970, a much smaller relative growth in this age group than in white-collar or in higher-status blue-collar occupations. Thus, whereas an increased proportion of young men began their work careers in relatively low-skilled labor jobs, a much smaller percentage of young women had entered similar female-type low-status jobs, such as domestic or other routine service or manual occupations (exclusive of babysitters).

Trends in Age/Race Composition of Workers, by Occupation

The more detailed statistics on the age/race composition of the labor force, by sex, for each of the 57 occupations are shown in Tables 3.21, 3.22, and 3.23. In 1960, as well as earlier periods, a number of occupations characteristically included larger proportions of youthful workers. These were typically occupations which required limited work experience or skill and which provided opportunities for part-time employment, within easy access of workers' homes. Thus, particularly high concentrations of workers, aged 16-24 years, were found among babysitters, retail clerks, the less-skilled food service occupations, automobile service and parking attendants, other non-manufacturing laborers, and in many office clerical occupations. Conversely, smaller-than-average proportions of youthful workers were found in professional and managerial occupations, among skilled craftsmen, and among manufacturing industry workers.

This pattern of concentration in youth-type occupations was generally retained for the large cohort of young workers who began their work careers in the decade of the 1960s. However, whereas large numbers of girls and young women were able to find jobs in various clerical and sales occupations, many young men found employment—whether by choice or necessity—in the lower-status laborer and service-type jobs, which we have classified in group 5. These occupations are characterized, normally, by extremely high turnover rates. In addition, the generally favorable labor market conditions of the 1960s, combined with the reductions in barriers against employment of blacks in higher-status occupations, had resulted in a large net outflow of both white and nonwhite adult workers from these occupations to higher-wage jobs.*

——————

*These observations are based on the results of a cohort analysis of net occupational shifts between 1960 and 1970, for male workers in

TABLE 3.18

Distribution of Experienced Civilian Labor Force in Each Occupational Status Group,
by Broad Age Group and Race, 1960-70—Total, Both Sexes

Occupational Status Group	Total	Ages 16-24			Ages 25 and Over		
		Total	White	Nonwhite	Total	White	Nonwhite
				Number (000)			
Total							
1960	64,366	9,655	8,625	1,030	54,711	49,046	5,665
1970	75,113	14,722	13,145	1,577	60,391	54,006	6,385
Net change	10,747	5,067	4,520	547	5,680	4,960	720
Group 1							
1960	7,398	777	747	30	6,621	6,281	340
1970	10,641	1,575	1,479	96	9,066	8,438	628
Net change	3,243	798	732	66	2,445	2,157	288
Group 2							
1960	19,810	3,229	3,110	119	16,581	16,026	555
1970	24,711	5,115	4,670	445	19,596	18,583	1,013
Net change	4,901	1,886	1,560	326	3,015	2,557	458
Group 3							
1960	14,545	1,469	1,353	116	13,076	12,232	844
1970	15,686	2,274	2,070	204	13,412	12,345	1,067
Net change	1,141	805	717	88	336	113	223
Group 4							
1960	14,454	2,587	2,298	289	11,867	10,450	1,417
1970	15,755	3,466	2,978	488	12,289	10,572	1,717
Net change	1,301	879	680	199	422	122	300
Group 5							
1960	8,159	1,615	1,142	473	6,544	4,031	2,513
1970	8,320	2,363	1,972	391	5,957	3,994	1,963
Net change	161	748	830	-82	-587	-37	-550

Percent Distribution

Total							
1960	100.0	15.0	13.4	1.6	85.0	76.2	8.8
1970	100.0	19.6	17.5	2.1	80.4	71.9	8.5
Group 1							
1960	100.0	10.5	10.1	0.4	89.5	84.9	4.6
1970	100.0	14.8	13.9	0.9	85.2	79.3	5.9
Group 2							
1960	100.0	16.3	15.7	0.6	83.7	80.9	2.8
1970	100.0	20.7	18.9	1.8	79.3	75.2	4.1
Group 3							
1960	100.0	10.1	9.3	0.8	89.9	84.1	5.8
1970	100.0	14.5	13.2	1.3	85.5	78.7	6.8
Group 4							
1960	100.0	17.9	15.9	2.0	82.1	72.3	9.8
1970	100.0	22.0	18.9	3.1	78.0	67.1	10.9
Group 5							
1960	100.0	19.8	14.0	5.8	80.2	49.4	30.8
1970	100.0	28.4	23.7	4.7	71.6	48.0	23.6

Note: All 1960 and 1970 data are net totals, excluding not reported and allocated comparability; detail may not add to totals due to rounding.

Source: Bureau of the Census public use sample tapes, 1960, 1970.

145

TABLE 3.19

Distribution of Experienced Civilian Labor Force in Each Occupational Status Group, by Broad Age Group and Race, 1960–70—Male Workers

Occupational Status Group	Total	Ages 16-24			Ages 25 and Over		
		Total	White	Nonwhite	Total	White	Nonwhite
				Number (000)			
Total							
1960	43,400	5,859	5,208	651	37,541	34,112	3,429
1970	47,016	8,087	7,241	846	38,929	35,262	3,667
Net change	3,616	2,228	2,033	195	1,388	1,150	238
Group 1							
1960	4,549	410	396	14	4,139	3,980	159
1970	6,290	749	705	44	5,541	5,258	283
Net change	1,741	339	309	30	1,402	1,278	124
Group 2							
1960	10,876	1,185	1,142	43	9,691	9,397	294
1970	12,097	1,560	1,427	133	10,537	10,065	472
Net change	1,221	375	285	90	846	668	178
Group 3							
1960	12,665	1,254	1,140	114	11,411	10,740	671
1970	13,066	1,699	1,568	131	11,367	10,544	823
Net change	401	445	428	17	-44	-196	152
Group 4							
1960	9,913	1,695	1,517	178	8,218	7,207	1,011
1970	10,090	2,149	1,856	293	7,941	6,841	1,100
Net change	177	454	339	115	-277	-366	89
Group 5							
1960	5,397	1,279	977	302	4,118	2,828	1,290
1970	5,473	1,938	1,697	241	3,535	2,561	974
Net change	76	659	720	-61	-583	-267	-316

Percent Distribution

Total							
1960	100.0	13.5	12.0	1.5	86.5	78.6	7.9
1970	100.0	17.2	15.4	1.8	82.8	75.0	7.8
Group 1							
1960	100.0	9.0	8.7	0.3	91.0	87.5	3.5
1970	100.0	11.9	11.2	0.7	88.1	83.6	4.5
Group 2							
1960	100.0	10.9	10.5	0.4	89.1	86.4	2.7
1970	100.0	12.9	11.8	1.1	87.1	83.2	3.9
Group 3							
1960	100.0	9.9	9.0	0.9	90.1	84.8	5.3
1970	100.0	13.0	12.0	1.0	87.0	80.7	6.3
Group 4							
1960	100.0	17.1	15.3	1.8	82.9	72.7	10.2
1970	100.0	21.3	18.4	2.9	78.7	67.8	10.9
Group 5							
1960	100.0	23.7	18.1	5.6	76.3	52.4	23.9
1970	100.0	35.4	31.0	4.4	64.6	46.8	17.8

Note: Detail may not add to totals due to rounding.

147

TABLE 3.20

Distribution of Experienced Civilian Labor Force in Each Occupational Status Group, by Broad Age Group and Race, 1960–70—Female Workers

Occupational Status Group	Total	Ages 16–24			Ages 25 and Over		
		Total	White	Nonwhite	Total	White	Nonwhite
			Number (000)				
Total							
1960	20,966	3,857	3,459	398	17,109	14,886	2,223
1970	28,097	6,716	5,957	759	21,381	18,656	2,725
Net change	7,131	2,859	2,498	361	4,272	3,770	502
Group 1							
1960	2,849	370	353	17	2,479	2,296	183
1970	4,351	822	774	48	3,529	3,181	348
Net change	1,502	452	421	31	1,050	885	165
Group 2							
1960	8,934	2,037	1,966	71	6,897	6,638	259
1970	12,614	3,544	3,229	315	9,070	8,540	530
Net change	3,680	1,507	1,263	244	2,173	1,902	271
Group 3							
1960	1,880	237	201	36	1,643	1,474	169
1970	2,620	526	471	55	2,094	1,850	244
Net change	740	289	270	19	451	376	75
Group 4							
1960	4,541	881	772	109	3,660	3,256	404
1970	5,665	1,337	1,139	198	4,328	3,711	617
Net change	1,124	456	367	89	668	455	213
Group 5							
1960	2,762	331	160	171	2,431	1,210	1,221
1970	2,847	382	248	134	2,465	1,463	1,002
Net change	85	51	88	-37	34	253	-219

Percent Distribution

Total							
1960	100.0	18.4	16.5	1.9	81.6	71.0	10.6
1970	100.0	23.9	21.2	2.7	76.1	66.4	9.7
Group 1							
1960	100.0	13.0	12.4	0.6	87.0	80.6	6.4
1970	100.0	18.9	17.8	1.1	81.1	73.1	8.0
Group 2							
1960	100.0	22.8	22.0	0.8	77.2	74.3	2.9
1970	100.0	28.1	25.6	2.5	71.9	67.7	4.2
Group 3							
1960	100.0	12.6	10.7	1.9	87.4	78.4	9.0
1970	100.0	20.1	18.0	2.1	79.9	70.6	9.3
Group 4							
1960	100.0	19.4	17.0	2.4	80.6	71.7	8.9
1970	100.0	23.6	20.1	3.5	76.4	65.5	10.9
Group 5							
1960	100.0	12.0	5.8	6.2	88.0	43.8	44.2
1970	100.0	13.4	8.7	4.7	86.6	51.4	35.2

Note: Detail may not add to totals due to rounding.
Source: Bureau of the Census, public use sample tapes, 1960, 1970.

TABLE 3.21

Percent Distribution of the Experienced Civilian Labor Force 16 Years and Over in Each Occupation, by Broad Age Group and Race, 1960, 1970—Total, Both Sexes

Occupation	Year	Ages 16-24			Ages 25 and Over		
		Total	White	Nonwhite	Total	White	Nonwhite
Total, experienced civilian labor force	1960	15.0	13.4	1.6	85.0	76.2	8.8
	1970	19.6	17.5	2.1	80.4	71.9	8.5
Group 1, total	1960	10.5	10.1	0.4	89.5	84.9	4.6
	1970	14.8	13.9	0.9	85.2	79.3	5.9
Engineers	1960	5.8	5.7	0.1	94.2	92.9	1.3
	1970	5.8	5.4	0.4	94.2	91.1	3.1
Teachers, excluding college	1960	9.4	8.9	0.5	90.6	83.4	7.2
	1970	17.9	16.8	1.1	82.1	74.0	8.1
Medical personnel[a]	1960	11.3	10.4	0.9	88.7	83.5	5.2
	1970	15.8	15.0	0.8	84.2	77.5	6.7
Other professional and technical workers[b]	1960	12.0	11.7	0.3	88.0	84.1	3.9
	1970	14.8	13.9	0.9	85.2	80.1	5.1
Group 2, total	1960	16.3	15.7	0.6	83.7	80.9	2.8
	1970	20.7	18.9	1.8	79.3	75.2	4.1
Managers, officials, and proprietors, nonfarm	1960	3.1	3.1	0.0	96.9	94.6	2.3
	1970	5.2	4.8	0.4	94.8	91.8	3.0
Clerical, total	1960	24.3	23.3	1.0	75.7	72.1	3.6
	1970	29.7	26.8	2.9	70.3	65.2	5.1
Bookkeepers	1960	19.3	19.2	0.1	80.7	79.6	1.1
	1970	16.4	15.1	1.3	83.6	81.6	2.0
Secretaries, stenographers, typists	1960	31.2	30.0	1.2	68.8	66.4	2.4
	1970	36.8	33.8	3.0	63.2	60.2	3.0
Office machine operators	1960	27.8	26.5	1.3	72.2	68.3	3.9
	1970	35.0	31.3	3.7	65.0	57.5	7.5

(Group 2 continued)

Telephone operators	1960	27.0	26.4	0.6	73.0	71.6	1.4
	1970	39.2	32.0	7.2	60.8	56.7	4.1
Cashiers	1960	30.6	30.0	0.6	69.4	67.8	1.6
	1970	40.4	37.7	2.7	59.6	54.5	5.1
Postal clerks, mail carriers	1960	7.0	6.0	1.0	93.0	81.7	11.3
	1970	12.1	8.0	4.1	87.9	73.7	14.2
Other clerical[c]	1960	22.3	21.1	1.2	77.7	73.3	4.4
	1970	27.7	24.8	2.9	72.3	65.9	6.4
Sales, total	1960	17.0	16.4	0.6	83.0	81.3	1.7
	1970	19.0	18.0	1.0	81.0	78.1	2.9
Retail clerks	1960	22.8	22.0	0.8	77.2	75.1	2.1
	1970	28.7	27.4	1.3	71.3	67.8	3.5
Other sales	1960	11.3	10.9	0.4	88.7	87.3	1.4
	1970	10.9	10.2	0.7	89.1	86.7	2.4
Policemen, firemen[d]	1960	5.2	5.2	0.0	94.8	91.5	3.3
	1970	12.1	11.4	0.7	87.9	83.6	4.3
Group 3, total	1960	10.1	9.3	0.8	89.9	84.1	5.8
	1970	14.5	13.2	1.3	85.5	78.7	6.8
Craftsmen and foremen, total	1960	8.1	7.7	0.4	91.9	87.5	4.4
	1970	11.6	10.7	0.9	88.4	82.8	5.6
Foremen, not elsewhere classified	1960	2.1	2.1	0.0	97.9	96.2	1.7
	1970	5.6	5.2	0.4	94.4	89.5	4.9
Mechanics, excluding auto	1960	10.0	9.4	0.6	90.0	84.5	5.5
	1970	9.7	9.1	0.6	90.3	84.6	5.5
Machinists	1960	7.6	7.6	0.0	92.4	87.9	4.5
	1970	9.6	8.4	1.2	90.4	85.2	5.2

(continued)

151

(Table 3.21 continued)

Occupation	Year	Ages 16-24			Ages 25 and Over		
		Total	White	Nonwhite	Total	White	Nonwhite
(Group 3 continued)							
Metalworking crafts, excluding mechanics, machinists	1960	7.3	7.0	0.3	92.7	87.7	5.0
	1970	10.2	9.7	0.5	89.8	86.2	3.6
Carpenters	1960	8.1	7.6	0.5	91.9	86.2	5.7
	1970	9.6	9.0	0.6	90.4	83.8	6.6
Electricians, brickmasons, excavating machine operators[e]	1960	7.4	6.9	0.5	92.6	87.7	4.9
	1970	10.8	9.9	0.9	89.2	83.2	6.0
All other craftsmen[f]	1960	11.0	10.4	0.6	89.0	85.2	3.8
	1970	19.6	18.1	1.5	80.4	74.1	6.3
Farmers, farm managers, and unpaid farm workers, total	1960	7.9	6.5	1.4	92.1	85.8	6.3
	1970	3.3	3.1	0.2	96.7	92.6	4.1
Barbers, bartenders, practical nurses[g]	1960	17.5	15.1	2.4	82.5	71.4	11.1
	1970	32.3	29.4	2.9	67.7	58.1	9.6
Operatives, total	1960	16.2	14.6	1.6	83.8	77.0	6.8
	1970	19.5	17.3	2.2	80.5	70.4	10.1
Deliverymen, routemen	1960	26.0	22.5	3.5	74.0	68.4	5.6
	1970	24.0	21.7	2.3	76.0	68.5	7.5
Checkers, examiners, and inspectors	1960	11.6	10.6	1.0	88.4	84.1	4.3
	1970	12.9	11.6	1.3	87.1	79.6	7.5
Operatives, nondurables manufacturing, including chemical, petroleum[h]	1960	15.4	14.2	1.2	84.6	78.7	5.9
	1970	23.5	20.9	2.6	76.5	65.9	10.6
Operatives, transport equipment manufacturing	1960	14.0	12.5	1.5	86.0	74.2	11.8
	1970	16.6	14.1	2.5	83.4	68.4	15.0

	Year						
Group 4, total	1960	9.8	72.3	82.1	2.0	15.9	17.9
	1970	10.9	67.1	78.0	3.1	18.9	22.0
Craftsmen, total	1960	9.0	79.1	88.1	0.7	11.2	11.9
	1970	9.4	72.9	82.3	1.2	16.5	17.7
Auto mechanics	1960	7.4	78.8	86.2	0.8	13.0	13.8
	1970	8.0	72.1	80.1	0.9	19.0	19.9
Construction painters, plasterers, cement and concrete finishers, roofers, paperhangers	1960	11.1	79.3	90.4	0.5	9.1	9.6
	1970	11.8	75.3	87.1	1.6	11.3	12.9
Transport operatives, total	1960	12.9	70.0	82.9	1.9	15.2	17.1
	1970	10.9	69.5	80.4	1.8	17.8	19.6
Truck and tractor drivers	1960	12.9	73.9	86.8	1.9	11.3	13.2
	1970	11.7	76.5	88.2	2.0	9.8	11.8
Auto service and parking attendants	1960	11.4	45.0	56.4	2.4	41.2	43.6
	1970	4.2	42.0	46.2	2.0	51.8	53.8
Taxi drivers, bus drivers[i]	1960	14.3	77.2	91.5	1.2	7.3	8.5
	1970	14.6	74.2	88.8	1.2	10.0	11.2
Other operatives, total	1960	7.7	76.2	83.9	1.6	14.5	16.1
	1970	10.3	69.9	80.2	3.4	16.4	19.8
Packers	1960	9.7	65.7	75.4	2.9	21.7	24.6
	1970	11.5	63.1	74.6	4.9	20.5	25.4
Welders, flamecutters	1960	6.8	86.6	93.4	0.8	5.8	6.6
	1970	8.9	79.2	88.1	1.1	10.8	11.9
Operatives, metalworking industries[j]	1960	6.7	77.3	84.0	1.1	14.9	16.0
	1970	9.2	74.4	83.6	2.4	14.0	16.4
Operatives, lumber, furniture, stone, clay, and glass industries	1960	10.9	69.2	80.1	2.9	17.0	19.9
	1970	17.9	49.7	67.6	6.1	26.3	32.4

(continued)

(Table 3.21 continued)

Occupation	Year	Ages 16-24			Ages 25 and Over		
		Total	White	Nonwhite	Total	White	Nonwhite
(Group 4 continued)							
Operatives, food and tobacco industries	1960	14.6	12.4	2.2	85.4	71.3	14.1
	1970	19.0	14.6	4.4	81.0	65.8	15.2
Operatives, textiles, apparel, and leather industries	1960	15.7	14.4	1.3	84.3	78.9	5.4
	1970	19.9	15.7	4.2	80.1	71.5	8.6
Operatives, nonmanufacturing industries	1960	14.4	12.8	1.6	85.6	78.1	7.5
	1970	21.7	18.2	3.5	78.3	68.7	9.6
Shipping and receiving clerks, messengers, and office boys	1960	25.1	22.6	2.5	74.9	61.9	13.0
	1970	29.5	24.3	5.2	70.5	58.6	11.9
Services, total	1960	26.8	22.9	3.9	73.2	62.1	11.1
	1970	30.8	27.3	3.5	69.2	56.5	12.7
Guards and watchmen, crossing guards, and bridge tenders	1960	4.4	3.2	1.2	95.6	92.0	3.6
	1970	8.4	7.5	0.9	91.6	80.1	11.5
Housekeepers and babysitters	1960	27.5	23.4	4.1	72.5	56.7	15.8
	1970	23.2	19.6	3.6	76.8	54.8	22.0
Waiters and counter and fountain workers	1960	29.7	26.0	3.7	70.3	62.8	7.5
	1970	37.6	35.2	2.4	62.4	56.0	6.4
Hospital attendants	1960	22.4	16.5	5.9	77.6	57.6	20.0
	1970	31.6	24.9	6.7	68.4	48.8	19.6
Laborers, metalworking industriesk	1960	18.9	16.3	2.6	81.1	58.8	22.3
	1970	29.2	25.6	3.6	70.8	54.4	16.4

	Year						
Group 5, total	1960	19.8	14.0	5.8	80.2	49.4	30.8
	1970	28.4	23.7	4.7	71.6	48.0	23.6
Nonfarm laborers, total	1960	24.1	19.6	4.5	75.9	53.3	22.6
	1970	37.9	32.7	5.2	62.1	45.8	16.3
Laborers, lumber, furniture, stone, clay, and glass industries	1960	21.8	14.7	7.1	78.2	55.6	22.6
	1970	22.8	19.5	3.3	77.2	57.7	19.5
Laborers, nondurables manufacturing, including chemicals, petroleum	1960	23.1	18.4	4.7	76.9	59.6	17.3
	1970	32.3	25.6	6.7	67.7	52.9	14.8
Construction laborers	1960	18.5	14.8	3.7	81.5	55.6	25.9
	1970	26.5	22.9	3.6	73.5	51.5	22.0
Laborers, nonmanufacturing industries	1960	28.0	23.8	4.2	72.0	49.7	22.3
	1970	44.7	38.9	5.8	55.3	41.1	14.2
Farm laborers—paid	1960	30.5	22.4	8.1	69.5	48.9	20.6
	1970	30.2	26.3	3.9	69.8	50.0	19.8
Personal services, total	1960	12.7	6.7	6.0	87.3	46.6	40.7
	1970	20.4	16.0	4.4	79.6	49.4	30.2
Cooks	1960	9.2	6.1	3.1	90.8	68.6	22.2
	1970	19.9	16.1	3.8	80.1	63.9	16.2
Kitchen workers	1960	27.3	17.3	10.0	72.7	54.8	17.9
	1970	41.4	36.4	5.0	58.6	43.6	15.0
Janitors and sextons	1960	12.3	8.2	4.1	87.7	59.9	27.8
	1970	26.0	21.6	4.4	74.0	54.5	19.5
Cleaners, charwomen, porters, chambermaids, and elevator operators	1960	13.9	6.3	7.6	86.1	41.5	44.6
	1970	18.4	12.7	5.7	81.6	49.4	32.2
Laundry and dry cleaning operatives	1960	13.5	7.9	5.6	86.5	53.3	33.2
	1970	14.2	9.8	4.4	85.8	54.0	31.8
Private household workers, not elsewhere classified	1960	10.7	4.1	6.6	89.3	27.7	61.6
	1970	7.2	3.3	3.9	92.8	29.6	63.2

(continued)

Notes to Table 3.21

[a]Includes physicians, dentists, medical and dental technicians, and all other health personnel classified as professional.

[b]Includes all other professional and technical workers, not elsewhere classified.

[c]Includes all other clerical and kindred workers, not elsewhere classified, except shipping and receiving clerks, messengers, and office boys.

[d]Includes marshals and constables; sheriffs and bailiffs.

[e]Includes grading and road machinery operators, plumbers and pipefitters, and structural metalworkers.

[f]Includes all other craftsmen and foremen, not elsewhere classified, except those in status group 4.

gIncludes hospital attendants, recreation and amusement workers, ushers, and all other service workers not elsewhere classified.

hIncludes operatives not elsewhere classified in the following nondurable goods industries: paper and allied products; printing and publishing; chemicals and allied products; petroleum and coal products; rubber and plastic products; and not specified nondurables manufacturing.

iIncludes rail conductors, subway motormen, mine motormen, railroad brakemen, railroad switchmen, boatmen and canalmen, and sailors and deck hands.

jIncludes operatives, not elsewhere classified, in the following industries: metal industries; machinery, except electrical; electrical machinery; professional and photographic equipment; miscellaneous manufacturing.

kSame industrial distribution as for operatives in note j.

Source: Bureau of the Census, public use sample tapes, 1960, 1970.

TABLE 3.22

Percent Distribution of the Experienced Civilian Labor Force 16 Years and Over in Each Occupation, by Broad Age Group and Race, 1960, 1970—Male Workers

Occupation	Year	Ages 16–24			Ages 25 and Over		
		Total	White	Nonwhite	Total	White	Nonwhite
Total, experienced civilian labor force	1960	13.5	12.0	1.5	86.5	78.6	7.9
	1970	17.2	15.4	1.8	82.8	75.0	7.8
Group 1, total	1960	9.0	8.7	0.3	91.0	87.5	3.5
	1970	11.7	11.0	0.7	88.3	83.8	4.5
Engineers	1960	5.8	5.7	0.1	94.2	92.9	1.3
	1970	5.5	5.2	0.3	94.5	91.5	3.0
Teachers, excluding college	1960	6.7	5.9	0.8	93.3	85.6	7.7
	1970	18.2	17.2	1.0	81.8	75.8	6.0
Medical personnel[a]	1960	4.4	3.8	0.6	95.6	92.7	2.9
	1970	8.7	7.8	0.9	91.3	85.9	5.4
Other professional and technical workers[b]	1960	11.3	11.1	0.2	88.7	85.2	3.5
	1970	12.7	11.9	0.8	87.3	82.7	4.6
Group 2, total	1960	10.9	10.5	0.4	89.1	86.3	2.8
	1970	12.8	11.7	1.1	87.2	83.3	3.9
Managers, officials, and proprietors, nonfarm	1960	3.2	3.2	0.0	96.8	94.8	2.0
	1970	5.0	4.7	0.3	95.0	92.4	2.6
Clerical, total	1960	19.2	18.0	1.2	80.8	75.5	5.3
	1970	23.4	20.7	2.7	76.6	69.4	7.2
Bookkeepers	1960	18.1	18.1	0.0	81.9	79.5	2.4
	1970	16.0	13.4	2.6	84.0	81.1	2.9
Secretaries, stenographers, typists	1960	24.0	21.3	2.7	76.0	72.0	4.0
	1970	25.7	22.8	2.9	74.3	67.9	6.4
Office machine operators	1960	38.2	36.4	1.8	61.8	58.2	3.6
	1970	35.4	32.4	3.0	64.6	55.7	8.9

(Group 2 continued)

Telephone operators	1960	—	—	—	—	—	—
	1970	—	—	—	—	—	—
Cashiers	1960	49.5	47.5	2.0	50.5	50.5	0.0
	1970	54.6	52.3	2.3	45.4	40.9	4.5
Postal clerks, mail carriers	1960	7.2	6.1	1.1	92.8	80.9	11.9
	1970	11.0	7.4	3.6	89.0	76.7	12.3
Other clerical	1960	19.1	17.9	1.2	80.9	76.2	4.7
	1970	24.1	21.5	2.6	75.9	69.3	6.6
Sales, total	1960	16.1	15.7	0.4	83.9	82.4	1.5
	1970	16.2	15.4	0.8	83.8	80.9	2.9
Retail clerks	1960	28.4	27.6	0.8	71.6	69.4	2.2
	1970	33.8	32.4	1.4	66.2	61.7	4.5
Other sales	1960	10.8	10.5	0.3	89.2	88.0	1.2
	1970	10.1	9.5	0.6	89.9	87.5	2.4
Policemen, firemen	1960	5.3	5.3	0.0	94.7	91.8	2.9
	1970	11.4	10.7	0.7	88.6	84.6	4.0
Group 3, total	1960	9.9	9.0	0.9	90.1	84.8	5.3
	1970	12.8	11.8	1.0	87.2	80.9	6.3
Craftsmen and foremen, total	1960	8.1	7.7	0.4	91.9	87.6	4.3
	1970	11.3	10.5	0.8	88.7	83.2	5.5
Foremen, not elsewhere classified	1960	2.1	2.1	0.0	97.9	96.3	1.6
	1970	5.3	4.9	0.4	94.7	90.0	4.7
Mechanics, excluding auto	1960	10.0	9.4	0.6	90.0	84.4	5.6
	1970	9.4	8.9	0.5	90.6	85.2	5.4
Machinists	1960	7.4	7.4	0.0	92.6	88.2	4.4
	1970	9.7	8.5	1.2	90.3	84.9	5.4

(continued)

159

(Table 3.22 continued)

Occupation	Year	Ages 16-24			Ages 25 and Over		
		Total	White	Nonwhite	Total	White	Nonwhite
(Group 3 continued)							
Metalworking crafts, excluding mechanics, machinists	1960	7.4	7.1	0.3	92.6	87.6	5.0
	1970	10.2	9.7	0.5	89.8	86.3	3.5
Carpenters	1960	8.0	7.5	0.5	92.0	86.3	5.7
	1970	9.4	8.8	0.6	90.6	84.0	6.6
Electricians, brickmasons, excavating machine operators[e]	1960	7.4	6.9	0.5	92.6	87.8	4.8
	1970	10.6	9.8	0.8	89.4	83.4	6.0
All other craftsmen[f]	1960	11.2	10.6	0.6	88.8	85.2	3.6
	1970	19.8	18.2	1.6	80.2	74.2	6.0
Farmers, farm managers, and unpaid farm workers, total	1960	8.2	6.9	1.3	91.8	85.9	5.9
	1970	3.9	3.7	0.2	96.1	92.7	3.4
Barbers, bartenders, practical nurses[g]	1960	19.6	17.0	2.6	80.4	71.4	9.0
	1970	32.7	29.5	3.2	67.3	58.8	8.5
Operatives, total	1960	17.5	15.7	1.8	82.5	75.2	7.3
	1970	19.7	17.8	1.9	80.3	69.7	10.6
Deliverymen, routemen	1960	25.4	21.8	3.6	74.6	68.8	5.8
	1970	24.1	21.9	2.2	75.9	68.4	7.5
Checkers, examiners, and inspectors	1960	13.1	12.3	0.8	86.9	83.7	3.2
	1970	13.3	12.8	0.5	86.7	77.4	9.3
Operatives, nondurables manufacturing, including chemicals, petroleum[h]	1960	15.6	14.3	1.3	84.4	78.4	6.0
	1970	19.5	18.0	1.5	80.5	69.5	11.0
Operatives, transport equipment	1960	15.2	13.7	1.5	84.8	72.2	12.6
	1970	18.3	15.3	3.0	81.7	66.4	15.3

Group 4, total						
	1960	17.1	15.3	1.8	82.9	72.7	10.2
	1970	21.3	18.4	2.9	78.7	67.8	10.9
Craftsmen, total	1960	12.0	11.4	0.6	88.0	78.9	9.1
	1970	17.5	15.9	1.6	82.5	73.0	9.5
Auto mechanics	1960	13.8	13.1	0.7	86.2	78.7	7.5
	1970	20.0	19.0	1.0	80.0	72.1	7.9
Construction painters, plasterers, cement and concrete finishers, roofers, paperhangers	1960	9.7	9.2	0.5	90.3	79.2	11.1
	1970	13.5	12.0	1.5	86.5	74.5	12.0
Transport operatives, total	1960	17.3	15.4	1.9	82.7	69.7	13.0
	1970	21.1	19.2	1.9	78.9	67.9	11.0
Truck and tractor drivers	1960	13.2	11.3	1.9	86.8	73.9	12.9
	1970	12.3	10.2	2.1	87.7	76.0	11.7
Auto service and parking attendants	1960	44.3	41.9	2.4	55.7	44.1	11.6
	1970	57.3	55.4	1.9	42.7	38.9	3.8
Taxi drivers, bus drivers[i]	1960	9.2	7.9	1.3	90.8	75.8	15.0
	1970	12.2	10.9	1.3	87.8	71.0	16.8
Other operatives, total	1960	17.5	16.0	1.5	82.5	74.8	7.7
	1970	21.0	17.6	3.4	79.0	68.7	10.3
Packers	1960	34.0	32.0	2.0	66.0	54.8	11.2
	1970	33.6	25.1	8.5	66.4	52.6	13.8
Welders, flamecutters	1960	5.7	5.2	0.5	94.3	87.2	7.1
	1970	11.9	11.2	0.7	88.1	79.3	8.8
Operatives, metalworking industries[j]	1960	17.1	16.3	0.8	82.9	76.3	6.6
	1970	18.7	16.0	2.7	81.3	72.4	8.9
Operatives, lumber, furniture, stone, clay, and glass industries	1960	21.6	18.3	3.3	78.4	67.6	10.8
	1970	24.9	20.3	4.6	75.1	55.3	19.8

(continued)

161

(Table 3.22 continued)

Occupation	Year	Ages 16-24			Ages 25 and Over		
		Total	White	Nonwhite	Total	White	Nonwhite
(Group 4 continued)							
Operatives, food and tobacco industries	1960	20.3	18.4	1.9	79.7	66.8	12.9
	1970	19.9	16.0	3.9	80.1	65.0	15.1
Operatives, textiles, apparel, and leather industries	1960	20.1	18.1	2.0	79.9	75.2	4.7
	1970	26.6	21.9	4.7	73.4	66.0	7.4
Operatives, nonmanufacturing industries, total	1960	15.6	14.1	1.5	84.4	77.1	7.3
	1970	21.4	17.7	3.7	78.6	69.9	8.7
Shipping and receiving clerks, messengers, and office boys	1960	23.9	21.0	2.9	76.1	61.9	14.2
	1970	30.1	25.5	4.6	69.9	58.1	11.8
Services, total	1960	19.5	14.5	5.0	80.5	68.4	12.1
	1970	28.6	23.8	4.8	71.4	56.6	14.8
Guards and watchmen, crossing guards, and bridge tenders	1960	3.5	3.5	0.0	96.5	93.5	3.0
	1970	8.2	7.1	1.1	91.8	80.7	11.1
Housekeepers and babysitters	1960	—	—	—	—	—	—
	1970	—	—	—	—	—	—
Waiters and counter and fountain workers	1960	40.8	32.9	7.9	59.2	44.7	14.5
	1970	56.5	51.2	5.3	43.5	25.2	18.3
Hospital attendants	1960	23.3	12.1	11.2	76.7	49.1	27.6
	1970	44.9	34.7	10.2	55.1	36.7	18.4
Laborers, metalworking industries[k]	1960	18.6	15.8	2.8	81.4	59.4	22.0
	1970	21.4	17.8	3.6	78.6	60.1	18.5

Group 5, total	Year						
	1960	23.7	18.1	5.6	76.3	52.4	23.9
	1970	35.4	31.0	4.4	64.6	46.8	17.8
Nonfarm laborers, total	1960	24.1	19.6	4.5	75.9	53.2	22.7
	1970	38.6	34.0	4.6	61.4	45.1	16.3
Laborers, lumber, furniture, stone, clay, and glass industries	1960	21.7	14.5	7.2	78.3	55.8	22.5
	1970	22.4	19.7	2.7	77.6	57.9	19.7
Laborers, nondurables manufacturing, including chemical, petroleum	1960	22.9	18.3	4.6	77.1	58.5	18.6
	1970	31.2	26.2	5.0	68.8	53.9	14.9
Construction laborers	1960	18.7	15.0	3.7	81.3	55.5	25.8
	1970	25.9	22.7	3.2	74.1	52.0	22.1
Laborers, nonmanufacturing industries	1960	28.0	23.9	4.1	72.0	49.9	22.1
	1970	45.5	40.2	5.3	54.5	40.3	14.2
Farm laborers—paid	1960	30.3	22.9	7.4	69.7	50.7	19.0
	1970	32.8	29.0	3.8	67.2	49.4	17.8
Personal services, total	1960	17.4	10.9	6.5	82.6	51.8	30.8
	1970	15.9	10.4	5.5	84.1	58.8	25.3
Cooks	1960	15.7	12.0	3.7	84.3	63.9	20.4
	1970	43.1	37.5	5.6	56.9	40.9	16.0
Kitchen workers	1960	38.8	24.8	14.0	61.2	42.6	18.6
	1970	72.6	64.9	7.7	27.4	17.1	10.3
Janitors and sextons	1960	13.6	9.1	4.5	86.4	58.5	27.9
	1970	22.5	19.0	3.5	77.5	56.3	21.2
Cleaners, charwomen, porters, chambermaids, and elevator operators	1960	19.6	10.0	9.6	80.4	35.4	45.0
	1970	28.5	21.9	6.6	71.5	43.7	27.8
Laundry and dry cleaning operatives	1960	15.5	8.6	6.9	84.5	55.2	29.3
	1970	17.4	14.8	2.6	82.6	55.6	27.0
Private household workers, not elsewhere classified	1960	—	—	—	—	—	—
	1970	—	—	—	—	—	—

(continued)

Notes to Table 3.22

[a]Includes physicians, dentists, medical and dental technicians, and all other health personnel classified as professional.

[b]Includes all other professional and technical workers, not elsewhere classified.

[c]Includes all other clerical and kindred workers, not elsewhere classified, except shipping and receiving clerks, messengers, and office boys.

[d]Includes marshals and constables; sheriffs and bailiffs.

[e]Includes grading and road machinery operators, plumbers and pipefitters, and structural metalworkers.

[f]Includes all other craftsmen and foremen, not elsewhere classified, except those in status group 4.

gIncludes hospital attendants, recreation and amusement workers, ushers, and all other service workers not elsewhere classified.

hIncludes operatives not elsewhere classified in the following nondurable goods industries: paper and allied products; printing and publishing; chemicals and allied products; petroleum and coal products; rubber and plastic products; and not specified nondurable manufacturing.

iIncludes rail conductors, subway motormen, mine motormen, railroad brakemen, railroad switchmen, boatmen and canalmen, and sailors and deck hands.

jIncludes operatives, not elsewhere classified, in the following industries: metal industries; machinery, except electrical; electrical machinery; professional and photographic equipment; miscellaneous manufacturing.

kSame industrial distribution as for operatives in note j.

Note: Percentages not shown where base number is less than 50,000.

Source: Bureau of the Census, public use sample tapes, 1960, 1970.

TABLE 3.23

Percent Distribution of the Experienced Civilian Labor Force 16 Years and Over in Each Occupation, by Broad Age Group and Race, 1960, 1970—Female Workers

Occupation	Year	Ages 16-24			Ages 25 and Over		
		Total	White	Nonwhite	Total	White	Nonwhite
Total, experienced civilian labor force	1960	18.4	16.5	1.9	81.6	71.0	10.6
	1970	23.9	21.2	2.7	76.1	66.4	9.7
Group 1, total	1960	13.0	12.4	0.6	87.0	80.6	6.4
	1970	19.2	18.0	1.2	80.8	72.9	7.9
Engineers	1960	—	—	—	—	—	—
	1970	—	—	—	—	—	—
Teachers, excluding college	1960	10.5	10.1	0.4	89.5	82.5	7.0
	1970	17.8	16.7	1.1	82.2	73.2	9.0
Medical personnel[a]	1960	15.8	14.7	1.1	84.2	77.5	6.7
	1970	19.9	19.1	0.8	80.1	72.7	7.4
Other professional and technical workers[b]	1960	14.2	13.7	0.5	85.8	80.6	5.2
	1970	20.6	19.2	1.4	79.4	72.7	6.7
Group 2, total	1960	22.8	22.0	0.8	77.2	74.3	2.9
	1970	27.9	25.5	2.4	72.1	67.8	4.3
Manangers, officials, and proprietors nonfarm	1960	2.7	2.7	0.0	97.3	93.0	4.3
	1970	7.6	6.7	0.9	92.4	87.4	5.0
Clerical, total	1960	26.5	25.6	0.9	73.5	70.6	2.9
	1970	31.2	28.3	2.9	68.8	64.3	4.5
Bookkeepers	1960	19.5	19.4	0.1	80.5	79.6	0.9
	1970	16.5	15.5	1.0	83.5	81.7	1.8
Secretaries, stenographers, typists	1960	31.5	30.3	1.2	68.5	66.1	2.4
	1970	34.4	31.7	2.7	65.6	62.6	3.0

(Group 2 continued)

Office machine operators	1960	25.6	24.4	1.2	74.4	70.5	3.9
	1970	35.0	31.0	4.0	65.0	58.1	6.9
Telephone operators	1960	26.6	26.0	0.6	73.4	72.0	1.4
	1970	40.0	32.6	7.4	60.0	56.7	3.3
Cashiers	1960	25.5	25.2	0.3	74.5	72.4	2.1
	1970	37.7	35.0	2.7	62.3	57.1	5.2
Postal clerks, mail carriers	1960	5.1	5.1	0.0	94.9	89.8	5.1
	1970	16.0	9.9	6.1	84.0	63.4	20.6
Other clerical[c]	1960	25.0	23.9	1.1	75.0	71.0	4.0
	1970	29.6	26.5	3.1	70.4	64.1	6.3
Sales, total·	1960	18.5	17.6	0.9	81.5	79.4	2.1
	1970	23.5	22.3	1.2	76.5	73.7	2.8
Retail clerks	1960	19.3	18.5	0.8	80.7	78.7	2.0
	1970	27.0	25.7	1.3	73.0	70.0	3.0
Other sales	1960	14.4	13.5	0.9	85.6	83.1	2.5
	1970	13.4	12.5	0.9	86.6	84.4	2.2
Policemen, firemen[d]	1960	—	—	—	—	—	—
	1970	—	—	—	—	—	—
Group 3, total	1960	12.6	10.7	1.9	87.4	78.4	9.0
	1970	20.6	18.5	2.1	79.4	69.9	9.5
Craftsmen and foremen, total	1960	8.5	7.3	1.2	91.5	86.6	4.9
	1970	14.3	12.6	1.7	85.7	77.8	7.9
Foremen, not elsewhere classified	1960	2.5	2.5	—	97.5	95.0	2.5
	1970	7.2	6.3	0.9	92.8	85.7	7.1
Mechanics, excluding auto	1960	—	—	—	—	—	—
	1970	—	—	—	—	—	—
Machinists	1960	—	—	—	—	—	—
	1970	—	—	—	—	—	—

(continued)

(Table 3.23 continued)

Occupation	Year	Ages 16-24			Ages 25 and Over		
		Total	White	Nonwhite	Total	White	Nonwhite
(Group 3 continued)							
Metalworking crafts, excluding mechanics, machinists	1960	—	—	—	—	—	—
	1970	—	—	—	—	—	—
Carpenters	1960	—	—	—	—	—	—
	1970	—	—	—	—	—	—
Electricians, brickmasons, excavating operators[e]	1960	—	—	—	—	—	—
	1970	—	—	—	—	—	—
All other craftsmen[f]	1960	9.7	8.2	1.5	90.3	83.5	6.8
	1970	15.7	14.2	1.5	84.3	75.8	8.5
Farmers, farm managers, and unpaid workers, total	1960	6.0	2.8	3.2	94.0	84.8	9.2
	1970	2.9	2.9	0.0	97.1	87.1	10.0
Barbers, bartenders, practical nurses[g]	1960	16.2	13.9	2.3	83.8	71.2	12.6
	1970	27.5	25.0	2.5	72.5	61.9	10.6
Operatives, total	1960	12.2	11.1	1.1	87.8	82.4	5.4
	1970	18.2	15.7	2.5	81.8	73.3	8.5
Deliverymen, routemen	1960	—	—	—	—	—	—
	1970	—	—	—	—	—	—
Checkers, examiners, and inspectors	1960	10.1	9.0	1.1	89.9	84.6	5.3
	1970	13.8	11.5	2.3	86.2	81.0	5.2
Operatives, nondurables manufacturing, including chemicals, petroleum[h]	1960	14.8	13.8	1.0	85.2	79.5	5.7
	1970	24.2	21.3	2.9	75.8	64.3	11.5
Operatives, transport equipment manufacturing	1960	5.7	4.3	1.4	94.3	88.5	5.8
	1970	14.9	13.2	1.7	85.1	72.7	12.4

168

	Year						
Group 4, total	1960	19.4	17.0	2.4	80.6	71.7	8.9
	1970	23.7	20.2	3.5	76.3	65.4	10.9
Craftsmen, total	1960	9.1	6.1	3.0	90.9	84.8	6.1
	1970	16.6	16.6	0.0	83.4	77.8	5.6
Auto mechanics	1960	—	—	—	—	—	—
	1970	—	—	—	—	—	—
Construction painters, plasterers, cement and concrete finishers, roofers, paperhangers	1960	—	—	—	—	—	—
	1970	—	—	—	—	—	—
Transport operatives, total	1960	5.2	2.6	2.6	94.8	84.5	10.3
	1970	12.5	10.9	1.6	87.5	82.0	5.5
Truck and tractor drivers	1960	—	—	—	—	—	—
	1970	—	—	—	—	—	—
Auto service and parking attendants	1960	—	—	—	—	—	—
	1970	—	—	—	—	—	—
Taxi drivers, bus drivers[i]	1960	0.0	0.0	0.0	100.0	90.5	9.5
	1970	9.4	8.4	1.0	90.6	85.3	5.3
Other operatives, total	1960	13.2	11.6	1.6	86.8	79.1	7.7
	1970	18.6	14.8	3.8	81.4	71.3	10.1
Packers	1960	18.2	14.7	3.5	81.8	73.1	8.7
	1970	19.5	16.4	3.1	80.5	70.5	10.0
Welders, flamecutters	1960	—	—	—	—	—	—
	1970	—	—	—	—	—	—
Operatives, metalworking industries[j]	1960	13.3	11.5	1.8	86.7	79.8	6.9
	1970	17.8	14.8	3.0	82.2	73.2	9.0
Operatives, lumber, furniture, stone, clay, and glass industries	1960	8.9	8.9	0.0	91.1	79.7	11.4
	1970	35.7	26.2	9.5	64.3	48.8	15.5

(continued)

(Table 3.23 continued)

Occupation	Year	Ages 16-24			Ages 25 and Over		
		Total	White	Nonwhite	Total	White	Nonwhite
(Group 4 continued)							
Operatives, food and tobacco industries	1960	12.1	9.8	2.3	87.9	68.4	19.5
	1970	19.2	13.2	6.0	80.8	65.7	15.1
Operatives, textiles, apparel, and leather industries	1960	13.6	12.7	0.9	86.4	80.6	5.8
	1970	17.8	13.6	4.2	82.2	73.3	8.9
Operatives, nonmanufacturing industries, total	1960	8.1	6.0	2.1	91.9	83.5	8.4
	1970	18.9	16.1	2.8	81.1	67.5	13.6
Shipping and receiving clerks, messengers, and office boys	1960	34.1	34.1	—	65.9	65.9	—
	1970	24.2	18.5	5.7	75.8	62.9	12.9
Services, total	1960	28.9	25.3	3.6	71.1	60.3	10.8
	1970	31.6	28.4	3.2	68.4	56.3	12.1
Guards, watchmen, crossing guards, and bridge tenders	1960	—	—	—	—	—	—
	1970	—	—	—	—	—	—
Housekeepers and babysitters	1960	27.7	23.6	4.1	72.3	56.4	15.9
	1970	25.1	22.0	3.1	74.9	53.9	21.0
Waiters and counter and fountain workers	1960	27.6	24.7	2.9	72.4	66.2	6.2
	1970	36.7	34.5	2.2	63.3	58.3	5.0
Hospital attendants	1960	22.2	18.2	4.0	77.8	60.6	17.2
	1970	26.3	20.7	5.6	73.7	53.0	20.7
Laborers, metalworking industriesk	1960	22.6	22.6	0.0	77.4	51.6	25.8
	1970	25.8	22.6	3.2	74.2	54.8	19.4

	Year						
Group 5, total	1960	12.0	5.8	6.2	88.0	43.6	44.4
	1970	13.3	8.7	4.6	86.7	51.4	35.3
Nonfarm laborers, total	1960	26.0	20.4	5.6	74.0	53.6	20.4
	1970	30.8	22.6	8.2	69.2	53.8	15.4
Laborers, lumber, furniture, stone, clay, and glass industries	1960	—	—	—	—	—	—
	1970	—	—	—	—	—	—
Laborers, nondurables manufacturing, including chemical, petroleum	1960	25.0	19.4	5.6	75.0	69.4	5.6
	1970	26.4	17.0	9.4	73.6	56.6	17.0
Construction laborers	1960	—	—	—	—	—	—
	1970	—	—	—	—	—	—
Laborers, nonmanufacturing industries	1960	29.8	22.8	7.0	70.2	43.9	26.3
	1970	35.0	29.0	6.0	65.0	51.3	13.7
Farm laborers—paid	1960	32.1	18.5	13.6	67.9	35.8	32.1
	1970	40.9	29.6	11.3	59.1	25.3	33.8
Personal services, total	1960	10.1	4.4	5.7	89.9	44.0	45.9
	1970	11.1	6.9	4.2	88.9	52.0	36.9
Cooks	1960	5.6	2.8	2.8	94.4	71.1	23.3
	1970	7.5	4.4	3.1	92.5	75.8	16.7
Kitchen workers	1960	19.9	12.6	7.3	80.1	62.8	17.3
	1970	24.0	20.1	3.9	76.0	59.2	16.8
Janitors and sextons	1960	2.6	1.3	1.3	97.4	70.7	26.7
	1970	15.1	10.1	5.0	84.9	66.9	18.0
Cleaners, charwomen, porters, chambermaids, and elevator operators	1960	9.1	3.1	6.0	90.9	46.7	44.2
	1970	11.7	7.0	4.7	88.3	53.3	35.0
Laundry and dry cleaning operatives	1960	12.7	7.6	5.1	87.3	52.6	34.7
	1970	13.5	8.3	5.2	86.5	52.8	33.7
Private household workers, not elsewhere classified	1960	10.9	4.2	6.7	89.1	27.3	61.8
	1970	7.7	3.2	4.5	92.3	29.2	63.1

(continued)

Notes to Table 3.23

[a]Includes physicians, dentists, medical and dental technicians, and all other health personnel classified as professional.

[b]Includes all other professional and technical workers, not elsewhere classified.

[c]Includes all other clerical and kindred workers, not elsewhere classified, except shipping and receiving clerks, messengers, and office boys.

[d]Includes marshals and constables; sheriffs and bailiffs.

[e]Includes grading, and road machinery operators, plumbers and pipefitters, and structural metalworkers.

[f]Includes all other craftsmen and foremen, not elsewhere classified, except those in status group 4.

gIncludes hospital attendants, recreation and amusement workers, ushers, and all other service workers not elsewhere classified.

hIncludes operatives not elsewhere classified in the following nondurable goods industries: paper and allied products; printing and publishing; chemicals and allied products; petroleum and coal products; rubber and plastic products; and not specified nondurable manufacturing.

iIncludes rail conductors, subway motormen, mine motormen, railroad brakemen, railroad switchmen, boatmen and canalmen, and sailors and deck hands.

jIncludes operatives, not elsewhere classified, in the following industries: metal industries; machinery, except electrical; electrical machinery; professional and photographic equipment; miscellaneous manufacturing.

kSame industrial distribution as for operatives in note j.

Note: Percentage not shown where base number is less than 50,000.

Source: Bureau of the Census, public use sample tapes, 1960, 1970.

These high replacement needs were augmented, moreover, by requirements for an expanded work force in various personal service occupations, and in laborer jobs in nonmanufacturing industries. Thus, the group 5 workers experiencing very sharp increases in their proportion of youthful male workers between 1960 and 1970 included cooks and kitchen workers, janitors and other building or cleaning service personnel, and nonmanufacturing laborers.

An additional source of labor supply in certain of the group 5 occupations consisted of adult white women—a population group which also contributed substantially to overall labor force growth in the 1960s. White female workers, aged 25 years and over, accounted for increased proportions of the female work force among the following: nonmanufacturing laborers (excluding construction); cooks; cleaners, charwomen, chambermaids and allied building service occupations; and private household workers, not elsewhere classified (see Table 3.23).

Trends in Percentage of Nonwhite Workers, by Occupation

As shown in Table 3.24, the overall percentage of nonwhite workers in group 5 occupations declined from 36.5 percent in 1960 to 28.3 percent in 1970. The reduction was particularly sharp among

----

the experienced civilian labor force who were in the age group 25-44 years in 1960. A multiple regression analysis of the net changes in the number of male workers in each occupation in this age cohort (adjusted for net separations from the male labor force in this age group over the decade) was made, using the following independent variables: overall employment change in occupation, 1960-70 (EMP); full-time earnings in occupation in 1960 (EARN); and occupational status, based on our percentile rankings (STAT). The regression explained 55 percent of the variance (R^2) in net occupational mobility for this group:

$$\ln \text{MOBIL} = -5.0136 + .0763 \ln \text{EMP} + .4892 \ln \text{EARN}$$
$$(2.96) \qquad\qquad (1.93)$$

$$+ .1129 \ln \text{STAT}$$
$$(1.62)$$

The employment change and earnings variables were significant at the 95 percent level; the status variable, at the 90 percent level. (A log-linear form was used to minimize colinearity between the earnings and status variables.)

nonwhite women: In 1960, 51 percent of the female labor force in group 5 jobs consisted of nonwhite women, reflecting their heavy concentration in domestic service work, in farm labor, and in building and cleaning service occupations; this percentage was reduced to about 40 percent by 1970. This sharp overall reduction in the proportion of nonwhite women in group 5 occupations was due, in part, to divergent trends in labor force growth among the group 5 occupations, and, in part, to pronounced declines in the proportion of nonwhite women in specific occupations. Thus the female labor force in domestic service and in hired farm labor, which had included the highest concentrations of nonwhite women in 1960, declined sharply over the decade, whereas the labor force in certain other group 5 occupations such as food service, which employed smaller proportions of nonwhites, grew over the decade. An examination of the trend in nonwhite percentages among female workers in the specific group 5 occupations indicates significant declines in about half of these occupations, with no significant change in most of the remainder. Among the latter was domestic work (excluding babysitters) which—unlike other personal service occupations—did not succeed in attracting an increased proportion of young white workers.

In the case of male workers, the percentage of nonwhites in group 5 occupations declined in each of the specific occupations for which data are available, with particularly sharp reductions in their proportions among building service occupations and kitchen workers. For all group 5 occupations, the percentage of nonwhites among male workers declined from 29.5 percent in 1960 to 21.4 percent in 1970.

The net withdrawal of nonwhites from group 5 occupations was accomplished by increases in the percentage of nonwhites in each of the four higher occupational status groups. Among the group 1 and group 2 occupations, nonwhites made sharp relative gains in participation in some jobs in which they had been least represented in the past, for example, as engineers, bookkeepers, telephone operators, and cashiers. Among the group 3 and group 4 occupations, the largest increases in nonwhite participation occurred among manufacturing operatives, particularly in those manufacturing industries with high concentrations in the South (for example, textiles, lumber, furniture, chemicals, and petroleum) as well as in transportation equipment and other metalworking industries. Nonwhite gains in participation in most of the crafts and mechanical occupations were generally smaller than in the operatives groups. Only a few group 3 and 4 occupations experienced reductions in the percentage of nonwhite workers. These included farmers and farm managers, auto service and parking attendants, truck drivers, metalworking craftsmen, laborers in metalworking industries, waiters and counter and fountain workers, and the group including barbers, bartenders, beauticians, and practical nurses.

TABLE 3.24

Percent of Nonwhites in Each Occupational and Status Group, by Sex: 1960, 1970

Status Group and Occupation	Both Sexes		Male		Female	
	1960	1970	1960	1970	1960	1970
Total, experienced civilian labor force	10.8	11.1	9.8	9.9	12.9	12.9
Group 1	5.1	6.8	3.8	5.3	7.1	9.1
Engineers	1.5	3.5	1.5	3.3	—	—
All other professional and technical workers[a]	4.2	6.0	3.7	7.3	5.7	8.1
Teachers, excluding college	7.7	9.2	8.5	6.9	7.4	10.2
Medical personnel[b]	6.1	7.6	3.4	6.3	7.9	8.2
Group 2	3.4	5.9	3.2	5.0	3.7	6.8
Bookkeepers	1.2	3.2	2.4	5.5	1.0	2.8
Secretaries, stenographers, typists	3.7	6.0	6.7	9.3	3.6	5.9
All other sales workers, excluding retail clerks	1.8	3.0	1.5	3.0	3.5	3.2
Managers, officials, proprietors	2.4	3.4	2.1	2.9	4.3	5.9
All other clerical and kindred workers[c]	5.6	9.3	5.8	9.2	5.3	9.4
Office machine operators	5.2	11.2	5.5	11.9	5.1	10.9
Telephone operators	1.9	11.2	—	—	2.0	10.7
Policemen, firemen[d]	3.3	5.0	2.9	4.6	—	—
Sales clerks, retail trade	2.9	4.8	3.0	5.9	2.9	4.3
Cashiers	2.3	7.8	2.0	6.8	2.4	8.0
Postal clerks, mail carriers	12.3	18.3	13.1	15.9	5.1	26.7

Group 3						
Foremen, not elsewhere classified	6.8	8.1	6.2	7.3	10.9	11.6
All other craftsmen[e]	1.7	5.3	1.6	5.1	2.5	7.9
Mechanics, excluding auto	4.4	7.8	4.1	7.6	7.6	9.7
Deliverymen, routemen	5.9	6.0	5.9	4.8	—	—
Metalworking crafts, excluding mechanics, machinists	9.1	9.8	9.4	9.7	—	—
Farmers, farm managers, unpaid family workers	5.3	4.1	5.4	4.0	—	—
Electricians, brickmasons, excavating machine operators[f]	7.6	4.3	7.0	3.5	12.4	9.8
Machinists	5.3	6.9	5.3	6.7	—	—
Checkers, examiners	4.5	6.3	4.3	6.5	—	—
Operatives, chemical, petroleum industries[g]	5.2	8.8	4.0	9.9	6.4	7.5
Barbers, bartenders, practical nurses[h]	7.1	13.0	7.2	12.5	6.7	15.0
Operatives, transport equipment manufacturing	13.6	12.5	11.7	11.4	14.9	13.0
Carpenters	13.2	17.4	14.1	18.2	7.2	14.0
Group 4						
Taxi drivers, bus drivers[i]	6.7	13.9	12.0	13.6	11.3	10.0
Auto mechanics	11.7	16.0	16.1	18.1	7.4	14.5
Nonmanufacturing operatives, total[j]	15.0	8.8	8.2	8.7	—	6.3
Auto service and parking attendants	8.2	13.1	8.8	12.4	10.2	—
Operatives, metalworking industries[k]	13.8	6.1	14.0	6.1	8.6	15.4

(continued)

(Table 3.24 continued)

Status Group and Occupation	Both Sexes		Male		Female	
	1960	1970	1960	1970	1960	1970
(Group 4 continued)						
Guards and watchmen, crossing guards and bridge tenders	4.8	12.4	3.0	12.1	—	—
Housekeepers and babysitters	20.0	25.6	—	—	20.1	24.8
Waiters, counter and fountain workers	11.2	8.8	22.4	22.0	9.2	7.3
Shipping and receiving clerks, messengers and office boys	16.0	17.1	17.2	16.6	8.3	19.7
Laborers, metalworking industries[1]	24.9	19.9	24.8	19.8	—	—
Operatives, food and tobacco industries	16.9	19.6	14.7	18.9	21.8	21.1
Construction painters, plasterers, cement and concrete finishers, roofers, paperhangers	11.6	13.4	11.7	13.7	—	—
Hospital attendants	25.9	26.3	38.8	28.6	21.2	26.3
Truck and tractor drivers	14.9	13.8	14.8	13.8	—	—
Operatives, textiles, apparel, leather industries	6.7	12.8	8.0	11.7	6.5	13.1
Packers	12.6	16.4	13.2	21.3	12.2	13.1
Welders, flamecutters	7.6	10.0	7.6	9.5	—	—
Operatives, lumber, furniture, stone, clay, and glass industries	13.8	24.2	14.1	23.7	11.4	26.7

Group 5

Laborers, selected nonmanufacturing industries[m]	26.5	20.1	26.2	20.2	33.3	18.1
Janitors and sextons	31.9	23.8	32.4	23.1	28.0	28.1
Cooks	25.4	20.0	24.1	20.9	26.1	19.6
Construction laborers	29.6	25.6	29.5	25.3	—	—
Laborers, lumber, furniture, stone, clay, and glass industries	29.7	22.8	29.8	22.6	—	—
Laborers, Nondurables manufacturing, including chemicals, petroleum[n]	22.0	21.5	23.2	20.2	11.1	28.1
Farm laborers—paid	28.7	23.7	26.3	22.0	45.7	41.3
Kitchen workers	27.9	20.0	32.6	21.5	24.7	19.4
Laundry and dry cleaning operators	38.8	36.2	36.2	29.2	39.9	39.3
Cleaners and charwomen, porters, chambermaids, and elevator operators	52.2	37.9	54.6	32.9	50.2	39.8
Private household, not elsewhere classified	68.2	67.1	37.1	45.8	68.5	67.7

Header row values: 36.5 · 28.3 · 29.5 · 21.4 · 50.2 · 39.5

(continued)

Notes to Table 3.24

[a]Includes all other professional and technical workers, not elsewhere classified.

[b]Includes physicians, dentists, medical and dental technicians, and all other health personnel classified as professional.

[c]Includes all other clerical and kindred workers not elsewhere classified.

[d]Includes marshals and constables; sheriffs and bailiffs.

[e]Includes all other craft workers not elsewhere classified.

[f]Includes grading and road machinery operators, plumbers and pipefitters, and structural metalworkers.

[g]Includes operatives not elsewhere classified in the following nondurable goods industries: paper and allied products; printing and publishing; chemicals and allied products; petroleum and coal products; rubber and plastic products; and not specified nondurable manufacturing.

hIncludes hospital attendants, recreation and amusement workers, ushers, and all other service workers not elsewhere classified.

iIncludes rail conductors, subway motormen, mine motormen, railroad brakemen, railroad switchmen, boatmen and canalmen, and sailors and deck hands.

jIncludes operatives not elsewhere classified in the following industries: communications, utilities, public administration, agriculture, forestry, fishery, mining, construction, finance, insurance and real estate, wholesale and retail trade, personal services, entertainment and recreation services, business and repair services, and professional and related services.

kIncludes operatives, not elsewhere classified, in the following industries: metal industries; machinery, except electrical; electrical machinery; professional and photographic equipment; miscellaneous manufacturing.

lSame industrial distribution as for operatives in note k.

mIncludes laborers in all nonmanufacturing industries, except construction.

nIncludes laborers in all nondurable goods industries.

Note: Percentages not shown where base numbers are less than 50,000.

Source: Bureau of the Census, public use tapes, 1960, 1970.

Trends in Educational-Level Composition of Workers

Thus far, our discussion of changes in characteristics of workers, by occupation, has not taken into account the effects of the sharp educational upgrading of the labor force. Between 1960 and 1970, the percentage of workers in the experienced civilian labor force who were high school graduates increased from 50.7 percent to 64.5 percent. As a result, the average educational achievement of workers increased in virtually all occupations, continuing the long-term trend. Relative gains in the percentage of high school graduates were most pronounced in the middle- and lower-level occupational status groups, as indicated in Table 3.25. Thus, in group 3 occupations, the proportion of high school graduates rose from about 40 percent in 1960 to 55 percent in 1970, or by more than one-third; among group 4 occupations, the increase was from 31 percent to 44 percent, or about two-fifths, and in group 5 occupations, the corresponding rise was from 21 percent to 35 percent, or approximately two-thirds. Increases in the proportion of high school graduates in group 5 were most pronounced in occupations which experienced a relatively large inflow of young white workers, such as kitchen work and nonmanufacturing labor. Conversely, declining occupations such as domestic work and laundry work received the smallest increases in high school graduates.

Net Shifts in Composition of Group 5 Labor Force

After having examined the trends in labor force composition, by occupations, in relation to each of the major sociodemographic characteristics, a composite analysis of net labor force gains and losses, by sex, race, educational level, and broad age group is presented in Table 3.26, for the group 5 category, as a whole. From this analysis, several major conclusions concerning the changing sources of manpower for these low-status occupations can be drawn:

1. There was a large-scale net exodus of nonwhite workers, primarily adults, from low-status occupations. Between 1960 and 1970, the number of nonwhites in these occupations declined by 630,000, or 21 percent. Of this net loss, 550,000 consisted of workers 25 years and over; 80,000, of workers 16-24 years. (The latter reduction, in the face of the large growth in the overall size of this age group between 1960 and 1970, reflected—of course—a particularly sharp reduction in the proportion of young nonwhites who entered low-status occupations in the course of the decade.) About three-fifths of this net loss of 630,000 nonwhites was among men, mainly reflecting reductions in nonfarm laborers, and two-fifths among women, mainly from domestic service and farm labor.

2. A second source of loss consisted of adult white male workers, 25 years and over, whose participation in group 5 occupations declined by 280,000 or 10 percent over the decade, reflecting mainly declines in various laborer occupations, both farm and nonfarm. Thus, the combined losses of nonwhites and of adult white males from group 5 occupations amounted to more than 900,000.

3. These losses were more than offset by gains from two sources: a large inflow of young white workers (mainly males) and an increase in the number of adult white women. Between 1960 and 1970, the number of white male youths aged 16-24 years in group 5 occupations increased by 720,000 or 73 percent, while the number of young white women rose by 100,000 or about 50 percent. In addition, there was a net increase of adult white women, 25 years and over, in group 5 occupations amounting to 250,000 or 21 percent.

4. These shifts in labor force composition were accompanied by a particularly sharp increase in the proportion of high school graduates in the group 5 labor force. Reflecting the general trend towards lengthening of schooling, the white entrants into the labor force (both youth and female adults) consisted predominantly of high school graduates, while the group experiencing reductions consisted mainly of persons with less than 12 years of schooling. Thus, there was a net gain of 1,200,000 high school graduates in group 5 occupations and a net loss of 1,040,000 nongraduates. As a result, the percentage of high school graduates among group 5 workers rose from 21 percent to 35 percent between 1960 and 1970.

The Growth of Part-Time Employment

Our analyses of the net changes in labor force composition, by occupation, between 1960 and 1970, have defined labor supply, thus far, in terms of numbers of workers rather than in terms of the labor force time, or hours of work, provided by different elements of the working population. However, the large-scale shift in composition of the group 5 labor force from nonwhites (mainly adult workers) to white youth and adult white women also reflected a significant shift, in many of these occupations, from reliance upon full-time career members of the labor force to increased utilization of secondary workers who—in many cases—were only available for part-time or intermittent employment.

We have already seen that young workers aged 16-24 years, and adult women, in combination, accounted for a large proportion of the net overall growth of the labor force between 1960 and 1970. This was accompanied by a parallel growth in the number and proportion of

TABLE 3.25

Percent of Experienced Civilian Labor Force, 16 Years and Over, with 12 or More Years of Education, by Detailed Occupational Group, Subgroup, and Sex: 1960, 1970

Status Group and Occupation	Both Sexes		Male		Female	
	1960	1970	1960	1970	1960	1970
Total, experienced civilian labor force	50.7	64.5	47.6	62.1	56.9	68.4
Group 1	92.4	95.0	92.2	93.9	92.7	94.9
Engineers	93.1	96.4	93.2	96.4	—	—
All other professional and technical workers[a]	89.9	93.6	90.1	93.7	89.3	93.3
Teachers, excluding college	98.5	97.5	98.6	98.5	98.4	97.1
Medical personnel[b]	90.3	94.2	95.2	97.0	87.0	92.8
Group 2	70.2	80.7	67.6	79.4	73.3	81.9
Bookkeepers	83.0	86.8	86.1	88.0	82.3	86.6
Secretaries, stenographers, typists	90.0	92.0	78.7	86.4	90.4	92.2
All other sales workers, excluding retail clerks	69.8	80.4	72.0	81.6	55.3	75.5
Managers, officials, proprietors	65.4	79.2	65.7	79.7	64.0	76.6
All other clerical and kindred workers[c]	73.3	81.1	68.7	78.5	77.2	83.1
Office machine operators	76.4	87.5	87.2	91.7	74.0	85.8
Telephone operators	62.8	83.0	—	—	62.0	83.5
Policemen, firemen	60.3	81.1	60.1	81.4	—	—
Sales clerks, retail trade	55.3	66.8	61.0	68.2	51.6	66.2
Cashiers	59.5	66.6	68.3	71.4	57.2	65.0
Postal clerks, mail carriers	72.4	80.3	72.7	79.6	69.2	82.4

Group 3						
Foremen, not elsewhere classified	39.5	54.9	39.2	54.5	41.8	56.9
All other craftsmen[e]	49.6	62.3	50.1	63.2	43.0	51.8
Mechanics, excluding auto	47.0	58.5	47.1	58.9	46.6	54.4
Deliverymen, routemen	41.0	57.4	41.0	57.5	35.7	47.4
Metalworking, crafts, excluding mechanics, machinists	47.7	54.9	47.2	54.9	—	—
Farmers, farm managers, and unpaid farm workers	40.4	54.3	40.6	55.1	—	—
Electricians, brickmasons, excavating machine operators[f]	29.9	45.4	29.7	46.1	32.0	40.3
Machinists	37.2	52.4	37.1	52.3	60.0	62.5
Checkers, examiners	46.0	59.6	46.4	60.4	16.7	35.3
Operatives, nondurables manufacturing, including chemicals, petroleum[g]	43.9	56.3	49.4	64.6	38.7	46.4
Barbers, bartenders, practical nurses[h]	35.4	47.5	37.4	49.1	29.5	43.2
Operatives, transport equipment manufacturing	43.7	63.6	36.6	52.2	48.7	68.4
Carpenters	36.6	51.6	37.3	52.0	31.9	49.6
Group 4						
Taxi drivers, bus drivers[i]	30.3	42.3	30.3	42.3	100.0	50.0
Auto mechanics	30.6	43.6	30.5	43.9	30.9	43.1
Nonmanufacturing operatives, total[j]	35.2	46.0	32.2	43.9	71.4	54.7
Auto service and parking attendants	34.9	49.1	35.0	49.2	—	—
Operatives, metalworking industries[k]	32.5	46.2	32.3	47.6	33.2	41.0
	42.1	47.6	42.2	48.3	—	—
	33.0	48.1	33.5	48.7	31.7	47.1

(continued)

(Table 3.25 continued)

Status Group and Occupation	Both Sexes		Male		Female	
	1960	1970	1960	1970	1960	1970
(Group 4 continued)						
Guards and watchmen; crossing guards and bridge tenders	30.8	45.0	27.8	43.6	—	—
Housekeepers and babysitters	26.6	37.7	—	—	26.6	37.2
Waiters, counter and fountain workers	41.3	52.5	40.1	52.5	41.5	52.5
Shipping and receiving clerks, messengers, and office boys	42.5	61.4	39.8	60.2	61.4	67.6
Laborers, metalworking industries[1]	27.6	42.6	27.4	43.2	—	—
Operatives, food and tobacco manufacturing	26.0	36.8	28.2	39.9	21.3	30.7
Construction painters, plasterers, cement and concrete finishers, roofers, paperhangers	29.5	38.7	28.8	38.7	—	—
Hospital attendants	38.1	56.9	39.7	65.1	37.5	55.5
Truck and tractor drivers	26.7	39.0	26.8	38.9	—	—
Operatives, textiles, apparel, leather industries	19.8	27.8	21.2	23.9	19.1	29.0
Packers	30.4	40.2	29.9	43.0	30.8	35.5
Welders, flamecutters	28.5	42.8	28.5	42.6	—	—
Operatives, lumber, furniture, stone, clay, and glass industries	21.1	28.2	21.8	27.0	16.5	35.9

Group 5

	20.8	34.8	21.1	37.4	20.1	29.8
Laborers, selected nonmanufacturing industries[m]	25.1	44.2	24.8	44.0	31.6	47.4
Janitors and sextons	21.8	35.5	21.8	36.1	26.7	31.7
Cooks	27.7	38.5	27.3	46.3	27.9	34.7
Construction laborers	19.0	33.6	19.0	33.9	—	—
Laborers, lumber, furniture, stone, clay, and glass industries	17.6	33.3	16.9	32.7	—	—
Laborers, nondurables, including chemicals, petroleum[n]	22.8	35.8	22.9	36.6	22.2	31.6
Farm laborers—paid	15.8	27.0	15.8	26.3	15.4	34.6
Kitchen workers	20.9	43.1	28.7	41.7	15.7	43.8
Laundry and dry cleaning operatives	24.1	28.8	27.6	39.8	22.7	23.8
Cleaners and charwomen, porters, chambermaids, and elevator operators	22.0	31.4	23.2	34.8	21.0	30.1
Private household, not elsewhere classified	16.7	19.1	—	—	17.0	18.8

(continued)

187

Notes to Table 3.25

[a]Includes all other professional and technical workers, not elsewhere classified.

[b]Includes physicians, dentists, medical and dental technicians, and all other health personnel classified as professional.

[c]Includes all other clerical and kindred workers not elsewhere classified.

[d]Includes marshals and constables; sheriffs and bailiffs.

[e]Includes all other craft workers not elsewhere classified.

[f]Includes grading and road machinery operators, plumbers and pipefitters, and structural metalworkers.

[g]Includes operatives not elsewhere classified in the following nondurable goods industries: paper and allied products; printing and publishing; chemicals and allied products; petroleum and coal products; rubber and plastic products; and not specified nondurable manufacturing.

hIncludes hospital attendants, recreation and amusement workers, ushers, and all other service workers not elsewhere classified.

iIncludes rail conductors, subway motormen, mine motormen, railroad brakemen, railroad switchmen, boatmen and canalmen, sailors and deck hands.

jIncludes operatives not elsewhere classified in the following industries: communications, utilities, public administration, agriculture, forestry, fishery, mining, construction, finance, insurance and real estate, wholesale and retail trade, personal services, entertainment and recreation services, business and repair services, and professional and related services.

kIncludes operatives, not elsewhere classified, in the following industries: metal industries; machinery, except electrical; electrical machinery; professional and photographic equipment; miscellaneous manufacturing.

lSame industrial distribution as for operatives in note k.

mIncludes laborers in all nonmanufacturing industries, except construction.

nIncludes laborers in all nondurable goods manufacturing industries.

Note: Percentages not shown where base numbers are less than 50,000.

Source: Bureau of the Census, public use tapes, 1960, 1970.

189

TABLE 3.26

Net Changes in Group 5 Labor Force, 1960–70, by Sex, Race, Age Group, and Educational Level
(000)

Age and Years of School Completed	Total, Both Sexes			Male			Female		
	Total	White	Nonwhite	Total	White	Nonwhite	Total	White	Nonwhite
Total, ages 16 and over	160	790	-630	70	460	-370	80	340	-260
Less than 12 years	-1,040	-350	-690	-840	-400	-430	-210	50	-260
12 years and over	1,200	1,140	60	910	860	60	290	290	—
Ages 16-24	740	830	-80	670	720	-50	60	100	-40
Less than 12 years	30	130	-100	30	100	-70	-10	20	-30
12 years and over	710	700	20	640	610	20	70	80	-10
Ages 25 and over	-580	-40	-550	-600	-280	-320	30	250	-220
Less than 12 years	-1,070	-470	-590	-870	-500	-360	-200	30	-230
12 years and over	490	440	50	270	230	40	220	210	10

Note: Detail may not add to group totals due to rounding.
Source: Compiled by the author.

part-time workers. One measure of this trend is provided by statistics, based upon the Current Population Survey, which indicate an increase in the percentage of employed workers, working part time for noneconomic reasons, from 7.1 million, or 10.1 percent of the total in April 1960, to 10.7 million, or 13.1 percent, in April 1970. As shown in Table 3.27, the proportions of part-time workers have tended to be highest both in the less-skilled white-collar occupations (clerical and sales work) and in the less-skilled blue-collar or service occupations. Between 1960 and 1970, the sharpest relative gains in employment of part-time workers occurred among nonfarm laborers, service workers, and clerical workers, with much smaller increases in other categories. Thus, a relatively large proportion of the increase in part-time employment was concentrated in lower-status (group 5-type) occupations.

The sources of part-time manpower for group 5 occupations are indicated in Table 3.28, based on our tabulations of decennial census data for 1960 and 1970. (It should be noted that the latter statistics are not directly comparable to those shown in Table 3.27, since the census data include as part-time workers all those employed less than 35 hours during the census enumeration week for either economic reasons or other reasons. Nevertheless, the broad patterns of change between 1960 and 1970, based on these two measures, were found to be reasonably consistent.) Among the group 5 occupations shown in Table 3.28, the sharpest gains in the proportion of part-time workers occurred among nonfarm laborers, cooks and kitchen workers, cleaners and other building service workers, and laundry and dry cleaning operatives. The largest component of the part-time labor force in most of these occupations consisted of 16-24-year-olds. By 1970, nearly 22 percent of all nonfarm laborers (exclusive of those in durable goods manufacturing industries) consisted of 16-24-year-olds who worked at these jobs for less than 35 hours during the census week—more than twice the corresponding proportion in 1960. The proportion of young part-time workers more than doubled, too, among cooks and kitchen workers, from 7.1 percent to 16.1 percent, and registered substantial increases in the cleaning and building service occupations, as well. Adult women, 25 years and over, also increased their proportion of part-time workers among cleaners and building service workers, as well as among laundry operatives and domestics. Among domestics, fully one-half of those employed in 1970, exclusive of housekeepers and babysitters, had worked less than 35 hours in the census week.

Although the statistics on hours of work, derived from the census public use sample, do not warrant any detailed computations of labor force trends for specific occupations based on an equivalent full-time labor force index, since they refer to hours worked in the census

TABLE 3.27

Part-Time Employment for Noneconomic Reasons,
as Percent of Total Persons at Work, by Major
Census Occupational Group and Sex:
April 1960, April 1970

Occupational Group	Percentage Part-Time[a]					
	Total, Both Sexes		Male		Female	
	1960[b]	1970	1960[b]	1970	1960[b]	1970
Total, 16 years and over	10.1	13.1	5.5	8.5	19.6	25.8
Professional, technical and kindred workers	9.1	12.7	4.7	6.8	16.8	22.1
Managers and proprietors, excluding farm	3.7	4.1	2.2	2.6	12.9	12.5
Clerical workers	10.9	19.1	6.0	12.2	13.2	21.4
Sales workers	20.1	27.7	8.9	14.1	36.4	47.1
Craftsmen and foremen	2.6	3.1	2.4	2.8	11.1	15.9
Operatives	4.7	6.7	3.9	5.9	6.8	8.5
Nonfarm laborers	9.1	19.3	9.0	19.2	15.4	22.9
Service workers, excluding private household	18.0	30.7	10.9	21.6	24.2	36.6
Private household workers	35.3	58.2	—	—	35.6	58.3
Farm workers, total	18.6	21.7	11.9	17.9	54.8	43.0
Farm managers and proprietors	11.2	15.1	9.2	13.4	59.1	56.3
Farm laborers and foremen	28.5	30.2	16.8	25.8	54.1	40.7

[a]Includes those with a job and working less than 35 hours during survey week for the following reasons: labor dispute, bad weather, own illness, vacation, demands at home, school, no desire for full-time work, and full-time work only during peak season.

[b]Data adjusted to exclude 14-15-year-olds, based on ratios derived from the March 1966 Current Population Survey.

Note: Data not shown where base numbers were too small to allow calculation of a meaningful percentage.

Source: Unpublished tables from Census Bureau's Current Population Survey.

TABLE 3.28

Percent Distribution of Employed Workers in Group 5 Occupations, by
Hours Worked in Census Week, and by Age Group and Sex
for Part-Time Workers: 1960 and 1970

			Percent Distribution			
				Part Time		
	Total	Full Time		Ages	Ages 25 and Over	
Occupation	Employed	(35 Hours)	Total	16–24	Male	Female
Nonfarm laborers, excluding durable goods manufacturing						
1960	100.0	80.2	19.8	10.5	8.5	0.8
1970	100.0	71.5	28.5	21.8	5.7	1.0
Farm laborers (paid)						
1960	100.0	76.6	23.4	10.5	9.8	3.1
1970	100.0	75.0	25.0	13.7	7.0	4.3
Cooks and kitchen workers						
1960	100.0	77.8	22.2	7.1	1.5	13.6
1970	100.0	68.7	31.3	16.1	1.2	14.0
Janitors and sextons						
1960	100.0	78.4	21.6	7.1	9.2	5.3
1970	100.0	77.3	22.7	12.5	6.3	3.9
Cleaners and charwomen, porters, chambermaids, and elevator operators						
1960	100.0	79.1	20.9	4.2	2.3	14.4
1970	100.0	71.1	28.9	7.1	1.9	19.9
Laundry and dry cleaning operatives						
1960	100.0	87.3	12.7	2.2	1.1	9.4
1970	100.0	78.3	21.7	4.2	2.7	14.8
Private household workers, not elsewhere classified						
1960	100.0	53.6	46.4	3.9	1.0	41.5
1970	100.0	50.0	50.0	4.8	0.7	44.5

Source: Bureau of the Census, public use sample tapes, 1960, 1970.

193

enumeration week only, the data cited above, in combination with the CPS data for broader occupational groups, do support the following inferences:

1. Occupations such as domestics and hired farm laborers, which experienced a sharp reduction in terms of numbers of workers, probably experienced an even sharper reduction in terms of labor force man-years.

2. Occupations such as nonfarm laborers which, on balance, experienced little net change in numbers of workers, probably declined significantly in terms of full-time man-years available.

3. Finally, those low-status occupations, such as food service, whose numbers increased rapidly over the decade, probably experienced a more moderate increase in man-years worked, when allowance is made for the increased utilization of part-time workers, mainly youth, in place of full-time adult workers.

The Later Immigration

Immigration, which had been a negligible factor in labor force growth since the 1920s, increased moderately in the decade of the 1960s, as illustrated by the following summary statistics:

1. Immigration of aliens, as recorded by the Immigration and Naturalization Service (INS), increased from a total of 2.5 million in 1951-60 to 3.3 million in 1961-70.[4]

2. Net civilian immigration, as estimated by the Bureau of the Census, rose from 3.0 million in the 1950s to 3.9 million in the 1960s. This corresponded to a rate of 2.2 immigrants per 1,000 persons—the highest rate for any decade since termination of mass immigration in the 1920s. (The Census Bureau statistics include, in addition to aliens admitted for permanent residence, allowances for net movements of resident aliens, such as foreign students and businessmen; net inflows of Puerto Ricans; entries of temporary workers and of "parolees," such as Cuban refugees; and net emigration of U.S. citizens.[5])

This increased inflow more than offset separations from the labor force of foreign-born workers residing here in 1960, and as a result, the percentage of foreign-born workers in the experienced U.S. labor force, including Puerto Ricans, rose from 7.5 percent in 1960 to 8.4 percent in 1970, according to our tabulations based on the decennial census public use tapes.

The composition of the immigrant population entering in the
1960s, although similar to that of immediately preceding decades,
contrasted sharply with that of the earlier era of mass immigration
into the United States, prior to enactment of the restrictive laws of
the early 1920s. The national origins quota system, imposed on immigration from the Eastern Hemisphere—combined with the effects of
the postwar prosperity in Western Europe—had sharply curtailed the
proportion of immigrants from Europe from an average of 80 percent
of the total in the period 1901-30 to 53 percent in the 1950s, and to
34 percent in the period 1961-70. Immigration from Mexico, from
the West Indies, and from other Latin American countries had increased rapidly and accounted for 39 percent of all alien immigrant
entries in the decade of the 1960s, as against only 22 percent in the
1950s and 6 percent in the 1901-30 period. (The 1965 amendments to
the immigration law established an overall Western Hemisphere quota,
for the first time; however, this quota did not become fully effective
until 1968 and had a limited effect on the proportion of immigrants
entering from Latin American countries during the decade as a whole.)
Occupational preference systems, operating within the framework of
quota limitations which were reinforced by the 1965 amendments, had
moreover contributed to a sharp upgrading in occupational and educational levels of the later immigrants—particularly in facilitating
an increased inflow of highly educated professional and technical
workers. Thus, in sharp contrast to earlier periods such as 1901-10,
when professional and technical workers constituted less than 2 percent of the total immigrant inflow, the proportion of professional and
technical workers among immigrants with a reported occupation was
15.5 percent in 1951-60 and 23.0 percent in 1961-70. The latter percentage was twice as great as the percentage of professional and
technical workers in the experienced civilian labor force in 1960 (see
Table 3.29). At the same time, the growing number of immigrants
from Mexico and from other neighboring West Indian and Latin American countries (other than Cuba) continued to include a large proportion of workers with limited skills and educational backgrounds, as
reflected in a higher-than-proportionate frequency, among immigrants,
of such occupations as private household workers and laborers.

The above statistics refer to the occupation reported by immigrants at the time of entry and do not necessarily reflect the jobs
occupied by such immigrants in the United States. To assess the
impact of later immigration upon the labor force in various occupations, tabulations were made of the distribution of foreign-born
workers in 1960 and 1970, by occupation and region of origin, based
on the decennial census public use sample tapes. The proportions
of foreign-born workers in each occupation and occupational status

TABLE 3.29

Occupational Distribution of Immigrants, 1951–60 and 1961–70,
Compared with Occupational Distribution of Experienced
Civilian Labor Force, 14 Years and Over, 1960
(percent distribution)

Occupational Group	Alien Immigrants 1951–60	1961–70	Experienced Civilian Labor Force, 1960
Total, with occupation reported	100.0	100.0	100.0
Professional and technical	15.5	23.0	11.3
Managers, officials, and proprietors, nonfarm	4.5	4.5	8.5
Clerical and sales	16.7	16.7	22.4
Craftsmen and foremen	16.5	14.1	14.3
Operatives	14.1	11.1	20.0
Nonfarm laborers	11.2	8.8	5.5
Service workers, excluding private household	5.9	7.4	8.9
Private household workers	7.9	8.7	2.8
Farm			
Farmers and farm managers	4.1	1.8	2.8
Farm laborers and foremen	3.6	3.9	2.4

Sources: Data on immigrants: U.S. Department of Commerce,
Bureau of the Census, Statistical Abstract of the United States, 1971
(Washington, D.C.: U.S. Government Printing Office, 1971), p. 91;
data on civilian labor force, Bureau of the Census, Census of Population, 1960, Subject Report, "Occupational Characteristics" (Washington, D.C.: U.S. Government Printing Office, 1963). table 1.

group, based on these tabulations, are shown in Table 3.30 for all
foreign-born workers and, separately, for those born in Latin America (that is, in all Western Hemisphere countries other than Canada).
The net changes in the proportion of foreign-born workers in the experienced civilian labor force between 1960 and 1970 provide an indication of the relative occupational distribution of later immigrants,
although these changes were influenced, too, by separations from the
labor force of foreign-born workers (mainly drawn from earlier immigrant cohorts) and by net occupational mobility among foreign-born
workers over the decade.

An examination of the statistics for the foreign-born labor force,
as a whole, reveals a much more favorable distribution, relative to
the overall occupational distribution of the labor force, than indicated
by our comparisons for earlier periods. In 1970, foreign-born professional workers accounted for a larger-than-proportionate share of
the labor force of medical and allied occupations and of engineers,
and for about the same proportion, in all other professional and technical occupations, as their overall percentage of the labor force. At
the same time, foreign-born workers also continued to account for
a larger-than-proportionate share of the labor supply in various
lower-status occupational groups, including operatives in low-wage
manufacturing industries, farm laborers, and service workers other
than private household.

Whereas the overall percentages of foreign-born workers, by
occupation, reflect the heterogeneous sources and skill levels of later
immigrant groups, the separate data for workers born in Latin American countries reveal a more consistent pattern of differential concentration in low-status occupations. Between 1960 and 1970, the
number of workers in the experienced civilian labor force, excluding
those with no specific occupation reported, who were born in Latin
American countries rose from about 400,000 to 900,000. Of the latter
total, over 200,000, or 22 percent, were in the group 5 occupations,
although these occupations, in 1970, accounted for only 14 percent of
the total experienced civilian labor force. A similar concentration of
Latin American-born workers was evident in the group 4 class of
occupations. As a result, whereas Latin American workers represented only 1.2 percent of all experienced civilian workers in 1970,
they accounted for 2.5 percent or more of the labor force in the
following occupations: hired farm laborers (7.6 percent), laundry
and dry cleaning operatives (2.9 percent), operatives in nondurable
goods manufacturing (2.8 percent), cleaners, charwomen, and allied
workers (2.7 percent), and other private household workers (2.5
percent).

The above statistics, moreover, probably understate to a significant degree the participation by foreign workers, and particularly,

TABLE 3.30

Percent of Experienced Civilian Labor Force, 16 Years and Over,
Born Outside the United States, by Status Group and in
Selected Occupations: 1960, 1970

Occupation	Foreign Born Total	Born in Latin America	Born Elsewhere
Experienced civilian			
labor force			
1960	7.5	0.6	6.9
1970	8.4	1.2	7.2
Status group 1: professional and			
technical workers[a]			
1960	6.6	0.4	6.2
1970	7.6	0.8	6.4
Engineers			
1960	7.0	0.0	7.0
1970	9.9	0.3	9.6
All other professional and			
technical workers			
1960	7.1	0.3	6.8
1970	8.3	0.9	7.4
Teachers, excluding college			
1960	3.0	0.3	2.7
1970	3.6	0.2	3.4
Medical personnel[b]			
1960	9.6	0.6	9.0
1970	10.1	1.6	8.5
Status group 2[c]			
1960	6.4	0.3	6.1
1970	6.5	0.7	5.8
Managers, officials,			
proprietors, total			
1960	8.4	0.3	8.1
1970	7.8	0.5	7.3
Clerical workers, total			
1960	5.1	0.4	4.7
1970	5.9	0.8	5.1
Secretaries, typists,			
stenographers			
1960	4.1	0.2	3.9
1970	6.4	0.9	5.5

Occupation	Foreign Born Total	Born in Latin America	Born Elsewhere
All other clerical[d]			
1960	5.4	0.5	4.9
1970	5.6	0.8	4.8
Sales workers, total			
1960	6.9	0.3	6.6
1970	6.6	0.7	5.9
Sales workers, excluding retail clerks			
1960	6.4	0.3	6.1
1970	5.9	0.5	5.4
Sales clerks, retail trade			
1960	7.4	0.3	7.1
1970	8.5	0.8	7.7
Status group 3			
1960	8.5	0.4	8.1
1970	7.8	1.0	6.8
Craftsmen and foremen, total			
1960	8.1	0.4	7.7
1970	7.5	1.1	6.4
Foremen, not elsewhere classified			
1960	5.0	0.1	4.9
1970	5.8	0.9	4.9
Craftsmen, not elsewhere classified[e]			
1960	10.7	0.4	10.3
1970	9.3	1.1	8.2
Mechanics, total			
1960	7.1	0.6	6.5
1970	5.8	1.0	4.8
Metalworking craftsmen, including machinists			
1960	10.2	0.3	9.9
1970	9.0	0.1	8.9
Construction craftsmen, excluding carpenters			
1960	7.7	0.5	7.2
1970	7.1	0.8	6.3

(continued)

(Table 3.30 continued)

Occupation	Foreign Born Total	Born in Latin America	Born Elsewhere
Carpenters			
1960	7.0	0.2	6.8
1970	8.3	1.6	6.7
Farmers, farm managers, unpaid family workers			
1960	8.3	0.3	8.0
1970	5.8	0.0	5.8
Barbers, bartenders, practical nurses[f]			
1960	11.5	0.9	10.4
1970	10.6	1.5	8.1
Checkers, examiners			
1960	5.8	0.0	5.8
1970	5.5	1.1	4.4
Status group 4			
1960	8.8	0.9	7.9
1970	10.0	3.4	6.6
Selected operative occupations, total			
1960	9.3	1.0	8.3
1970	12.0	2.0	10.0
Operatives—metalworking industries[g]			
1960	10.0	0.7	9.3
1970	9.5	1.8	7.7
Operatives—nondurable goods[h]			
1960	13.6	1.6	12.0
1970	16.1	2.8	13.3

Occupation	Foreign Born Total	Born in Latin America	Born Elsewhere
Truck and tractor drivers			
1960	3.0	0.5	2.5
1970	3.9	0.4	3.5
Packers			
1960	9.5	0.6	8.9
1970	11.7	2.3	9.4
Selected service occupations, total			
1960	8.0	0.5	7.5
1970	8.9	1.5	7.4
Housekeepers and babysitters			
1960	9.7	1.5	8.2
1970	10.4	2.7	7.7
Waiters, counter and fountain workers			
1960	7.8	0.1	7.7
1970	9.6	1.0	8.6
Hospital attendants			
1960	6.8	0.2	6.6
1970	7.3	1.8	5.5
Status group 5[i]			
1960	9.4	2.1	7.3
1970	8.8	2.5	6.3
Nonfarm laborers, total[j]			
1960	7.0	1.1[k]	5.9
1970	6.3	1.5	3.8

(continued)

(Table 3.30 continued)

Occupation	Foreign Born Total	Born in Latin America	Born Elsewhere
Farm laborers—paid			
1960	11.3	6.7	4.6
1970	12.2	7.6	4.6
Personal services, total			
1960	11.4	1.6	9.8
1970	11.0	3.0	8.0
Janitors and sextons			
1960	11.2	0.8	10.4
1970	10.2	1.6	9.6
Cooks and kitchen workers			
1960	14.0	1.7	12.3
1970	11.1	2.0	9.1
Cleaners and charwomen, porters, chambermaids, and elevator operators			
1960	11.2	0.8	10.4
1970	13.2	2.7	10.5
Laundry and dry cleaning operatives			
1960	8.6	1.5	7.1
1970	12.3	2.9	9.4
Private household workers, not elsewhere classified			
1960	9.0	2.2	6.8
1970	8.3	2.5	5.8

Notes to Table 3.30

[a]Includes all other professional and technical workers, not elsewhere classified.

[b]Includes physicians, dentists, medical and dental technicians, and all other health occupations classified as professional.

[c]Includes policemen, firemen; marshals and constables; sheriffs and bailiffs.

[d]Includes all other clerical and kindred workers not elsewhere classified.

[e]Includes all other craft workers not elsewhere classified.

[f]Includes hospital attendants, recreation and amusement workers, ushers, and all other service workers not elsewhere classified.

[g]Includes operatives, not elsewhere classified, in the following industries: metal industries; machinery, except electrical; electrical machinery; professional and photographic equipment; miscellaneous manufacturing.

[h]Includes operatives not elsewhere classified in the following nondurable goods industries: paper and allied products; printing and publishing; chemicals and allied products; petroleum and coal products; rubber and plastic products; and not specified nondurable manufacturing.

[i]Data are weighted averages of foreign born experienced civilian labor force, aged 16 and over, in farm laborer and personal service categories, and of foreign born employed in nonfarm laborer category.

[j]Data are percentages of employed foreign born in relation to total employed rather than experienced civilian labor force, used because of a coding error.

[k]Includes data for employed foreign born Mexicans only; other countries not available.

Note: Due to a coding omission, 300,000 taxi drivers and bus drivers were excluded from the 1960 tabulation. Also, published decennial census data for employed workers in the nonfarm laborer occupation were used in place of the tabulated data on experienced civilian labor force for this occupation for both 1960 and 1970, due to a miscoding. "Foreign born" is defined to include persons born in Puerto Rico and residing in mainland United States. These were, however, included in the "born elsewhere" column.

Sources: Based on 1960 and 1970 1/1,000 census public use samples, except as noted above.

those from Mexico and other Latin American countries, in the low-status labor force. The first, and most obvious source of this understatement consists of workers residing in Mexican border areas and who commute daily to jobs in southern California and other border areas within the United States. A spot survey conducted by the INS in the late 1960s enumerated a total of 47,876 such border commuters: other estimates of such commuters range as high as 75,000.[6] About two-fifths of the commuters in 1967 were reported as working in agriculture; the balance, in a variety of nonfarm pursuits, were reported as working as service workers, as industrial and construction workers, or as domestics.[7]

In addition, there is a wide range of evidence indicating the presence in the U.S. population and labor force of large numbers of illegal aliens—immigrants who entered the country illegally or who overstayed their authorized period as visitors, students, or other temporary entrants. The most tangible evidence of the extent of illegal immigration consists of the statistics on deportation of apprehended aliens, compiled by the NS. The number of such deportations rose from 465,000 in fiscal years 1961-65 to 1,142,000 in fiscal years 1966-70.[8] A very large percentage of these deportees consisted of Mexicans apprehended in the Southwest border states; however, increasing numbers of illegal aliens have been apprehended in other sections of the country, including the Northeast and Midwest. Exceptionally high rates of population growth in Mexico and elsewhere in Latin America, and the much higher wage levels in the United States even for unskilled labor, have served as strong inducements for illegal as well as legal immigration from these areas. Another major factor in the growth of illegal entries and deportations was the termination of the bracero program in 1964. This program, initiated during World War II, had provided for importation of contract Mexican agricultural laborers to meet the wartime farm labor shortage; it had been continued during the post-World War II period in response to demands of agricultural interests in the Southwest border region and was formally terminated when the labor market situation in that region could no longer justify such a program.

The contribution to labor supply of those aliens actually apprehended and deported has probably been modest. Most aliens have been apprehended in border areas after very brief stays, of a few weeks or less; the statistics moreover apparently include large numbers of repeaters. However, it is generally recognized that only a fraction of the illegal aliens are actually apprehended. Based on a review of its operating experience and on certain necessarily arbitrary assumptions, the INS arrived at an estimate of approximately 1.0 million illegal aliens residing in the United States in early 1972, of whom about three-fourths (mainly Mexicans) were assumed to be illegal entrants and most of the remainder were individuals, such as

tourists or students, who had overstayed their visas.[9] Manuel Aragon,
Jr., in a statement presented to the Commission on Population Growth
and the American Future, gave an independent estimate of between one
million and 1.5 million illegal residents in the United States of Mexican
origins, based on his analysis of local INS reports and on an independent study by the Chicano Studies Department at California State College,
Los Angeles.[10] A House subcommittee, chaired by Representative
Peter W. Rodino, Jr., conducted extensive hearings on the problem
of illegal aliens during 1971-72 and concluded that "although the number of illegal aliens in this country cannot be accurately measured,
it is generally accepted that there are presently between one and two
million aliens illegally in the United States."[11] In the following three
years, estimates—or guesses—concerning the number of such aliens
residing here escalated. Thus, in February 1975, the commissioner
of the INS advised the House Subcommittee on Immigration: "We really
don't know how many illegal aliens there are in this country. The
estimates range from four million to twelve million: the actual number is probably somewhere in between—perhaps about eight million
or so."[12]

Irrespective of the precise number of illegal aliens in the United
States, there is a general consensus among informed sources concerning certain relevant characteristics:

1. Such persons mainly enter the United States, or stay here
illegally, to improve their economic status. A very large proportion
are young adults and are either working or seeking work.

2. Occupationally, such workers are disproportionately concentrated in the less desirable unskilled or semiskilled jobs, typically
in menial service occupations, in farm labor or casual nonfarm labor,
and in low-wage manufacturing industries.

3. Geographically, the largest concentration of such workers
consists of Mexicans in the Southwest border area. However, substantial numbers, including many West Indian immigrants, are apparently located in eastern seaboard cities, for example, New York,
Washington, and Miami, as well as in certain midwestern industrial
cities, such as Chicago.

From the standpoint of our statistical analysis of labor supply by
occupation, it is reasonable to assume that most such illegal residents
are not included in the official census enumerations, or if counted,
are not likely to accurately report their country of origin. Some confirmation of this assumption is provided by an analysis by Donald S.
Akers of the Bureau of the Census, who derived estimates of net
immigration from Mexico for the decade 1950-60 based on alternative
sources, including (1) official U.S. immigration statistics, (2) analysis

of U.S. census of population statistics on the population born in
Mexico, using a cohort survival method; (3) analysis of the census
statistics on those persons with Spanish surnames in the five southwestern states, also using a cohort survival method; and (4) analysis
of official Mexican census and vital statistics data, as an alternative
method of arriving at the net outflow to the United States. His estimates of net immigration based on these four sources are shown
below.[13]

Source	Estimated Net Mexican Immigration, 1950-70
Immigration statistics	313,000
U.S. census	
Country of birth	205,000
Spanish surname	350,000
Mexican census and vital statistics	473,000

Akers's analysis of the Mexican census and vital statistics, in
comparison with the official U.S. immigration data, thus suggested
that unrecorded (illegal) immigration from Mexico may have amounted
to 150,000 in the decade of the 1950s. Akers further suggested that,
because of improvements in coverage of Mexican population and vital
statistics between 1950 and 1960, his estimate based on the latter data
may have been biased downward. Although Akers cautiously avoided
any definite conclusions from these data, it appears evident that the
census data based on country of origin, which resulted in an estimate
100,000 less than the official U.S. immigration statistics for the
decade, do have a significant downward bias. Since the census data
served as our source for analysis of the foreign-born labor force by
occupation, it is reasonable to assume that the size of the foreign-
born labor force in low-status (group 5) occupations in 1970, as well
as its growth between 1960 and 1970, were substantially greater than
reflected in the census counts for those years.

It should be noted that the problem of undercount of foreign-born
workers in the United States is a special aspect of the broader problem
of incompleteness in census enumerations. By use of a variety of
demographic techniques, Jacob Siegal of the Bureau of the Census has
estimated the total undercount in the 1970 census at 5.3 million, or
2.5 percent of the total U.S. population, as compared to an undercount
of 2.7 percent in the 1960 census and 3.3 percent in 1950. The degree
of underenumeration has been consistently higher for blacks, and
particularly for adult black males, than for other defined population
groups. Thus, Siegal estimates that the census underreported the

number of black males aged 25–44 in the U.S. population by approximately 18.5 percent in 1960 and by 18.0 percent in 1970.[14] Such nonenumerated persons, if in the labor force, are likely to be concentrated in unskilled, casual labor-type jobs, and—hence—are likely to cause a particularly serious relative understatement of the labor force in the group 5 occupations. However, Siegal's analysis suggests that the percentage of underenumeration in the 1960 and 1970 censuses for the population of working age has been fairly stable, and may in fact have declined slightly. Thus, although the absolute magnitude of the labor force attached to group 5 occupations is probably understated by the official census data—both in absolute numbers and in relation to other occupational groups—there is no reason to believe that this factor has significantly biased our analysis of overall trends in the size of this labor force group or the shifts in its composition, by race, sex, or age groups. In contrast, the limited available data on illegal immigration in the 1960s combined with indications of incomplete coverage of the number of legal workers here who were born in Mexico, point to a probably significant understatement of the growth of this particular component of the group 5 labor force during the decade.

SUMMARY

In this chapter we have presented data on the changing composition of labor supply by occupation during 1960–70, from two separate—but related—perspectives: first, the changes in occupational distribution of various social and demographic groups in the labor force, resulting in measures of overall changes in their respective occupational status; and second, the changes in composition of the labor force within occupations, or occupational groups. From either vantage point, it is evident that very significant changes occurred in the composition of the work force in many low-status occupations.

The most significant of these changes were (1) extensive replacement of nonwhite workers, and of adult white men, in low-status jobs by young white workers, particularly males; (2) a substantial improvement in occupational status of nonwhite workers over the decade, particularly among better-educated young workers, aged 16–24; (3) increased utilization of part-time workers in many of these occupations, including both students and adult women; and (4) an increase in the proportion of foreign-born workers, mainly immigrants from Mexico and other Latin American countries, in low-status occupations.

The first of these developments, reflected in a substantial exodus of black workers from the lowest-status jobs and in significant increases in their participation in white-collar occupations, may well be the most significant, in terms of its long-range social consequences. Some of the influences contributing to this breakthrough have been suggested by our analysis, namely, the progress made in closing their educational attainment gap in relation to white workers and the favorable labor market climate of the second half of the 1960s. Perhaps of equal importance was the catalytic impact of the civil rights movement of the 1960s and of resulting government and private initiatives in the field of equal employment opportunity. The net effect was the generation of a social and psychological climate among white workers and employers—as well as among blacks—which was conducive to increased acceptance of blacks in occupations and industries which had been effectively foreclosed to them in the past.

The second dynamic force at work was a direct consequence of the post-World War II baby boom, which—predictably—brought in its wake a record-breaking number of youthful entrants into the labor force during the 1960s. This new postwar generation was also the most-educated generation in our history, as measured by the yardstick of years of schooling completed. However, the very fact that a large proportion of these youth continued their full-time education into their late teens and early twenties created a large supply of workers whose employment options were limited to the types of jobs amenable to part-time work schedules and which were geographically accessible to such youth. These youth, therefore, constituted a ready source of unskilled, casual labor for both low-level white-collar and blue-collar or service jobs, often serving as replacements for full-time adult nonwhite (as well as white) workers, who left these jobs in favor of better-paying jobs in higher-status occupations.

Finally, we have noted the increased role of the later immigration, particularly from Mexico, the West Indies, and other Latin American countries, as an additional source of manpower for low-status occupations. Although the contribution of later immigrants to the overall supply of lower-status workers appears to have been modest at the national level—even after allowing for some considerable underreporting in the census statistics—it is clear from collateral evidence that this manpower source has been much more significant in areas such as southern California and New York City, to which these workers have gravitated in substantial numbers.

Before proceeding with an assessment of the manpower supply outlook in the next chapter, we should note some limitations in the scope of our analysis of the experience of 1960-70. First, our analysis thus far has been largely based on data on net changes in the labor force, by occupation, between successive decennial censuses, and has not examined the process by which these changes were accomplished. Secondly, we have not yet systematically attempted to relate these occupational trends in the labor force to other relevant labor market variables, such as trends in differential wages or unemployment by occupation. The remainder of our study will include efforts to analyze these variables within the broader framework of labor supply and labor market theory.

NOTES

1. Based on estimates by Stanley Lebergott, decennial percentage increases in the total labor force, aged 10 years and over, were as follows: 1900-10, 28.9 percent; 1910-20, 11.0 percent; 1920-30, 17.4 percent; 1930-40, 15.3 percent; 1940-50, 16.3 percent. Stanley Lebergott, Manpower in Economic Growth: The American Record Since 1800 (New York: McGraw-Hill, 1964), p. 510.

2. U.S. Department of Commerce, Bureau of the Census, The Social and Economic Status of Negroes in the United States, 1970, BLS Report no. 394, Current Population Reports, Series P-23, no. 38 (Washington, D.C.: U.S. Government Printing Office, 1971), p. 74.

3. For evidence on the extent to which employment in these sectors is negatively correlated with the general level of demand for labor, see Arthur M. Okun, "Upward Mobility in A High-Pressure Economy," Brookings Papers on Economic Activity, no. 1 (Washington, D.C.: Brookings Institution, 1973), table 2.

4. Statistical Abstract, p. 89.

5. Irene B. Taeuber, "Growth of the Population of the United States in the Twentieth Century," in Demographic and Social Aspects of Population Growth, Commission on Population Growth and the American Future, Research Reports, vol. 1 (Washington, D.C.: U.S. Government Printing Office, 1973), p. 122.

6. Charles B. Keely, "Immigration: Considerations on Trends, Prospects and Policy," in Demographic and Social Aspects of Population Growth, op. cit., p. 183.

7. Hearings before the Select Commission on Western Hemisphere Immigration. The Impact of Commuter Aliens (Washington, D.C.: U.S. Government Printing Office, 1968), pt. 1, p. 8.

8. U.S. Department of Justice, Immigration and Naturalization Service, 1971 Annual Report (Washington, D.C.: U.S. Government Printing Office, 1972), table 23.

9. U.S. Congress, House, Hearings before Subcommittee No. 1 of the Committee on the Judiciary, House of Representatives, 92nd Congress, 2nd Session, on Illegal Aliens, Part 5, March 1972, pp. 1323-1325.

10. Testimony by Manuel J. Aragon, Jr., before the Commission on Population Growth and the American Future, Los Angeles, May 3, 1971.

11. U.S. Congress, House, <u>Report on Amending the Immigration and Nationality Act, and for Other Purposes</u>, 92d Cong., 2d sess., Report no. 92-1306, August 17, 1972, p. 3.

12. Statement by Leonard F. Chapman, Jr., commissioner, Immigration and Naturalization Service, before the House Subcommittee on Immigration, Citizenship and International Law, February 4, 1975.

13. Donald S. Akers, "Immigration Data and National Population Estimates for the United States," <u>Demography</u> 4, no. 1 (1967): 269.

14. Jacob S. Siegal, "Estimates of Coverage of the Population by Sex, Race and Age in the 1970 Census" (Paper presented at the annual meeting of the Population Association of America, New Orleans, April 26, 1973).

4

LABOR SUPPLY AND
OCCUPATIONAL
WAGE DIFFERENTIALS

While the preceding chapter has identified a number of significant changes in the composition of the labor force of lower-level occupations during the 1960-70 decade, we have not yet assessed the labor market implications of these shifts. For example, was the outflow of nonwhites from lower-level jobs—and their replacement by youthful white workers as well as by adult white women—accompanied by any significant change in the overall labor supply-labor demand balance in these occupations, as reflected in such indicators as changes in relative wages or in relative unemployment levels? Similarly, it is moot to investigate the effects, if any, of the educational upgrading of the labor force in many lower-level occupations upon differential wages in such occupations. From such assessments we might derive insights as to the implications of foreseeable future sociodemographic trends on the labor market for low-level occupations.

The classical economists' models of labor market behavior are, unfortunately, of limited assistance in such an analysis. These theories, as noted in Chapter 1, tended to explain the structure of occupational wage differentials in terms of such variables as (1) differences in training and educational investments required; (2) differences in nonpecuniary aspects of occupations; and (3) obstacles to free labor mobility among occupations from such factors as apprenticeship or licensing rules, governmental regulations, discriminatory practices, and so on. These explanations were, however, cast within the framework of a static equilibrium analysis, designed to define the long-term wage structure, rather than its shorter-term variations. On the premise that supply of various categories of labor is relatively fixed over short periods of time, economists—such as Marshall—have postulated that fluctuations in labor demand, rather than labor supply factors, are the primary determinants of short-term shifts in relative wages.

Neither the long-term equilibrium model, nor the premise of stability in short-term labor supply, has provided an adequate framework for explanation of observed occupational wage trends over a period of decades. Beginning with Paul Douglas's landmark study in the 1920s, a number of institutional economists conducted extensive empirical research on longer-term trends in the occupational wage structure. These earlier studies, covering a period of decades prior to the post-World War II era, generally concluded that there had been a significant trend towards narrowing of occupational wage differentials. One general explanation advanced was that the sharp rise in educational attainment of the labor force had increased the supply of workers qualified for entry into the white-collar occupations and into other preferred skilled occupations at a faster rate than the growth of demand in these occupations. Concurrently, the stoppage of large-scale immigration—although partially offset in its impact by the increased internal migration of black workers—was cited as a major factor checking the growth in labor supply for low-level jobs. These forces tending to narrow wage differentials appeared to be particularly operative in periods of full employment, such as World War II and the early postwar years.[1]

In contrast to this longer-term trend, studies focusing on post-World War II experience have more typically revealed a fairly stable pattern of occupational wage differences or some widening of these differences, depending upon the time periods and occupations selected for study. Thus, an analysis by Arthur Sackley and Thomas W. Gavett of occupational wage trends for broad categories of white-collar and blue-collar workers, covering the period 1959-69, arrived at the following conclusions:

> In summation, occupational wage information from BLS [Bureau of Labor Statistics] and other sources generally confirms the trend indicated by Census data, which show a slightly faster rise in the 1960's in the pay for white-collar jobs requiring extended educational preparation than in wages for blue-collar and white-collar jobs requiring little or no training. Certain low-paid occupations are an exception in that their pay rose at better than the average increase for the overall category.[2]

These trends were attributed to a combination of labor supply and labor demand influences. On the demand side, there had been a relatively large increase in employment in certain skilled occupations, such as professional and clerical work. On the supply side, the authors cited such factors as (1) the shortage of trained professionals and managers as a consequence of lower birth rates during the 1930s; (2) increased labor force participation of women; and (3) the large-scale entry into the labor force during the 1960s of the less-trained segments of the postwar baby boom generation, which augmented the supply of labor for low-wage occupations—whereas those members of this population group who had gone on to college did not begin to enter the full-time labor force in large numbers until the close of the decade.

From this brief discussion, it will be apparent that most of the empirical assessments of occupational wage trends have identified changes in the composition and characteristics of the work force as important determinants of change in the structure of occupational wage differences. However, these analyses have suffered from common limitations due to inadequacies of historical wage data, of related data on characteristics of the work force in various occupations, and of other relevant labor market parameters. Thus, explanations offered for either narrowing of wage differentials (prior to the 1950s) or stable or widening wage differentials (since the 1950s) have typically been advanced as reasonable inferences or hypotheses, rather than as empirically verified conclusions.

In the present chapter we shall attempt to further explore this relationship, in the context of our special interest in lower-level occupations. Two sets of analyses have been conducted for this purpose. The first further examines 1960–70 occupational wage trends for broad occupational groups, utilizing CPS data on earnings of full-time year-round workers as the measure of wage rate change. Our objective in this analysis is to determine the degree of association between relative wage changes and such factors as relative employment growth and changes in the characteristics of the work force of various occupations. The second is a more intensive analysis of relative wages in selected lower-level occupations, based on a cross-sectional study of interarea differences in such wages in 1969. In the latter analysis, we have again attempted to determine the extent to which variations in the characteristics of the available work force, as distinct from other relevant and measurable labor market factors, have been associated with interarea variations in relative wages.

OCCUPATIONAL WAGE TRENDS, 1960–70

Prior to the 1950s, occupational wage statistics were available only for a small number of occupations, such as the building and printing trades, and were often further limited to those in the unionized sector of the occupation. Empirical studies of longer-term occupational wage trends were therefore limited in scope and typically focused

on wage differentials between the skilled and unskilled in selected
blue-collar occupations or industries. Since the 1950s, the Census
Bureau has conducted annual sample surveys of income of families
and individuals, which have provided data on earnings of workers by
occupation. These data were further refined, beginning in 1958, to
show separately the median earnings of male and female workers
employed full time (35 hours or more) on a year-round basis, that
is, 50-52 weeks, classified by the occupation of the job held longest
by such workers. These data can be used as an approximate measure of occupational wage differences (at least among full-time workers) and thus provide—for the first time—a series covering the full
range of occupations of the labor force. One major limitation of
this data source, however, is the fact that, because of sample size,
these occupational earnings data are available only for large occupational groupings or subgroups. Thus, for any comparison of 1960-70
trends, full-time year-round earnings data have been published for
only 19 separate occupational groups, for male workers, and for 13
groups, for female workers. These correspond to the standard major
census occupational groups, with some further limited disaggregation
within such large groups as operatives, male craftsmen, and female
clerical workers.

These trends are shown in Table 4.1 for men and women by the
major census occupational groups. Relative earnings indices have been
computed for 1960 and 1970, expressing the median earnings of men
and women in a given occupational group relative to the corresponding
medians for all male and female year-round full-time workers. Inspection of this table indicates a high degree of stability in the overall
structure of occupational wage differentials between the two years.
The rank ordering of earnings by major occupational group for men and
women remained virtually unchanged between 1960 and 1970 and the
standard deviations of occupational earnings—based on the full range
of 19 male occupations and 13 female occupations—were found not to
differ significantly between 1960 and 1970. Nevertheless, there were
some significant intergroup differences in relative earnings growth
rates, as measured by the ratio of the 1970 relative earnings index
to that for 1960. Generally, relative earnings growth was greater
than average both among certain of the more highly-paid occupations,
such as professional and managerial workers, and some of the lowest-
paid occupational groups, such as male workers in farm occupations
and female workers in private household and sales jobs. In contrast,
blue-collar workers, as well as clerical workers of both sexes, experienced a less-than-average growth in relative earnings. Earnings
of male and female service workers, other than those in private
households, grew at an approximately average rate, as did earnings
of male sales workers.

TABLE 4.1

Median Annual Earnings of Year-Round, Full-Time Workers and
Indices of Change in Relative Earnings, by Occupational
Group, Male and Female: 1960-70

	Earnings		Relative Earnings Indices		
Occupational Group	1960	1970	1960	1970	Change (1960 = 100)
Males, total	$5,368	$8,966	100.0	100.0	100
Professional and technical workers	7,115	12,255	132.5	136.7	103
Managers, proprietors, and officials, nonfarm	6,648	11,665	123.8	130.1	105
Clerical workers	5,291	8,652	98.6	96.1	97
Sales workers	5,842	9,765	108.8	108.9	100
Craftsmen and foremen	5,826	9,253	108.5	103.2	95
Operatives	4,997	7,644	93.1	85.3	92
Laborers, excluding mine and farm	4,017	6,462	74.8	72.1	96
Service workers, excluding private household	4,088	6,964	76.2	77.7	102
Farmers and farm managers	2,004	3,881	37.3	43.3	116
Farm laborers and foremen	1,686	3,355	31.4	37.4	119
Females, total	3,257	5,323	100.0	100.0	100
Professional and technical workers	4,358	7,850	133.8	147.5	110
Managers, proprietors, and officials, nonfarm	3,514	6,369	107.9	119.7	111
Clerical workers	3,575	5,539	109.8	104.1	95
Sales workers	2,389	4,174	73.3	78.4	107
Operatives	2,969	4,465	91.2	83.9	92
Private household workers	1,156	1,990	35.5	37.4	105
Service workers, excluding private household	2,340	3,875	71.8	72.8	101

Note: Earnings data not shown for occupational groups with low sample size, for example, male private household workers.

Source: U.S. Department of Commerce, Bureau of the Census, Current Population Reports—Consumer Income, Series P-60, no. 39 (Washington, D.C.: U.S. Government Printing Office, 1963).

215

An initial hypothesis we attempted to test was one which presumed that these differential occupational wage changes could be explained by differential changes in labor demand, as reflected in actual employment trends. This hypothesis is consistent with one which assumes a significant degree of occupational mobility in labor supply and that wages do operate—under these conditions—as an effective mechanism for allocation of labor among various categories of occupations. Relative employment growth indices, as derived in Table 4.2, have been compared with the corresponding earnings growth indices, in Table 4.4. A direct comparison of the rank ordering of these two indices provides very little support for this hypothesis. Using a crude measure of rank correspondence, of ± 1, only five out of ten male occupational groups, and one out of seven female occupational groups, satisfied this test. Among the male occupations, the two farm occupational groups—farmers and farm managers, and farm laborers and foremen—had experienced the most rapid employment decline and also the most rapid increase in relative earnings. Conversely, craftsmen ranked second in employment growth but next to last in terms of relative earnings growth. Among female occupations, clerical workers ranked second in employment growth but next to last in earnings growth, whereas the reverse pattern applied to women in the managerial occupations. Female private household workers, whose employment had dropped sharply over the decade, had, at the same time, experienced an above-average growth in earnings. These comparisons—although based on a very limited number of observations—are sufficient to suggest that factors other than changes in relative demand played a major role in differential occupational wage rate changes over the 1960s.

A second hypothesis which we subjected to this crude test was that differential wage rate changes were a function of changes in the tightness of the labor market for various occupations, as measured by differential changes in unemployment rates of experienced workers in each occupational group between 1960 and 1970. As shown in Table 4.3, the overall pattern of unemployment rate differentials among occupational groups had remained fairly stable between 1960 and 1970, with no change in rank ordering. White-collar occupations—normally characterized by relatively low unemployment rates—did experience relatively higher unemployment rates in 1970 than in 1960, possibly due in part to the 1969-70 cutback in defense employment, with its large white-collar component. Conversely, most blue-collar and service worker occupations experienced a somewhat less-than-average increase in their unemployment rates. Again, a simple comparison of the rank orderings in Table 4.4 provides no support for the hypothesis of an inverse relationship between unemployment and wage rates. Only two male occupational groups (sales workers,

TABLE 4.2

Annual Average Employment and Relative Employment Growth Indices, by Occupational Group and Sex: 1960-70

Occupational Group	Employment (000)		Employment Index, 1970 (1960 = 100)	Relative Employment Growth Index
	1960	1970		
Males, total	44,485	48,960	110.0	100
Professional and technical workers	4,768	6,841	143.5	130
Managers, proprietors, and officials, nonfarm	5,967	6,968	116.8	106
Clerical workers	3,154	3,482	110.4	100
Sales workers	2,707	2,763	102.1	93
Craftsmen and foremen	8,338	9,826	117.8	107
Operatives	8,652	9,605	111.0	101
Laborers, excluding mine and farm	3,583	3,589	100.1	91
Service workers, excluding private household	2,873	3,245	112.9	103
Farmers and farm managers	2,670	1,670	62.7	57
Farm laborers and foremen	1,728	928	53.7	49
Females, total	22,196	29,666	133.7	100
Professional and technical workers	2,706	4,298	158.8	119
Managers, proprietors, and officials, nonfarm	1,099	1,320	120.1	89
Clerical workers	6,629	10,233	154.4	115
Sales workers	1,695	2,091	123.4	92
Operatives	3,333	4,304	129.1	97
Private household workers	2,171	1,519	70.0	52
Service workers, excluding private household	3,260	4,909	150.6	113

Source: U.S. Department of Labor, Bureau of Labor Statistics, Employment and Earnings (Washington, D.C.: U.S. Government Printing Office, 1971).

TABLE 4.3

Unemployment Rates and Indices of Change in Unemployment
Rate Differentials for Workers in the Experienced
Civilian Labor Force, by Occupational Group,
Male and Female: 1960-70

Occupational Group	Unemployment Rates 1960	Unemployment Rates 1970	Relative Unemployment Indices 1960	Relative Unemployment Indices 1970	Change (1960 = 100)
Males, total	4.9	3.9	100.0	100.0	100
Professional and technical workers	1.7	1.8	34.7	46.2	133
Managers, proprietors, and officials, nonfarm	1.3	1.2	26.5	30.8	116
Clerical workers	3.8	3.4	77.6	87.2	112
Sales workers	2.7	2.7	55.1	69.2	126
Craftsmen and foremen	5.2	3.8	106.1	97.4	92
Operatives	7.0	5.9	142.9	151.3	106
Service workers, excluding private household	5.9	5.1	120.4	130.8	109
Farm laborers and foremen	6.0	6.0	122.4	153.8	126
Laborers, excluding farm and mine	12.4	9.4	253.1	241.0	95
Females, total	5.1	5.0	100.0	100.0	100
Professional and technical workers	1.7	2.3	33.3	46.0	138
Managers, proprietors, and officials, nonfarm	1.7	2.1	33.3	42.0	126
Clerical workers	3.8	4.3	74.5	86.0	115
Sales workers	5.2	5.3	102.0	106.0	104
Operatives	10.5	9.5	205.9	190.9	92
Private household workers	4.9	4.3	96.1	86.0	89
Service workers, excluding private household	6.1	5.7	119.6	114.0	95

Sources: Data for 1960 are from U.S. Department of Labor, Bureau of Labor Statistics, Employment and Earnings (Washington, D.C.: U.S. Government Printing Office, November 1961), p. 103; 1970, from Bureau of Labor Statistics, Handbook of Labor Statistics, 1973 (Washington, D.C.: U.S. Government Printing Office, 1974), p. 149.

TABLE 4.4

Comparison of Indices of Change in Relative Earnings,
Employment Growth, and Unemployment Rates,
1960-70

Occupational Group	Relative Earnings Change		Relative Employment Growth		Relative Unemployment Growth	
	Index	Rank	Index	Rank	Index	Rank (inverse order)
Males, total	100	—	100	—	100	—
Professional and technical workers	103	4	130	1	133	9
Managers, proprietors, and officials, nonfarm	105	3	106	3	116	6
Clerical workers	97	7	100	6	112	5
Sales workers	100	6	93	7	126	7.5
Craftsmen and foremen	95	9	107	2	92	1
Operatives	92	10	101	5	106	3
Laborers, excluding mine and farm	96	8	91	8	95	2
Service workers, excluding private household	102	5	103	4	109	4
Farmers and farm managers	116	2	57	9	—	—
Farm laborers and foremen	119	1	49	10	126	7.5
Females, total	100	—	100	—	100	—
Professional and technical workers	110	2	119	1	138	7
Managers, proprietors, and officials, nonfarm	111	1	89	6	126	6
Clerical workers	95	6	115	2	115	5
Sales workers	107	3	92	5	104	4
Operatives	92	7	97	4	92	2
Private household workers	105	4	52	7	89	1
Service workers, excluding private household	101	5	113	3	95	3

Source: Compiled by the author from data in Tables 4.1-4.3.

service workers) and two female groups (clerical workers, sales workers) showed a close correspondence ($\pm$ 1) in their relative earnings and their relative unemployment rate change rankings.

In order to further test the relationship between 1960-70 earnings changes and various labor supply and demand variables, a series of multiple regressions was conducted, using as the dependent variable in each case, the percentage change in year-round full-time wage and salary income (ΔW_i) in the 19 occupations (for men) and the 13 occupations (for women) for which such data were published by the Census Bureau. To minimize sampling errors, earnings averages for 1959-61 and 1969-71 were used. These were tested iteratively in various models in relation to the following independent variables:

1. percent employment change in occupation, 1960-70 (ΔN_i)
2. unemployment rate change in occupation, 1960-70 (ΔUNR_i)
3. change in percentage of women employed in occupation, 1960-70 (ΔFN_i)
4. change in percentage of nonwhites employed in occupation, 1960-70 (ΔNW_i)
5. change in percentage employed part time in occupation, 1960-70 (ΔPT_i)
6. change in median educational attainment in occupation, 1960-70 (ΔED_i)
7. percent of workers in occupation who were union members in 1970 ($UNION_i$).

Data for these variables were derived from the census CPS reports, supplemented by decennial census data. We postulated that earnings growth would vary positively with employment growth and with the growth in the educational level of the occupation's work force, but that it would vary inversely with the change in the proportion of women, of nonwhites, and of youth and/or part-time workers in the occupation. Because of the very small number of observations and of problems of intercorrelation, only three or four of the above variables could be included in any one test.

The results generally confirmed the findings based on our initial inspection of earnings changes by major occupational group, that is, that no simple model could satisfactorily explain the changes in relative earnings between 1960 and 1970, for relatively broad occupational groupings. The amount of variance explained ($\bar{R}^2$) did not exceed .34 in any of these tests. More important, the few labor supply variables which met or approached the accepted confidence levels did not perform consistently in the separate models for male and female workers.

These limitations are illustrated by the results of two of the regressions which provided among the highest $\bar{R}^2$ values for men and women, respectively, of those tested:

Males (19 occupations)

$$\Delta W_i = .6832^{**} + .2002 \ \Delta N_i$$

$$(18.1) \qquad (1.57)$$

$$-4.1465 \Delta NW^{**} + .0152 \Delta UNR_i$$

$$(-3.01) \qquad\qquad (1.51)$$

$$\bar{R}^2 = .26$$
$$f(3.15) = 3.129 \qquad\qquad\qquad (4.1)$$

Females (13 occupations)

$$\Delta W_i = .2149^{**} - .2367 \Delta N^{**} + 1.6902 \ \Delta NW^{**}$$

$$(3.00) \qquad (-2.15) \qquad\quad (2.61)$$

$$-1.9243 \Delta PT^*$$
$$(-1.94)$$

$$\bar{R}^2 = .34$$
$$f(3.9) = 3.068 \qquad\qquad\qquad (4.2)$$

In equation 4.1, for male workers, the only explanatory variable which met standard tests of significance, at the .90 confidence level (indicated by one asterisk) or higher (two asterisks), was the relative growth of nonwhite workers in the occupation. Although the sign was in the expected negative direction, the magnitude of the influence of shift in racial composition was found to be small: a one percentage point increase in the average percentage of nonwhite men in occupations was, on the average, associated with a reduction of .05 percentage points in the growth of male earnings. Employment growth also varied in the expected direction, for men, although its effect was also very small and it marginally failed to meet the .90 confidence level.

In equation 4.2, for female workers, three variables were found to be significant: employment growth, the change in percentage of nonwhites, and the change in the percentage of part-time workers. However, two of these variables—employment growth and change in percentage of nonwhites—varied in the opposite direction from that postulated and which had been observed in equation 4.1, for men.

Only one variable—growth in percentage of part-time workers—had the expected negative effect upon growth in earnings of full-time year-round workers. One additional variable for women—the relative change in educational level—tested significantly, in a separate formulation, but this was in the negative direction; that is, greater relative growth in the educational attainment of women in a given occupational group was associated with a lesser relative increase in earnings.

The lack of generalizable findings from this necessarily limited analysis simply tends to confirm the findings of other studies of trends in the wage structure. For example, a study by the Organization for Economic Cooperation and Development covering mainly post-World War II experience in ten countries, including the United States, had found some evidence of a positive association between employment and wage growth in particular industries and occupations, but in general found that "there is no evidence of a strong systematic statistical relationship between changes in earnings among individual industries and variations in total employment. . . . Moreover, in most instances where the data provide evidence of a statistically significant relationship, it is clear that the explanatory role of relative wages is overshadowed by the influence of other factors."[3]

It is, of course, possible to offer reasonable explanations for some of the differential occupational wage trends during the decade of the 1960s, based on specific factors relevant in each occupation or industry. Thus, the rapid growth in earnings of professional workers during the 1960s is explainable by the strong expansion of demand in such fields as teaching and engineering, and the limited growth in supply of college graduates, as a result of the relatively small size of the age group reaching college graduation age during most of this decade. Occupations such as clerical jobs, on the other hand, experienced a much smaller relative wage growth because they were able to utilize the much larger and growing pool of female workers (of all ages), who were not college graduates and who regarded these jobs as preferable to blue-collar or service occupations. At the other extreme of the occupational spectrum, relatively large percentage increases in earnings for certain low-wage occupations—such as male farm workers and female household workers—in the face of sharp reductions in employment, suggested that large-scale withdrawals of workers from these occupations and reluctance of young workers to enter these low-wage, low-status occupations may have been the decisive factors. Finally, expansion of coverage of minimum wage laws during the 1960s to several million additional workers may have contributed to the larger-than-average increases in earnings for certain other low-wage groups such as female sales and service workers.

Interarea Differences in Relative Wages

Our second approach to analysis of occupational wage differentials was based on a series of cross-sectional models, limited to a number of more specific lower-level occupations. A total of 10 occupation/sex categories were selected for this purpose: chambermaids and maids (female); cleaning service workers (male); cooks (male and female); construction laborers (male); hospital attendants (male and female); laundry and dry cleaning operatives (male and female); sewers and stitchers (female). Of these occupations, all but two are classified in our status group 5, and these accounted for approximately 30 percent of the experienced civilian labor force in group 5 occupations in 1970. The remaining two occupations—hospital attendants and sewers and stitchers—fall within the group 4 category. The selection of specific occupations was based on two main considerations:

1. Data availability—all occupations selected are widely distributed geographically; hence, published census employment data were available on them in all, or nearly all, of the metropolitan areas selected for analysis.
2. Industry concentration—these occupations are highly concentrated in one or two major (two-digit) industries, thus reducing the degree of interarea wage variation which might be attributable to interarea differences in industry mix.

Additional considerations in selection of occupations for this analysis were assurance of a range of occupations reflecting differing labor force characteristics (that is, predominantly male, predominantly female, or with a mixed sex composition) and difference in growth characteristics (that is, expanding versus contracting occupations).

A fully articulated econometric analysis of the labor market for these occupations would logically require a simultaneous model in which (1) labor demand in a specific occupation and area is expressed as a function of wages and of various demand-specific variables (for example, number of households, family income, industry mix); (2) labor supply is expressed as a function of wages and of the various relevant labor supply factors (for example, sociodemographic characteristics of the area's labor force, alternative labor market opportunities); and (3) occupational wage rates in turn are determined as a function of the relevant labor supply and demand equations. Such a system of equations did not prove to be feasible for present purposes. One of the technical limitations encountered was the difficulty in obtaining a valid measure of labor supply by occupation. This can

differ significantly from reported statistics on either employment or
experienced civilian labor force, by occupation. The latter is simply
the sum of employed workers in a given occupation and experienced
unemployed workers last employed in that occupation. The latter in
turn clearly need not correspond to the number actually available for
or seeking work in a given occupation at a given wage level, or at
varying wage levels.

As an alternative, a reduced-form wage equation was employed,
which includes as explanatory variables a combination of variables
hypothesized to affect labor supply and labor demand in various occupations, but which only purports to identify the most significant influ-
ential variables. To illustrate, it appeared reasonable to include a
variable such as family income in our model, because of its possible
relevance to labor supply of secondary family members and because
of its relevance to labor demand, notably in personal service occupations such as laundry workers. The reduced-form equation does not
however permit us to isolate each of these influences, only the net
effect.

The dependent variable for this model was the ratio of earnings
of full-year workers in the given occupation to a standardized earnings
measure for each area. The latter was computed separately for men
and women, based on an average of earnings of full-year workers in
16 male occupations and in 13 female occupations. National employment totals by occupational group, and for detailed occupations were
used as the weighting factors. These occupations include a range of
nonprofessional and nonmanagerial jobs typically found in all larger
metropolitan areas.* The resulting averages may be considered as

---

*Algebraically, $W_{ij}/W_{STD} = \dfrac{\sum\limits_{i=1}^{n} N_{iUS} \cdot W_{ij}}{\sum\limits_{i=1}^{n} N_{iUS}}$

where N_{iUS} is the share of occupation i in the respective census
occupational group (sales clerks nationally ÷ total female sales
workers nationally, for example), W_{ij} is as defined above. The occupations used for females included clerks; bookkeepers; secretaries;
assemblers; checkers, examiners, and inspectors; laundry and dry
cleaning operatives; packers and wrappers; sewers and stitchers;
miscellaneous operatives in durable goods manufacturing; cleaning
service workers; food service workers; health service workers; and

reasonable approximations of general occupational earnings differentials among standard metropolitan statistical areas (SMSAs) for full-year workers. In turn, the ratio of the earnings of workers, in a specific occupation, to this standardized earnings measure (W_{ij}/W_{STD}) provides a uniform measure of relative earnings in the given occupation.

We hypothesized that relative wages in lower-level occupations were a function of the following types of variables: (1) race and ethnic composition of the occupation and/or SMSA; (2) relative labor market opportunities of minority groups in the SMSA; (3) age composition of the occupation's and/or SMSA's labor force; (4) educational attainment of workers in the occupation and/or SMSA; (5) general labor market conditions in the SMSA; (7) average payments of aid to families with dependent children (AFDC) in the SMSA; (8) extent of unionization of the occupation; and (9) selected other occupation-specific variables which might account for differences in relative wages.

The data base for this model consisted mainly of published 1970 decennial census data for 68 SMSAs with populations of 250,000 or more. SMSAs, rather than states, were selected as the geographical unit of observation because of their greater relevance for labor market analysis. The limitation of the sample SMSAs was dictated by the fact that the 1970 census did not include published labor force data by occupation for smaller SMSAs. Moreover, since the census does not include published data on work force characteristics by occupation, or by race, for those SMSAs where the frequency of a given occupation (or characteristic) is below certain thresholds, the actual number of areas included in the equations for specific occupations ranged between 57 and 66.

In view of the exploratory nature of the model being tested, two or more alternative formulations of many of the sets of variables surveyed above were included in our data base. For example, the racial/ethnic composition measures used included (1) percent of black workers employed in the specified occupation $(PCTBLK_{ij})$; (2) percent of black workers in the area's labor force $(PCTBLK_j)$; (3) percent of Spanish-origin workers in the area's labor force; and

---

private household workers. For males the occupational groups included sales representatives, retail trade; salesmen, retail trade; clerical workers, total; construction craftsmen; automobile mechanics; metal craftsmen, excluding mechanics; assemblers; welders and flamecutters; machine operatives; miscellaneous specified; operatives, miscellaneous machinery, including electrical; truck drivers and deliverymen; construction laborers; freight stock and material handlers; cleaning service workers; food service workers; protective service workers.

TABLE 4.5

List of Independent Variables Tested in
Reduced-Form Wage Equation Models

Variable	Description
Race/ethnic group	
$PCTBLK_j$	Percent of blacks (sex-specific) in standard metropolitan statistical area (SMSA) labor force, 1970
$PCTBLK_{ij}$	Percent of blacks in occupation, 1970
$\dfrac{PCTBLK_{ij}}{PCTBLK_j}$	Relative concentration of blacks in occupation, 1970
$MEBRELW_j$	Ratio of median earnings of black to white year-round workers in SMSA, 1969
$PCTLFSPO_j$	Percent of Spanish-origin workers in labor force of SMSA, 1970*
$PCTFBLA_j$	Percent of persons in SMSA who are foreign born and of Latin American origin, 1970
$\Delta\ NWPOP60 - 70_j$	Change in percentage of nonwhite persons in SMSA population, 1960–70
Age	
$PCTYOUTH_j$	Percent of persons (sex-specific), ages 16–24, in SMSA labor force, 1970
$PCTYOUTH_{ij}$	Percent of persons (sex-specific), ages 16–24 in occupation, 1970
$\dfrac{PCTYOUTH_{ij}}{PCTYOUTH_j}$	Relative concentration of youth (sex-specific), occupation, 1970
$LEPR16 - 24_j$	Civilian labor force participation rate of persons, 16–24 years of age (sex-specific), 1970
$LEPR25 +_j$	Civilian labor force participation rate of persons, 25 years and older (sex-specific), 1970
Education	
$PCTED12P_j$	Percent of SMSA labor force with 12 or more years of education (sex-specific), 1970
$\dfrac{BLKED12P_j}{CLF_j}$	Percent of blacks in total SMSA labor force with 12 or more years of education relative to persons in the labor force (sex-specific), 1970
$BRELWED12P_j$	Percent of blacks in SMSA labor force with 12 or more years of education relative to percent of whites with 12 or more years of education (sex-specific), 1970
Age/education	
$(PCTYOUTH_{ij})\times$ $(PECTED12P_j)$	Percent of those in occupation, 16–24 years of age, weighted by percent of SMSA labor force with 12 or more years of education (sex-specific), 1970

Variable	Description
Labor market	
UNR_j	SMSA unemployment rate (sex-specific), 1970
$PCTM16-21NISNILF_j$	Percent of males in SMSA, 16-21 years of age, who are not in school and unemployed or not in labor force, 1970
Income/earnings	
$INCFAMH_j$	Median annual income of families with male head, in SMSA, 1969
$AFDC_j$	Average monthly benefit from aid to families with dependent children, by SMSA, 1972
$PCTHIW_j$	Percent of SMSA labor force employed in selected high-wage industries (sex-specific), 1970
$MEDFAMINCOME_j$	Median family income in SMSA, 1969
$MEDEABM_j$	Median earnings of nonwhite males in SMSA, 1969
Region	
$SOUTH_j$	Southeast, Southwest SMSAs = 1; otherwise = 0
Unionization	
$PCTUNION_{ij}$	Union membership (selected unions) as ratio to employed workers in occupation, by state, 1970
Growth	
$\Delta EMP60-70_{ij}$	Percent change in SMSA occupational employment, 1960-70
Industry mix	
$PCTSSRHOTELS_j$	Retail expenditures on hotels and lodgings relative to selected services, by SMSA, 1967
$PCTSSREATDRK_j$	Percent of total retail sales receipts due to eating and drinking establishments, by SMSA, 1967
$PCTMULTIFAM_j$	Percent of families living in multiunit dwellings in SMSA, 1970
MIX_j	Value of new residential construction relative to value of new nonresidential construction in SMSA, 1970

*Spanish origin based on Spanish surname or Spanish language use.

Sources: Except as otherwise specified, all data for this and subsequent tables are from Bureau of the Census, Census of Population, 1970 (various volumes), and Country and City Date Book, 1972. Estimates of union membership by state, for selected unions, from unpublished BLS data. Estimates of residential and nonresidential construction by SMSA (MIX_j) from unpublished data, Construction Division, Bureau of the Census.

(4) percent of foreign-born workers of Latin American origin in the area's labor force. In all, a total of 30 separate independent variables were incorporated into our data base, as specified in Table 4.5.

Although the data base provided by the detailed 1970 census area labor force data was reasonably comprehensive it still presented a number of important limitations for our purposes:

1. Annual earnings of all workers employed 50-52 weeks in 1969, classified by their principal occupations in 1969, served as our proxy for relative wage rates.* This measure thus includes earnings of workers who were employed year-round, but on a part-time basis, in contrast to the CPS annual earnings data for full-time year-round workers, cited earlier in this chapter. The unavailability of occupational earnings data classified by annual hours worked required an assumption that full-year workers in a given occupation worked the same number of hours per year in each area. The magnitude of the possible resulting biases is suggested by CPS data on work experience of persons, 14 years and over, with earnings in 1969. Of all such workers who worked year-round, that is, 50-52 weeks in 1969, 6.2 percent of all males and 18.4 percent of all females, worked at part-time jobs.[4] This implies a larger potential bias in our relative wage measure for female than for male occupations. From collateral information, it is also reasonable to infer that the bias is greater, generally, in those lower-level occupations with a high proportion of part-time workers, such as cooks or cleaning service workers. (See Table 3.28.)

2. The detailed census occupational classifications, although more useful than the broad occupational groups used in our analysis of 1960-70 earnings changes, were still too broad in most cases for careful measurement of occupational earnings differentials by area. For example, sewers and stitchers in the New York City area include a large proportion of skilled workers employed in the high fashion segments of the apparel industry; those employed in the South include a higher proportion of less-skilled workers employed in the more standard mass production components of the industry, such as work clothing and men's shirts.

3. Demand-specific variables associated with the selected low-level occupations could not be adequately specified in most cases.

---

*Unfortunately, with very limited exceptions, no alternative direct measures of wage rates or hourly earnings for these occupations were available, corresponding in occupational coverage and in area detail to the Census data on characteristics of the work force by occupation.

The absence of an occupation/industry matrix at the SMSA level was a significant handicap in our analysis of those occupations which are distributed among two or more industries with differing industry wage structures. (Certain proxy variables on industry mix were introduced, however, for some of the occupations, where pertinent data were available.)

4. Unionization—which is recognized as an important variable in most wage structure studies—could only be estimated indirectly and partially from available BLS data. Geographical distributions of union membership, if available at all, are normally limited to the state level. In most instances, there is no precise correspondence between the jurisdiction of a given union and a specific census occupation or industry. To develop a measure for this potentially important variable we were thus compelled to use the ratio of state membership in the union identified as including the largest number of members in a particular occupation or industry, and the employment in that occupation or industry, by state, as reported in the 1970 census.

Our final methodological note concerns the estimation of the reduced-form wage equation. A stepwise regression technique was employed, rather than a fixed model. Its effect was to include the maximum number of significant variables—among the whole range of variables available—which contributed to the explanation of inter-area variations in relative earnings for the specified occupations. This form excludes certain variables—which although separately significant—do not contribute to maximization of explained variance.

The results of this analysis are presented in summary form in Table 4.6. Of the variables included in our data base, only 19 variables, grouped under ten broader categories, met our tests of significance in one or more of the ten occupation/sex categories, and no more than five explanatory variables were included in an equation for any single occupation. All of the resulting equations met statistical tests of significance at the .99 confidence level with coefficients of determination ($\bar{R}^2$) ranging from .69 for male construction laborers, to only .16 for female sewers and stitchers.

The elasticities in Table 4.5 measure the impact, for example, of a one percent variation in a specified significant variable upon changes in relative wages (at the mean)—holding other factors constant. An inspection of this table indicates that, for the limited range of occupations under study, the influence of various labor market factors upon relative wages is quite variable. These results are discussed below for each of the major categories of variables.

TABLE 4.6

Reduced-Form Wage Equation Elasticities for Significant Variables, Calculated at Means (Dependent Variable: $W_{ij}/WSTD_j$)

Occupational Category	Race/Ethnic				Age			Education		Age/Education
	$PCTBLK_{ij}$	$\Delta NWPOP$ $60-70_j$	$PCTLFSPO_j$	$\dfrac{FYEB_j}{FYEW_j}$	$PCTYOUTH_{ij}$	$\dfrac{PCTYOUTH_{ij}}{PCTYOUTH_j}$	$LFPR16\text{-}24_j$	$PCTED12_{ij}$	$\dfrac{PCT}{BLKED12_j}$	$PCTYOUTH_{ij}$ $\times PCTED12_{ij}$
Male										
Hospital attendants	—	—	.034[a]	—	—	—	-.371[c]	-.542[b]	—	—
Construction laborers	-.302[a]	—	—	.356[a]	—	-.112[a]	—	—	—	—
Cooks	—	.042[a]	—	—	-.165[a]	—	—	—	-.045[a]	—
Laundry and dry cleaning operatives	-.088[a]	—	—	—	-.054[a]	—	—	—	—	—
Cleaning service workers	-.073[a]	—	—	.324[b]	—	—	—	—	—	—
Female										
Hospital attendants	—	—	—	—	—	—	-.599[a]	—	—	—
Sewers and stitchers	.023[b]	—	—	—	—	—	—	—	—	—
Cooks	.042[b]	—	—	—	-.271[b]	—	.250[a]	—	-.081[a]	—
Charwomen, chambermaids	—	—	—	—	-.107[a]	—	—	—	-.068[b]	—
Laundry and dry cleaning operatives	—	—	-.008[b]	—	—	—	—	—	—	—

	Labor Market		Income		Region	Unionization	Growth	Industry Mix		
Occupational Category	UNR_j	PCTM16-21 NISNILF	$FAMINC_j$	$AFDC_j$	$SOUTH_j$	$PCTUNION_j$	$\Delta EMP60\text{-}7Q_j$	PCTSSR $HOTELS_j$	PCTSSR $EATDRK_j$	$\bar{R}$
Male										
Hospital attendants	—	—	—	—	.054[b]	—	—	—	—	.335[a]
Construction laborers	—	—	—	—	—	—	—	—	—	.605[a]
Cooks	—	-.076[b]	—	—	—	—	—	.054[a]	—	.492[a]
Laundry and dry cleaning operatives	—	—	.200[b]	—	—	—	—	—	—	.258[a]
Cleaning service workers	—	—	—	—	—	.010[c]	—	—	—	.690[a]
Female										
Hospital attendants	-.160[b]	—	-.600[a]	—	—	—	—	—	—	.265[a]
Sewers and stitchers	—	—	—	—	.030[a]	.035[b]	—	—	—	.164[a]
Cooks	—	—	—	.071[a]	—	—	—	—	.215[a]	.585[a]
Charwomen, chambermaids	—	—	.471[a]	—	—	-.017[b]	—	—	—	.328[a]
Laundry and dry cleaning operatives	-.099[a]	—	—	—	—	.018[a]	.149[a]	—	—	.298[a]

[a] Significant at .99 level of confidence.
[b] Significant at .95 level of confidence.
[c] Significant at .90 level of confidence.

Source: Compiled by the author.

231

Racial-Ethnic Factors

Based on prevailing theories of the dual or segmented labor market, we hypothesized that relative wages in lower-level occupations would be lower in those areas which included large concentrations of black or Spanish-origin workers in the occupation, particularly where alternative job opportunities for such workers are inferior. Some support for this premise was found in two or three of the male occupations, but in none of the female occupations. A higher concentration of black workers in the occupation ($PCTBLK_{ij}$) was found to be associated with a lower relative wage for that occupation in the case of construction laborers, male laundry and dry cleaning operatives, and male cleaning service workers. The impact on relative wages was considerable for construction laborers (that is, an elasticity of -.302); it was quite small in the remaining two occupations (that is, -.088 for laundry and dry cleaning workers, and -.073 for male cleaning service workers).

For two of these three male occupations, construction laborers and cleaning service workers, the ratio of full-year earnings of all male black workers in the SMSA to those of white workers proved more significant in explaining interarea variations in relative wages than did the proportion of black workers employed, as evidenced by elasticities of .356 and .324, respectively. The latter variable was designed as a measure of relative earnings opportunities for black workers in each area. Hence, this finding implies that—at least in the two specified occupations—as black workers approach parity in labor market opportunity, significant increases in relative wages in certain low-level occupations, in which they have been previously concentrated, may be expected.

The results for the selected female occupations—on the other hand—do not provide any support for the "overcrowding" hypothesis. In fact, in two of the five female occupations analyzed—sewers and stitchers, and cooks—a higher concentration of black female workers in the occupation, in particular areas, was associated with a higher, rather than lower, relative wage, albeit with very low elasticities. This may be due, in part, to the lesser reliability of annual year-round earnings data for women as a wage rate proxy. Moreover, in the case of sewers and stitchers, we believe that the positive relationship of relative wages to percentage of blacks employed may be a consequence of the movement of the apparel industry to southern communities characterized by low general wage levels, and which have also increasingly utilized indigenous black female workers in their labor force, as described in Chapter 6. Hence, the small, but significant, positive relationship between the proportions of black women in sewing occupations and relative wages, may have resulted from the fact that interregional differences in general occupational wage levels (as measured by our standardized occupational wage index) are slightly greater than in the apparel industry alone—possibly as a consequence of such factors as union organization and the minimum wage.

Concentrations of Spanish-origin workers in particular areas also were not found to have the expected negative effect upon relative wages in the selected occupations. In one occupation—male hospital attendants—a larger proportion of Spanish-origin workers was associated with slightly higher relative wages, possibly reflecting either employer preferences for such workers (as compared to blacks) or the fact that Spanish-origin workers, including many later immigrants, have tended to move into expanding or labor-short occupations.

Youth

A larger supply of youthful workers aged 16-24 years was expected to have a depressing effect upon wage levels in low-level occupations, on the premise that youth without specialized training—in common with minority workers—tend to be overcrowded in these occupations. Moreover, it would be reasonable to expect an adverse differential for youth, even in less-skilled jobs, because of their lesser experience and productivity. Several measures of the youth labor supply were included in our data base, that is, the percentage of youth in the specified occupation ($PCTYOUTH_{ij}$); the ratio of the percentage of youth in the occupation to the percentage of youth in the area's labor force as a whole ($PCTYOUTH_{ij}/PCTYOUTH_j$); and the labor force participation rate of youth in each area ($LFPR\ 16\text{-}24_j$). In addition, because of the observed covariation between age and educational attainment by occupation, a compound variable ($PCTYOUTH_{ij} \times PCTED12_{ij}$) was also tested. These youth variables— in varying forms—proved to be significant, and in the expected direction, in almost all of the occupations studied.

The interpretation of these relationships is however clouded by the nature of the dependent variable used. Since we have been obliged to use annual earnings of year-round—but not necessarily full-time workers—as our proxy for occupational wage levels, it is possible that interarea differences in occupational earnings were affected, to some extent, by variations in the proportion of regular part-time workers employed in certain occupations, such as cooks or domestic workers (which typically utilize large proportions of part-time employees). Since youth are a major component of the part-time labor force, the regressions may have reflected interarea variations in hours worked per year, rather than in wage rates. However, in view of the fact that regular part-time workers constitute only 10 percent of the total labor force of workers employed 50-52 weeks, it is possible that though this factor has caused some upward bias in the resulting elasticities, the youth variable would have been significant and in the expected direction even if unbiased estimates of relative wage rates were available. To illustrate, the youth concentration variable proved significant in the wage equation for construction laborers, even though only 6 percent of this occupation's year-round labor force consists of regular part-time workers (based on unpublished BLS data, derived from CPS annual income surveys).

Educational Attainment

We had hypothesized that a more educated labor force would, generally, have the effect of reducing the labor supply and of increasing relative wages in lower-level occupations. Educational attainment, in our model, was measured alternatively as the percentage of workers in each occupation with 12 or more years of education ($PCTED12_{ij}$) and as the percentage of black workers in the area with 12 or more years of education ($PCTBLKED12_j$). The first of these variables ($PCTED12_{ij}$) was found to be significant in relation to relative wages only in the case of male hospital attendants, but with an unexpected negative sign. In three other occupations—male cooks, female cooks, and charwomen and chambermaids—a higher proportion of black workers with 12 or more years of school was also associated with a lower relative wage, although with low elasticities. It is likely that these findings resulted from the inherent difficulty of isolating the separate effect of educational attainment from that of age distribution. In any event, the data provide no support for our hypothesis that an increase in the proportion of high school graduates in the labor force will, per se, result in a reduced labor supply and, hence, higher relative wages for lower-level occupations.

Unemployment

We assumed that areas with higher unemployment rates would tend to have lower relative wages in low-level occupations, other factors being equal. This relationship was validated in two of the five female occupations, hospital attendants and laundry operatives, with elasticities of -.10 and -.16, respectively. It did not prove to be significant for any of the male occupations. An alternative labor market measure, the percentage of males, 16-21 years, who were neither in school nor in the force, did prove to be significant for male laundry operatives, although with a low elasticity (-.08).

Income

Average family incomes or alternative sources of income, such as AFDC, were assumed to have an impact upon relative wage levels in low-level occupations, both through their influence upon labor supply and upon labor demand, in certain of the industries employing workers in such occupations. On the labor supply side, we hypothesized that higher alternative income levels, for example, through earnings of other family members of AFDC, would tend to raise the reserve wage of workers whose job choices were limited to low-level occupations. On the demand side, higher levels of family income were postulated as increasing the demand for personal services, hence, serving also to increase relative wages in occupations, related to personal service activities. Thus, generally, a positive relationship was postulated.

The results for these variables proved to be mixed, however. The family income variable ($FAMINC_j$) met our tests of significance, in the expected positive direction, in only two occupations—male laundry and dry cleaning workers, and charwomen and chambermaids. It was significant, but negative, in the case of female hospital attendants—higher-level group 4 workers. The AFDC variable was significant and positive for only one occupation, female cooks. It should be noted, however, that alternative model formulations for selected occupations, as described in Chapter 6, did identify the AFDC variable as significant in explaining interarea wage and/or employment differentials among two other low-wage female occupations: domestic maids, and sewers and stitchers in southern cities.

Region

A dummy variable identifying southern SMSAs was included in the model on the premise that this variable would reflect the effects of a combination of regional economic and institutional factors, relevant to wage structures, and which were not otherwise adequately specified in the model. BLS area wage studies have consistently shown wider differentials between unskilled and skilled workers' wage rates in the South than in northern cities; hence, a negative sign for the South dummy was expected. This variable proved to be significant in only two of the occupations—male hospital attendants and female sewers and stitchers. In both, the variable was actually positive, but with low elasticities. This would suggest that other more specific variables included in our model, such as racial/ethnic factors, income levels, and degree of unionization, were more important in explaining interarea wage differentials than location in the South, per se.

Unionization

Higher rates of union membership were expected to be positively associated with relative wage levels in our model. As noted earlier, the union membership ratios by area were approximated by state-level ratios of reported membership in selected unions to employment for those occupations or industries where relevant union membership data were available. These unionization ratios were found to be significant in the expected direction in three of the eight occupations for which such ratios could be derived, that is, male cleaning service workers, female sewers and stitchers, and female laundry and dry cleaning operatives. The unexpected negative sign was found in one occupation, charwomen and chambermaids. All elasticities were very low (in the .01 to .03 range), possibly due in part to the inadequacy of the union membership data for our purposes.

Growth

We also hypothesized that a different rate of growth in an occupation between 1960 and 1970, other factors being equal, would be associated with a change, in the same direction, in its relative wages. This proved to be a significant independent variable in only one occupation group, female laundry and dry cleaning operatives, with an elasticity of .15. The reliability of this variable was undoubtedly affected, to some degree, by the effects of the previously mentioned changes in census occupational classification and reporting procedures.

Industry Mix

Proxy variables designed to allow for interarea variations in the industrial distribution of workers by occupation were incorporated in our data base for seven occupation/sex groups. These variables included the percentage of selected service industry receipts coming from hotels and motels (incorporated for cooks, laundry workers, and charwomen and chambermaids); the percentage of total retail sales receipts from eating and drinking establishments (for cooks) and the ratio of the value of residential to that of nonresidential structures (for construction laborers). The mix variable proved significant for cooks, indicating that higher relative concentrations of hotels or eating and drinking establishments in an area were associated with higher relative wages for cooks. In separate models, described in Chapter 6, the residential-nonresidential mix proved to be a significant variable in explaining interarea differentials for construction laborers. Moreover, from collateral information, it is probable that introduction of detailed industry distributional data

for sewers and stitchers would have considerably improved the effi-
ciency of our relative wage model for that occupation group as well.

SOME TENTATIVE CONCLUSIONS

In this chapter, we have attempted to develop quantitative measures of the relationship between specified labor supply variables and
occupational wage structures based both on a comparison of changes
by broad occupational groups, for the 1960-70 decade, and on a more
detailed comparison of interarea differences in relative earnings in
1969, for selected lower-level occupations. Any attempt to generalize
from these findings must be carefully qualified in view of the many
limitations of the available data base and of our model specifications.
The following observations must therefore be interpreted as tentative
findings, supported by some empirical data.

Generally, our analysis has tended to confirm findings of other
investigations concerning the relative stability of occupational wage
structures, at least over relatively short time spans, such as a decade.
Thus, the substantial changes in labor supply during the decade of the
1960s were accompanied by only limited changes in relative wages for
major occupational groups. Similarly, our cross-sectional analysis
for 1969-70 generally resulted in relatively low elasticities for those
labor supply variables which proved to be significant. It is probable
that many institutional factors impinging upon the wage-setting processes, as well as a relatively high degree of adaptability of the labor
force, contributed to the general overall stability of the occupational
wage structure.

Nevertheless, both the 1960-70 comparisons and the cross-sectional analyses have provided significant indications of labor supply
impacts upon relative wages in specific occupations—and, by inference—upon occupational employment levels, as well. Some of these
indications are described below.

Hired farm laborers and private household workers both experienced greater-than-average wage increases in the decade of the 1960s,
despite sharp reductions in their employment levels. Both of these
occupations have been at or near the bottom of the occupational hierarchy in terms of pay and status; they have relied upon blacks and
other disadvantaged population groups for their labor supply in the
past. Neither occupation was covered by minimum wage laws or was
unionized to any appreciable extent during this decade. It is reasonable to infer that the increase in relative earnings and some portion
of the employment reduction in both occupations were direct consequences of the expansion of job opportunities for many of these work-

ers in higher-wage, higher-status occupations, as well as of the reluctance of young minority group members to work as farm laborers or in households. (For a more detailed analysis of the labor supply of domestic maids, see Chapter 6.)

Our analyses also provided some partial support for the overcrowding hypothesis, that is, that the concentration of black workers in low-status occupations has had the effect of reducing relative wages in such occupations. The supporting evidence was however limited to male workers. Thus, in three of the five male low-level occupations included in our cross-sectional model—construction laborers, cleaning service workers, and laundry and dry cleaning operatives—relative wages were lower in those SMSAs where a larger proportion of blacks were employed in these occupations. In the first two of these occupations, we found even more significant positive relationships between a general measure of local labor market opportunities for black male workers (that is, the ratio of their full-year earnings to those of white males), and the relative wage level in the specified occupation. Similarly, our model of occupational wage changes for male workers between 1960 and 1970 established a significant negative relationship between wage growth and the increase in nonwhite employment by occupation. Neither of these findings were found to be applicable in the case of female workers in the limited range of occupations covered by our analyses.

Differential concentrations of youth and/or part-time workers in particular occupations appeared to have had a depressing effect upon earnings of year-round workers in some of these occupations. The evidence for this finding from our cross-sectional analysis is clouded because of the likelihood that these relationships reflected the combined effect of both increased labor supply pressure and lower hours of work, associated with higher utilization of young workers in these jobs. However, our analysis of 1960-70 occupational earnings changes for female workers—limited to those working year-round on full-time jobs—also found that earnings rose less in those occupations which included larger concentrations of part-time workers.

Higher unemployment rates or related indicators of labor market surplus were found to have a significant (but numerically small) depressing effect upon relative wages in three of the ten lower-level occupation/sex groups included in our cross-sectional analysis, but were not found to be a significant explanatory variable in our analysis of occupational wage trends for 1960-70. It should be noted that our cross-sectional data base was limited to unemployment rate observations in a particular week, that is, the 1970 census survey week, and therefore provided—at best—a limited measure of the impact of labor market conditions upon relative wages by occupation.

Finally, we should note that, although we had hypothesized a positive relationship between interarea differences in educational levels of workers in particular lower-level occupations and relative wages, this relationship was not confirmed by our cross-sectional studies. In fact, where significant relationships were found, they were in the (unexpected) negative direction. This may be due in part to the intercorrelation between the educational level and the youth variables in our stepwise regression model. Nevertheless, it is important to note that these analyses—as well as our 1960-70 wage trend analysis—provide no confirmation that an increase in educational attainment of workers will reduce the labor supply and increase the wages of workers in lower-level occupations in the absence of alternative preferred employment opportunities for such workers. Neither of these analyses addressed collateral issues such as the possible impact of overqualification of workers upon job satisfaction or labor turnover.

NOTES

1. For a discussion of these longer-term trends, see particularly: Paul Douglas, Real Wages in the United States, 1890-1920 (1930; reprint ed., Clifton, N. J.: Augusta M. Kelley). Lloyd G. Reynolds and Cynthia H. Tafts, The Evolution of Wage Structure (New Haven: Yale University Press, 1956), pp. 355-58; and Melvin W. Reder, "The Theory of Occupational Wage Differentials," American Economic Review, December 1955, pp. 833-52.

2. Arthur Sackley and Thomas W. Gavett, "Blue-Collar/White-Collar Pay Trends Analysis of Occupational Wage Differences," Monthly Labor Review, June 1971, p. 10.

3. Organization for Economic Cooperation and Development, Wages and Labor Mobility (Paris, 1965), p. 16.

4. U.S. Department of Commerce, Bureau of the Census, "Income in 1969 of Families and Persons in the United States," Current Population Reports, Series P-60, no. 75 (Washington, D. C.: U.S. Government Printing Office, 1970), table 54.

5

**PROJECTIONS OF
OCCUPATIONAL LABOR
SUPPLY AND DEMAND
TO 1985**

At the outset of the present study, we offered a hypothesis that as a result of a number of emerging social and demographic trends, the earlier manpower sources for staffing lower-level occupations, such as blacks, immigrants, rural inmigrants, and other disadvantaged groups in the labor force, were declining, and that continuation of these trends might require a number of significant labor market adjustments to meet anticipated needs of the economy for lower-level manpower in future decades. Our detailed examination of recent trends in occupational labor supply indicated that these trends were operative in the 1960s but that their effect was, at least temporarily, counterbalanced by the exceptionally large inflow of new entrants into the labor force, many of whom replaced nonwhites as well as white adults in the lower-status occupations. As a consequence, our analysis of differential wage trends by occupation and collateral labor market data did not provide any clear indications of supply constraints upon the aggregate level of employment in lower-level occupations during the decade, although employment and wages in specific occupations—such as domestic service and farm labor—were probably influenced by these sociodemographic trends.

Looking at the 1975-85 period, we can however anticipate some significant shifts in the balance of supply and demand factors affecting low-level occupations. On the supply side, there will be a substantial reduction in the rate of inflow of young workers into the labor force from the peak rates of the 1960s, as well as a reduced net inflow of adult women. Further, despite some slowdown in college enrolment rates, the educational attainment of the labor force will continue to rise, as young workers with longer periods of formal schooling replace less-educated older workers in the course of the decade. The outlook is also for a further reduction in the net migration of workers

from farm to city, and for a leveling off—or possible curtailment—
of legal immigration of low-level manpower from nearby Latin American countries, as a result of newly implemented revisions in the
immigration laws. All of these factors will tend to constrain the
overall supply of workers for low-level jobs under conditions of high
aggregate demand for labor.

The first part of this chapter describes the methods used to
project the expected distribution of the labor force, in 1980 and 1985,
by broad occupational status group, taking into account the trends in
occupational distribution of major sociodemographic groups, as well
as the projected changes in labor force composition. These projections are then compared with projections of employment, or labor
requirements, to provide a preliminary assessment of possible occupational imbalances. The final section of the chapter discusses the
probable nature and direction of labor market adjustments which may
be required in various occupations.

EXPECTED DISTRIBUTION OF LABOR FORCE
BY OCCUPATION

The effect of such characteristics as sex, age, education, race,
and nativity upon the occupational distribution of workers has been
systematically described in earlier chapters of this study. Workers
with limited education and work experience, as well as those subject
to various forms of job discrimination because of their racial or ethnic
background, have been constrained in their choices to the less desirable, lower-paying occupations and industries. Conversely, those
with better education and more work experience—and who were not
subject to such job discrimination—have normally been concentrated
in the higher-status occupations and have not been available for lower-
level jobs, at least during periods of high aggregate labor demand.
To illustrate, in 1970 only 1.3 percent of white female workers 25
years and over with 13 years or more of education were in group 5
occupations, as compared to 65.1 percent of nonwhite women with
less than nine years of schooling. (See Table 3.4.)

These patterns, as we have observed, have not been fixed but
have changed over a period of decades in response to shifts in the
composition of the labor force and to changes in the occupational
distribution of available jobs, and due to a number of social and institutional forces. We can expect that in the future—as in the past—the
actual occupational distribution of workers will be the result of a
complex interaction of the many supply and demand variables operating
upon the labor market and of concurrent changes in relative wages.

The extent to which exogenous labor supply variables, such as changes in the age structure of the labor force or in its educational distribution, will influence the future availability of workers for specific occupations or their relative wages can only be partially estimated from available empirical evidence. Nevertheless, from the evidence in Chapter 4, it seems probable that major shifts in these sociodemographic variables will exert a significant impact on labor supply and employment trends in some of these occupations and on the overall availability of workers for lower-level jobs.

From this point of departure, estimates have been developed of the expected distribution of the labor force by broad occupational groups in 1980 and 1985, based on (1) projections of the labor force by age, sex, race, and educational attainment; and (2) projections of occupational participation rates, for each of these population subgroups. The methods and sources used in these projections and the resulting trends are described below.

Labor Force Projections by the Bureau of Labor Statistics

BLS projections to 1985 of the labor force by age, sex, and educational attainment, published in 1973, were adopted as a point of departure.[1] Since the BLS labor force projections referred to the total labor force, including the armed forces, and were on an annual average basis, comparable to annual average CPS data, a further series of adjustments was needed for comparability in coverage and seasonal level to corresponding decennial census statistics for the experienced civilian labor force in 1960 and 1970. A reconciliation between the BLS total labor force projections and our projections of the experienced civilian labor force for March 1980 and March 1985 is presented below:

	1980	1985
Total labor force, annual average, comparable to CPS (millions)	101.8	107.7
Less: armed forces projection	2.0	2.0
Less: adjustment for difference between March 1980 labor force and annual average labor force	3.4	4.2

	1980	1985
Civilian labor force, March 1980	96.4	101.5
Less: experienced workers, occupation not reported	4.3	3.6
Less: inexperienced civilian labor force	0.6	0.4
Experienced civilian labor force, with occupation reported, comparable to decennial census	91.5	97.5

The BLS projections for the total labor force indicate that the overall rate of labor force growth during the 1970–80 decade will be only slightly less than the high growth rate of the 1960s (see Table 5.1), reflecting the continued movement into the labor force of the large post–World War II generation born in the 1950s and early 1960s, as well as further increases in female labor force participation. The rate of labor force growth is, however, expected to decline sharply during the decade of the 1980s, mainly as a result of reduced entries into the labor force, reflecting the sharp reduction in births and birth rates during the 1960–70 decade. As a result the average annual percentage increase (arithmetically computed) will decline from 3.7 percent in the 1970–80 decade to 1.2 percent between 1980 and 1985. The shifts in labor force composition associated with these overall trends are described below.

Age

Labor force growth will be most rapid in the 25–34 age group, reflecting the maturing of those born during the post–World War II baby boom. Workers in this age group, which includes many who have begun or will begin full-time work activity in the 1970s upon completion of school or college, are projected to increase by 51.5 percent between 1970 and 1980 as contrasted to a projected increase of 18.5 percent for the total labor force. Conversely, the number of young workers aged 16–24 years will increase by only 19 percent in the 1970s, reflecting the initial impacts upon the labor force of the slowdown in birth rates which began in the early 1960s. Within the 16–24 age group, the teenage labor force, aged 16–19 years, will experience a particularly sharp reduction in its growth rate, from 46.4 percent in the 1960–70 decade to only 9.1 percent between 1970 and 1980.

This pattern will be intensified during the 1980–85 period, which will experience the full impact upon labor force entries of the birth rate reductions. During this period, the number of 16–19-year-olds

TABLE 5.1

Percent Changes in Total Labor Force, 16 Years
and Over, by Age and Sex: 1960–70, and
Projected for 1970–85

Sex and Age Group	1960–70	1970–80	1980–85
Both sexes	19.1	18.5	5.8
16–19 Years	46.4	9.1	–14.1
20–24 Years	63.7	25.9	–2.8
25–34 Years	17.1	51.5	11.1
35–44 Years	0.1	11.5	23.8
45–54 Years	15.6	–3.4	–0.9
55–64 Years	19.9	13.4	1.1
65 Years and Over	–4.7	2.4	3.1
Men	11.1	15.2	5.5
16–24 Years	45.3	14.8	–6.0
25–54 Years	4.1	18.0	11.4
55 Years and Over	4.7	5.3	0.1
Women	36.2	24.3	6.3
16–24 Years	76.3	26.0	–5.2
25–54 Years	24.4	24.5	12.3
55 Years and Over	33.0	20.9	3.7

Source: Denis F. Johnston, "The U.S. Labor Force: Projections to 1990," Monthly Labor Review, July 1973, table 2, p. 5,
based on annual average data, comparable to CPS.

in the labor force is projected to decline by 14.1 percent, while those
in the 20-24 age group will drop by 2.8 percent. There will also be
a sharp reduction in the rate of growth in the 25-34 age group, from
an average percentage annual increase of 5.2 percent in the 1970s to
2.2 percent in the 1980-85 period.

The sharp reduction in new labor force entrants, implicit in these
comparisons, has an important bearing upon the availability of workers
for lower-level jobs, since—as we have seen—young workers, and
particularly those in the student-age groups, have been a major and
growing source for many of these jobs. It also has broader implications for the extent of adaptability of our labor supply to shifts in the
economy's labor requirements in view of the much greater mobility
of young workers as evidenced by virtually all studies of worker mobility patterns.[2]

Sex

The BLS labor force projection assumes a slowing down in the
overall growth of labor force participation of women during the period
1970-85, as compared to the preceding decade, partly based on the
increased concentration of the female working-age population in the
25-34 group, within which many women have not been available for
work because of child-rearing responsibilities. As a result, women
are expected to account for a smaller percentage of total labor force
gains than in the 1960s. This pattern will be accentuated for the civilian labor force, moreover, in view of the assumed reduction in
armed forces active-duty strengths, from about 3.2 million in 1970
to 2.0 million in 1980 and 1985. Women, particularly those reentering
the labor force after interruptions for marriage and child rearing,
have typically been constrained in their choices to lower-paid jobs,
either in white-collar or in blue-collar or service occupations. Thus,
between 1960 and 1970, there was a net increase of 250,000 in the
number of adult white female workers, 25 years and over, in group
5 occupations. The projected slowdown in growth in this source of
labor supply can be expected to further contribute to a tightened labor
supply situation in many low-status service-type occupations, as well
as in lower-paid clerical and sales occupations, which are predominantly staffed by women.

Race

Based on our projections for the experienced civilian labor force,
the proportion of nonwhite workers will increase from 10.7 percent
in 1970 to 11.3 percent in 1980 and to 11.6 percent in 1985. This
results from a lesser decline in nonwhite, than in white, birth rates

during the early 1960s—and hence, in a larger proportion of nonwhites among new labor force entrants in the late 1970s and 1980s, as well as from an assumed reduction in the rate of decline in labor force participation of nonwhite men, as compared to the 1960-70 experience.

In view of the continued higher concentration of nonwhites in low-status occupations, an increase in their labor force proportion would be expected, other factors being equal, to augment the labor supply for lower-level jobs. This effect is likely to be more than offset, however, by the higher educational level of new nonwhite entrants to the labor force and by a continuation of the exodus of black workers from the lowest-status menial-type occupations.

Educational Attainment

The projections of the 1980 and 1985 experienced civilian labor force, by educational attainment, reflect a continued overall trend towards a more educated labor force as measured by length of formal schooling, with a further gradual narrowing in the educational gap between white and nonwhite workers. (See Table 5.2.) Thus by 1985, 77.6 percent of all experienced workers in the civilian labor force, 25 years and over, will have completed at least 12 years of education as contrasted with only 48.3 percent in 1960, and 61.5 percent in 1970. The projected percentage of nonwhite workers, 25 years and over, with a completed high school education is expected to continue to rise sharply to 61.6 percent by 1985, and by that year will approximate the corresponding percentage among white workers in 1970.

It should be noted that no separate projections of educational attainment, for workers aged 16-24 years, have been developed for purposes of this study. This is due in part to the lack of comparable historical data on educational attainment for this age group of workers and, in part, to the much greater uncertainty surrounding projections of enrollment and educational attainment for this age class. School enrollment trends suggest a continued increase in the proportion of youth completing high school, but a pronounced slowdown in growth of the proportion enrolling in college, particularly in the case of white males. It is not clear whether these trends have been due to special circumstances, such as the termination of the draft and the 1970-71 recession, or whether they reflect a longer-range modification in attitudes towards the desirability of higher education, conditioned by the greater difficulty experienced in the 1970s by college graduates in obtaining entry into higher-status employment.

TABLE 5.2

Distribution of the Experienced Civilian Labor Force, 25 Years and
Over, by Sex, Race, and Educational Attainment:
1960, 1970, and Projected for 1980, 1985

Sex/Race	Number (000)	Years of School Completed (percent distribution)		
		Less than 12	12	13 and Over
Total, both sexes				
1960	54,662	51.7	26.7	21.6
1970	60,335	38.5	34.5	27.0
1980	73,178	26.6	40.8	32.6
1985	80,268	22.4	41.3	36.3
White				
1960	48,999	49.2	28.0	22.8
1970	53,952	36.3	35.5	28.2
1980	65,078	24.5	41.8	33.7
1985	71,108	20.3	42.2	37.5
Nonwhite				
1960	5,663	72.8	15.9	11.3
1970	6,383	57.2	26.4	16.4
1980	8,100	43.8	32.5	23.7
1985	9,160	38.4	34.7	26.9
Male, total				
1960	37,566	53.9	24.3	21.8
1970	38,929	39.9	31.5	28.6
1980	45,834	27.2	37.5	35.3
1985	50,027	22.5	38.3	39.2
White				
1960	34,132	51.7	25.3	23.0
1970	35,283	37.8	32.2	30.0
1980	41,160	25.1	38.2	36.7
1985	44,716	20.4	38.8	40.8
Nonwhite				
1960	3,434	76.0	14.0	10.0
1970	3,646	60.5	23.7	15.8
1980	4,614	45.8	31.2	23.0
1985	5,311	40.0	34.2	25.8
Female, total				
1960	17,094	46.9	32.0	21.1
1970	21,396	35.9	40.1	24.0
1980	27,344	25.6	46.3	25.1
1985	30,241	22.3	46.1	31.6
White				
1960	14,865	43.1	34.0	22.3
1970	18,659	33.4	41.6	25.0
1980	23,918	23.4	48.1	28.5
1985	26,392	20.2	47.7	32.1
Nonwhite				
1960	2,229	68.0	18.8	13.2
1970	2,737	52.6	30.0	17.4
1980	3,426	41.0	34.3	24.7
1985	3,849	36.4	35.4	28.2

Sources: Based on decennial census data for 1960 and 1970, and on extrapolations
by author for 1980 and 1985.

Projected Distribution of Labor Force by Occupation

The general method followed in our projections of the expected occupational distribution of the labor force was to examine the 1960-70 changes in the occupational distribution of workers, stratified by age group, sex, and educational attainment, and to extrapolate the occupational participation rates, that is, percentages in specific occupations of each of these subgroups, to 1980 and 1985.

Two broad age groups were employed for this purpose: ages 16-24 and ages 25 and over. The occupational participation rate trends for the 16-24 group in 1960-70, by sex, were further disaggregated for workers in more specific age groupings—16-17 years, 18-19 years, and 20-24 years—based on available published decennial census data, and then separately extrapolated to 1980 and 1985. This further disaggregation was considered desirable because of the pronounced contrast in labor force growth trends projected for teenage workers, as compared to those aged 20-24 years, and because the former group included a large proportion of part-time student workers who have been differentially concentrated in many lower-level occupations. The projections for workers 25 years and over were disaggregated by sex, race (white and nonwhite), and three broad educational attainment groups (less than 12 years, 12 years, and 13 or more years of school completed).

The method used in extrapolating occupational participation rates (OPR) for each of these demographic groups premises a declining rate of change in these occupational participation rates, as compared to that experienced in the 1960-70 decade. This assumption appears reasonable because of some of the unique characteristics of the 1960-70 decade: (1) the shift from an economy operating well below full employment levels at the beginning of the decade to one characterized by much higher levels of aggregate labor demand, at the end of the decade; and (2) the significant breakthrough in occupational opportunities for many black workers during the decade, as a consequence of the civil rights movement and of related socioeconomic factors. Alternative procedures, such as those based primarily on a simple linear extrapolation of trends in occupational participation rates were initially followed in our preliminary (phase 1) projections to 1980, but proved inappropriate when extended to 1985 since this method would—in some instances—have resulted in negative occupational participation rates for some population subgroups, for example, for youth in farm occupations.

The actual formula used defines the occupational participation rate as the percentage of workers in a given population subgroup (j), who are in a given occupation group. Given the rates for 1960 and 1970, the rates in any subsequent year are determined by the following formula:

$$OPR_{ij} = a + b \log (TIME)$$

where for 1960 TIME = 1; for 1970, TIME = 11; for 1980, TIME = 21; and for 1985, TIME = 26

This formulation implies that the rate of change decreases over time at the rate of $-b/TIME$. The parameter b is estimated as follows:

1. for rates which increased between 1960 and 1970, b = $[OPR(70) - OPR(60)]/\log (11)$
2. for rates which decreased between 1960 and 1970, b = $[OPR(60) - OPR(70)]/\log (11)$

For increasing rates a equals the rate in 1960; for decreasing rates, a is equal to minus that rate in 1960.

The implied shape of the functions relating occupational participation rates to time is demonstrated in Figure 5.1, for both an increasing and declining rate. In each instance, the 1960-70 trend is continued, but at a progressively declining rate of change. * The effect of the procedure, thus, is to give much greater weight in the resulting occupational labor force trend projections to the effects of inherently more reliable projections of trends in the demographic composition of the labor force, as contrasted to the more uncertain trends in occupational participation rates.

A closely related methodological consideration was to define the level of occupational grouping which is relevant in any attempt to project future occupational labor supplies. Earlier in our study, separate projections were developed for each of the 57 occupational subgroups used in our occupational status classification scheme. We suggested, however, that any attempt to project occupational supply-demand imbalances, at this level of detail, was not likely to prove meaningful, particularly within the lower-level occupational categories, because of evidence of the high degree of occupational adaptability of American workers to changing patterns of employment opportunity. Thus, in its 1966 survey of 5,000 male workers aged 45 to 59, the Census-Ohio State University National Longitudinal Survey found that

---

*The authors are indebted to Mark Kendall of the National Planning Association for development of this procedure.

FIGURE 5.1

Illustrative Projections of Occupational Participation Rates to 1985

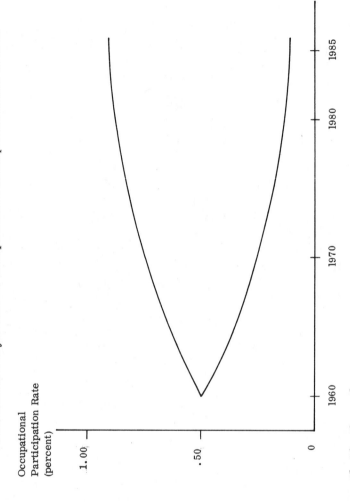

Source: Compiled by the author.

only 13 percent were in the same three-digit occupation as that of their
first postschool job. As might be expected, a majority of these men,
57 percent, had moved up the job ladder in the course of their work
careers to occupations of significantly higher status (that is, with
SES scores 15 points or more higher, based on the Duncan socioeconomic index), while an additional 15 percent had moved laterally.
Only 15 percent of the men had moved to significantly lower-status
occupations.[3] A more detailed analysis of these occupational shifts
indicated that most of the movements across major occupational
groups were among broadly related categories of occupations. Among
men who began their careers as professionals, most of the movers
went into other white-collar jobs, primarily as managers and proprietors. Among those who began as operatives, the most frequent
moves were to other blue-collar or to service occupations.

These survey findings, as well as collateral research, thus
suggest that disparities between the projected growth of labor supply
and of labor demand among occupations with substantially similar
status and wage levels are likely to be readily corrected through normal labor market processes, particularly if such occupations are
found in the same local labor markets and utilize similar sources of
labor supply. By the same token, imbalances among occupational
status groups, which would require a substantial lowering of occupational status or wage levels for sizable groups of workers, would be
more difficult to correct under conditions of high aggregate labor
demand. In particular, mature workers, with substantial investments
in education, training, and job experience (who will account for a
growing proportion of the future work force) would be especially re-
luctant to accept a substantial lowering of occupational status, except
after protracted periods of job search.

Based on the above reasoning, the projections of the expected
experienced civilian labor force, although derived from more detailed
estimates for some 17 occupational subgroups, are limited in this
chapter to the five major occupational status groups, and—separately—
to the ten standard major census occupational groups. The major
trends are discussed below.

Occupational Status Groups

The proportion of workers who will be available in the two higher-
status groups, groups 1 and 2, will continue to grow, from 47.2 percent, in 1970, to 53.8 percent of the experienced civilian labor force
in 1985, reflecting the combined effect of such factors as increased
education, the reduced proportion of youth in the labor force, and
the projected continuation of the 1960-70 pattern of upward mobility
of nonwhite workers. The proportion in group 3, which includes

mainly craftsmen and certain higher-paid operatives, would remain relatively stable, comprising 19.7 percent of the experienced civilian labor force in 1985, as compared to 21.1 percent in 1970. Conversely, those in the two lowest occupational status groups, groups 4 and 5, are expected to decline, from 31.6 percent in 1970 to 26.6 percent in 1985. (See Table 5.3.)

These shifts in the potential availability of workers, by broad status group, result from the sharply divergent projected rates of growth, among these groups—ranging from projected 1970-85 percentage increases of 66 percent and 40 percent for groups 1 and 2, respectively, to 12 percent for group 4 and only 3 percent for group 5. The projected trends for male and female workers are generally parallel. However, growth rates for women in group 3 and 4 occupations are expected to be significantly greater than for men. The number of women available in these two categories is projected to increase by about 24 percent between 1970 and 1985, as compared to an increase of about 15 percent for men.

The impact of changes in the size and composition of the labor force upon availability of workers for low-level occupations is likely to be most pronounced during the 1980-85 period, when overall labor force growth rates will decline sharply. Thus, as compared to a projected increase of 6.6 percent in the total experienced civilian labor force between 1980 and 1985, the number of workers available for group 5 occupations is expected to decline by nearly 3 percent, while those in group 4 would increase by less than one percent. The major factor contributing to the decline in the group 5 labor force between 1980 and 1985 is the projected reduction in the number of young workers, aged 16-24, an age group which—as we have seen— has contributed disproportionately to the supply of workers for many lower-level occupations.

Census Occupational Groups

Tables 5.4, 5.5, and 5.6 present comparable projections for ten major census occupational groups. Even this limited disaggregation of our occupational labor force projections indicates a broader disparity in potential labor supply growth rates than reflected in the trends for the five broad status groupings. The supply of professional and technical workers—corresponding to group 1 in our status classification—is projected to increase by nearly 66 percent between 1970 and 1985, more than twice as rapidly as the overall rate of growth of the experienced civilian labor force. Two other white-collar occupational groups—managers and administrators, and clerical workers— are also projected to experience above-average rates of growth in labor supply. Sales workers, however, are expected to grow at a

TABLE 5.3

Projections of the Experienced Civilian Labor Force, by Major Occupational Status Group and Sex, 1980 and 1985, Compared with 1970

Occupational Status Group	Number (millions)			Percent Distribution			Percent Changes		
	1970	1980	1985	1970	1980	1985	1970-85	1970-80	1980-85
Total, both sexes	75.1	91.5	97.5	100.0	100.0	100.0	29.8	21.8	6.6
Group 1	10.6	15.1	17.6	14.2	16.5	18.1	65.8	41.4	17.2
Group 2	24.8	32.0	34.8	33.0	35.0	35.7	40.1	28.9	8.7
Group 3	15.9	18.4	19.2	21.1	20.1	19.7	21.1	16.2	4.2
Group 4	15.6	17.3	17.4	20.7	18.9	17.9	11.9	11.2	0.7
Group 5	8.2	8.7	8.5	10.9	9.5	8.7	2.9	5.9	-2.8
Males, total	47.0	56.0	59.5	100.0	100.0	100.0	26.6	19.1	6.3
Group 1	6.3	8.9	10.4	13.4	15.9	17.5	65.4	41.3	17.0
Group 2	12.1	15.4	17.0	25.8	27.4	28.5	39.9	26.7	10.5
Group 3	13.2	15.1	15.7	28.2	27.0	26.4	18.9	14.4	3.9
Group 4	10.0	10.9	10.9	21.4	19.5	18.4	9.0	8.8	0.2
Group 5	5.3	5.7	5.5	11.3	10.1	9.2	2.6	6.6	-3.7
Females, total	28.1	35.5	38.0	100.0	100.0	100.0	35.2	26.3	7.0
Group 1	4.4	6.2	7.3	15.5	17.4	19.1	66.3	41.6	17.5
Group 2	12.7	16.6	17.8	45.2	46.8	46.8	40.3	31.0	7.1
Group 3	2.6	3.3	3.5	9.4	9.3	9.1	32.0	25.3	5.3
Group 4	5.5	6.4	6.5	19.7	18.0	17.1	17.3	15.4	1.6
Group 5	2.9	3.0	3.0	10.3	8.5	7.9	3.4	4.7	-1.2

Note: Data exclude workers not reported by occupation.
Sources: Data for 1970 adapted from Bureau of the Census, public use samples. Data for 1980 and 1985 are projections by the author.

TABLE 5.4

Projections of the Experienced Civilian Labor Force, by Census Occupational Group, 1980, 1985, Compared with 1970—Both Sexes

Census Occupation Group	Number (millions)			Percent Distribution			Percent Change		
	1970	1980	1985	1970	1980	1985	1970-85	1970-80	1980-85
Total, both sexes	75.1	91.5	97.5	100.0	100.0	100.0	29.8	21.8	6.6
White-collar workers									
Professional and technical	10.6	15.1	17.6	14.2	16.5	18.2	65.8	41.4	17.2
Managers and administrators	6.4	8.4	9.5	8.5	9.1	9.7	47.5	30.2	13.2
Sales workers	8.0	9.9	10.2	10.7	10.8	10.4	27.2	23.2	3.2
Clerical workers	11.8	15.4	16.6	15.7	16.9	17.0	40.5	30.5	7.6
Blue-collar workers									
Craft and kindred workers	10.5	12.2	12.8	13.9	13.3	13.1	21.9	16.4	4.7
Transport operatives	2.7	3.0	3.0	3.6	3.3	3.0	9.5	10.3	-0.7
Operatives (excluding transport)	10.3	11.5	11.8	13.7	12.6	12.1	14.8	11.9	2.6
Nonfarm laborers	3.4	3.8	3.6	4.6	4.1	3.7	6.0	9.0	-2.8
Service workers, total	8.6	9.9	10.1	11.4	10.8	10.3	12.1	14.9	1.9
Farm workers, total	2.7	2.5	2.4	3.6	2.7	2.4	-13.0	-9.3	-4.0

Sources: Data for 1970 adapted from Bureau of the Census, public use samples. Data for 1980 and 1985 are projections by the author.

TABLE 5.5

Projections of the Experienced Civilian Labor Force, by Census Occupational Group, 1980, 1985, Compared with 1970—Male Workers

Census Occupation Group	Number (millions)			Percent Distribution			Percent Change		
	1970	1980	1985	1970	1980	1985	1970–85	1970–80	1980–85
Total, male	47.0	56.0	59.5	100.0	100.0	100.0	26.6	19.1	6.3
White-collar workers									
Professional and technical	6.3	8.9	10.4	13.4	15.9	17.5	65.4	41.3	17.0
Managers and administrators	5.4	7.0	8.0	11.5	12.6	13.4	47.5	29.9	13.5
Sales workers	3.3	4.0	4.3	7.0	7.2	7.3	32.5	23.5	7.3
Clerical workers	4.4	5.2	5.4	9.0	9.3	9.1	27.7	22.8	4.0
Blue-collar workers									
Craft and kindred workers	10.0	11.6	12.1	21.3	20.7	20.4	21.2	15.9	4.6
Transport operatives	2.0	2.1	2.1	4.3	3.8	3.6	5.2	4.4	0.7
Operatives (excluding transport)	7.0	7.8	8.0	14.8	13.9	13.5	15.2	12.2	2.7
Nonfarm laborers	3.2	3.5	3.4	6.8	6.2	5.6	4.5	7.9	-3.1
Service workers, total	3.1	3.6	3.6	6.7	6.5	6.1	15.4	15.2	0.2
Farm workers, total	2.5	2.4	2.1	5.2	4.0	3.6	-13.3	-9.5	-4.1

Sources: Data for 1970 adapted from Bureau of the Census, public use samples. Data for 1980 and 1985 are projections by the author.

TABLE 5.6

Projections of the Experienced Civilian Labor Force, by Census Occupational Group, 1980, 1985, Compared with 1970—Female Workers

Census Occupation Group	Number (millions)			Percent Distribution			Percent Change		
	1970	1980	1985	1970	1980	1985	1970-85	1970-80	1980-85
Total, female	28.1	35.5	38.0	100.0	100.0	100.0	35.2	26.3	7.0
White-collar workers									
Professional and technical	4.4	6.2	7.3	15.5	17.4	19.1	66.3	41.6	17.5
Managers and administrators	1.0	1.3	1.5	3.6	3.7	3.7	47.4	31.9	11.8
Sales workers	4.7	5.8	5.8	16.8	16.4	15.4	23.4	22.9	0.4
Clerical workers	7.6	10.2	11.2	27.0	28.8	29.5	47.6	34.9	9.5
Blue-collar workers									
Craft and kindred workers	0.5	0.6	0.6	1.6	1.7	1.7	37.6	28.2	7.3
Transport operatives	0.7	0.9	0.8	2.4	2.4	2.2	22.6	27.8	-4.0
Operatives (excluding transport)	3.3	3.7	3.8	11.9	10.4	10.0	13.8	11.1	2.4
Nonfarm laborers	0.2	0.3	0.3	0.8	0.8	0.8	26.5	24.8	1.4
Service workers, total	5.5	6.3	6.4	19.4	17.6	16.9	18.1	14.8	2.9
Farm workers, total	0.3	0.3	0.3	1.0	0.8	0.7	-10.0	-3.2	-7.0

Sources: Data for 1970 from Bureau of the Census, public use samples. Data for 1980 and 1985 are projections by the author.

significantly lower rate, partly because of the reduced proportion of youth in the labor force, who now fill a significant proportion of the lower-paid jobs in sales work.

All of the blue-collar occupational categories are projected to have a less-than-average increase in labor force in the period 1970-85, ranging from 22 percent for craftsmen to only 6 percent for nonfarm laborers. The service workers group, which encompasses a particularly heterogeneous range of occupations in terms of pay and status, is projected to grow by 12 percent while workers available for farm occupations are expected to decline by 13 percent, continuing their long-term declining trend.

COMPARISON OF OCCUPATIONAL LABOR FORCE
AND EMPLOYMENT PROJECTIONS

The BLS has, for a number of decades, conducted a program of long-range forecasting of employment by occupation for use in its occupational outlook studies and for related purposes. The latest of these projections, published in summary form in December 1973, were adapted for use in comparison with our projected trends in labor force availability by occupational group. The BLS employment projections, which are linked to the BLS labor force projections cited above, assume that "fiscal, monetary and manpower training and educational programs will achieve a satisfactory balance between relatively low unemployment and relative price stability," as illustrated by an assumed 4 percent unemployment rate and a 3 percent annual increase in the implicit GNP price deflator; another key assumption is that efforts to solve environmental problems and energy shortages "may consume more productive resources but will not have more than a marginal effect on long-term economic growth."[4]

The methodology followed in the BLS projections includes the following major steps: (1) GNP is derived as the product of three major variables: projected total employment, projected hours of work, and projections of output per man-hour; (2) GNP is distributed through use of a macroeconomic model which extrapolates trends in major GNP components, along with selected exogenous estimates, for example, for governmental expenditures; (3) employment estimates by industry are based on an input-output matrix, which translates potential demand for all final goods and services into industry output requirements and—in turn—into employment requirements; and (4) employment by occupation is derived from occupational staffing patterns by industry (occupation-industry matrices) for 1960 and 1970, which are extrapolated to 1985, and modified by more specific data on employment and technological trends by occupation, where pertinent.

The resulting projections may generally be described as estimates of prospective demand for workers by occupation, in a full-employment economy, based on the stated assumptions. It should be noted, however, that labor supply considerations have at least indirectly influenced the BLS occupational estimates, to the extent, for example, that past shifts in unit labor requirements and in occupational staffing patterns for particular industries have been influenced by the relative supply of labor for these industries and occupations. In effect, however, the BLS methodology assumes that these forces will tend to operate in the same manner in the future, as in the past, and makes no direct allowance for the effect of changes in exogenous labor supply factors, such as those described in the preceding section. For this reason, it seems appropriate to compare these demand-oriented projections with our own estimates of the expected supply of workers by broad occupational group, as a means of identifying prospective occupational imbalances.

In adapting the BLS occupational employment projections for this purpose, it was necessary to disaggregate a number of BLS occupations and to combine others to correspond to the occupational status groups used in the present study. These were based generally on an assumption of fixed relationships between component occupations and the larger occupation/industry groups, based on 1960 and 1970 data. Thus, in the case of our groups of operatives, by industry cluster, specialized industry-occupation matrices were developed from the 1960 and 1970 data, and extrapolated to 1985, using as controls the corresponding BLS employment projections by industry and occupation.

The resulting employment projections by occupational status group for 1980 and 1985 are expressed as percentage changes, in Table 6.7, over corresponding BLS estimates for 1970, rather than in absolute numbers, mainly because the BLS data represent annual average employment estimates, comparable with CPS levels, whereas our projections of the experienced civilian labor force have been adjusted for comparability with decennial census data, exclusive of workers whose detailed occupation was not reported. *

----

*The small differences between the projected overall percentage growth in the labor force and in employment shown in this table are the net result of differences in the projected unemployment rate and armed forces levels, as compared to 1970, and the various statistical adjustments made in moving from annual average civilian labor force levels for 1980 and 1985 to the decennial census-based estimates of the experienced civilian labor force.

TABLE 5.7

Comparison of Projected Percentage Changes in Labor Force and Employment, by Major Occupational Status Group, 1970–85

Occupational Status Group	Experienced Civilian Labor Force (ECLF)			Employment			Difference (ECLF – Employment)		
	1970–85	1970–80	1980–85	1970–85	1970–80	1980–85	1970–85	1970–80	1980–85
Total	29.8	21.8	6.6	29.3	21.0	6.1	0.5	0.8	0.5
Group 1	65.8	41.4	17.2	50.5	35.0	11.6	15.3	6.4	5.6
Group 2	40.1	28.9	8.7	41.3	32.3	7.0	-1.2	-3.4	1.7
Group 3	21.1	16.2	4.2	19.0	13.0	5.4	2.1	3.2	-1.2
Group 4	11.9	11.2	0.7	18.3	14.3	4.1	-6.4	-3.1	-3.4
Group 5	2.9	5.9	-2.8	5.5	7.0	-1.3	-2.6	-1.1	-1.5

Sources: Employment data adapted from unpublished Bureau of Labor Statistics (BLS) projections for detailed occupations, by industry, compatible with December 1973 BLS labor force and employment projections. For adjustment procedures, see text.

The comparisons for the entire period 1970-85 in Table 5.7 indicate a large potential surplus of available workers for group 1 occupations resulting from a projected labor force growth of 66 percent as compared to 51 percent growth in projected employment. At the lower extreme of the job structure, the growth in potential requirements for group 4 and group 5 occupations is expected to exceed the projected growth of available workers by 6.4 percent and 2.6 percent, respectively. The trends for the two intermediate occupational status groups—group 2 and 3—are in closer overall balance.

The disparity between a projected surplus of workers in high-level jobs, and a shortage, in lower-level jobs, is more clearly evident in the comparisons for the 1980-85 period. Both the group 1 and 2 occupations—which correspond closely to the white-collar category, exclusive of such jobs as shipping clerk and messenger—are expected to experience a more rapid growth in labor supply than in jobs; while groups 3-5 would all experience deficits in labor force growth as compared to projected job needs.

Similar comparisons of projected labor force and employment trends are presented in Table 5.8 based on the standard census occupational groups. These comparisons indicate wider divergences between labor force and employment growth rates between 1970 and 1985 than those based on our broader status groupings. Among the white-collar occupations, labor supply growth is expected to substantially exceed employment growth in three groups—professional and technical workers, nonfarm managers, and clerical workers. Labor force growth, however, is expected to lag behind demand in the case of sales workers, reflecting the large projected employment growth in this occupational group, as well as the fact that our labor force projections indicate a somewhat less-than-average growth in supply. The latter is attributable mainly to the reduced labor force growth among youth and women, who have staffed a large proportion of the lower-paid sales jobs.

In the case of the remaining census occupational groups, these comparisons suggest prospective deficits in labor force growth in two occupational groups, service workers (-16.0 percent) and craftsmen (-6.6 percent), in contrast to a projected large surplus of farm workers. In the latter occupational group, the surplus is a consequence of a projected sharp reduction, of 41.9 percent, in farm employment, as compared to a smaller projected reduction, of 19.3 percent, in our farm labor force estimates.* The comparisons for the two remaining

---

*It is probable that the BLS projection for farm employment will be substantially increased in revised projections, as a result of subsequent trends in agricultural production, prices, and employment.

TABLE 5.8

Comparison of projected percentage changes in Labor Force and Employment, 1970–85.
by One-Digit Census Occupational Groups

Census Occupational Group	Experienced Civilian Labor Force (ECLF)			Employment			Difference (ECLF–Employment)		
	1970–85	1970–80	1980–85	1970–85	1970–80	1980–85	1970–85	1970–80	1980–85
Experienced civilian labor force	29.8	21.8	6.6	29.6	23.3	5.9	0.2	-1.5	0.7
Professional, technical, and kindred	65.8	41.4	17.2	53.3	35.3	13.3	12.5	6.1	3.9
Nonfarm managers	47.5	30.2	13.2	27.4	22.5	4.0	20.1	7.7	9.2
Clerical workers	45.5	32.5	9.8	33.3	29.2	3.2	12.2	3.3	6.6
Sales workers	27.2	23.2	3.2	44.0	30.8	10.1	-16.8	-7.6	-6.9
Craftsmen, foremen, and kindred workers	23.6	17.5	5.2	30.2	22.2	6.6	-6.6	-4.7	-1.4
Operatives (including transport)	18.3	15.8	2.2	13.8	11.6	2.0	4.5	4.2	0.2
Nonfarm laborers	7.4	10.3	-2.6	6.0	6.0	0.0	1.4	4.3	-2.6
Service workers	17.1	14.9	1.9	33.1	26.2	5.5	-16.0	-11.3	-3.6
Farm workers, total	-19.3	-12.1	-8.2	-41.9	-27.3	-20.0	22.6	15.2	11.8

Source: 1970 employment data by occupational group drawn from unpublished BLS estimates adjusted for comparability with published estimates since January 1971, based on revised occupational classification and enumeration procedures.

occupational groups—operatives and nonfarm laborers—suggest a closer correspondence between labor force and employment trends for the entire 1970-85 period than for any of the other major census occupational groups. However, in the case of nonfarm laborers, a projected surplus in labor force growth during the 1970-80 period, of over 4 percent, would be reversed in the 1980-85 period, reflecting the reduced number of young workers available for such jobs.

The extent to which the above comparisons provide a meaningful indicator of possible future labor market difficulties depends, in part, upon the degree of confidence which can be placed on any longer-term projections of labor demand, as well as of labor supply, by occupation. It is therefore moot to enquire into the reliability of the BLS projections of employment, by occupation. Three sets of comparisons are available for this purpose: (1) a retroactive comparison of earlier BLS projections for the decade of the 1960s with actual employment trends; (2) a comparison between two later BLS projections of employment by occupation for 1980; and (3) a comparison between the 1973 projection for the entire decade of the 1970s with actual employment trends in the period 1970-74.

For the first of these comparisons, we have available an assessment by Sol Swerdloff, who compared BLS projections for 1970, issued early in the 1960s, with actual trends during the decade. These projections, as of 1960, could not anticipate the massive increases in defense spending for the Vietnam War and for space exploration, or the extent of increased federal funding in areas such as education, health, and allied social services. Nor did they allow, in the case of such occupations as domestic service, for the impact of labor supply factors upon actual employment trends, which resulted in an unexpected decline in household employment, attributed by Swerdloff to "unwillingness on the part of young better-educated Negro women to accept domestic work as do many older Negro women."[5]

Despite these limitations, Swerdloff concluded that "the broad occupational trends projected in the 1960 report have materialized pretty well."[6] Specifically, employment increased most rapidly in the white-collar occupations; blue-collar and service worker employment experienced a more moderate growth, with virtually no increase for nonfarm laborers; and farm employment declined sharply. All of these broader trends were in accordance with the predicted general pattern of occupational employment growth. However, deviations between actual and projected trends for some of the individual occupational groups, such as household workers and farm workers, were quite substantial.

A second set of comparisons can be made between two successive BLS projections for 1980—the first, published in 1970, using 1968 data as a point of departure and the second, published in December 1973,

based on actual data for 1972. These are shown in Table 5.9 for nine
major census occupational groups. It will be evident that, as in the
previous comparison, the differential pattern of employment growth
by major occupation remained fairly consistent. Notably, most white-
collar groups—as well as service occupations—were expected to experience above-average employment growth under both projections;
craftsmen were expected to grow at a rate identical with that of total
employment in each projection; while the other occupational groups,
including operatives, nonfarm laborers, and farm workers, were
expected to experience below-average growth or to decline. The deviation in projected annual growth rates between the two sets of projections was 0.4 percent or less for five of the nine major occupational
groups; on the other hand, it was quite large for nonfarm laborers
and farm workers, 0.7 percent and -1.3 percent, respectively.

The final set of comparisons shows the difference between the projected annual growth rate between 1970 and 1980, based on the most
recent 1973 projections and the actual rate in the period 1970-74. To
make this comparison, it was necessary to revise the originally reported CPS employment data by occupation for 1970 to allow for the
effects of revisions in occupational classification and enumerating
procedures, similar to those in the 1970 Census which were introduced into the Current Population Survey in 1971. These are necessarily subject to some error. Allowance must also be made for the
difference in time periods, and for the fact that 1974 marked the onset
of a major economic recession. The degree of variation between actual
employment trends between 1970-74 and those projected for the entire
period 1970-80 (using 1972 as a base year), was therefore somewhat
greater than in our first set of comparisons. Nevertheless, the actual
annual rate of employment change deviated by 0.4 points or less for
six of the nine major occupational groups. The most pronounced dis-
crepancy was in the farm-workers occupational group. In contrast to
a projected annual rate of decline of 3.1 percent, employment in this
group activity rose at a rate of 2.6 percent between 1970 and 1974.
Employment growth was also greater than projected for service workers and nonfarm laborers.

Despite the limitations of the above comparisons, they do provide
some confirmation for the broad differentials in growth rates, reflected in the longer-term BLS employment projections by occupation.
In fact, if the most recent trends can serve as a guide, the economy's
demand for workers in certain occupational groups including large
proportions of lower-level jobs, such as farm workers and service
workers, may be somewhat greater than indicated in the 1973 BLS
projections.

At the same time, the hazardous nature of longer-term manpower
projections will be quite evident. The most critical uncertainty lies,

TABLE 5.9

Annual Employment Growth Rates by Occupational Group:
Comparison of Bureau of Labor Statistics
Projections for 1970-80 and Actual
Employment Trends, 1970-74
(Annual Rates)

| Occupational Group | BLS projections 1970-80* | | Actual employment change 1970-74* | Differences | |
| | | | | Actual |
	1970 projections	1973 projections		1973 projections minus 1970 projections	change 1970-74, minus 1973 projections
Total	1.9	2.0	2.2	0.1	0.2
Professional and technical	3.4	3.1	2.7	-0.3	-0.4
Managers, nonfarm	1.4	1.7	1.3	0.3	-0.4
Sales	1.7	2.6	2.7	0.7	0.3
Clerical	2.3	2.7	2.4	0.4	-0.3
Craft and kindred	1.9	2.0	3.5	0.1	1.5
Operatives, including transport	1.0	1.1	0.9	0.1	-0.2
Nonfarm laborers	-0.1	0.6	0.8	0.7	0.2
Service workers	3.0	2.4	3.1	-0.6	0.7
Farmworkers	-1.8	-3.1	2.6	-1.3	5.7

*Sources: Actual employment by occupational group for 1970 and 1974 from Manpower Report of the President, April 1975, Table A-15. BLS projections for 1980 from Tomorrow's Manpower Needs, vol. 4 (revised 1971), BLS Bulletin 1737, Appendix 1, and from Neal Rosenthal, "Projected Changes in Occupations," Monthly Labor Review, December 1973, p. 19. For computation of annual rates based on the 1973 projections and of actual changes, 1970-74, revised employment estimates for 1970, comparable to 1970 census classifications, were used, based on unpublished BLS data. All annual rates were computed by the author.

of course, in the extent of deviation of aggregate economic activity
from a full-employment path. In an economy burdened by an unemployment rate of 8.5 percent in 1975, the most pressing labor market
problems are clearly those resulting from inadequate demand for
nearly all occupations, and this is likely to continue to be true if unemployment rates were to persist at or near 1975 levels. Even if satisfactory economic growth levels are restored later in the decade, such
factors as increased costs of energy and other raw materials, as well
as the scope and direction of federal energy programs, may significantly affect differential growth rates in particular industries and
occupations. Until our longer-term energy program goals and the
direction of related economic and fiscal policies become more clearly
defined, longer-term economic and manpower needs projections will
be subject to particularly wide margins of uncertainty.

The hazards of longer-term projections of manpower demand are
compounded when such projections are in turn used as a basis of comparison with projections of potential labor supply by occupation. The
limitations of the latter projections have been discussed earlier in
this chapter, including, particularly, our limited knowledge concerning
the adaptability of the labor force to conditions in which relative surpluses of workers develop for the more desirable, higher-status occupations as contrasted to potential deficits in lower-status jobs.

The above cautions inevitably lead one to the ultimate question as
to the potential usefulness of any systematic effort to anticipate future
trends in manpower supply and demand, by occupation, in a dynamic
and complex society. Howard R. Bowen, in a provocative article,
has challenged certain assumptions underlying such projections, including the premises that "the character of the economy and its skill
requirements can be predicted for periods long enough to be pertinent
to educational planning" and that "the economy requires a more or
less fixed inventory of occupational skills at each state in its evolution."[7] Bowen contends that there will be an accommodation between
the economy's needs for goods and services, and the types of jobs
which workers in that society want to do; that is, between labor demand
and labor supply factors.

> The economy adjusts to the manpower available. Every
> economy learns to use its particular mix. If it cannot
> get people to do repetitive assembly-line jobs, incen-
> tives are created to automate or change these jobs. If
> it cannot get people to do stoop labor or dig ditches,
> it has incentives to invent and substitute suitable
> machines. If it cannot find people to be pliant house-
> hold servants, it simply goes without them and produces
> packaged foods, household appliances, and housing of

different size and design. If it cannot find people to
collect garbage, it will invent new ways to handle solid
waste disposal or, better yet, to eliminate unnecessary
containers, Sunday papers, and other refuse that use up
precious resources and degrade the environment. [8]

Thus, any labor market pressures or shortages resulting from
a reduced availability of workers for certain unpleasant jobs would
result in an accommodation of the economy—either through appropriate wage rate adjustments, product substitution, increased capital
intensity, or simply doing without certain market goods and services.
These complex interactions are difficult, or perhaps impossible, to
quantify in a single comprehensive model of the occupational labor
market.

Despite these limitations, the broad imbalance between the occupational distribution of the labor force implied by our demographically
based projections and that resulting from projections of labor demand
by occupation, under full-employment conditions, does suggest that
some significant adjustments may be required. Our examination of
1970-74 experience, as well as the inherently conservative assumptions underlying our demographically based projections of labor force
by occupational status group, suggest that the resulting comparisons
may well have understated, rather than overstated, the potential for
future imbalances under full-employment conditions. The nature of
the resulting adjustments in turn can be expected to depend upon the
respective elasticities of supply and demand for labor in particular
industries and occupations. If the supply of labor for a particular
occupation is highly elastic, a relatively small differential increase
in wages would attract the additional workers needed. On the other
hand, if the supply of workers is relatively inelastic and employers
are not in a position to substantially increase relative wage levels,
or modify conditions of work to make these jobs more attractive,
employment will be reduced. In the latter case, as suggested by
Bowen, the needs of the economy may still be met in a variety of
ways: by product substitution, by substitution of capital for labor,
by changing the skill mix of workers required to produce a particular
good or service through industrial relocation, or increased reliance
upon imports. Other possible adjustments include modifications in
employee recruitment and selection standards, increased use of
part-time workers, or relaxation of immigration restrictions upon
entry of low-level manpower.

We can anticipate, based on past experience, that, to the extent
needed, some combination of these forms of adjustment will occur
over a period of time and that the particular path taken will vary
from industry to industry, and from area to area, depending upon a

number of economic, social, and technological variables. Although
any attempt to systematically forecast these possible adjustments
over the full range of occupations is not practicable, some insights
as to their possible direction can be derived both from our previous
analysis of the sensitivity of relative wages to various labor supply
factors (Chapter 4) and from a more detailed discussion of experience
in selected lower-level occupations, in the following chapter.

NOTES

1. Denis F. Johnston, "Education of Workers: Projections to
1990," Monthly Labor Review, November 1973, pp. 22-31.

2. A review of this literature appears in the Manpower Report
of the President, 1974 (Washington, D. C.: U.S. Government Printing
Office, 1974), chap. 4.

3. Herbert S. Parnes et al., The Pre-Retirement Years: A
Longitudinal Study of the Labor Market Experience of Men, vol. 1,
Manpower Research Monograph no. 15 (Washington, D. C.: U.S.
Government Printing Office, 1970).

4. Jack Alterman, "The United States Economy in 1985: An
Overview of BLS Projections," Monthly Labor Review, December
1973, pp. 4-5.

5. Sol Swerdloff, "How Good Were Manpower Projections for the
1960's," Monthly Labor Review, November 1969, pp. 17-22.

6. Ibid.

7. Howard R. Bowen, "Manpower Management and Higher Education," Educational Record 54, no. 1 (1973): 10.

8. Ibid.

6

ALTERNATIVE PATTERNS
OF LABOR MARKET
ADJUSTMENT:
FOUR CASE STUDIES

In Chapter 4, we described the efforts to deduce, through econometric analysis of cross-sectional data, the impact of sociodemographic variables upon relative wages and employment in a number of lower-level occupations. It has been apparent that these labor supply variables have not operated in a uniform and consistent manner upon occupational wage differentials and/or employment. Even after allowance for imperfections both in the empirical data base and in model specifications, it appears likely that a fundamental limitation in this cross-sectional approach has been its inability to take into account the full range of relevant market and institutional factors operating dynamically to influence labor supply, labor demand, and wages in various occupations and labor markets.

To provide some of these additional insights we have selected four occupations for more intensive examination on a case study basis: household maids, construction laborers, apparel operatives, and hospital attendants. Our selection of these groups was designed to provide—

1. a range of status levels from very low status, group 5 workers, such as household maids, to somewhat higher status, group 4 workers, such as hospital attendants;
2. comparisons between predominantly male-type occupations, such as construction laborers, and occupations with predominantly female staffing;
3. industry representation, to include both occupations in service industries and those in goods-producing industries;
4. contrasts between rapidly growing occupations, such as hospital attendants, and those with static or declining employment levels.

In each of the four occupations, we have examined relevant data on the characteristics of the occupation, employment and wage trends, and changes in labor force composition. The interaction of these and other factors has been analyzed by use of econometric models, where applicable. Based on these analyses and on prospective trends in labor force growth, some inferences have been made concerning future employment and wage trends. [1]

HOUSEHOLD MAIDS

Occupational Characteristics

Household maids, or domestics, are defined in this study to include persons working for hire in private households, in performance of cleaning, laundering, cooking, routine child care, and other personal care services and related household duties. All but a small percentage of household workers are female; hence, it has been convenient to limit our analysis of household workers to maids. Babysitters who do not perform other household duties have also been excluded from this analysis because of the distinctive labor supply source for babysitting (predominantly white teenage youth) and because of its typically casual nature. *

By most criteria, household maids fall at or near the bottom of the occupational hierarchy. For example:

1. The median cash hourly earnings of private household workers, except babysitters, were reported at $1.34 in May 1971. This contrasted with a then prevailing minimum wage of $1.60 per hour under the Fair Labor Standards Act. Even after allowance for the value of fringe benefits, such as food and carfare, these earnings were probably lower than for any other sizable occupational group in the labor force. [2]

---

*Mattila in his study defines household maids or domestics to include all private household workers, as reported in the decennial censuses, other than babysitters, where the latter are separately identified. Also excluded are private household employees engaged as gardeners, chauffeurs, or in related outside activities. Our classification, for purposes of occupational status ranking, also excludes housekeepers from the category of private household workers not elsewhere classified.

2. Formal education or specialized training requirements for entry into routine domestic jobs are either nonexistent or very low. Most of the skills entailed in household work are normally acquired by girls and young women, at least in rudimentary fashion, in their own households.

3. Domestic work has been predominantly staffed by a part-time and intermittent labor force. In May 1971, over one-half of this labor force worked less than 15 hours per week and nearly four-fifths, less than 35 hours per week.[3] Among the small proportion of live-in maids, however, nearly one-half reported work weeks of 45 hours or longer—a typical pattern which was probably much more pronounced in earlier decades, when live-in workers represented a much larger proportion of the domestic work force.

4. By the nature of their employment, domestic workers are subjected to personalized and, often, erratic supervision, particularly with the almost complete absence of any form of governmental safeguards or union organization. Until the 1970s, they were afforded few, if any, of the protections available to most other workers under state and federal laws. They were excluded from coverage under minimum wage, unemployment insurance, and workmen's compensation legislation, with very limited exceptions. *

Domestic service thus, in almost all respects, provides a prototype of the kind of employment which has been characterized as part of the secondary labor market. All of these factors have also contributed to the low status ranking of household workers, whether based on socioeconomic status, prestige, or on our own criteria, as described in Chapter 1 of this study (see Table 1.3).

In the latter context, the low social status of domestic service in the United States and its general identification as a menial occupation, has also in part been directly attributable to the composition of its work force. In 1910, when immigration was at its peak, more than a fifth of the female servants were foreign born, with a particularly high concentration of women of Irish and Scandinavian origin. Over one-third were black, and over two-fifths of all black female workers were in this occupation (see Table 2.3). With the cessation of large-scale immigration after World War I and the beginning of the mass

----

*A major breakthrough in this respect was the extension of minimum wage and overtime pay coverage to most domestic workers, other than babysitters employed on a casual basis, under the 1974 amendments to the Fair Labor Standards Act.

movement of the black population from southern farms to northern
cities, black women became the single most important labor supply
source for domestic labor, particularly in the larger cities where a
large proportion of these jobs were concentrated. By 1930, nearly
one-half of all female domestics were black while the foreign-born
proportion had declined to less than 15 percent. The concentration
of black women in the domestic service labor force became even more
pronounced after World War II. By 1970, fully two-thirds of all female
household workers (excluding babysitters) were nonwhite.

The household maid occupation has certain additional characteristics which make it particularly interesting from the standpoint of
analysis of occupational supply and demand behavior. First, because
it is highly decentralized and because it has neither been organized
nor subject to governmental wage regulation it is—as Mattila has
noted—"probably as competitive as any other labor market in existence."[4] Secondly, it is a one-industry occupation, whose inputs consist entirely of labor services to private households; hence, the theory
of consumer demand should be directly applicable to the analysis of
demand for domestic worker services. Finally, as noted by George
Stigler in his pioneering study of this occupation, domestic service
is an occupation, which—based mainly on apocryphal rather than
empirical data—appears to have been afflicted by chronic problems
of labor shortage, attributable—at least in part—to the low social
status of the occupation.[5]

Factors Affecting Employment Trends

Employment of household maids has declined sharply, although
unevenly over a period of decades. Based on decennial census data,
the number of private household workers, excluding babysitters, rose
from 1,579,000 in 1900 to 2,413,000 in 1940, but then declined to
981,000 in 1970.[6] In relation to the number of households, domestics'
employment fell from 9.9 per 100 households in 1900 to 6.9 in 1940
and to 1.5 in 1970. These comparisons, moreover, understate the
true employment decline in this occupation in terms of full-time
equivalent man-years due to the sharp reduction in annual hours of
work per domestic worker. Early in the century, a considerable proportion of domestics were probably live-in maids, with the very long
hours of work characteristic of this occupation. As noted above,
live-in maids now account for only a small proportion of total female
household workers. Because of extensive part-time work among the
more typical day workers, the median weekly hours per domestic
are now very low, that is, less than 15 hours per week in 1972.

Closer inspection of these trends suggests that both demand and supply factors have contributed to this long-term decline. From the demand standpoint, there has been a progressive growth in a wide range of substitutes for domestic servants, ranging from labor-saving household appliances and equipment of all types, and increased availability of commercial personal services, for example, laundries and quick-food restaurants, to the extensive growth in preprocessed foods. As noted by Mattila, the prices of these substitutes for domestic servants increased much less between 1939 and 1970 than did domestic wage rates. For example, as compared to a 615 percent increase in domestic wage rates, the price of commercial laundry services rose by 259 percent and those of household appliances by only 20 percent.[7] Another contributing factor tending to reduce labor requirements for domestics was the long-term decline in family size associated with the secular decline in birth rates.

However, not all demand-related factors would necessarily have been expected to reduce requirements for domestic service. Analysis of family expenditures data suggests that expenditures for domestic service tend to be moderately elastic in relation to size of family income. Thus among urban families of four persons, the average percentage of income spent for domestic service in 1961 rose from less than 1 percent among families with income under $10,000 to 2.8 percent for families with incomes of $15,000 and over.[8] Other factors being equal, one would thus have expected an increase in employment of domestics to accompany the rising secular trend in family incomes—particularly in view of the increased participation of married women in gainful employment. Yet, the number of domestics in the labor force fell most sharply during the wartime decades of 1910-20, 1940-50, and 1960-70—periods characterized by sharp rises in employment and family income levels as well as by pronounced increases in participation of women in the labor force. In contrast, the number of domestics rose—both absolutely and per household—in the decades 1920-30 and 1930-40.[9] The trend during the 1930s, particularly, appears to be clearly associated with the sharp decline of alternative job opportunities for women during the Great Depression and the pressures upon them to contribute to family income in the face of pervasive unemployment and underemployment among male family members.

Collateral data also support an interpretation that the declining trend in household maid employment was induced, at least in part, by labor supply constraints. Based on BLS data, wage rates of domestics rose significantly more rapidly than did average hourly earnings of manufacturing production workers during periods such as 1939-48 and 1964-70, which were also marked by sharp reductions in household worker employment. Moreover, between 1960 and 1970, unemployment rates for all private household workers declined from 5.3 percent to 4.2 percent, whereas the unemployment rate for all women, 16 years and over, actually increased slightly, from 5.3 percent to 5.4 percent, between these two years.[10] If employment reductions had been solely due to curtailed demand, a decline in relative wages and an increase in relative unemployment for this occupation would have been expected.

The limited evidence from data over time is thus consistent with a hypothesis that the demand for domestics is highly elastic in relation to the relative wages of domestics and that, given the competitive market for domestics, both wage rates and employment of domestics have been particularly sensitive to supply conditions. In turn, the supply of domestics—given the low wages and the low status of the occupation—has been significantly influenced both by general labor market conditions and by changes in the availability of low-caste labor supply groups, such as black women and later immigrants, for this type of employment.

Cross-Sectional Studies

The above inferences had already been drawn by Stigler, based on a penetrating analysis of the limited data base available to him, in the 1940s. Later, Mattila attempted to extend this analysis by construction of cross-sectional econometric models, using the more extensive data resources of the 1960 and 1970 censuses, as well as collateral data. An initial analysis by Mattila, designed to estimate the employment effects of extending minimum wage coverage to household workers, was based mainly on the following models.[11]

1. Demand: The number of employed household maids per household was assumed to be a function of (a) real wages of domestics, (b) family income, (c) the price of substitutes for maid services (for example, laundry services, food away from home), and (d) the female labor force participation rate, on the assumption that higher employment rates for women increased the demand for domestic services.

2. Supply: Household maids in the experienced civilian labor force per household were used as the dependent variable for the supply model. This initial model assumed that supply of household maids was a function of (a) wages of domestics, (b) the percentage of black women in the labor force, and (c) alternative income sources of domestics, as estimated by income of nonwhite males and income of nonwhite females.

The data base for this analysis consisted of forty SMSAs for which BLS consumer price data on hourly wage rates of domestics

and prices of other personal services were available, with the other
variables derived from the 1960 census of population.

Mattila's major finding in this initial study was that demand for
maids was quite elastic with respect to domestics' wages, with elasticities ranging from -1.2 to -3.0, depending upon model specifications. Based upon estimates of existing hourly earnings distributions
of maids, Mattila concluded that even under a conservative (-1.3)
elasticity assumption, a minimum wage ranging from $1.20 to $2.00
per hour could have very substantial disemployment effects, of from
-12 percent to -58 percent, whether in the form of reduced employment or reduced weekly hours.

Other findings by Mattila, based on this initial analysis, were
that (1) income elasticity of demand, based on area cross-sectional
data, was not as consistently evident as in the family expenditures
data and—in any event—appeared to be outweighed by the greater inverse demand elasticity to domestic wages; (2) supply of domestics,
by SMSA, was strongly and positively associated with the percentage
of black women in the labor force in each SMSA and was negatively
related to earnings of nonwhite men in these areas; and (3) supply of
domestics did not appear to be significantly affected by intercity variations in domestics' real wage rates, holding other factors constant.

For purposes of the present study, Mattila has updated and revised his econometric analyses on the basis of 1970 census data, has
incorporated a number of additional variables in his basic models,
and has explored several other labor supply-relevant models. Following are some additional insights derived from his new study:

1. Whereas the revised supply model—in common with the earlier
model—did not find any significant relationship between supply of
household maids and real wage rates for domestics (deflated by each
area's consumer price index), the revised model did find a highly
significant relationship between supply of maids and the relative wage
of domestics as measured either by the ratio of domestics' wages to
those of female janitors in business and industry in each area, or by
the ratio of 1969 median annual earnings of full-year domestics to
the standardized occupational earnings measure for each area. (See
Chapter 4.)

2. The supply of domestics was also found to be significantly and
inversely correlated with the level of AFDC payments by SMSA, although the elasticities were relatively low, ranging between -0.2 and
-0.7 under alternative models.

3. The influence of the proportion of black women in the labor
force upon the supply of domestics was refined in this revised analysis
by defining this variable as the percentage of women in the labor force
who are blacks with less than 12 years of education. This factor again

proved to be highly significant and positively associated with supply
in almost all models, with elasticities about twice as large in southern
cities than in nonsouthern cities—probably indicative of the somewhat
more restricted range of job opportunities for poorly educated black
women in southern cities than in the North.

    4. A separate analysis was made of the factors affecting the
supply of black women for domestic work using (a) the number of
black female domestics per household, and (b) their relative concentration in domestic work, as the dependent variables. One of the
findings based on the former formulation was that, in areas where
the education of black women more closely approached that of white
female workers, the proportion of black women working as domestics
was significantly lower.

    5. The results of the revised demand model were generally con-
sistent with the earlier analysis, although with higher elasticities, in
relation to both domestics' wages (negative) and family income (positive), than for 1960.

    6. Finally, Mattila attempted to analyze factors affecting inter-
area differences in relative earnings of domestics, as measured by
the ratio of annual earnings of domestics employed 50-52 weeks to
those of all female workers employed year-round. The findings are
tentative because of data limitations. They did, however, suggest
that areas with higher levels of AFDC payments and with higher educational levels among black women also had significantly higher relative earnings levels for domestics.

    In summary, Mattila's findings are most definitive in demon-
strating the sensitivity of supply—and hence of employment—of domestic service workers to alternative income and job opportunities for
black women, who have been the primary labor supply source for
domestic work. These alternatives have been measured in different
ways in the various econometric models, but almost all formulations
have confirmed the strength of this relationship.

Employment and Earnings Outlook

    Based on the above analyses, it is reasonable to assume a con-
tinued declining trend in employment of domestics, in combination
with some moderate increase in their relative earnings under conditions of full or near full employment. Among important specific contributing supply factors will be (1) the continued decline in the number
and proportion of poorly educated black women in the labor force,
who have been a prime labor supply source for this work; (2) the
probable impact of new federal minimum wages for domestics, particularly in the South, assuming even a modest degree of enforcement,

and (3) the probablility that existing geographical differentials in AFDC
payments will also narrow, thus again tending to reduce the disproportionate utilization of domestics in the South.

The degree to which this reduction will be dependent upon availability of alternative job opportunities is also suggested by the sharp
contrast in occupational distribution of employed nonwhite women,
aged 18-24 years and not enrolled in school, by size of area. The
previously mentioned National Longitudinal Survey, in its initial 1968
study of this group, found that less than 0.5 percent of young nonwhite
women residing in large SMSAs (with labor force of 500,000 or more)
were employed as domestics, as contrasted with 14 percent of those
in areas with a labor force of 100,000-499,000 and with 22 percent of
those in areas with less than 100,000 workers.[12] This virtual dis-
appearance of young black women from the labor force of domestics
in large cities during the 1960s stands in sharp contrast to the experience of preceding generations of black women, and is undoubtedly associated both with the rapid rise in their educational attainment in large
cities and with their rapid influx into clerical and other white-collar
jobs in such cities. In view of the persistence of very high unemployment rates among young black women in large metropolitan areas—
in contrast with relatively low rates for domestic workers—we must
also note the widespread rejection of domestic service by such women
because of its menial status, low wages, and long commuting distances,
and because of availability of alternative income sources, including
AFDC.

One consequence of these trends, it has been suggested, may be
a greater impetus to provide measures to upgrade both the productivity
of domestic service and its status. During the 1960s, considerable
attention was given by the Department of Labor to these objectives.
The upgrading of domestic service was selected as a target for action
by the President's Committee on the Status of Women. Funding was
provided for a National Committee on Household Employment and for
eight pilot projects designed to train domestic workers and to help
them obtain better-paying and higher-status domestic jobs. The
training provided ranged from four to sixteen weeks. Those completing
the training were in turn offered placement assistance. These projects
met with limited success; loss rates during training were high, averaging more than one-third. Moreover, many of the graduates did not
choose to enter or remain in domestic jobs. Nevertheless, over one-
half of the graduates were still working at the termination of the projects and a majority were earning rates well above the prevailing
average for domestic maids.

These small-scale projects and similar promotional efforts to
upgrade domestic worker employment have, however, made no measurable impact to date upon prevailing practices or upon the overall

status of this occupation.[13] In fact, the experience of these projects
has served to illustrate the many inherent difficulties in such a process, stemming both from the characteristics of the labor supply and
of the typical employing household. Unless wages and working conditions, as well as productivity of domestics, can be substantially up-
graded, domestic service is likely to continue as a job of last resort,
attracting mainly women with few vocational skills who are interested
in part-time or intermittent work rather than in a full-time occupational career.

One source for augmenting the dwindling domestic labor supply
for this occupation has consisted of those immigrants, mainly from
nearby countries in Latin America and the West Indies, who have
entered this country either legally or illegally and who possess limited
education or vocational skills. Despite the generally higher overall
occupational and educational status of legal immigrants, nearly 9
percent of all such immigrants in the period 1961-70 who reported
an occupation identified themselves as household workers (see Table
3.29). Moreover, our analysis of the occupational distribution of
foreign-born workers who reported as their place of origin Latin
American countries indicated a greater-than-average concentration
in household jobs. Thus, in 1970, this group accounted for 2.5 percent
of private household workers, although they represented only 1.2
percent of the total experienced civilian labor force (see Table 3.30).
However, as documented by David North and William Weissert in their
follow-up study of 1970 immigrants, it is clear that a large proportion
of immigrant women who engaged in household work in their country
of origin do not enter this employment here, or—if they do—move on
to better-paying jobs as soon as they acquire the needed language or
educational qualifications.[14] This labor supply source has been significant in some areas with high concentrations of immigrants, for
example, in northern seaboard cities such as New York and in border
communities of the southwestern states. In the absence of a general
lowering of immigration barriers or very large-scale inflows of illegal
aliens, it is unlikely, however, that immigrants will substantially
expand the overall national supply of domestic workers.

APPAREL INDUSTRY OPERATIVES

Occupational Status

The apparel manufacturing industry was selected for detailed
analysis because—in most respects—it has been the prototype of

low-wage industrial employment in this country. The term "sweat-shop," in fact, had its origins in the descriptions of working conditions prevailing in the small tenement shops which characterized the new factory clothing industry in the decades immediately preceding World War I.[15]

Unionization, in combination with federal and state labor laws, has resulted in great improvements in working conditions and in amelioration of many of the other adverse features associated with the origins of the industry, although there are still many submarginal enterprises, particularly in the nonunionized sector of the industry. Nevertheless, apparel industry operatives, although at a higher status level than most low-skilled service workers or laborers, still rank at or near the bottom of the job hierarchy among the major semiskilled operative occupations, as illustrated by the following comparisons:

1. Earnings: The apparel industry ranks lowest in wage levels among the major manufacturing industries. Average hourly earnings of apparel industry production workers were $2.78 in 1973 as compared to an average of $4.07 in all manufacturing industries.[16]

2. Training and education: Little or no formal training is required for entry into most apparel operative jobs. In a 1962 survey, only 8.7 percent of all apparel operatives reported that they had received any formal training for their jobs and only 4.1 percent considered formal training as the most helpful way of learning this work.[17] Educational levels of apparel industry operatives are correspondingly low. In 1970, the median years of school completed by female apparel operatives was 9.3 years, as compared with an average of 9.8 years for women operatives in all manufacturing industries.[18]

3. Promotional opportunity: Employment as an apparel operative or sewing machine operator is typically a dead-end job, with little or no opportunity for occupational progression. As noted by Charles Brecher, "positions as machine operators are entry jobs which lead to practically no promotional positions."[19]

4. Turnover: As a result of these conditions, and of the seasonal and/or irregular production patterns characteristic of many branches of the industry, turnover rates in apparel manufacturing have tended to be among the highest of any major manufacturing industry.[20]

Economic Characteristics

These and other adverse employment conditions have their roots in the economic structure of the industry. The industry, as a whole, is characterized by a basically simple and relatively static technology, centered around the sewing machine, with use of additional equipment for such functions as cutting and pressing. Capital requirements are low as illustrated by the fact that the value of gross plant and equipment per apparel workers was only about $3,000 in 1973, or about one-ninth of the corresponding ratio for all manufacturing. The low capital requirements and the absence of major economies of scale have facilitated entry into the industry and, at the same time, have accounted for the small average firm size, which was less than 60 employees in 1973.[21]

This composite picture does conceal some important variations among major sectors of the apparel manufacturing industry. The fashion-oriented women's apparel industries—dresses, blouses, coats and suits, and furs—constitute one distinct sector. The many thousands of styles generated in these industries each year have imposed severe limits on the rationalization of production methods. Production runs are short and materials, such as fabrics, buttons, and trims, are highly diversified. With production schedules geared to rapid filling of retail orders for perishable merchandise, employment tends to be highly uneven, particularly during periods of slack general business activity. The more expensive price lines, which require more styling and handiwork, are still generally produced by skilled operators who perform the sewing operations for a whole garment. The less expensive volume price lines follow a section system of manufacture, in which each operator performs a highly specialized sewing task, often with specialized sewing machines or attachments. Little skill or training is required for the latter operations.

A common organizational form in these branches of the industry is the contractor system under which the principal entrepreneur—the jobber—designs and markets the product and procures the materials, but contracts out the actual production of the garments. This arrangement has the obvious advantage to the jobber of imposing upon the contractor all the costs and managerial problems associated with irregularity of production, as well as the responsibility for recruitment, supervision, and compensation of the production work force. In contrast, the conventional manufacturer, or inside shop, performs all of the above operations in a single organizational entity.

These fashion-oriented branches of the industry have also had in common a stronger centrifugal orientation, as evidenced by the fact that—despite accelerated outmigration—over one-half of total national employment in the women's outerwear industries was still concentrated in the three Middle Atlantic states of New York, New Jersey, and Pennsylvania in the early 1970s, and predominantly in the New York City metropolitan area. This has been explained by such factors as ready availability of skilled labor, of a large variety of diversified materials, and of large concentrations of retail store buyers in a single location, and the need for speedy deliveries of seasonal-style merchandise. [22]

At the opposite extreme have been those branches of the industry, such as men's shirts and work clothing, which are much less influenced by style factors and—hence—have been able to schedule long production runs. These industries are characterized by larger firm sizes, as illustrated by an average of about 190 employees per establishment in the work clothing industry and about 170 in men's shirt and nightwear factories. [23] The breakdown of work processes and the use of highly specialized sewing equipment is considerably more advanced. With low skill requirements and a limited need to be located near major market centers, labor supply has been the major factor in the locational orientation of these factories. This is illustrated by their relatively high geographical concentration in the southeastern states and—typically—in smaller cities or rural communities where they have been able to tap large reserves of low-wage female labor.

Employment and Labor Supply Trends

The early origins and growth of the factory clothing industry are inextricably bound with the history of immigration into the United States, and particularly with the successive waves of Jewish immigration from Central and Eastern Europe. It was the German-Jewish middle-class immigrants who were the early entrepreneurs in the emerging ready-to-wear women's and men's clothing industries in the latter decades of the nineteenth century, when these industries were initially localized in such cities as New York, Philadelphia, Boston, Chicago, and Rochester. In turn, it was the poor Jewish immigrants from the ghettos of Poland and Russia—many of whom had been employed as tailors or seamstresses in their countries of origin—who provided the initial supplies of cheap factory labor, both skilled and unskilled, as these industries expanded during the decades immediately preceding World War I.

Summary census statistics on the distribution of the apparel industry's operatives as of 1910 provide some indication of its reliance upon immigrant labor. Of a total of 436,000 workers reported as sewing machine operators or in other apparel operative occupations, 203,000, or nearly 47 percent, were foreign born, and an additional 113,000, or 26 percent, were natives born of immigrant parents. [24] From other evidence, it is clear moreover that the immigrant concentration was much higher in the women's outerwear and men's coat and suit industries, as contrasted to such decentralized branches as work clothing and other cotton garments. In contrast, employment of

blacks in apparel factories was negligible during this period: less than
2 percent of all apparel industry employees were blacks in 1910 and
these were probably mainly utilized as laborers or in unskilled service-type jobs.[25]

Another aspect of the early labor supply for the apparel industry
was the relatively large proportion of men initially employed in this
low-wage field. In 1910, about 55 percent of all apparel industry
workers were men. Collateral census data—limited to apparel industry
operatives—indicate that about two-thirds of these male apparel workers were foreign born, whereas over 60 percent of female apparel
industry operatives were native born.[26] The male apparel industry
workers were concentrated in the more style-oriented sectors of the
industry, localized in New York and other immigration centers,
whereas the less style-oriented branches of the industry were much
more decentralized and hence utilized a much larger proportion of
native-born female workers. In succeeding decades, as the proportion
of foreign-born workers declined, apparel operatives have become
predominantly female. In 1970, 89 percent of all apparel industry
operatives were women, mainly engaged in sewing machine operations
(see Table 6.1).

Unlike many other lower-level occupations, the proportion of
blacks employed in apparel manufacturing has been relatively low.
It rose significantly, however, from 7.5 percent to 10.2 percent between 1960 and 1970, according to census data. One factor contributing
to the relatively limited utilization of blacks in this industry has been
a continued reliance on other disadvantaged minority groups, notably
those of Spanish origin, in those areas where these groups are concentrated. In 1970, Spanish-origin workers accounted for 11.0 percent
of the work force of apparel operatives—a much higher proportion than
their representation in the employed work force as a whole.

Until 1966, the apparel manufacturing industry had experienced a
secular growth in employment. This was stimulated, initially, by the
shift from home sewing or custom work by seamstresses or tailors
to factory manufacture of ready-to-wear products. Subsequently, it
was maintained by growth in population and real per capita income.
Between 1910 and 1940, the number of gainful workers in the apparel
industry approximately doubled, rising from 370,000 to 707,000,
according to estimates by Edwards from decennial census statistics.[27]
A further sharp expansion of apparel industry employment was recorded in the following two and a half decades, when the total number
of production workers in apparel manufacturing rose from 819,000 in
1940 to a peak of 1,246,000 in 1966, according to BLS establishment-
based statistics.[28] However, between 1966 and 1973, production
worker employment in the industry declined by about 83,000, to

TABLE 6.1

Apparel Industry Employment Trends, 1910–70

	Number (000)			Percent	Black as Percent of
Year	Total	Male	Female	Female	Total
Total apparel industry employees					
1940	781	265	515	65.9	2.5
1950	1,065	311	754	79.8	7.1
1960	1,159	294	865	74.6	7.5
1970	1,219	273	946	77.6	10.2
Apparel industry operatives					
1960	893	139	754	84.4	n.a.
1970	790	99	808	89.1	11.5

Note: Census data on employed apparel industry operatives of Spanish origin, available only for 1970, indicate that a total of 100,000 workers of Spanish origin were employed in this occupation, corresponding to 11.0 percent of total apparel industry operatives.

Sources: Data for total employees from Elaine Wrong, The Negro in the Apparel Industry, The Racial Policies of American Industry, Report no. 31, Industrial Research Unit, Wharton School (Philadelphia: University of Pennsylvania Press, 1974), tables 9, 17, from decennial censuses. Data for apparel industry operatives from Bureau of the Census, Census of Population, 1960, "Occupation by Industry" PC(2)7C (Washington, D.C.: U.S. Government Printing Office, 1963), table 2 and Census of Population, 1970 PC(2)7B (Washington, D.C.: U.S. Government Printing Office, 1972), table 1.

1,163,000, with reductions distributed among almost all industry branches, other than men's and boys' furnishings.

The Role of Import Competition

This employment reduction, in the face of a continued upward trend in apparel purchases by American consumers, has been attributed to the sharp increase of imports of apparel since the 1960s, primarily from low-wage countries such as Taiwan, South Korea, Hong Kong, Japan, and Mexico. Imports of certain low-priced apparel items had created severe competitive problems for some branches of the industry for a number of decades. For example, the importation of scarves from Japan beginning in the mid-1950s had the effect of virtually wiping out domestic production of this item.[29] Thereafter, other items of apparel began to be imported at an increasing rate. The precise degree of import penetration during this period is difficult to estimate because of the absence of a common pricing or valuation base for imports in relation to domestic shipments. However, estimates by the Research Department of the International Ladies Garment Workers Union (ILGWU), based upon a conversion of apparel imports to domestic price equivalents, provide a reasonable approximation. (See Table 6.2.) They indicate a gradual increase in the volume of imports as a percentage of domestic consumption, from less than 4 percent in 1956 to 12 percent in 1965 and to nearly 25 percent in 1972. In an initial effort to check the growth of these imports, a multinational arrangement was concluded, under the auspices of the General Agreement on Tariffs and Trade (GATT), which established quota limits on exports to the United States of cotton textiles, cotton apparel, and other fabricated cotton products. However, these controls did not extend to textiles and apparel using wool or man-made fibers. It was in the latter categories that imports mushroomed in the following decade. Thus, the ILGWU has estimated the following percentage increases in apparel imports between 1961 and 1972, based on square yards of fabric used in their manufacture:

Type of Apparel	Percentage Increase in Imports, 1961-72
All	605
Cotton	110
Wool	168
Man-made fibers	5,553

TABLE 6.2

Imports, Domestic Production, and Exports of Apparel
(Knit and Woven), United States
(in millions of 1957-59 dollars)

Year	Imports	Domestic Production	Exports	Imports as Percent of Domestic Production	Imports as Percent of Domestic Consumption
1956	395.7	10,055.5	68.0	3.9	3.8
1957	435.4	10,214.1	71.1	4.3	4.1
1958	547.2	9,922.9	72.3	5.5	5.3
1959	869.8	10,557.5	75.9	8.2	7.7
1960	920.8	10,693.8	86.7	8.6	8.0
1961	744.7	10,891.5	83.3	6.8	6.4
1962	1,175.4	11,498.6	70.7	10.2	9.3
1963	1,230.4	11,635.4	74.7	10.6	9.6
1964	1,450.8	12,172.9	83.3	11.9	10.7
1965	1,741.9	12,877.0	96.3	13.5	12.0
1966	1,868.2	13,122.0	105.9	14.2	12.6
1967	2,146.8	13,480.2	107.4	15.8	13.8
1968	2,499.2	13,744.4	115.4	18.1	15.5
1969	3,098.8	13,721.0	140.1	22.6	18.6
1970	3,268.6	13,126.8	127.9	24.9	19.7
1971	3,819.8	13,533.0	133.7	28.2	22.2
1972	4,681.9*	14,344.3*	158.3*	32.6*	24.8*

*Preliminary
Source: Unpublished estimates, by Research Department of
International Ladies Garment Workers Union, New York.

The degree of import penetration has been generally greater for
most categories of women's and girls' apparel than for men's clothing
and it has been greater for apparel items relying mainly on man-made
fabrics, such as sweaters, blouses, and raincoats, than for those
relying on cotton, such as men's work clothing and underwear. Apparel
items requiring higher-than-average degrees of skill and styling such
as women's dresses and men's suits, on the other hand, have experienced smaller inroads from foreign competition, to date.

The causes of this massive influx of imports clearly stem from
the much lower wage rates in the major apparel exporting countries,
as compared to those in the United States. The extent of these differentials is suggested by the following 1974 BLS comparisons of hourly
compensation rates for textile production workers in selected competing countries:

Estimated Compensation per Hour Worked, 1972 ($ U.S.)

United States	3.22
Italy	2.02
Japan	1.25
Mexico	.92
Hong Kong	.44*
Korea	.25-.26
Taiwan	.20

*Based on published average hourly earnings; may exclude
some fringe benefits.

Other contributing factors were the general shift from reliance on
natural fabrics to man-made fabrics, the rapid post-World War II
development of the needed capital and entrepreneurial skills in the
low-wage exporting countries and major strides in world wide communications and air transport, which have further reduced the locational advantages of domestic apparel producers. Moreover, in view
of the prevailing labor-intensive technology in domestic apparel manufacturing, it is not apparent that the domestic industry enjoys any
marked labor productivity advantage as compared to its major foreign
competitors.[30]

In an effort to check the growing impact of foreign competition
upon jobs of domestic apparel workers, the leading apparel unions
initiated a major campaign, together with domestic apparel manufacturing interests, to limit the imports of apparel produced from
man-made fibers and wool, as well as from cotton. In 1971, these
pressures resulted in negotiation of a series of bilateral agreements
by the United States with four major exporting countries—Japan, South

Korea, the Republic of China (Taiwan) and Hong Kong. These agreements, in combination with the impacts of dollar devaluation, resulted in moderate reductions in unit volume of apparel imports in the following two years. Subsequently, a general agreement was negotiated under GATT in 1973 by which import restraints for apparel using wool and man-made fibers, allowing for growth rates of 6 percent per year or less, could be established between importing and exporting countries under bilateral agreements.

At this writing, it is still not practicable to assess the longer-range implications of these agreements. The present agreements are of limited duration and are based on physical units rather than value. These considerations suggest that there will be continued heavy import competition for domestic apparel manufacturers in the years ahead, with possible shifts of emphasis on the part of apparel exporting countries from low-unit-cost to higher-unit-cost items, and with possible emergence of new (non-quota-limited) sources of cheap-labor competition for the domestic industry.

Geographical Shifts in Apparel Employment

The significant movement of apparel production from domestic to foreign sources, described above, has been paralleled by a major geographical redistribution of the apparel industry within the United States. As noted earlier, the availability of a large pool of cheap, easily trained immigrant labor had been a prime factor in the initial localization of major segments of the apparel industry in New York City and in other large eastern seaboard cities. This locational advantage was reduced, however, in the early 1920s as a result of two concurrent factors: (1) the virtual stoppage of immigrant inflows during World War I and the sharp reduction in immigration under the immigration laws enacted in the early 1920s, and (2) the growth of apparel unionism in the established centers of the industry. Victor Fuchs, in his study of manufacturing location trends between 1929 and 1954, has noted that two patterns of geographical redistribution were evident in the apparel industry during this period: "Those apparel industries that are heavily dependent upon the New York City garment center either for part of the production process or for styling and distribution tended to have their largest comparative gains in the states surrounding New York or in the South Atlantic states (e.g., women's and children's clothing). Those industries that were not as dependent on New York tended to grow rapidly in the East South Central states (e.g., men's and boys' clothing)."[31] On the other hand, those industry branches which were very dependent on style, skilled labor, and external economies (for example, furs) showed no decrease in concentration in New York. Based on a multivariate analysis of ten locational factors, Fuchs concluded that "as in the case of textiles, the desire to avoid unions and to utilize the less expensive labor of the South appear to have been the major influences determining the direction of redistribution."[32]

Prior to the 1950s, these shifts in geographical distribution were relatively gradual and coincided with continued strong secular growth in overall apparel manufacturing employment. Thus, between 1940 and 1950, the New York City SMSA's share of total apparel employment dropped from 36.2 percent to 33.3 percent; but the number of apparel workers employed in New York continued to increase, from 283,000 to 354,000, according to decennial census data. Beginning in the 1950s, however, the overall rate of apparel industry employment growth slowed down appreciably and—at the same time—the rate of relocation accelerated rapidly. As a result, employment in the New York apparel industry dropped severely both in absolute numbers and in its share of the national total. Between 1950 and 1970, apparel industry employment in the New York City SMSA declined from 311,000 to 173,000, while its share of total apparel employment fell by more than one-half, from 29.2 percent to 14.2 percent. (See Table 6.3.) Similar, although less severe, reductions occurred in New England and in the Midwest. The Middle Atlantic region, exclusive of the New York SMSA, experienced a much more limited reduction, since continued movement of certain branches of the industry to Pennsylvania (typically to depressed coal mining communities) tended to offset sharp employment reductions elsewhere in these states.

In contrast to this declining pattern in the North, the southern states, as a group, experienced a major expansion in apparel industry employment. Between 1950 and 1970, the number of employed apparel workers in the southern states increased by about 280 percent, from 180,000 to 501,000, while their share of total apparel employment rose from 16.9 percent to 41.1 percent. The growth of the southern apparel industry appears to have been widespread throughout the southeastern and southwestern states, but was particularly rapid in states such as North Carolina, South Carolina, Tennessee, Florida, Alabama, and Mississippi. Apparel employment in these six states grew nearly fivefold, from 69,500 in 1950 to 335,400 in 1970. The southern apparel industry has, moreover, tended to locate mainly in smaller cities and towns, rather than in large metropolitan centers, paralleling the locational pattern of the textile industry in this region. One notable exception has been the Miami SMSA, where apparel industry employment expanded from 5,300 in 1960 to 15,700 in 1970. This appears to have been a direct consequence of the sharp growth during the decade in the Cuban refugee population in Miami which—in common with earlier immigrant groups—provided an adaptable low-wage labor supply for this industry in Miami, as well as a source of entrepreneurial skills.

TABLE 6.3

Apparel Industry Employment by Region: 1950, 1960, and 1970

Region	1950		1960		1970	
	Number (000)	Percent	Number (000)	Percent	Number (000)	Percent
New York standard metropolitan statistical area	311	29.2	255	22.0	173	14.2
Middle Atlantic, excluding New York standard metropolitan statistical area	279	26.2	271	23.4	258	21.2
New England	78	7.3	84	7.2	68	5.6
South	180	16.9	335	28.9	501	41.1
Midwest	161	15.1	139	12.0	130	10.7
Far West	53	5.0	64	5.5	73	6.0
United States*	1,065	100.0	1,159	100.0	1,219	100.0

*Regional totals do not add to U.S. totals because some states were excluded from regions.

Source: Adapted from Elaine Wrong, The Negro in the Apparel Industry, The Racial Policies of American Industry, Report no. 31, Industrial Research Unit, Wharton School (Philadelphia: University of Pennsylvania Press, 1974), tables 22, 25.

A more detailed analysis of differential geographical trends in apparel employment between 1959 and 1971 by industry branch, based on establishment data published in County Business Patterns, is presented in Table 6.4. These comparisons indicate that, with few exceptions, the northern states experienced significant losses of apparel jobs in all branches of the industry and that the southeastern and southwestern states were the major gainers.

The broad pattern of geographical redistribution during this period continued, however, to resemble that described by Fuchs in his analysis of earlier trends in this industry, between 1929 and 1954. Notably, those industries which were least dependent upon the New York garment center because of style factors or related marketing considerations, such as men's and boys' furnishings and work clothing, experienced consistent employment losses in all the major northern production areas and moved, particularly to southwestern states such as Texas, although southern states, generally, experienced sharp employment growth in this branch. Conversely, industry branches which were more style oriented, such as women's and misses' outerwear, experienced a less-than-average employment loss in the established production centers, with relatively sharper gains in the southeastern than in the Southwestern, states. The continued importance of convenient geographical access to the New York garment center for some components of this industry is illustrated by the fact that Pennsylvania experienced a moderate employment increase of 22.7 percent in the women's outerwear branch between 1959 and 1971 in contrast to declines in most other branches.

The Role of Labor Market Factors

The root causes for the massive geographical redistribution of apparel industry employment, both externally and internally, are by almost all accounts associated with the geographical differentials in wage rates and in labor costs in this highly competitive, labor-intensive industry. The contrast between wage rates in the major apparel exporting countries, competing in the U.S. market, with those in the United States has already been noted. Within the United States, apparel industry wage differentials between North and South, and between the large metropolitan centers and smaller communities, are also considerable—although, of course, within a much more modest range of variation. The extent of these differentials is illustrated by the following comparisons, based on BLS wage surveys:

1. In the women's and misses' dress manufacturing industry, among 12 cities surveyed, average hourly earnings of section-system sewing machine operators in August 1971 ranged from lows of $1.88

TABLE 6.4

Percent Changes in Apparel Industry Employment, 1959–71, by Industry Branch, for Selected Geographical Divisions and States

Selected Divisions and States	Total Apparel	Men's and Boys' Suits	Men's and Boys' Furnishings	Women's and Misses' Outerwear	Women's and Children's Undergarments	Children's Outerwear
United States	11.4	-6.0	28.1	12.2	-.4	-.9
Selected Divisions						
Middle Atlantic	-14.7	-15.9	-10.0	-6.8	-29.8	-29.0
Southeast	75.2	n.a.	43.2	170.1	81.0	126.8
Southwest	95.4	8.9	165.6	75.5	n.a.	- 12.6
Selected States						
New York	-23.5	-26.6	-7.0	-19.3	-34.2	-33.9
Pennsylvania	-.1	.2	-10.2	22.7	-15.2	-27.1
New Jersey	-12.4	-30.4	-7.2	-1.0	-42.9	-18.5
Massachusetts	-22.4	-19.4	-13.2	-19.5	-39.6	-38.3
Illinois	-29.1	-21.1	-36.5	-33.9	-62.9	-68.3
North Carolina	135.5	n.a.	89.2	335.7	53.0	159.0
South Carolina	71.0	n.a.	22.9	85.0	34.7	34.8
Georgia	62.9	100.4	51.8	115.0	79.0	162.4
Tennessee	70.4	47.5	40.8	302.6	118.5	775.2
Texas	86.2	8.9	153.3	72.1	89.4	-21.1
California	24.6	22.0	18.8	26.3	14.7	-.9

Source: U.S. Department of Commerce, Bureau of the Census, County Business Patterns, 1969 (Washington, D.C.: U.S. Government Printing Office, 1970).

in Miami and $2.03 in Dallas to highs of $2.83 in Chicago and $3.22 in New York City. [33]

2. In the men's and boys' suit and coat manufacturing industry, average hourly earnings of sewing machine operators in April 1973 ranged from a low of $2.64 in the southeastern states to a high of $3.52 in the Middle Atlantic states. [34]

3. In the trousers manufacturing industry, hourly earnings similarly ranged from $1.84 in North Carolina to $2.55 in the Middle Atlantic region. [35]

These interarea differences in earnings do not necessarily correspond to differentials in unit labor costs, because of the likelihood that—under the prevailing piece-rate system of pay—workers in the higher-wage areas are more experienced and productive than those in low-wage areas. Nevertheless, in view of the limited amount of skill involved in most of these machine-sewing operations, it may be assumed that unit labor cost differentials are quite substantial and have provided the major impetus for industry relocation. The importance of a labor cost differential of, for example, 20 percent in the competitive position of different apparel production centers is illustrated by the fact that payroll costs accounted for 54 percent of total value added in the apparel industry in 1972, while profit-to-sales margins averaged 2.3 percent. [36]

Regional wage differentials alone cannot, however, fully explain the sharp and sustained migration of the apparel industry in the 1950s and 1960s. Such differentials existed in earlier decades as well. It seems probable that the high rate of outmovement has been prompted by a number of additional economic and locational factors, including the increased postwar concentration of raw materials sources (particularly the new synthetic textiles plants) in the southern states, the heavy competitive pressures upon the domestic apparel industry stemming from increased foreign competition, and the rapid extension of our national highway network (thus reducing the need for market proximity).

In addition, there is considerable evidence that labor factors—other than those directly reflected in wage rate differentials—may also have played an important role. The two major unions in the apparel industry—the ILGWU and the Amalgamated Clothing Workers of America (ACWA)—were initially organized in the years prior to World War I; they developed considerable strength in the 1920s and, after a period of eclipse during the depression years, emerged as a dominant force in New York and other major northern and midwestern apparel manufacturing centers. They have, however, met with limited success in organizing workers in the cities and towns of the South, as well as in some of the out-of-town districts in northern states, as

illustrated by the fact that only 30.7 percent of all apparel industry
workers were reported to be union members in a census survey conducted in March 1971,[37] as contrasted to high degrees of unionization
in the established apparel centers. This has not only served to per-
petuate regional wage rate differentials, but has given employers in
the established centers the further motivation to relocate in order to
escape from a whole range of related constraints under collective
bargaining agreements. Additional considerations, noted in various
press articles, include rising crime in the New York garment district
and related problems of congestion, high rentals, and urban blight.[38]

    These problems appear to have been compounded in the late 1960s
by evidence of considerable labor recruitment difficulties in the metropolitan apparel industry even in the face of declining employment
levels. Elaine Wrong in her study of black employment in the industry
noted recurring employer complaints of scarcity of job applicants in
the course of field visits in cities such as New York, Chicago, Philadelphia, Los Angeles, and San Francisco.[39] Some supporting evidence
is provided by BLS job vacancy statistics, compiled for several years
beginning in 1969. Job vacancy rates during 1969-73 were consistently
higher in apparel manufacturing than in other manufacturing industries,
as shown in Table 6.5. In fact, the long-term vacancy rate—a more
sensitive indicator of recruitment difficulties—was at least twice as
high as the corresponding average for all manufacturing industries,
despite the fact that apparel manufacturing experienced a significant
employment decline during this period.

Apparel Labor Market Contrasts: New York Standard Metropolitan
Statistical Area Versus North Carolina

    In order to provide additional insight on labor market factors
influencing the relocation of the apparel industry and related labor
supply implications, we have selected two apparel manufacturing areas
for comparison: the New York City SMSA and North Carolina. The
New York area, as noted above, has experienced a severe reduction
in apparel employment; North Carolina has experienced a rapid growth
and ranked first among southern states in total apparel manufacturing
employment in 1970. Table 6.6 compares selected characteristics of
these two areas.

    Between 1960 and 1970, total apparel industry employment, as
reported in the decennial censuses, declined by more than one-third
in the New York City SMSA, from 255,000 to 173,000; it nearly doubled
in North Carolina, rising from 33,000 to 63,000. In New York, the
apparel industry work force has included an exceptionally large proportion of older workers, as evidenced by a median age (for female
employees) of 45.0 years in 1960, as compared to a median age of

TABLE 6.5

Job Vacancy Rates in Apparel Manufacturing and in
All Manufacturing Industries, 1969-72

| | Total Job Vacancy Rates | | Long-Term Vacancy Rates | |
| | Apparel | All | Apparel | All |
Year	Manufacturing	Manufacturing	Manufacturing	Manufacturing
1969	1.9	1.3	1.2	.6
1970	1.4	.7	.7	.3
1971	1.2	.5	.6	.1
1972	1.4	.7	.6	.2
1973	1.7	.9	.7	.3

Note: Vacancy rates are computed by dividing the number of vacancies by the sum of employment and vacancies and multiplying the quotient by 100. Long-term job vacancies are those that have remained unfilled for 30 days or more.

Sources: U.S. Department of Labor, Bureau of Labor Statistics, Handbook of Labor Statistics, 1973 (Washington, D.C.: U.S. Government Printing Office, 1974), table 53 and Employment and Earnings, March 1974 (Washington, D.C.: U.S. Government Printing Office, 1974), table E3.

41.4 years for all female workers in that area. Moreover, despite the high labor turnover in the industry and its limited skill requirements, relatively few young workers entered the New York apparel industry in the following decade. As a result, the median age of New York female apparel workers rose sharply, to 48.4 years, as compared with a decline of about a half year in the median age of all employed women in the New York area. In contrast, the apparel industry work force in North Carolina consists predominantly of young women, and rose by only one year in median age between 1960 and 1970. These contrasts in age structure are to be expected, to some extent, in any comparisons of declining and expanding industries or occupations. However, in combination with collateral information about recruitment difficulties experienced by New York apparel manufacturers in the late 1960s, they do suggest that reluctance of younger workers to enter this industry may have contributed to some degree to the reduction in apparel employment in the New York area.

The trends in racial composition of the apparel work force in these two areas also show a significant contrast. In New York, the percentage of nonwhite workers rose only slightly, from 11.2 percent

TABLE 6.6

Selected Characteristics of Apparel Workers, New York
Standard Metropolitan Statistical Area and
North Carolina: 1960, 1970

Characteristic	New York City Area		North Carolina	
	1960	1970	1960	1970
Employed workers, apparel manufacturing (000)	254.6	172.9	33.0	62.9
Nonwhites as percent of total apparel workers	11.2	11.7	4.6	16.2
Median age, female apparel workers	45.0	48.4	38.1	38.1
Median annual earnings, All Women				
All occupations	2,876	4,770	1,820	3,413
Apparel workers	2,438	3,826	1,953	3,251
Ratio to earnings in all occupations	.85	.80	1.07	.95
Median annual earnings, nonwhite women				
All occupations	2,344	4,501	754	2,128
Apparel workers	2,329	3,826	n.a.	2,808
Ratio to earnings in all occupations	.99	.85	—	1.32
Median annual earnings, Puerto Rican women (New York City only)				
All occupations	n.a.	3,958	—	—
Apparel workers	n.a.	3,615	—	—
Ratio to earnings in all occupations	—	.91	—	—

Note: Median annual earnings data refer to wage and salary workers with any earnings in 1959 and 1969, respectively.

Source: 1960 and 1970 Censuses of Population, Detailed Characteristics, New York and North Carolina, 1960: Tables 128, 130; 1970: Tables 187, 189.

to 11.7 percent, between 1960 and 1970. In North Carolina, the percentage of nonwhite workers rose sharply from 4.6 percent to 16.2 percent. This sharp increase paralleled the experience of most southern states in this industry with the notable exception of those with large Spanish-origin or other white ethnic populations, such as Florida, Texas, and Louisiana. [40] It also closely paralleled the trend in the southern textile industry, which resembles the apparel industry in many of its work force characteristics.

Several explanations have been offered for the relatively limited growth in the percentage of nonwhites in the New York apparel industry: the general contraction in job opportunities in the industry; apparent employer preferences for Puerto Rican workers (who accounted for about the same proportion of the work force there as did nonwhites); and the rapid growth of New York welfare rolls, including a disproportionate number of black women. [41] In turn, the rapid growth in the nonwhite ratio in North Carolina and other southern states has been attributed to a combination of rapid apparel industry employment growth and reduced availability of white women for these low-wage jobs—with a possible assist from the impact of federal equal employment opportunity programs.

The extent to which differences in comparative earnings opportunities for women in each area affected the industry's labor force composition and growth potential can be further illustrated by the earnings comparisons in Table 6.6. In the New York City area, median annual earnings of female apparel workers in 1959 were $2,438, nearly 20 percent higher than those of their counterparts in North Carolina but 15 percent below the median earnings of all New York female workers. Thus, by this criterion, apparel employment was unattractive to a large majority of women in the New York City area. In North Carolina, however, apparel worker earnings in 1959 were 7 percent above the corresponding median for all female workers, thus making work in apparel factories relatively desirable for a majority of women there.

By 1969, the relative earnings status of apparel workers had declined both in New York and North Carolina. In New York, female apparel worker earnings were 20 percent below the average for all female workers. In North Carolina, the ratio shifted from a positive differential of 7 percent in 1959 to an adverse differential of 5 percent in 1969, reflecting the general economic expansion of the state and the resulting broadening of job horizons for women there.

The above earnings comparisons refer to women of all races and ethnic origins. In the case of nonwhite women, the available data for 1969 indicate a striking contrast in relative earnings opportunities between New York and North Carolina. In New York, apparel industry employment was nearly as undesirable an employment option for nonwhite women as for white women, although more desirable to Puerto Rican women, based on relative earnings ratios for them. However, in North Carolina, nonwhite women in the apparel industry earned 32 percent more than the average for all North Carolina non-white women—reflecting the continued concentration of the latter in low-wage jobs such as domestic work.

These comparisons, when related to such trends as the inflow of nonwhite women into southern apparel factories in the 1960s, thus tend to support the hypothesis that apparel factory jobs became relatively less attractive to white southern women, in turn compelling employers to modify earlier hiring practices and open up operative jobs to increasing numbers of nonwhites, to whom such jobs still represented a step up the ladder.

Interarea Differences in Apparel Employment Trends: An Econometric Approach

In an effort to broaden our assessment of the factors contributing to the geographical shifts in the industry, a number of econometric models were tested using our data base of over 60 large SMSAs, with 250,000 or more population, described in Chapter 4. In these models, the dependent variable was the percentage change in apparel industry employment between 1960 and 1970 (E_{60-70}). We postulated that this growth rate was a function of—

1. apparel operatives' earnings, as approximated by full-year median earnings of female sewers and stitchers in 1969 (W_s);
2. median 1969 earnings of all women with earnings (W_f);
3. female unemployment rates in each area (UNR);
4. average AFDC payments per family (AFDC);
5. percentage growth in area's total labor force between 1960 and 1970 (LF_{60-70}).

After a series of tests, the most successful formulation of the apparel wage variable (W_{fs}) was one which expressed this as a ratio to AFDC payments (that is, W_{fs}/AFDC), thus reflecting the gross income advantage of apparel industry wages as compared to welfare payments. The results are shown below, for all 61 SMSAs, and—separately—for southern and nonsouthern SMSAs in this sample. Elasticities at the mean are shown below the coefficients for each variable. The following notations are used to indicate statistical significance: * = .90, ** = .95, and *** = .99—confidence intervals.

All SMSAs (61)

$$E_{60-70} = -1.724 + 1.363LF_{60-70} + 27.592UNR_{70} + 0.0256W_{fs}/AFDC - 0.0000760W_f$$
$$\phantom{E_{60-70} = -1.724 + } (0.903)^{***} \quad\quad (2.901)^{***} \quad\quad (1.490)^{***} \quad\quad\quad (-0.616)$$

$$\bar{R}^2 = .316^{***}$$

Nonsouthern SMSAs (36)

$$E_{60-70} = -2.601 + 1.673LF_{60-70} + 33.128UNR_{70} + 0.0123W_{fs}/AFDC + 0.000116W_f$$
$$\phantom{E_{60-70} = -2.601 + } (1.836)^{***} \quad\quad (6.822)^{***} \quad\quad (1.076) \quad\quad\quad\quad (1.900)$$

$$\bar{R}^2 = .350^{***}$$

South (25)

$$E_{60-70} = 8.296 + 0.105LF_{60-70} - 31.574UNR_{70} + 0.0281W_{fs}/AFDC - 0.00202W_f$$
$$\phantom{E_{60-70} = 8.296 + } (0.0494) \quad\quad (-1.903) \quad\quad (1.260)^{**} \quad\quad\quad (-8.887)^{**}$$

$$\bar{R}^2 = .196^*$$

Thus, for the combined sample of 61 areas, the above findings indicate that apparel employment growth was greatest in areas of higher unemployment, in areas where the relationship of apparel workers' wages to public assistance payments was more favorable, and where labor force growth, generally, was more rapid. These factors in combination explained nearly one-third of the observed variance and all were highly significant, at the .95 confidence level or above.

In the nonwouthern areas, only two of these variables were significant—the unemployment rate and the labor force growth rate. Neither the apparel wage relative to AFDC nor general female earnings were significant at the .90 confidence level. This model accounted for 35 percent of the total variance in apparel employment trends in the nonwouthern SMSAs.

In the southern SMSAs, two variables proved significant in accounting for variations in apparel employment growth. These were the full-year median earnings of all women in the area's labor force, which proved strongly and negatively correlated with apparel employment growth, and the relationship between apparel workers' earnings and AFDC, which was positively correlated with employment growth. The overall model accounted for only about one-fifth of the observed variation in apparel employment growth but was significant at the

.90 confidence level. It should be noted, however, that separate regressions in the South, using the ratio of apparel employment growth to the area's overall labor force growth and limited to the above significant variables, resulted in an $\bar{R}^2$ value of .41, significant at the .99 confidence level.

The above analysis provides substantial confirmation of our hypothesis concerning the importance of labor market variables as major contributing factors in the geographic redistribution of the apparel industry during the 1960s. The fact that the model did not explain a greater share of the total variation in apparel employment trends must be attributed in part to inherent limitations in the available data base. In particular, we should note the omission from this data base of many smaller areas, particularly in the South, which experienced significant growth in apparel employment, but for which the relevant data were not available from published census sources. An effort was made, too, to test the effect of interarea differences in unionization, but this proved largely unsuccessful, possibly because of the lack of union membership data by SMSA, as opposed to data by state. Finally, we should note that the possible effects of growth in the Spanish-origin labor force upon apparel industry trends could not be included in the model, because of absence of comparable data for this population group for 1960. Other limitations of the data base have been discussed in more detail in Chapter 4.

Some of the specific findings stemming from this analysis are described below:

1. Apparel employers have moved differentially to areas where large reserves of low-wage female labor exist. This is indicated separately in the positive association between 1970 unemployment rates and employment growth in nonsouthern areas, and in the strong negative association between median earnings of all women and employment growth in the South. In the South, apparel employees have also moved into areas where AFDC payments are lower, in relation to apparel worker earnings.

2. It is clear, too, that these separate labor market variables have had a differential impact upon intraregional differences in apparel employment growth. For example, it is probable that the significant positive relationship to overall labor force growth in nonsouthern areas may be due to the greater relative growth in regional apparel markets in areas such as the West Coast, which continued to enjoy a relatively rapid rate of overall population growth during the 1960s.

3. Similarly, the highly significant positive relationship between 1970 female unemployment rates in nonsouthern areas and apparel industry employment trends—and the absence of the relationship in the South—may be due, in part, to the fact that such unemployment rates

did not provide a satisfactory measure of female labor reserves in the more rural South.

4. Finally, we must assume that intraregional and interarea differences in product mix as well as many other specific character-istics of area labor markets, such as proximity to textile and other material sources, also contributed to these locational trends and were inadequately reflected in our models.

Employment and Labor Supply Outlook

As suggested by our discussion of apparel industry trends, the longer-term employment outlook in the domestic apparel manufacturing industry will critically depend upon the extent of future import compe-tition. Apparel expenditures by American consumers have accounted for about 7 percent of total personal consumption expenditures: BLS projections, for example, provide for an increase in personal con-sumption expenditures for nondurable goods from $300 billion in 1972 to $469 billion in 1985, in constant dollars. [42] The fact that population growth through 1980 will be most rapid in the young adult group—which is normally much higher than average in per capita apparel expend-itures—has been noted as an additional favorable market factor. Based on these considerations, the Department of Commerce anticipated, in 1971, a relatively favorable growth outlook for the industry in the 1970s, provided that the growth rate of imports could be slowed. [43] Similarly, the BLS has projected an employment level of 1,587,000 for the apparel industry in 1985, an increase of 16 percent over 1970. [44]

Quite apart from cyclical fluctuations in aggregate business activity, the uncertain outlook for import competition in the domestic apparel market has made any longer-term projections of domestic apparel production and employment particularly hazardous. This is compounded, too, by the vagaries associated with changing styles and consumer preferences, which may particularly impact upon the fashion-oriented branches of the industry. These uncertainties, in turn, probably account for the fact that in years subsequent to 1971, the Department of Commerce has omitted any discussion of the apparel industry outlook from its annual industrial outlook reports.

From the labor supply standpoint, our labor force projections do suggest, however, some prospective constraints on employment growth among apparel operatives. Based on our projections of the labor force by occupational group, the number of female workers in all operative occupations (other than transport) is expected to increase by 14 percent between 1970 and 1985, as compared to a projected in-crease of 16 percent in apparel worker requirements. The supply of apparel operatives, moreover, can be expected to increase at a lower rate than the average for all female operatives, in view of the low wage and status ranking of this occupation. Thus, under conditions of high aggregative labor demand and of some stability in the level of apparel imports, the apparel industry may be expected to experience labor recruitment difficulties in the 1980s similar to those evidenced in the late 1960s and early 1970s. This could be compounded, moreover, by high separations from the labor force in established apparel manufacturing centers, due to the large proportion of older workers in their labor force.

In view of the highly competitive nature of this industry and its geographic mobility, any squeeze on low-wage female labor supply for the industry in existing locations can be expected to prompt continued movements of the industry to remaining areas with reserves of low-wage female labor, as well as increased utilization of minority group workers, where available. Such factors as the rate of economic development of the deep South, the extent of unionization, and the extent to which earnings of minority group women will catch up with those of other women, will be important variables.

Enactment of welfare reform proposals, establishing minimum levels of welfare payments substantially above those now prevailing in many southern states, would tend to raise the reserve wage of female workers there. As indicated in our econometric analysis, the relationship between apparel workers' earnings and AFDC payments was identified as a key variable, affecting differential rates of employment growth. A national minimum welfare payment level could therefore have the effect of slowing down the movement of apparel plants to low-wage communities and raising the relative wage of apparel workers, generally.

CONSTRUCTION LABORERS

The Changing Nature of the Construction Laborer's Job

From the era of the pyramids on, the construction laborer has provided a historical prototype of heavy unskilled manual work, performed frequently under onerous conditions, by the lowest class or caste groups in society. This traditional image of the construction laborer's job is succinctly summarized in one of the training pamphlets of the Laborers' International Union of North America (LIUNA)—the largest union of organized construction laborers:

Not too long ago, a laborer contributed principally one
thing to his job—muscle. The tools he used—pick,
shovel, hand tamperer, crowbar—were muscle tools.
A man who had never used them before might be awk-
ward for a few days, but he became pretty good with
them by the time his blisters broke and he developed
calluses. This laborer could get by without even
knowing how to read or write. . . . "45

A considerable, although unmeasured, proportion of all construction laborer jobs probably still correspond reasonably closely to this
description. However, the progressive introduction of mechanical,
power-operated equipment for a wide range of specialized construction
tasks has reduced the "back-breaking" aspects of many of these jobs
and has imposed an increased requirement for at least a moderate
degree of initial training. Thus, the 1970 census occupational classification guide lists approximately 275 job titles which fall under the
occupational category of construction laborer. These range from the
more traditional unskilled labor jobs, such as brick carrier, hole
digger, and shoveler, to jobs such as concrete vibrator operator and
sandblast operator, which require operation of costly power-driven
equipment. The latter types of jobs probably now constitute a substantial proportion of all jobs performed by construction laborers and are
often analogous in skill requirements to those performed by semiskilled operatives in many industrial occupations.

Some confirmation of the mixed skill composition of the construction laborer occupation is provided by the results of a 1963 Labor
Department-CPS survey of occupational training of American workers.
As was to be expected all but a small percentage of construction laborers responded that training for their job could best be acquired by
either casual methods or informal on-the-job instruction. Nevertheless, only 13.4 percent indicated that no training of any type was
needed for their occupation, as contrasted to 18.4 percent of laborers
in manufacturing occupations and 25.2 percent in non-manufacturing
occupations, other than construction.46

The nature of the construction laborer's job, and the relative
utilization of laborers as compared to skilled workers, vary considerably among the major branches of the construction industry.
Private residential building is the largest single component of the
industry, as measured by dollar value of new construction, and has
constituted between one-third and two-fifths of total annual new construction activity. Private nonresidential building (commercial, industrial, institutional) has accounted for between one-fifth and one-
fourth of the total. Other major components—public utilities, public
buildings, and highways—have each accounted for about 10 percent of
the total dollar volume.47

Private residential building is still conducted predominantly by small specialized contractor firms, whereas larger firms predominate in nonresidential construction and in public works construction activities. The latter are more highly capitalized, make more extensive utilization of construction machinery, and, in turn, tend to have a lower relative requirement for construction laborers. This is illustrated by a comparative analysis of the percentage of total construction man-hours accounted for by on-site laborers, helpers, and tenders in several categories of construction work surveyed by the BLS over the decade of the 1960s. This ratio ranged from 20.7 percent for hospitals to 36.0 percent for single-family housing. (See Table 6.7.)

In many respects, private residential building—and particularly construction of single-family homes—constitutes a distinct noncompeting sector of the industry, as compared to larger-scale construction activities. Although comprehensive occupational wage statistics by industry branch are not available, construction laborers' wages in private residential building, by most indicators, are substantially lower than in other major sectors. This results, in part, from the differential extent of unionization in these two sectors. Whereas about 30 percent of all construction laborers were reported to be union members in a BLS survey conducted in 1970, spokesmen for the LIUNA have estimated that only about one-fifth of those engaged in residential building are union members, as contrasted to possibly 40 percent or more of those engaged in the nonresidential sector. The latter types of construction are, moreover, much more likely to be subject to the provisions of the Walsh-Healey Act which tend to link wage levels under federal government contracts to those established under local collective bargaining agreements. The impact of unionization upon construction laborers' wage rates, in turn, is suggested by a BLS survey conducted in 1972, which indicated that straight-time average hourly earnings for unionized construction laborers averaged approximately 40 percent higher than for nonunion laborers in the same SMSAs. It is probable, however, that—even in the absence of unionization—significant intraindustry variation in wage rates would be observed, in view of the somewhat higher skill levels required of laborers in the more mechanized branches of the industry and the greater premium placed by firms in these branches on assuring a reliable labor supply.

Despite these considerable intraoccupational variations, earnings of construction laborers, as a group, compare unfavorably with those workers in more skilled occupational categories. Of a total of 631,000 male construction laborers reported in the 1970 census, only 47 percent had worked for a full year (50-52 weeks) in 1969, reflecting both a high proportion of seasonal and part-year workers in the occupation and its high incidence of unemployment.[48] Median earnings of full-year

TABLE 6.7

Man-hours of On-Site Laborers, Helpers, and Tenders as a
Percent of Total Man-hours per $1,000 of Contract for
Selected Construction Projects, by Region

Type of Construction Project and Year	United States	Region			
		Northeast	North Central	South	West
Hospitals (1960)	27.7	24.6	26.2	32.0	18.6
College housing (1961)	31.8	24.9	29.5	40.5	24.7
Elementary and secondary schools (1961)	29.1	27.8	27.2	38.7	23.0
Federal office buildings (1962)	32.5	28.3	31.6	33.7	25.1
Public housing (1964)	30.9	23.3	25.3	40.8	22.0
Hospitals (1971)	20.7	23.9	23.4	35.5	17.2
Single-family housing (1969)	36.0	n.a.	n.a.	n.a.	n.a.

Sources: Adapted from data appearing in the following BLS publications on labor and material requirements for various categories of construction: "School Construction," BLS Bulletin 1199 (GPO, 1961), "College Housing Construction," BLS Bulletin 1441 (GPO, 1965), "Hospital Construction," BLS Bulletin 1340 (GPO, 1964), "Public Housing Construction," BLS Bulletin 1402 (GPO 1964), "Hospital and Nursing Home Construction," BLS Bulletin 1961 (GPO, 1971), "Single Family Housing," Monthly Labor Review (September 1971), pp. 12–14.

construction laborers were $6,199 in 1969—about 27 percent below
those of full-year construction craftsmen and 17 percent below those
of male nontransport operatives. On the other hand, full-year construction laborers' earnings were about 1 percent higher than those
of all nonfarm laborers and substantially above those of male workers
in the personal service and farm laborer occupations included in our
status group 5.[49] These earnings comparisons are thus quite consistent with our occupational status ranking of construction laborers
at the upper range of group 5.

Other characteristics of this occupation, too, have contributed to
its relatively low status ranking. Construction workers have typically
experienced the highest unemployment rates of any large occupational
group in the labor force as a consequence of the industry's high degree
of seasonality, of the vulnerability of the industry to wide cyclical
fluctuations, and of the casual nature of hiring arrangements, particularly in the unorganized sectors of the industry. Thus, in March
1970, 13.2 percent of construction laborers were unemployed, as
compared with unemployment rates of 8.2 percent for all nonfarm
laborers and 3.6 percent for all male workers in the experienced
civilian labor force (ECLF), 16 years and over.[50]

Finally, the construction industry is among the most hazardous
of the nation's industries, with work injury rates (in terms of man-
days lost), nearly three times as high as the average for all manufacturing industries in 1970. The construction industry rate was exceeded only by mining, lumber, and motor transportation, among
major industries, and by police and fire departments.[51] Although
separate injury rates by occupation are not available, it is thus probable that construction laborers are more vulnerable to work injury
than all but a few of the lower-level occupations in our group 5 or
group 4 categories.

Employment and Labor Supply Trends

Until the late 1950s the decennial censuses provided the only
source of data on the construction laborer work force. Changes in
occupational classification practices and in related census enumeration
procedures have limited the usefulness of these data for longer-term
trend comparisons. According to census statistics the number of employed construction laborers declined from 663,000 in 1950 to 650,000
in 1960 and to 601,000 in 1970. Over these two decades, their proportion of the total employed male labor force fell from 1.62 percent in
1950 to 1.26 percent in 1970. In contrast, CPS statistics indicate an
increase in annual average employment of construction laborers from

784,000 in 1960 to 812,000 in 1970, and a smaller decline in their proportion of total male employment—from 1.79 percent in 1960 to 1.65 percent in 1970. (See Table 6.8.)

Some of the disparity in the 1960-70 trend between the two sources may be due to differences in each of these two census years between construction laborer employment levels at the time of census enumeration, in the last week of March (when construction activity is relatively low, seasonally) and the corresponding annual average levels, as reflected in CPS data. It is probable, too, that—although there was no significant change in census occupational classifications for this group between 1960 and 1970—related changes in census enumeration and editing procedures may have affected the comparability of the CPS data. It is possible, for example, that extensive reliance upon self-enumeration procedures in the 1970 census may have resulted in a considerable upgrading of reported occupations, particularly among young workers, as compared to the 1960 census, when self-enumeration was first introduced on a nationwide scale. This bias would not be present to the same extent in the CPS, which has relied upon direct interviews with household members throughout this period. Furthermore, a comparison of the CPS annual average data for construction laborers since 1960 with the trend in total payroll employment in the contract construction industry suggests that the CPS series provides the more reliable measure of employment trends in this occupation. (See Table 6.9.)

In any event, both the census data and the CPS/BLS annual data indicate that construction laborers have declined relative to the total construction industry work force. Based on census data, the ratio of construction laborers to total construction industry employment fell from 19 laborers per 100 total employed construction workers in 1950, to 17 per 100 in 1960 and 13 per 100 in 1970. Although directly comparable industry employment trend data are not available for the CPS series, the comparisons in Table 6.9 indicate that between 1960 and 1973, payroll employment in contract construction rose by 26.5 percent, as contrasted to an increase of only 8.2 percent for construction laborers, as measured by the CPS.

The declining relative requirement for construction laborers undoubtedly reflects a much longer-term trend, similar to that in other components of the low-skilled blue-collar labor force. It is closely associated with the major technological changes in the construction industry, including progressive substitution of power equipment for hand labor; the introduction of labor-saving materials, such as reinforced concrete in lieu of masonry; the larger scale of construction projects; and the increased role of off-site assembly in the industry. These trends have been most apparent in the nonresidential sectors of the industry.

TABLE 6.8

Trends in the Construction Laborer Work Force: 1950-70

(numbers in thousands)

Year	Construction Laborers	Decennial Census		Annual Averages	
		Employed Construction Laborers		Employed Construction Laborers	
		Number	Percent of Total Employed Males	Number	Percent of Total Employed Males
1950	763	663	1.62	—	—
1960	791	650	1.48	784	1.79
1970	693	601	1.26	812	1.65

Sources: U.S. Department of Commerce, Bureau of the Census, Census of Population, 1960, U.S. Summary, "Detailed Characteristics," (Washington, D.C.: U.S. Government Printing Office, 1963), tables 201, 202; Census of Population, 1970, "Occupational Characteristics" (Washington, D.C.: U.S. Government Printing Office, 1972), tables 1, 38; and unpublished Current Population Survey tabulations, courtesy of Bureau of Labor Statistics.

TABLE 6.9

Employment of Construction Laborers and Total Construction
Industry Employment: Annual Averages, 1960-73

Year	Construction Laborers		Contract Construction Industry Employment	
	Number (000)	Index, 1960=100	Number (000)	Index, 1960=100
1960	784	100.0	2,885	100.0
1961	737	94.0	2,816	97.6
1962	728	92.9	2,902	100.6
1963	712	90.8	2,963	102.7
1964	770	98.2	3,050	105.7
1965	785	100.1	3,186	110.4
1966	712	90.8	3,275	113.5
1967	730	93.1	3,208	111.2
1968	739	94.3	3,285	113.9
1969	801	102.2	3,435	119.1
1970	812	103.6	3,381	117.2
1971	823	105.0	3,411	118.2
1972	872	111.2	3,521	122.0
1973	848	108.2	3,649	126.5

Note: Excludes small number of female construction laborers.
Sources: Bureau of the Census, Current Population Survey; and
Bureau of Labor Statistics data, based on Manpower Report of the
President, 1974 (Washington, D.C.: U.S. Government Printing
Office, 1974), table C-1.

It should be noted, however, that not all technological change has operated to reduce the proportion of unskilled workers required in building projects. Thus, in the case of single-family housing construction, a BLS survey in 1969 found that the percentage of total man-hours for laborers, helpers, and tenders had increased since an earlier 1962 survey, as a result of increased use of prefabricated materials which had served to reduce the relative requirement for carpenters or other skilled craftsmen. [52]

As in other low-level occupations, the labor supply for construction laborer jobs has been drawn disproportionately from the most disadvantaged elements of the labor force—immigrants, nonwhites, and the least educated. In 1910, nearly one-half (49 percent) of all construction laborers were either foreign born or black. [53] With the sharp reduction of immigration following World War I, the proportion of foreign-born white workers in the occupation dropped sharply in subsequent decades, from 30 percent in 1910 to 8.5 percent by 1950. They were replaced both by native white workers and by black workers. The proportion of the latter rose from 19.0 percent to 25.9 percent over this period.

Construction laborers, as a group, were also characterized by a very low level of educational attainment. In 1960, only 19.0 percent of all construction laborers had completed 12 or more years of schooling, as contrasted with an average of 47.6 percent for all experienced male workers and of 21.1 percent among those in group 5 occupations, as a whole.

The decade of the 1960s witnessed a significant shift in the composition of the construction laborer work force. Based on decennial census data, the proportion of young workers, aged 16-24 years, in this occupation rose from 18.5 percent in 1960 to 26.5 percent in 1970. This increase was due entirely to an inflow of young white men into construction laborer jobs, and, in turn, contributed to a particularly sharp increase in the proportion of high school graduates among construction laborers, from 19.0 percent in 1960 to 33.6 percent in 1970. At the same time, the overall proportion of nonwhites in the occupation fell from 29.6 percent in 1960 to 25.6 percent in 1970, reflecting relatively high withdrawal rates on the part of adult nonwhite men from the construction laborer work force. These trends are noted in Table 6.10, and, in more detail, in Chapter 3.

In view of the disparity in overall trends in construction laborer employment during the 1960s between the decennial census and the CPS, we have also shown, in Table 6.10, available CPS data on the compositional characteristics of employed construction workers. The latter data, based on annual average employment levels, show a much higher proportion of young workers in the employed construction laborer work force than does the decennial census, reflecting the large

TABLE 6.10

Trends in Composition of Construction Laborer Work Force

Construction Laborers	Percent of Total Construction Laborers
Decennial census data, ECLF	
Percent aged 16–24	
1960	18.5
1970	26.5
Percent nonwhite	
1960	29.6
1970	25.6
Percent with 12 or more years education	
1960	19.0
1970	33.6
CPS annual average data, employed workers	
Percent aged 16–24	
1960	26.0
1970	33.4
1973	43.8
Percent nonwhite	
1960	30.6
1970	25.1
1973	22.1

Sources: Decennial census data from Bureau of Census public use tapes, 1960, 1970. CPS data from unpublished BLS translations.

proportion of youth who work as construction laborers during the peak summer months of construction activity. Between 1962 and 1970, the percentage of 16-24-year-olds among employed construction laborers rose from 26.0 percent to 33.4 percent, an increase paralleling that shown by the decennial census between 1960 and 1970. Moreover, this proportion continued to rise sharply, to 43.8 percent in 1973, as a result of an increase of 99,000 in the number of 16-24-year-olds employed as construction laborers between 1970 and 1973, concurrent with a reduction of 64,000 among those 25 years and over.

Similarly, the CPS data suggest a continued withdrawal of black workers from this occupational group. Between 1960 and 1970, the percentage of nonwhites among employed construction laborers fell from 30.6 percent to 25.1 percent, a slightly greater reduction than indicated by the comparable decennial census data. It continued to drop, to 22.1 percent, in 1973. Even in 1973, however, nonwhite workers continued to be disproportionately represented in the employed construction laborer work force by a ratio of about two to one.

In summary, the period since 1960 has witnessed a significant transformation of the construction laborer work force from one staffed predominantly by mature male workers with low educational levels— and including a large proportion of blacks—to one increasingly reliant upon better-educated white youth, particularly during peak seasonal periods of construction activity.

Earnings

Until 1972, when the BLS conducted an initial survey of both union and nonunion construction laborers' wage rates in selected SMSAs, data on wage rates and hourly earnings of construction laborers, as well as for other construction crafts, were largely based on BLS surveys of union wage rates in these occupations. Over a period of decades, there has been—at least until the 1960s—a long-term decline in the differential between union wage rates for construction laborers and helpers and those for journeymen in the skilled construction crafts. Thus, between 1913 and 1952, real wages for unionized helpers and laborers are estimated to have increased by 182 percent as compared to 98 percent for journeymen, according to D. Haber and H. Levinson.[54] The skilled-unskilled wage rate differential tended to narrow more rapidly during wartime periods of general labor shortage, that is, during World War I and World War II; it tended to widen during periods of depression, notably during the early 1930s.

This long-term trend towards a narrowing of skill differentials in wage rates in the construction trades was paralleled by similar trends for the labor force as a whole, and has been generally attributed to such labor supply factors as the stoppage of large-scale immigration and the rapid educational upgrading of the labor force. These served to reduce the supply of workers for low-level jobs, on the one hand, while increasing the proportions qualified for both white-collar and the more skilled blue-collar jobs.[55]

An analysis by Dan Gustman and Martin Segal has indicated a further significant decline in the skilled-unskilled wage rate differential between 1953 and 1961, but no clearcut trend during the decade of the 1960s. Annual fluctuations in this relationship were found to be correlated with cyclical movements in construction industry unemployment. During periods of upswing in construction labor demand, skilled wage rates were found to increase more rapidly than rates for unskilled workers—thus tending to slow down, or reverse, the longer-term historical trend.[56]

A general assumption in the literature on construction industry wage trends is that the demand for labor in the industry is inelastic, particularly with respect to specific construction occupations.[57] This does not appear to be an unreasonable assumption in view of the fact that on-site labor costs account for only about 26 percent to 30 percent of construction costs, depending upon the type of project, and that wages of construction laborers represent only a modest fraction of the total construction payroll.

Nevertheless, there is some evidence suggesting that the relative utilization of unskilled or semiskilled construction laborers, as compared to skilled craftsmen, does vary in relation to the respective wage rates for these categories of labor. For example, the wage differential between construction laborers and skilled craftsmen, such as carpenters, has been much wider in the South than in other regions—a pattern typical of the occupational wage structure, generally, in this region. At the same time, a number of BLS surveys of both residential and nonresidential construction projects have consistently indicated that construction laborers, helpers, and tenders account for a higher proportion of total on-site man-hours in the South than in other regions. For example, a 1964 BLS survey of labor requirements for public housing projects indicated that laborers, helpers, and tenders constituted 41 percent of on-site man-hours in the South, as contrasted to about 25 percent in the north central region, 23 percent in the northeastern states, and 22 percent in the west. (See Table 6.7.) These variations appear to be accounted for in part by a number of interregional differences affecting construction technology including (1) the greater use of load-bearing masonry in the South, with its higher man-hour requirements; (2) the small size of contracts in the South, implying less use of labor-saving equipment; and (3) the greater number of man-hours required in nonmetropolitan locations (more frequent in the South). Although the empirical data base does not permit a complete identification of these and other factors affecting regional variations in occupational staffing, it appears probable that the greater availability of low-wage construction laborers in the South—typically nonunion and black—has been a significant contributing factor.[58]

In view of the wide observed regional differentials in relative wages for unskilled workers in the construction industry, we have attempted, through use of econometric models, to determine the extent to which labor supply factors have contributed to these variations. For this purpose, median annual earnings data, by SMSA, have been used as a proxy for actual wage rates or hourly earnings. The major portion of this analysis was based on published census data for 68 SMSAs with 250,000 or more population, used as the data base for the econometric studies described in Chapter 4. Relative occupational earnings for construction laborers were computed separately, as a ratio to earnings of carpenters ($W_{ij}/WCARP_j$) and to a standardized occupational wage level for each SMSA ($W_{ij}/WSTD_j$), based on an average of median earnings in selected male occupations in each SMSA, using fixed national employment weights. (See Chapter 4.)

The various models tested postulated that relative wages of construction laborers were a function of—

1. certain characteristics of the occupational labor supply of each SMSA, that is, the proportions of construction laborers who were black ($PCTBLACK_{ij}$), who were aged 16-24 ($YOUTH_{ij}$), or who had 12 or more years of education ($ED12P_{ij}$);

2. the percentage of the occupation who were unionized ($PCTUNION_j$);

3. general labor market conditions in the SMSA as measured by relative unemployment rates for construction laborers as compared to those of carpenters ($UNRCNLBR/UNRCARP_j$) and by the labor force participation rates for males aged 16-24; and

4. relative labor market opportunities for black male workers, as compared to white male workers, as measured by the respective proportions who were high school graduates in the SMSA ($ED12BM/ED12WM_j$) and by the ratio of median annual earnings of black males to white males in the SMSA.

Certain of the models also introduced additional possible explanatory variables, such as the proportion of construction contracts awarded for nonresidential versus residential construction (MIX_j), the proportion of the SMSA labor force employed in higher-wage industries ($PCTHIW_j$), and the proportion of construction laborers who were of Spanish origin.

Our hypothesis, generally, was that differential concentrations of youth and of blacks among construction laborers as well as higher relative unemployment rates in the group would tend to depress relative wage rates for construction laborers, whereas such factors as a higher concentration of better-educated workers, greater relative economic opportunities for black workers, and a greater degree of unionization in the group would tend to raise relative wage rates. Major findings of these studies are described below.

1. Labor supply factors, in combination with the unionization variable, were found to explain a major portion of the inter-SMSA differences in relative earnings of construction laborers, as indicated by coefficients of variation ($\bar{R}^2$) of .641 and .774 on alternative

formulations of this model. (See Tables 6.11 and 6.12.) These coefficients are considered very satisfactory for cross-sectional models
of this type, particularly in view of inherent limitations of the available
data base. They were superior to similar coefficients derived from
our analyses of interarea differences in relative wages in other selected low-level occupations.

2. In the model using the ratio of earnings of construction laborers to those of carpenters as a dependent variable, we found that—
both for the full sample of all SMSAs and for the nonsouthern SMSAs,
separately analyzed—the most significant single explanatory variable
was the relative education of black males to that of white males in the
SMSA. Relative wages of construction laborers rose as the education
of black males approached that of whites, with an elasticity at the
mean of .30 in the overall model. Relative wage rates for construction
laborers also tended to rise with the degree of unionization of these
workers relative to that of carpenters. Conversely, higher concentrations of young workers among construction laborers (relative to
carpenters), as well as high relative unemployment rates for construction laborers tended to reduce relative earnings of construction laborers. Elasticities for the latter variable were however quite low.
It should also be noted that the regressions for the southern SMSAs
did not produce significant results under this and alternative formulations.

3. In the model using the ratio of construction laborers' earnings
to the standardized area's earnings average, we also found that higher
concentrations of youth and of black workers had a depressing effect
upon relative wages, whereas higher concentrations of better-educated workers as well as a higher degree of unionization (in the nonsouthern areas) were associated with higher relative wages. A greater
concentration of the male labor force in higher-wage industries was
also associated with higher relative wages for the construction laborers.

4. Finally, a comparison of cross-sectional models for 1960 and
1970 was made, based on the ratio of median earnings of all construction laborers to those of carpenters, since data for full-year workers
only were not published in 1960. The most significant explanatory
variable in these models was found to be the median earnings of blacks
relative to those of white male workers, which provided a measure of
relative economic opportunity of blacks in the various SMSAs. The
elasticity of this variable, moreover, rose from .34 in 1960 to .53 in
1970, suggesting more sensitivity of the unskilled-skilled wage differential in 1970 to reductions in labor market discrimination against
black workers. Other variables found to be significant—but with much
lower elasticities—were differential unemployment rates (1970 only)
and percentage of black males in the labor force.

TABLE 6.11

Elasticities from Wage Differential Model Using Ratio of Earnings of Full-Year Construction Laborers to Standardized Occupational Earnings Index, by Region, 1970

Dependent Variable for Regions, $\dfrac{W_{ij}}{WSTD_j}$	Mean	Independent Variable							$\bar{R}^2$	F
		$ED12P_{ij}$	$PCTBLK_{ij}$	$YOUTH_{ij}$	$WSTD_j$	$PCTHIW_j$	$PCTUNION_j$	MIX_j		
All standard metropolitan statistical areas	.7583	.1654*	-.0491*	-.1137*	—	.2268*	.0335	.0045	.774	32.986*
Nonsouthern	.7787	.1421*	-.0501*	-.1020*	—	.1302	.0782*	.0198	—	19.285*
South	.7314	.1059	-.0471	.2800	—	.2217	1.1196	.0567	.279	2.483

*Significant with .95 level of confidence.
Note: See this chapter and Table 4.6 for definitions of variables used above and in Tables 6.12 and 6.13.
Source: Compiled by the author.

TABLE 6.12

Elasticities from Wage Differential Model Using Ratio of Earnings of Construction Laborers to Earnings of Carpenters as Dependent Variable

Dependent Variable Form	Independent Variable									
	$\frac{UNRCNSLBR}{UNRCARP}_j$	$\frac{CNSLBR1624}{CARPENT1624}_j$	$\frac{PCTUNIONCNSLBR}{PCTUNIONCARPENT}_j$	$\frac{ED12BM}{ED12WM}_j$	$\frac{WBM}{WWM}_j$	$LFMPCTBLK_j$	$PCTED12_j$	$PRM1624_j$	$\bar{R}^2$	F
1970 $WCNSLBR^c$, $WCARPENT_{fy}$, all										
standard metropolitan statistical areas (SMSAs)	-.0386[a]	-.0437	.0891[a]	.3030[a]	.1047	—	—	—	.641	20.979[a]
Nonsouth	-.0484[a]	-.0814[a]	.0746[b]	.2754[a]	.0326	—	—	—	.501	7.433[a]
South	.0685[b]	-.1132	.0986	-.0163	-.2483	—	—	—	.061	1.300
$WCNSLBR^d$, $WCARPENT_{me}$, all										
SMSAs 1970	-.0837[a]	—	—	—	.5345[a]	-.0538[a]	-.0180	-.1997	.548	14.589[a]
1960	-.0671	—	—	—	.3409[a]	-.0494[a]	.0119	-.2264	.376	7.757[a]

[a] Significant with .95 level of confidence.
[b] Significant with .90 level of confidence.
[c] "Fy" refers to earnings of full-year workers as defined by the Census Bureau; note that a full-year worker does not imply necessarily a full-time worker.
[d] "Me" refers to median annual earnings of all workers, including both full-year and part-year workers.
Source: Compiled by the author.

Factors Affecting Composition of Construction Laborer Work Force

    The preceding analyses demonstrated that interarea differences in the characteristics of the construction laborer work force (race, age, education), as well as other labor market variables, have been significantly associated with differences in relative earnings of construction laborers. A corollary of this analysis is to attempt to identify, in turn, the key factors which are associated with differences in the relative concentrations of blacks, youth, or better-educated workers in construction laborer jobs. The overall availability of workers with these characteristics for employment in lower-level occupations is expected to change significantly in the 1980s—hence an identification of the factors contributing to their differential participation in a specific lower-level occupational group, that is, construction laborers, may provide useful insights concerning their responsiveness to such inducements as increases in relative wages, if these are needed to attract additional workers.

    In the case of youth, for example, it is relevant to know what factors have been most closely associated with the sharp increase in the proportion of youth employed as construction laborers. Since the available time series data is very limited for such an analysis, we have attempted to derive some insights from analysis of our cross section of SMSAs in 1970. Simply stated, were the interarea differences in the proportion of youth in construction laborer jobs solely a function of differences in the proportion of young workers in each area's labor force, or were other factors, such as differences in labor market conditions, in relative wages, or in relative availability of competing labor force groups, also significant?

    The empirical findings for the youth-concentration equation (in Table 6.13) indicate that, as expected, the percentage of youth in construction laborer jobs varied directly with their overall proportion in the SMSA labor force (elasticity, 1.33); that it was higher in areas where relative wages of construction laborers were lower (elasticity, -.55); and that it was lower in areas where more youth were neither in school nor at work. These findings in turn imply that the influx of youth into construction laborer jobs was indeed a key factor checking the relative growth in construction laborers' wages during the 1960s. Conversely, the projected decline in the percentage of young workers in the labor force, other factors being equal, can be expected to result in a somewhat more-than-proportionate reduction in their availability for construction laborer jobs and in an increase in relative wages. The findings also suggest the potential for increasing the supply of such youthful workers for construction laborer jobs by tapping the labor reserve of unemployed out-of-school youth.

FOUR CASE STUDIES

FOUR CASE STUDIES

317

The educational concentration variable, in Table 6.13, is defined as the proportion of high school graduates in construction laborer jobs as a ratio to the corresponding proportion for all men in the area's labor force. The most significant finding in this analysis was the relative high propensity of better-educated men to take construction laborer jobs, at least temporarily, in response to higher wage rates for such work, as evidenced by an elasticity of 1.8, in relation to the relative wage rate, $E_{C/S}$. Thus, an increase in the overall educational level of the labor force, per se, is not indicated as a significant obstacle to filling these jobs, under assumed conditions of relatively inelastic demand for construction laborers.

The results from the third concentration equation—that for black workers—tend to confirm the relationship expected from crowding theories, that is, that a high proportion of blacks, or other disadvantaged minorities, in a given population is associated with a lower relative wage for that occupation. However, the most important explanatory variables in this model are those which measure the relative economic status of black workers in various labor markets. The median earnings of black men relative to white men provides a useful index for this purpose. The relationship proved particularly significant in the nonsouthern areas where a 1 percent increase in the black-white earnings ratio was associated with about a 2.5 percentage point decline in the concentration of blacks in construction laborer jobs. Conversely, the black concentration index shows a significant, but relatively inelastic relationship, to the ratio of black workers' earnings as construction laborers to earnings of all black workers (WBM_{ij}/WBM_j). On balance, these relationships thus confirm the hypothesis that the proportion of black workers in construction laborer jobs will continue to decline as a result of narrowing of both the educational and income gaps between black and white workers.

Employment Outlook

Projections of construction industry output and employment, under full-employment assumptions, generally anticipate substantial growth in this sector: BLS projections issued in December 1973 thus provide for an increase of 39 percent in construction industry gross output (in constant 1972 dollars), from $56.0 billion in 1972 to $77.9 billion in 1985. Productivity in contract construction is projected to grow at very moderate rates: 1.5 percent per year between 1972 and 1980, and 0.8 percent between 1980 and 1985. After allowance, in addition, for a small assumed increase in average annual hours per construction worker, the BLS has projected an increase in total contract construction payroll employment of 19 percent, from 4,352,000 in 1972 to 5,184,000, in 1985.[59] In turn, BLS staff have projected an increase

TABLE 6.13

Elasticities from Education, Age, and Black-Concentration Equations—Standard Form

Dependent Variable	Mean	$\dfrac{W_{ij}}{WSTD_j}$	$\dfrac{WBM_{ij}}{WBM_j}$	$\dfrac{BMED12P}{CLF_j}$	$\dfrac{FYEBM_j}{FYEWM_j}$	$INCFAMHD_j$	$\dfrac{YOUTH_{ij}}{YOUTH_j}$	$YOUTH_j$	$PRM1624_j$
$ED12P_{ij}$	.2969	1.7569[a]	—	-.0946[a]	—	—	.3609[a]	—	—
$YOUTH_{ij}$	.2594	-.5462[b]	—	—	-.6645	.2890	—	1.3316[a]	—
$BLKCONC_{ij}$	2.8268	-.8468[a]	.1900[a]	—	-1.7671[a]	—	—	.2311	.4514
NS	2.5794	-1.7595[a]	.2461[a]	—	-2.4703[a]	—	—	.9856	-.7808
S	3.1669	.7992	.0982	—	-1.6097[a]	—	—	.6048	1.0270[b]

Independent Variable

Dependent Variable	Mean	Independent Variable							$\bar{R}^2$	F
		$LIFPCTSPO_j$	$PCTM16NLF_j$	$ED12P_j$	$\%\Delta(N_{ij}/N_j)$	UNR_j	$PCTUNION_{ij}$	$\Delta POPNW_j$		
$ED12P_{ij}$	.2969	—	—	.1345	$-.0002^a$	.0196	—	—	.697	19.410^a
$YOUTH_{ij}$	.2594	.0099	$-.2602^a$	—	.0000	—	—	—	.483	7.335^a
$BLKCONC_{ij}$	2.8268	-.0197	—	—	—	—	$.2282^a$	.0052	.266	3.541^a
NS	2.5794	.0477	—	—	—	—	$.9344^a$	-.0212	.317	2.854^a
S	3.1669	-.0534	—	—	—	—	.0785	.0395	.298	2.397

[a] Significant with .95 level of confidence.

[b] Significant with .90 level of confidence.

Source: Compiled by the author.

in employment of construction laborers from an annual average of about 870,000 in 1972 to about 1.0 million in 1985.

This BLS projection of growth in construction laborer requirements, of about 15 percent between 1972 and 1985, can be contrasted with our projection that the number of males available for all categories of nonfarm laborer jobs will increase by only 5 percent between 1970 and 1985 (see Chapter 5). More specifically, the analysis of trends among construction laborers has revealed that employment in this work force increased because of a large-scale inflow of young white workers, offsetting the withdrawal of older men, particularly blacks—many of whom apparently progressed to higher-wage, higher-status occupations. Such factors as the generally high level of labor demand in the late 1960s, as well as rising educational levels and reduced discrimination against blacks in higher-level occupations contributed to the significant declines in the number of older men among construction laborers.

If high employment levels are restored before the end of the 1970s, these factors would again be operative. At the same time, the overall labor supply of young men is projected to decline, beginning in the late 1970s, as illustrated by a projected reduction of 13 percent in the male labor force aged 16-21 years, between 1980 and 1985. Moreover, a reduced supply of those entrants into the labor force in the 1980s will tend to more than proportionately reduce the percentage of these young men available for construction laborer jobs in the absence of higher relative wages or other inducements. (This is suggested by the elasticity of 1.33 on the youth population variable in our youth-concentration equation, in Table 6.13.) Thus, it is evident that, to meet the BLS-projected employment levels, construction employers will have to recruit a significantly higher proportion of the available low-level male labor force than in past years. One of the consequences will be a probable resumption of the longer-term trend towards narrowing of the unskilled-skilled labor wage differential in the construction industry.

It should be noted, however, that there is a very large potential for more effective utilization of available labor resources in this occupation, through decasualization of the work force (as in longshoring), through systematic efforts to reduce seasonality, and through improved labor market organization—all of which should contribute to both a reduction of the chronically high unemployment rate in this occupation and to an increase in its attractiveness as compared to other lower-skilled jobs. Improved opportunities for on-the-job training and for upgrading of laborers to journeyman jobs would also increase the ability of employers to recruit young men for this work.

Our assessment, thus far, has assumed an inelastic demand for construction laborers, based on a premise of complementarity of laborer requirements to those for skilled labor. Our analysis of regional differences in the relative utilization of construction laborers (Table 6.7) suggested that, in addition to other factors, the lower wage level for construction laborers in the South has resulted in a higher utilization of unskilled labor, in lieu of more capital-intensive construction methods or materials. This implies that any substantial increase in construction laborers' wages in the South may provide the impetus for increased labor productivity growth there, hence, reducing the overall requirement for construction laborers.

In summary, therefore, our assessment suggests that if overall construction activity does expand, as indicated by the foregoing projections, this will result in a considerably tighter labor market for unskilled construction labor in the 1980s than in the preceding decade and in a probable increase in relative wages for construction laborers. In addition, there are other socially desirable options which will be available to employers, to organized labor, and to labor market agencies which will facilitate meeting these manpower needs and which should be systematically encouraged by private and public manpower policies.

HOSPITAL ATTENDANTS

Occupational Status

Hospital attendants include workers classified as nursing aides, orderlies, and attendants in the 1970 census.[60] They perform a variety of duties requiring limited training that contribute to the comfort and care of patients in hospitals and other health facilities, including such personal care duties as serving meals, making beds, bathing and dressing patients, and giving massages, as well as taking temperatures and setting up medical equipment. They are at the lower end of the occupational hierarchy among health care personnel, working in a supporting role to registered nurses (RNs) and licensed practical nurses (LPNs) and, in turn, enabling the nurses to devote more time to work that requires professional and technical training.

The occupational status of hospital attendants, based on our analysis of the labor force composition of this occupation in 1960, places them at about the twentieth percentile in the rank ordering of occupational groups or close to the midvalue of our status group 4. (See Table 1.3.) This is a significantly higher status than that of the three other lower-level occupations analyzed in detail above. The following characteristics of hospital attendants, when viewed as a composite, tend to confirm this rank ordering.

Earnings

Hospital attendants rank relatively low in wage levels, even in relation to other lower-level workers. A useful approximation of their relative annual full-time wages is provided by a special tabulation, based on 1960 decennial census data of workers employed 48 weeks or more in 1959, and who also worked 35 hours or more in the census survey week, in 1960. Based on this measure, hospital attendants ranked lower than any other occupational subgroup in our group 4 category, other than housekeepers and babysitters, and waiters and counter and fountain workers. Hospital attendants' earnings were also lower than those of many of the group 5 workers.

One factor contributing to these low earnings has been the high concentration of female workers among hospital attendants. In 1970, women comprised 85 percent of hospital attendants, a much higher proportion than in most other lower-level occupational groups, other than private household workers. However, even comparisons limited to female workers indicate that annual earnings of hospital attendants employed 50-52 weeks in 1969 were lower than those of women in other major low-level census occupational groups, other than private household workers and other personal service workers.

Training and Education

In contrast to their relatively low ranking in terms of wages, hospital attendants rank significantly higher than most group 4 or group 5 workers in terms of such criteria as their training requirements and average educational level. In the 1963 Labor Department-census survey of formal occupational training, a majority of hospital attendants identified on-the-job learning as the source of their own training and as the "most helpful way" of learning their jobs. However, only 5 percent of the hospital attendants surveyed indicated that no training was needed for their occupation, as contrasted to 28 percent of the private household workers, 22 percent of the janitors, 18 percent of the laborers, and 9 percent of all operatives and kindred workers.[61] Moreover, about 56 percent of female hospital attendants in the experienced civilian labor force had completed 12 or more years of education in 1970, as contrasted to only 43 percent of women in all group 4 occupations and 30 percent of women in group 5 occupations. (See Table 3.25.)

Other Status Criteria

In addition to pay and training, many other—less measurable—
attributes of the hospital attendant's work have affected the scale of
preference of workers for this job, as compared to alternative lower-
level jobs open to them. By most standards, many of the tasks performed by hospital attendants would be regarded as unpleasant and
dull. This is illustrated by Studs Terkel's case study of one young
woman working as a nurse's aide who described her duties as "makin'
beds and bed pans and rotten stuff like that."[62] The absence of any
structured promotional opportunities for higher-skilled hospital positions is another contributing factor. Thus, in describing various categories of jobs in the "secondary" labor market, Peter Doeringer and
Michael Piore cite "menial jobs in hospitals" as typical of jobs in
"secondary" internal labor markets; these markets are defined as
those which "do possess formal internal structures, but they tend to
have many entry ports, short mobility clusters, and the work is generally low paying, unpleasant or both."[63]

On the positive side, work associated with care of the ailing—
even if routine and unplesant, at times—has traditionally been considered more prestigious than similar types of duties elsewhere. Performance of these duties in hospitals or similar facilities, by the same
token, requires a greater standard of discipline and training. Moreover, although unionization is still of limited scope among hospital
attendants, it is likely that institutionalized personnel policies and
procedures provide somewhat more, in the way of employee safeguards
and fringe benefits, than is available to workers in other lower-level
service occupations, such as domestics, cleaners, and food service
workers.

These considerations—many of which cannot be readily quantified—
probably account in combination for the fact that various surveys of
occupational prestige rank hospital attendants substantially higher than
most other lower-level workers. Thus, Paul Siegel, in his systematic
compilation of prestige scores for all census occupations, ranked
hospital attendants in the sixth decile of the labor force, whereas
nearly all of the other lower-level occupations in our group 4 and 5
categories fell into the lowest three or four deciles of the labor force,
in terms of prestige.[64]

Employment and Labor Supply Trends

Hospital attendants have experienced the most rapid growth rates
of any of the lower-level workers in our study. Based on decennial

census data, the number of hospital attendants in the experienced civilian labor force has approximately doubled in each decade since 1940, when these workers were first separately enumerated—growing from 102,000 in 1940 to 216,000 in 1950, to 408,000 in 1960, and to 752,000 in the 1970 census. [65] For the decade of the 1960s, BLS estimates, based on somewhat different definitions and source data, indicate an increase of 84 percent in employment of hospital attendants, as contrasted to an overall employment increase of 19 percent.

The major factor in this rapid growth during the 1960s has been the overall expansion of employment in the medical and health services industry, as a result of the increasing hospitalization and health insurance coverage of the population, including the Medicare and Medicaid programs; increases in real per capita income; and advances in medical technology. In addition, hospital attendants have increased as a proportion of total employment within the medical and health industry, from 15.2 percent in 1960 to 17.6 percent in 1970, for reasons examined in detail below.

This employment growth was accompanied by the following changes in the characteristics of hospital attendants as a group:

1. The proportion of women working as hospital attendants rose from 73.8 percent in 1960 to 84.6 percent in 1970.

2. The overall percentage of nonwhites working as hospital attendants rose slightly from 25.2 percent to 26.6 percent, and continued to be about two and a half times as great as their proportion in the labor force as a whole. This resulted from an increase in the proportion of nonwhite women, among hospital attendants, and from a reduction in the proportion of nonwhite men.

3. Among male hospital attendants, there was a marked shift from employment of men 25 years and over, to employment of younger men, aged 16-24 (predominantly white) resulting in a reduction in the median age of male hospital attendants from 37.3 years to 32.3 years. The median age of female hospital attendants was higher than for men in both 1960 and 1970 and declined only slightly—from 39.7 years to 38.6 years.

4. The median educational level of employed hospital attendants rose substantially over the decade—from 10.6 years of schooling to 12.2 years for men and from 10.8 years to 11.8 years for women.

These trends suggest that the primary source of recruits for this growing occupational group in the 1960s consisted of both young and more mature female workers, and included both new entrants into the labor force as well as those who had moved up from other lower-status occupations. Among the latter, nonwhite women probably contributed a greater-than-proportionate share. In the case of male hospital

attendants, however, the evidence suggests a significant net outmovement of adult male workers, particularly nonwhites, from this low-
wage occupation and their replacement by new male entrants into the
labor force as well as women. Thus, the relatively large increase in
the female labor force during the 1960s, as well as the inflow of youth,
facilitated recruitment of hospital attendants.

These labor supply sources appear to have been generally adequate
to meet employer recruitment needs. A number of health manpower
studies conducted during the 1960s—although noting problems of high
turnover rates among hospital attendants—generally have not indicated
any major recruitment problems for low-skilled personnel as contrasted to severe shortages of registered nurses and licensed practical
nurses. Confirming evidence is provided by the relatively large increases in wage rates for the latter categories of personnel, whereas
wage rates for hospital attendants experienced an average rate of increase, despite the sharp growth in their employment. Thus, between
1959 and 1969, annual earnings of female hospital attendants rose by
56 percent, as compared to 90 percent for licensed practical nurses
and 72 percent for registered nurses.

These trends, in turn, tend to support the inferences by Rosenthal
and Sommers that the relatively sharper increases in employment of
hospital attendants than of trained nurses between 1960 and 1970 resulted from a reallocation of some duties, previously performed by
nurses, to nurses' aides and other hospital attendants, in view of the
widening wage differential between the two categories of personnel and
the increased availability of untrained females and youth.

Labor Market Factors Affecting Relative Employment and Wages of Hospital Attendants

The inferences, noted above, concerning the relationship between
relative employment and relative earnings of hospital attendants, on the
one hand, and the supply of workers for attendants' jobs on the other,
have been tested by use of a number of econometric models. Although
precise variables used varied in each test, the general approach in all
was based on the premise that, as in other segmented labor markets,
the supply of workers available for work as hospital attendants was
drawn disproportionately from certain population groups, for example,
nonwhites, youth, and women with limited education or specialized
training. Such individuals have often had a restricted choice of working
in a specific lower-level job, such as that of hospital attendant (provided such jobs are available), of working in other lower-level jobs
for which they qualify, or of not working at all. Thus, to the extent
that the employment of hospital attendants is a function of labor supply
conditions and relative wages, employment would be expected to be

higher—relative to the total size of the hospital or health services industry—where the supply of such workers is greater and where alternative job opportunities (or nonemployment sources of income) are less attractive.

The empirical data base for these analyses, as for most of the other econometric models in this study, consisted of 1970 census data for our sample of over 60 SMSAs with populations of 250,000 or more. The major findings are described below.

Relative Employment. Relative employment of female hospital attendants (REL EMP) is defined as the ratio of hospital attendants employed in each SMSA to total employment in lower-level occupations in that SMSA, that is, those classified in groups 4 and 5 in our occupational status grouping. The model postulates that this varies both as a function of total hospital employment in the area (HOSP) and in relation to certain other specified labor market characteristics of each SMSA. The latter include (1) percentage of females in the area's labor force (FEM); (2) percentage of nonwhites and Spanish-origin persons in the area's labor force (NW); (3) median educational level of women in the labor force (EDUC); (4) median earnings of hospital attendants in 1969, employed 50-52 weeks, as a ratio to a nationally weighted average of earnings of all group 4 and 5 employed workers in that SMSA (REL WAGE); (5) unemployment rate for women in the SMSA (UNEMP); and (6) percent increase of total hospital employment relative to total employment growth in the SMSA between 1960 and 1970 (GROWTH). The results are shown below, with one asterisk indicating significance at .90 and two asterisks, at .95.

$$
\text{REL EMP} = 0.2643 + 0.3640 \text{ HOSP**} - 0.0478 \text{NW*} + 0.2304 \text{FEM**}
$$
$$
\quad\quad (-2.7020)\ (2.4581)\quad\quad\quad (-1.5926)\quad\quad (2.5600)
$$
$$
+ 0.0142 \text{EDUC**} + 0.0343 \text{REL WAGE**} + 0.5889 \text{UNEMP**}
$$
$$
\quad (2.1149)\quad\quad\quad (1.7051)\quad\quad\quad\quad (3.4486)
$$
$$
- 0.0006 \text{ GROWTH}
$$
$$
(-0.5045)
$$

$$
\bar{R}^2 = .233
$$

Although the total explained variation in relative employment of female hospital attendants was low, it is noteworthy that all variables were significant except for the growth variable. The signs of all the significant variables were also in the expected direction, with the exception of the nonwhites variable, where a positive relationship had been hypothesized. The implications to be drawn are that—apart from the obvious relationship to total hospital employment in the area—

more women are likely to be employed as hospital attendants, rather than in other lower-level jobs, in areas where female unemployment rates are higher, where women constitute a larger share of the total labor force, where their educational level is above average, and where the wages of hospital attendants are higher relative to other low-level occupations. Their relative employment as hospital attendants is, however, likely to be lower in areas with a higher percentage of non-whites in the labor force—possibly because of a relatively larger aggregate employment in low-level jobs in such areas, resulting from crowding of black workers into these jobs (for example, domestics).

Attempts to apply a similar model separately to male hospital attendants proved unsuccessful.

Relative Wages. A similar effort was made to determine the extent to which relative wages of hospital attendants, as compared to those of other group 4 and group 5 workers (as approximated by the census data on median earnings of full-year workers in 1969) were influenced by certain labor market characteristics. Separate equations, in parallel forms, for female and male hospital attendants explained about one-fifth of the variation in each case. (A modified form, in the case of males, raised the $\bar{R}^2$ to about .35.) For female hospital attendants, full-year wages were found to be significantly lower (relative to those in other group 4 and group 5 occupations) in areas with higher proportions of women in the labor force and to be significantly higher in areas with greater proportions of nonwhites. (The finding is attributed by Rosenthal and Sommers to the likelihood that as the proportion of nonwhite women in an area's labor force increases, this is likely to exert a greater depressing influence on other less desirable low-level jobs into which they are crowded, than it does upon hospital attendants, thus raising the relative wage for the latter.) In the case of male hospital attendants, relative earnings were found to be significantly lower in areas where greater proportions of youth, aged 16-24, were in the labor force, and significantly higher in areas with higher percentages of nonwhites and where public assistance payments to families were greater. Variables such as educational level were found to be insignificant in both equations, as was the level of public assistance in the case of female hospital attendants. Also, the relative proportion of women in the labor force had no significant effect on relative wages of male hospital attendants.

In addition to these findings, based on the specific models described above, insights were derived from the more generalized low-level labor force models described in Chapter 4. Most of the empirical tests of these models failed to prove applicable to hospital attendants, partly, we believe, because of the higher status of these workers, as compared to others included in this comparative analysis. However, this approach did yield significant results in explaining interarea differences in the relative concentration of young women, aged 16-24 years, among hospital attendants. We found that youth concentration among female hospital attendants was significantly higher in areas where relative wages of hospital attendants were higher (based on a broadly standardized area occupational wage measure) and where median annual earnings of full-year black female workers in 1969 more closely approximated those of white women. Youth concentration was significantly lower, as might be expected, in areas where employment of hospital attendants had grown less rapidly and also in areas with higher concentration of Spanish-origin female workers. These variables in combination explained about one-third of the variance in the youth concentration variable ($\bar{R}^2 = .329$).

Any generalizations based on the above findings must be carefully qualified both because of the generally low $\bar{R}^2$'s, as noted, and because the coefficients of elasticity for many of the variables identified as significant were also relatively low. Nevertheless, one general observation is that both relative employment and wages have been found to be sensitive to some degree to relevant demographic labor supply variables, as well as to other factors such as area unemployment rates. The findings tend to confirm the hypothesis that the large inflow of women into the labor force during the 1960s was a key factor facilitating the relative rapid growth in employment of hospital attendants as compared to other skilled health occupations, while tending to check the relative growth in wages for hospital attendants. The empirical evidence also tends to suggest that, among hospital attendants, young workers, mainly white, were substitutes for minority group workers and were more likely to be employed in areas where the proportion of minority workers was low and/or where earnings opportunities for minority workers were more favorable.

Employment Outlook

The longer-range employment outlook for hospital attendants continues to be highly favorable. The BLS has projected an annual employment growth rate of 3.6 percent for hospital attendants, more than twice the projected growth rate for total employment under full-employment conditions. Enactment of national health insurance legislation would further enhance the prospects for a rapid increase in the need for hospital attendants, as well as for other health service personnel.

The projected shifts in composition of the labor force between 1970 and 1985 suggest, however, that hospitals and similar institutions may experience more difficulty in recruitment of hospital attendants, under existing relative wages, than they did during the 1960s. One important consideration is a projected slowdown in the rate of labor

force growth for women, who now comprise 85 percent of hospital
attendants. The BLS labor force projections indicate that women will
account for only 46 percent of the increase in labor force between 1970
and 1985, as compared with 60 percent of the growth over the 1960-70
decade. Moreover, as a result of reduced marriage and birth rates,
a greater proportion of women will have had sustained periods of work
experience and, to this extent, be less amenable to entering or remaining in low-skilled and, essentially, dead-end jobs, such as those
of hospital attendants.

A further consideration is the projected reduction in the proportion
of young workers of both sexes who will be entering the labor force in
the 1980s. As in other lower-level occupations, young men as well as
women were an important source for the supply of hospital attendants
during the 1960s.

One favorable aspect of the labor supply outlook for this occupation
is the fact that it appears to enjoy more prestige than most other lower-
level groups; hence, in spite of its low wage structure, it was previously successful in attracting an increased proportion of nonwhite
women, in contrast to the reduction in nonwhite ratios experienced in
most other lower-level service occupations (groups 4 and 5). It is
likely, however, that young nonwhite women will be less content to
remain as hospital attendants in the absence of significant upgrading
opportunities.

Although a definitive projection of the combined impact of these
demographic and social trends upon the future employment and wages
of hospital attendants is not possible, Rosenthal and Sommers have
applied the coefficients of elasticity, derived from their relative wage
model for hospital attendants, to illustrate the partial effect of these
trends—under an implicit assumption of an inelastic demand function
for this occupation. This approach resulted in a projected increase in
the relative wage for hospital attendants of about 7 percent for women
and 10 percent for men, in relation to wages of workers in all lower-
level occupations (groups 4 and 5).

A similar set of estimates was derived, by use of the coefficients
developed from the relative employment equation for female hospital
attendants as well as the projected relative wage, to develop a supply-
oriented projection of future employment for hospital attendants. Based
on this procedure, Rosenthal and Sommers derived a potential shortage
of 164,000 hospital attendants, or 12 percent, in relation to the BLS
projected requirement for hospital attendants in 1985. In turn, this
would imply a further increase in relative wages of female hospital
attendants, of 35 percent, above that projected based upon relative
supply trends alone.

The procedures followed above cannot be regarded as providing a
definitive projection of future supply and demand conditions and of

relative wage trends among hospital attendants since the econometric models used did not result in a fully integrated system of supply and demand equations. Of equal importance, they did not directly take into account the implications of the prospective growth in supply of trained personnel qualified as registered nurses and licensed practical nurses. To the extent that a substitution of hospital attendants for these better-qualified personnel occurred in the 1960s, a reverse process may be anticipated in the 1980s.

While recognizing the limitations of the technical data base, Rosenthal and Sommers conclude that "the supply of hospital attendants in 1985 . . . may be insufficient to meet employment requirements as projected by BLS unless adjustments are made in the factors affecting supply." The most probable adjustments, in addition to an increase in relative wages for hospital attendants, are (1) increased employment of LPNs and RNs; (2) various measures to upgrade status and working conditions; and (3) increased upgrading opportunities, which would provide credit for experience as hospital attendants in advancement to more technical health service occupations.

NOTES

1. The material on household maids is adapted, in part, from a supplementary study by J. Peter Mattila. The analysis of hospital attendants is similarly adopted from a report by Neal Rosenthal and Dixie Somers.

2. U.S. Department of Labor, Employment Standards Administration, Private Household Workers (Washington, D. C.: U.S. Government Printing Office, 1974), p. A-11.

3. Ibid., p. A-27.

4. J. Peter Mattila, "The Effect of Extending Minimum Wages to Cover Household Maids," Journal of Human Resources, Summer 1973, p. 369.

5. George T. Stigler, Domestic Servants in the United States, 1900-1940, Occasional Paper 24 (New York: National Bureau of Economic Research, April 1946), p. 1.

6. Mattila, op. cit., table 1.

7. Ibid., p. 369.

8. U.S. Department of Labor, Bureau of Labor Statistics, Consumer Expenditures and Income, Urban United States, 1961, Survey of Consumer Expenditures, 1960-61, supp. 3, pt. C, to BLS Report 237-38 (Washington, D. C.: U.S. Government Printing Office, 1964), table 29F. Stigler estimated the income elasticity of demand for servants as 2.0, based on 1935-36 consumer expenditures data.

9. The trends for 1910-20 and for 1920-30 have been affected, however, by a probable undercount of domestics in the 1920 census. See Stigler, op. cit., app. A.

10. Manpower Report of the President, 1974 (Washington, D.C.: U.S. Government Printing Office, 1974), tables A-16 and A-17.

11. Mattila, op. cit.

12. Herbert S. Parnes et al., Years for Decision: A Longitudinal Study of the Educational and Labor Market Experience of Young Women, vol. 1, Manpower Research Monograph no. 24 (Washington, D.C.: U.S. Government Printing Office, 1971), pp. 129-30.

13. National Committee on Household Employment, National Pilot Program of Household Employment: Final Report of the Experimental and Demonstration Projects (Washington, D.C.: U.S. Government Printing Office, 1971), pp. 31-32.

14. David S. North and William G. Weissert, Immigrants and the American Labor Market (Report prepared for the Manpower Administration, U.S. Department of Labor [Washington, D.C.: Trans Century Corp., 1973]).

15. Louis Levine, The Women's Garment Workers (New York: B.W. Huebisch, 1927), chap. 4.

16. U.S. Department of Labor, Bureau of Labor Statistics, Employment and Earnings (Washington, D.C.: U.S. Government Printing Office, January 1974).

17. U.S. Department of Labor, Formal Occupational Training of Adult Workers: Its Extent, Nature, and Use, Manpower Automation Research, Monograph no. 2 (Washington, D.C.: U.S. Government Printing Office, 1964), table 11.

18. U.S. Department of Commerce, Bureau of the Census, Census of Population, 1970, "Occupation by Industry," PC(2)-7C (Washington, D.C.: U.S. Government Printing Office, 1972), table 2.

19. Charles Brecher, Upgrading Blue Collar and Service Workers, (Baltimore: Johns Hopkins Press, 1972), p. 19.

20. Bureau of Labor Statistics, Employment and Earnings, op. cit.

21. U.S. Department of Commerce, U.S. Industrial Outlook for 1974: With Projections to 1980 (Washington, D.C.: U.S. Government Printing Office, 1973), p. 206.

22. For a discussion of the role of these factors, see Raymond Vernon, Metropolis 1985: An Interpretation of the Findings of the New York Metropolitan Regional Study (Cambridge, Mass.: Harvard University Press, 1960), pp. 64-65.

23. U.S. Department of Commerce, op. cit., pp. 210-11.

24. Alba M. Edwards, Comparative Occupational Statistics for the United States, 1870 to 1940 (Washington, D.C.: U.S. Government Printing Office, 1943), tables 14, 15.

25. Elaine Wrong, The Negro in the Apparel Industry, The Racial Policies of American Industry, Report no. 31, Industrial Research Unit, Wharton School (Philadelphia: University of Pennsylvania Press, 1974), pp. 29-30.

26. Edwards, op. cit., tables 14 and 15.

27. Ibid., table 3.

28. Bureau of Labor Statistics, Employment and Earnings, United States, 1909-1970, Bulletin 1312-7 (Washington, D.C.: U.S. Government Printing Office, 1970).

29. International Ladies Garment Workers Union, Report of the General Executive Board to the 35th Convention, New York, May 31, 1974, p. 5.

30. Interview with Carl Pressland, economic consultant to American Apparel Manufacturers Association.

31. Victor P. Fuchs, Changes in the Location of Manufacturing in the United States Since 1929 (New Haven and London: Yale University Press, 1962), p. 252.

32. Ibid.

33. Monthly Labor Review, March 1973, p. 57.

34. Monthly Labor Review, May 1974, p. 71.

35. Monthly Labor Review, March 1972, p. 53.

36. U.S. Department of Commerce, U.S. Industrial Outlook for 1974: With Projections to 1980, op. cit., p. 208.

37. U.S. Department of Labor, Bureau of Labor Statistics, Selected Earnings and Demographic Characteristics of Union Members, 1970, Report 417 (Washington, D.C.: U.S. Government Printing Office, 1972), p. 8.

38. Cited in Wrong, op. cit., p. 20.

39. Ibid., p. 63.

40. Ibid., table 24.

41. Ibid., pp. 63, 97.

42. Ronald E. Kutscher, "The United States Economy in 1985," Monthly Labor Review, December 1973, p. 34.

43. U.S. Department of Commerce, U.S. Industrial Outlook, 1971 (Washington, D.C.: U.S. Government Printing Office, 1970), p. 163.

44. Based on unpublished estimates by the Bureau of Labor Statistics, October 1974.

45. Laborers' Education and Training Pamphlet No. 27, Laborers' International Union of North America, 1972, p. 1. We wish to thank Marion Parsons, national director of the LIUNA training program, for providing this and other union publications and his many helpful comments.

46. U.S. Department of Labor, Formal Occupational Training of Adult Workers, op. cit., p. 45.

47. Construction Review, December 1969, table A1, and July 1973.

48. U.S. Bureau of the Census, Census of Population, 1970, Special Report, "Occupational Characteristics, 1970," PC(2)-7A (Washington, D.C.: U.S. Government Printing Office, 1972), table 11.

49. Ibid., table 11.

50. Ibid., table 15.

51. U.S. Department of Labor, Bureau of Labor Statistics, Handbook of Labor Statistics, 1973, Bulletin 1970 (Washington, D.C.: U.S. Government Printing Office, 1974), table 163.

52. Robert Ball and Larry Ludwig, "Labor Requirements for Construction of Single Family Housing," Monthly Labor Review, September 1971, p. 13.

53. Edwards, op. cit., table 16.

54. D. Haber and H. Levinson, Production and Productivity in the Building Trades (Ann Arbor: University of Michigan Press, 1956), chap. 10.

55. See, for example, Lloyd G. Reynolds and Cynthia H. Taft. The Evaluation of Wage Structure (New Haven: Yale University Press, 1956). pp. 355-58.

56. Dan Gustman and Martin Segal, "The Skilled-Unskilled Wage Differential in Construction," Industrial and Labor Relations Review 27 (January 1974): 261-75.

57. Haber and Levinson, op. cit., p. 217. The authors note, however, the absence of empirical evidence to suggest this assumption.

58. See, for example, U.S. Department of Labor, Bureau of Labor Statistics, Labor and Material Requirements for Hospital and Nursing Home Construction, BLS Bulletin 1661 (Washington, D.C.: U.S. Government Printing Office, 1971) and Labor and Material Requirements for Public Housing Construction, BLS Bulletin 1402 (Washington, D.C.: U.S. Government Printing Office, 1964).

59. Ronald E. Kutscher, "Projections of GNP, Income, Output and Employment," in "The United States Economy in 1985," Monthly Labor Review, December 1973, pp. 27-42.

60. Except as otherwise noted, data cited in this section are adapted from Neal Rosenthal and Dixie Sommers, The Supply of Hospital Attendants, in The Labor Supply for Lower-Level Occupations, Appendix A-II, Supplementary Reports, prepared for the U.S. Department of Labor under Grant No. 21-11-73-02, National Planning Association, Washington, D.C., June 1975 (mimeographed).

61. U.S. Department of Labor, Formal Occupational Training of Adult Workers, op. cit., table 11.

62. Studs Terkel, Working (New York: Pantheon Books, 1972), p. 471.

63. Peter B. Doeringer and Michael J. Piore, Internal Labor Markets and Manpower Analysis (Lexington, Mass.: D.C. Heath and Co., 1971), p. 167.

64. Paul M. Siegel, "Prestige in the American Occupational Structure," (Ph. D. diss., University of Chicago, March 1971), table 5.

65. Data for 1940 and 1950 from David L. Kaplan and M. Claire Casey, Occupational Trends in the United States: 1890 to 1950, Census Working Paper no. 5 (Washington, D. C.: U. S. Government Printing Office, 1958), table 6; data for 1960 and 1970 from U.S. Bureau of the Census, Detailed Characteristics of the Population, Census of Population: 1950, 1960, 1970 (Washington, D. C.: U. S. Government Printing Office, 1971). Changes in census occupational classifications have had a limited effect upon intercensal comparability for this occupation.

CHAPTER

7

THE OUTLOOK FOR
LOWER-LEVEL EMPLOYMENT:
AN ASSESSMENT AND
SOME POLICY IMPLICATIONS

MAJOR FINDINGS

The point of departure of the present study was the premise that there exists a hierarchy of jobs in our society, based on the nature of the work performed, the rewards for this work, the conditions of work, and the prestige associated with the occupation. The precise delineation of this hierarchy varies somewhat depending upon the choice of criteria. Some of the criteria, such as relative wages or income, have been more amenable to quantitative measurement and have also seemed most pertinent to the study of such problems as poverty and inequality of income distributions. Other criteria, such as working conditions—although clearly relevant in any assessment of occupational labor supply—are far more difficult to apply in any simple metric and are more likely to be affected by the varying preferences or value systems of individual workers.

For our purposes, broad occupational status groups were defined in Chapter 1, based on the proportion of white workers with at least 12 years of education in each occupation, using data for a specific age group, those 25-34 years in 1960. Our premise was simple: within any age/sex group, employers had generally given preference to white over nonwhite workers (at least in 1960 and prior years), and to better-educated over less-educated workers. Workers with these preferred characteristics had a broader choice of jobs, as illustrated, for example, by their substantially lower unemployment rates. Hence, the differential concentration of such workers in various occupations provided a reasonable indicator of their collective occupational preference scale, reflecting—in Adam Smith's words—the "sum of the advantages and disadvantages" of various kinds of work.

335

Based on this occupational preference scale, the lowest level, group 5, workers were found to consist predominantly of laborers and of certain of the less-skilled personal service groups, such as domestics, cleaning service workers, cooks and kitchen workers, and laundry or dry cleaning operatives. Directly above them, in the occupational hierarchy, is a much larger group, including all but the most skilled and/or highest-paid blue-collar workers; certain semiskilled personal service workers with somewhat better pay and/or working conditions than those in the group 5 category (for example, waiters, housekeepers, hospital attendants), and certain low-skilled clerical workers, such as messengers and shipping clerks.

The group 5 jobs, as well as many in the lower level of the group 4 category, all embody, in varying degrees, a combination of factors which make jobs undesirable to most workers: low pay, little skill, little challenge, and little or no upward mobility. They are, in other words, the jobs of last resort which workers take in the absence of other preferred ways of earning a livelihood. Nevertheless, workers engaged in these jobs are contributing to some of the most basic and essential activities in our economy—harvesting and processing of our food supplies, provision of clothing and shelter, care for the sick and aged, and performance of a wide variety of other production and housekeeping functions. Moreover, although technological progress has steadily reduced requirements for unskilled labor in most goods-producing industries, there have been growing requirements for low-level manpower in the expanding service sector of the economy, including food service workers, hospital attendants, and cleaning and janitorial workers. Labor requirements for service activities have proved less amenable to rationalization through substitution of machines or other devices, or through shifts in locus of production, than those in the goods-producing sector.

From this point of departure, we examined in Chapter 2 the ways in which the American economy has met these low-level manpower needs at various stages of its evolution. With limited exceptions, employers had experienced little difficulty in recruiting an adequate supply of workers for most of these jobs because of the existence of a large pool of workers who had few other effective choices. Included in this pool were disproportionate numbers of black workers, immigrants, and migrants from farm to city. These groups of workers shared, in varying degrees, common handicaps of limited education, limited skills, and limited labor market information. Particularly for the black workers, these handicaps were reinforced by various forms of institutionalized discrimination. A supplementary source of adult labor supply for these jobs consisted, at all times, of those indigenous white workers who, because of various personal or social handicaps, had also been confined to the lowest rungs of the occupational ladder.

The roles of both youth and women also deserve special attention in any examination of sources of low-level labor supply. Children and women had historically played an important role in providing the unskilled labor for routine personal service jobs; for light manufacturing industries, such as textiles and apparel; and for unpaid work in family farms and businesses. Young workers of both sexes, as well as more mature women, shared common labor market disadvantages due to their more limited work experience and more uncertain job tenure, as compared to adult men. Women, in addition, had been further limited in their job choices by their more restricted mobility and by discriminatory employment patterns, which had largely confined them to female-type jobs, typically in helping or auxiliary roles.

The process of urbanization and concomitant social and economic trends served to modify these occupational patterns, to a considerable degree. An increasingly sophisticated economy demanded—and also made possible—a progressive increase in the length of schooling. An increasing proportion of youth of both sexes, particularly those from more advantaged backgrounds, were able to substitute formal education and professional training for earlier traditional on-the-job methods of acquiring vocational skills, thus enabling them to enter directly into the growing ranks of the higher-status white-collar occupations. Child labor and compulsory school attendance laws further limited the scope of low-level youth employment, notably in factory work and in certain hazardous occupations, while the steady decline in agricultural employment resulted in sharp reductions in their utilization in the farm labor force.

Whereas participation of youth in full-time jobs had thus experienced a steady decline, many of these same forces had served to broaden the opportunities for employment of women, particularly in the expanding white-collar and service occupations. Women in these occupations had, however, been consistently relegated to the less-skilled and lower-wage jobs in these occupations due—at least in part—to systematic discrimination in hiring and promotional opportunities. Thus, whereas women held a roughly proportionate share of all group 4 and 5 jobs in 1960, they were heavily concentrated in the poorest paid of these occupations, that is, in the low-wage personal service occupations and in semiskilled jobs in the apparel and textile industries.

Our more detailed analysis of experience during the decade of the 1960s in Chapter 3 revealed major changes in the pattern of labor supply for low-level jobs. A favorable labor market climate, in conjunction with such influences as increased education and the momentum of private and public equal employment opportunity programs, had made possible a substantial broadening in job opportunities for non-white workers, particularly for those with above-average educational attainment. The result was a net reduction of over 600,000, or more than one-fifth, in the number of black workers in the lowest-level group 5 occupations. Despite this exodus, the overall size of the group 5 labor force actually increased slightly between 1960 and 1970, mainly as a result of a net inflow of over 800,000 young white workers, aged 16-24 years—a direct consequence of the entry into working age of large numbers of the post-World War II baby boom generation. Increased labor force participation among adult white women, including many with limited education or work experience, provided an additional source of recruits for these jobs. In both categories, a substantial proportion of these new entrants consisted of part-time workers— students or housewives—many of whom engaged in these jobs on a temporary or transitional basis. These labor supply sources were supplemented by an increased inflow of legal as well as illegal immigrants, predominantly drawn from nearby Latin American countries, and of Puerto Ricans moving to New York City and other eastern seaboard cities.

In the second phase of our study (Chapters 4-7), we attempted, by a variety of research approaches, to assess the labor market and wage structure implications of these trends and, in turn, to examine the probable consequences of prospective changes in overall labor force structure and growth for the future supply of workers in lower-level occupations. In Chapter 4, trends during the 1960s in relative occupational wages, as well as interarea wage variations for selected lower-level occupations, were analyzed in an attempt to measure the sensitivity of the occupational wage structure to labor supply variables. We found, not unexpectedly, that trends in the structure of wage differentials were not readily amenable to explanation by use of available empirical data. The evidence indicated considerable stability in the overall occupational wage structure during the decade of the 1960s. Nevertheless, the analysis did find that relative wage trends and differentials in some occupations were sensitive, in varying degrees, to such labor supply factors as (1) differences in the proportions of black workers in certain lower-level occupations; (2) differences in relative labor market opportunities for black workers; (3) differences in availability of youth or part-time workers for these jobs; (4) differences in overall unemployment rates; and (5) differences in availability of alternative income sources. These findings and related studies do suggest that the apparent general stability in occupational wage structures during the 1960s was due, in part, to the ability of employers to substitute new or augmented sources of low-level labor supply (for example, youth and female part-time workers) for declining low-level manpower sources, such as upwardly mobile black workers.

From this perspective, we then attempted, in Chapter 5, to assess the quantitative implications of prospective changes in overall labor force composition for labor supply, by broad occupational groups, in relation to projections of labor demand (or employment) by occupation. Changes in overall labor force growth and composition, for a period of up to 15 years in the future, are more predictable than other longer-range socioeconomic trends, since they derive in large part from such demographic realities as recent trends in birth rates and the normal processes of labor force attrition. Other related labor force trends, such as the growth of educational attainment of the adult labor force, can also be projected with some confidence for a decade or more ahead. These projections, combined with extrapolations of 1960-70 trends in the broad occupational distribution of the various socio-demographic components of the labor force, provided the basis for estimates of the expected distribution of the labor force by broad occupational group. The major finding was that, in contrast to sharp projected increases in availability of workers for higher-status (predominantly white-collar) jobs between 1970 and 1985, we can expect substantial reductions in the proportion of workers who will be available for the lower-level group 4 and 5 occupations. This results from a confluence of forces specified in our projection model—but, most importantly, from the projected slowdown in growth in the number of young workers, who had accounted for a large and growing segment of the low-level labor force in the decade of the 1960s.

Comparisons of these labor supply projections with BLS projections of employment or labor demand by occupation, under a full-employment model, in turn resulted in potential surpluses of workers for high-level (group 1 and 2) occupations and potential shortages for lower-level (group 4 and 5) occupations.

Any projections of this type are based on numerous assumptions. The most critical of these in the current context is that the economy of the 1980s will revert to a condition of high aggregate labor demand, as illustrated by an assumed 4 percent unemployment rate. There are, moreover, many other uncertainties concerning the shape of our future economy which could significantly modify these findings. However, a comparison of actual employment trends for the years 1970 through 1974 with the BLS projection for the entire decade of the 1970s suggests that the latter may have understated future labor requirements for certain low-level occupations, such as farm work and service work and, to this extent, represent a conservative projection of the potential low-level manpower deficit under full-employment conditions.

From past experience, we can anticipate that, if the trends projected above do materialize, the labor market will tend to accommodate these altered labor supply conditions in a number of ways. Our more detailed case studies of four lower-level occupations, in Chapter 6, were designed to identify the multiplicity of forces operating

dynamically upon labor supply and demand in specific occupations and
to suggest the possible path of future labor market adjustment in each
case.

Household maids are probably unique among the low-level workers studied, both because of the highly competitive labor market for
domestics, and because they are a "one-industry" group. For both
reasons, the supply of and demand for domestic workers is more
amenable to structured econometric analysis. Such analyses, based
on cross-sectional data, confirmed that both supply of and demand for
domestics were highly elastic. As a result, increased education and
expanding employment opportunities for black women (the major labor
supply source in past decades), as well as increases in alternative
income sources such as AFDC, were identified as important factors
contributing to the sharp downtrend in domestic employment, concurrent with a moderate increase in the relative wages for domestic
work. The establishment of a minimum wage for domestics, in combination with the projected reduction in overall supply of low-level
labor, is expected to result in a continued employment downtrend,
under conditions of high aggregate labor demand. Prospects for augmenting the labor supply of career domestics through increased
training and upgrading appear to be limited, based on experience of
past pilot projects. Augmentation of supply through increased immigration—including both legal and illegal aliens—has provided an additional source of labor for domestic work in some areas; however, this
has been transitory to a large extent, in view of the high propensity
of most immigrants to move to better-paid, higher-status jobs as
soon as they acquire the needed language or vocational skills.

Apparel industry operatives provide a prototype of the labor
market forces at work in a low-wage female, light manufacturing
occupation. The geographical mobility of the apparel industry, facilitated by advances in transportation and communication, has been a
dominant factor affecting its adjustment to changing labor market conditions. The stoppage of mass immigration, the upward mobility of
the ethnic groups who had initially staffed this industry, and the establishment of strong apparel worker unions in the major production
centers appear to have been key factors setting in motion a geographic
redistribution of apparel industry employment since the 1920s. Intensified import competition, particularly from low-wage countries
in Eastern Asia, has had the effect of arresting employment growth
in this industry in the 1960s and of accelerating its geographical relocation from North to South, particularly in the less style-oriented
branches of the industry. In the South, the attempts of employers to
utilize available reserves of low-wage female labor were reflected in
our findings that apparel industry employment grew most rapidly in
low-wage areas with high unemployment, and where AFDC payments

were low relative to apparel worker earnings. In addition, the southern industry had significantly increased its employment of black women
in operative jobs, probably reflecting, in large part, limitations in
available labor reserves of low-wage white female labor for apparel
factory jobs. Based on this experience, we concluded that labor supply
constraints are likely to result in continued movements of the industry
in search of remaining areas of low-wage female labor and in increased utilization of disadvantaged minority groups where available.
These tendencies may be checked, however, by such factors as establishment of national minimum welfare payments or income floors, by
increased unionization, and by a more rapid overall economic development in southern production regions. Under the latter contingencies,
significant increases in relative wages for apparel operatives would
be required to attract the needed labor supply, particularly in the
South.

Construction laborers provide a good illustration of a low-level
male occupational group which has experienced major shifts in its
labor supply sources. For example, between 1960 and 1973, the proportion of nonwhites among construction laborers fell from 31 percent
to 22 percent, while the proportion of (predominantly white) young
workers, aged 16-24, employed as construction laborers, rose from
26 percent to nearly 44 percent. It is probable that the large inflow
of young men into the construction laborer work force during the
1960s, and the fact that construction laborers' hourly wage rates
compare favorably to those in many other low-status jobs, were major factors contributing to the stability of the skilled-unskilled construction workers' wage differential during the 1960s, in contrast to
the longer-term trend towards a narrowing of this differential in
earlier decades. This interpretation is reinforced by our cross-
sectional analyses of interarea differences in relative earnings of
year-round construction laborers, which indicated that these differences were significantly influenced by such factors as interarea
differences in alternative job opportunities for black workers and in
availability of youth for construction laborer jobs, as well as by other
identifiable wage-relevant variables, such as unemployment rates
and extent of unionization. These findings, in conjunction with projections of a substantial increase in demand for construction laborers
by 1985, point to the likelihood of a considerably tighter labor market
for construction laborers than that experienced in the second half of
the 1960s. One possible outcome is a resumption of the longer-term
trend towards narrowing of the skilled-unskilled wage differential for
construction workers—particularly in view of the relatively inelastic
demand function for this category of labor. Construction laborer jobs
could be made more attractive by efforts to decasualize the construction laborer work force and to provide increased upgrading opportuni-

ties. A tighter labor supply is also likely to foster accelerated introduction of labor-saving equipment and construction methods, particularly in the South, which currently utilizes larger proportions of
construction laborers than other regions.

Hospital attendants, in a number of respects, offer a significant
contrast to the three other lower-level occupations analyzed. Unlike
many other low-skilled workers, they have experienced a sharp and
sustained employment increase since 1940, growing by 85 percent in
the 1960-70 decade alone. The principal sources of additional labor
supply for these jobs consisted of women (who increased their share
of jobs among hospital attendants from 74 percent in 1960 to 85 percent
in 1970) and of young workers of both sexes. This sharp employment
growth was accomplished, moreover, with only moderate increases
in wage rates, as compared to those for such related occupations as
licensed practical nurses and registered nurses. It is clear that the
supply of hospital attendants was more adequate in the 1960s than the
supply of more skilled health care personnel. Some confirmation of
these interpretations was provided by cross-sectional models, indicating that relative wages of hospital attendants, as compared to those
of workers in all lower-level jobs, were lower in areas with larger
proportions of women in the labor force and with larger proportions
of youth. Hence, the large inflow of both women and youth into the
labor force, and their preference for jobs as hospital attendants as
compared to more menial-type jobs, were key factors facilitating recruitment during the 1960s. By the same token, the projected slowdown in entry of both women and youth into the labor force, in combination with an expected continued growth in demand for hospital
attendants, is expected to cause a reversal of this experience in the
1980s. Adjustments to a tighter supply of hospital attendants are
expected to include significant increases in relative wages, combined
with measures to upgrade the status of hospital attendants. In addition,
there may be some capability for reducing the proportion of hospital
attendants needed, as compared to nurses, thus reversing the trend
observed in the 1960-70 decade, in view of the projected sharp growth
in availability of professionally trained personnel.

To summarize, the indications derived both from our broader
statistical projections and from a closer examination of selected
lower-level occupations, point to the likelihood that we are entering
an era which will witness a significant shift in the balance of labor
supply and labor demand among major categories of occupations.
Although our society will continue to require the services of large
numbers of workers in low-level jobs, basic changes in the demographic structure and rate of growth of the labor force—combined
with a continued thrust to a more egalitarian welfare-oriented society—
are likely to progressively constrain the supply of workers who will

readily accept such jobs, in the absence of significant changes in their wages and working conditions.

Past experience also suggests some of the ways in which the labor market is likely to accommodate these altered conditions, if and where they develop. At the upper end of the job spectrum, as the supply of better-educated workers becomes more plentiful, employers are likely to respond by reducing relative wages and by raising selection standards. Conversely, as some lower-level jobs become harder to fill, a number of options will be open, depending in part upon the elasticity of demand for such work. In some occupations, such as domestic work, we can expect a further employment decline: an increasing proportion of families will be obliged to seek substitutes for the services of paid domestics, either through product substitution, such as increased use of commercial services, or by simply doing more of their own household chores. Conversely, in the case of workers such as construction laborers and hospital attendants, the more probable longer-range outcome is for an increase in relative wages, accompanied by other efforts to make their jobs somewhat more attractive. In the case of geographically mobile, low-wage industries, such as apparel manufacturing, adjustment might also take the form of continued shifts in the locus of production, either to states or regions containing residual reserves of low-wage labor or through increased reliance upon imports from low-wage countries.

POLICY IMPLICATIONS

If manpower projections are to be used as a guide to decision making, they should meet certain standards of reliability and credibility. It is reasonable to ask: What is the reliability of the projections of labor demand in various occupations, given the large number of assumptions and economic variables which must enter into these projections? How much confidence, moreover, can we place upon any attempts to forecast the future availability of workers by occupation, given the limited knowledge of the forces influencing occupational mobility and occupational choices?

If these projections are treated as forecasts for a specific year, such as 1985, the answer clearly is: very little. One need simply examine the actual fluctuations of unemployment rates in past decades to recognize that a projection based on a full-employment peacetime economy—and one with relative price stability—does not correspond with actual experience in all but a few years at best. It seems particularly unreal at a time when the unemployment rate, in 1975, was 8.5 percent and when some forecasts anticipate that it may remain above 6 percent for the balance of the decade.

If these projections are treated as contingent indicators of labor market trends which may emerge in the 1980s under conditions of high aggregate labor demand, we believe that they can be given considerably more weight. The most reliable parameter in our projections is the predictable sharp reduction in the number and proportion of youth and young adults in the labor force of the 1980s—the population group which provided the greatest increment of manpower for lower-level jobs in the 1960s. (The labor market strains associated with this large influx during the 1960s were in fact foreseen by U.S. Labor Department studies released at the beginning of the decade[1] and, to some degree, may have influenced policymakers in initiation of an active manpower policy for the United States, as illustrated by programs conducted under the Manpower Development and Training Act and various elements of the Economic Opportunity Act of 1964.) Concurrent trends—such as the increase in occupational aspirations of minority groups, of women, and more generally of all youth coming from lower-income or disadvantaged backgrounds—have acquired sufficient momentum to be considered as irreversible forces in our society. These trends have, moreover, been treated rather conservatively in our manpower projection model, partly because they could not all be quantified. Furthermore, we made no effort to allow for the implications of possible future changes in income maintenance policies, such as establishment of some form of national minimum welfare payment or guaranteed income. For these reasons, these projections may well understate, rather than overstate, the potential need for future labor market adjustments in a high-employment economy.

The outlook, as we see it, points to the emergence of significant labor market strains, which can pose serious problems for some categories of workers and employers, as well as for those concerned with the efficient functioning of the labor market. At the same time, it can create a climate conducive to both private and public initiatives for reducing and/or upgrading low-level jobs in our society.

The heart of the dilemma which may be facing us is the sharp contrast between the limited demands and limited rewards of many jobs, as presently constituted, and the abilities, skills, and aspirations of the members of our labor force. To the extent that we approach such major national goals as sustained full employment and equal access to jobs, irrespective of race, sex, or social origin, the supply of workers available for the least desirable jobs will decline. The prospective decline in the number of youthful entrants into the labor force will further reduce the supply of workers for these jobs, particularly if the sharp downtrend in marriage and birth rates continues.

Some of the problems associated with these trends are already visible; others, as follows, can be expected to become evident as we move into the decade of the 1980s, to illustrate:

1. The better-educated young workers who have entered the labor market in the 1970s or who will be entering it in the 1980s, can expect increased competition in seeking preferred jobs, depending upon their area of specialized training, and may be forced to stay in or accept jobs not utilizing their education. Surveys have indicated that over one-third of American workers consider that they are already educationally overqualified for their jobs and that these workers have significantly lower levels of job satisfaction than other workers.[2] An acceleration of these trends, in turn, can be expected to intensify problems associated with poor worker morale.

2. Minority workers and women, seeking a fair share of the preferred jobs, face increased competition from majority worker categories, with a consequent danger of increased confrontations on issues relating to equal employment opportunity. (These issues become even more critical in periods of substantial unemployment since such workers, because of lower seniority, are often the first to be laid off.)

3. Although employers will have a greater choice of applicants in many professional, managerial, and other higher-status occupational fields, they may be faced with high job vacancy and turnover rates—and with related problems of poor worker morale—in low-skilled, low-status jobs.

4. Public manpower agencies and employment services, whose primary clientele in the late 1960s consisted of youth and disadvantaged workers, could be faced with conflicting demands for their services on the part of better-educated workers seeking placement in higher-status jobs, and of employers, who—on the other hand—may mainly need assistance in filling their lower-level jobs.

5. Institutions of higher education, already beset by serious financial difficulties, will be forced to reevaluate their educational programs and their enrollment prospects in the light of the altered labor market outlook for college-trained personnel.

It is possible, however, to view the projected labor force trends from a much more positive perspective. For example, the declining flow of new entrants into the labor force in the 1980s can, of itself, aid in reducing unemployment rates, since youthful workers, as well as adult married women, contribute disproportionately to the overall volume of frictional unemployment.[3] More specifically, a reduced supply of workers for lower-level jobs can, as suggested in our case study analyses, set in motion a number of labor market adjustments which most observers would consider desirable.

In industries or occupations where the demand for low-status labor is wage elastic (such as domestic service) a more restricted labor supply will create an inducement for substitution of capital or of alternative products or services, hence, reducing the requirement for this category of labor. A considerable potential for such economies in utilization of low-level labor is present in many industries, based on existing methods and technologies. In occupations where demand is much less elastic in the short run, as is probably the case in such diverse occupations as construction laborers, hospital attendants, and hired farm workers, the outlook is for a significant narrowing of wage differentials, as compared to more skilled occupations. Many workers in these occupations now receive annual earnings which do not meet socially accepted minimums; hence, this trend is also in a desirable direction.

Finally, in a tight labor market situation, a combination of employer self-interest and increased union pressures can make possible a number of other initiatives to raise the status of workers in low-level jobs, including measures to increase job security, to improve working conditions, to facilitate worker upgrading, and to provide more flexible work schedules.

Some of the adjustments described above can be expected to develop as part of the normal process of decision making by individual employers and workers in a free labor market. Other changes, particularly those involving significant realignments of wage structures and of personnel policies, are likely to be considerably slower, because of information lags, institutional obstacles, or simple reluctance of employers and/or worker groups to change established practices. This suggests the desirability of a more active role by policymakers in government, business, and labor in creating a climate which will accelerate adoption of desirable changes.

Policy Recommendations

For this purpose, the National Planning Association (NPA) established, in late 1973, a Joint Committee on Lower-Level Jobs, chaired by Howard Bowen, and including in its membership representatives of business, labor, agriculture, and the academic community. The initial findings of the present study, as well as a number of related studies, provided a frame of reference for the committee's assessment of the lower-level job outlook. Its report was released in February 1975, under the signature of 79 members of the NPA Board

of Trustees and committees.[4] Its major recommendations were
centered around a strategy which "should continue to encourage the
elimination of these jobs where possible, through technological change,
should seek to improve continuing low-status jobs by restructuring
them, and should try to insure that no segment of society is unfairly
relegated to the undesirable work which remains."[5] More specifically,
the report recommended the following:

1. restructuring of jobs, including (a) greater diffusion of responsibility and control among individual workers or teams of workers; (b) changes in work methods or work assignments in order to
enlarge and diversify job content; and (c) improvements in working
conditions, including better work space, more flexible work schedules,
and extension of various amenities such as parking and lunch room
facilities;

2. increased utilization of transitory labor sources, such as
student workers, for low-level jobs, through more flexible work
scheduling, more flexible academic calendars, and work-study arrangements; other labor supply sources which might be recruited
through more flexible work scheduling include housewives available
for part-time work and retirees;

3. improvement of minimum wage and of occupational health
and safety standards, including their extension to any residual non-
covered worker groups;

4. training and job creation programs, particularly to assist
hard-to-employ persons in obtaining useful employment, as well as
to assist in upgrading workers now in low-status jobs;

5. continuing education programs to provide opportunities for
upward mobility for midcareer workers stuck in low-level jobs;

6. strengthening of measures to end job discrimination because
of race and sex, or because of lack of opportunity to acquire needed
job skills.

In addition to the above recommendations, eight representatives
of organized labor, included among the signatories of the report,
strongly advocated the more rapid unionization of workers now employed in low-level jobs as holding "the greatest promise of upgrading
their status quickly," and also proposed amendments to the National
Labor Relations Act to extend its coverage of all workers, to ex-
pedite its procedures, and to provide effective penalties for unfair
labor practices.

From the above discussion, it will be evident that any broad
policy strategy for dealing with low-level employment can encompass
a very wide range of specific approaches. Some of these proposed
measures, such as job restructuring, improvement of work standards,

and unionization, are designed to make such jobs more attractive, hence, upgrading them from their present low-level status. One other proposal—for attracting additional transitory workers to these jobs— addresses the potential labor supply problem more directly. Still other proposals in this list—quite apart from their intrinsic desir- ability—would however have the effect of further diminishing the sources of manpower for these jobs.

Two other options were considered by the NPA committee but unanimously rejected. The first was a modification of the existing immigration laws to make possible more flexible year-to-year quotas geared to anticipated manpower needs by occupation. The second option, according to the committee, was "to encourage some individuals to curtail or tailor their education to the needs of the labor market," through such approaches as encouraging acceptable educational alter- natives to the conventional four-year college program for individuals without a strong interest or aptitude in academic courses and through reduced employer emphasis on formal academic credentials. Both options could have the effect of increasing labor supply for lower- level jobs. The reasons for their rejection as desirable options are assessed below.

Immigration Policy

An expansion of quotas for admission of low-skilled workers, in the event of a developing shortage of workers for low-level jobs, was rejected because such a policy "would simply transfer the dirty work to a new, more disadvantaged group. In the long run, such a policy would exacerbate social problems by encouraging exploitation of low- wage workers and by adding numerous new individuals to the ranks of the disadvantaged who require society's support and by adding low-wage competition to the U.S. work force."[6] The report notes, particularly, the problems associated with the increased flow of illegal immigrants who tend to be trapped in the worst jobs and are most subject to exploitation. It supports pending legislation designed to impose sanctions upon employers who knowingly hire such aliens as well as measures to strengthen the enforcement capabilities of the Immigration and Naturalization Service.

There is considerable difference in opinion concerning current immigration issues. Economists who approach these issues from the theoretical perspectives of the neoclassical tradition are likely to be opposed to any artificial barriers to free movement of either goods or labor across national borders. Employers who hire such workers clearly do so because it is profitable for them. And the immigrants themselves, although exploited in terms of American standards, have continued to come here because of the sharp differential between

U.S. wages and those in their native countries. The major initiatives for stricter enforcement of immigration rules have come from U.S. labor organizations and workers, particularly in industries where competition from such immigrant workers has tended to undermine labor standards and has impeded union organization. More generally, however, public authorities and community leaders have noted the adverse effects of illegal immigration upon economic and social conditions and welfare burdens in the affected communities and the linkage with organized crime. [7]

The social overhead costs associated with a policy of encouragement of immigration to meet low-level job needs have also been dramatically illustrated by experiences of developed countries in Western Europe and elsewhere. The rapid post-World War II economic expansion of Western Europe had resulted in a depletion of the more readily available domestic labor reserves in these countries, particularly in view of the very low natural rates of labor force growth during this period—a demographic pattern analogous to that projected for the United States in the 1980s. Economic growth, low unemployment rates, and vocational training programs facilitated upward mobility of native-born workers in these countries, and, in turn, resulted in significant shortages of workers for the low-skilled and undesirable jobs. To fill this gap, Western European countries resorted to increased importation of foreign workers from the southern Mediterranean countries, the Balkans, and North Africa. This policy took various forms, ranging from formal contractual arrangements with these supplying countries to liberal work permit policies for individual immigrants, and was supplemented by a large, but unmeasured, flow of illegal immigrants. Estimates in 1975 place the total of such foreign workers in the nine Common Market nations at more than ten million, and, despite the slowdown resulting from the recession prior to then, some forecasts indicate a further growth to more than 20 million in the 1980s. [8]

By virtually all accounts, these foreign workers have been concentrated in the most undesirable occupations—"the uncomfortable, unskilled, dirty and dangerous jobs—the ones that native Western Europeans no longer want to do."[9] There is ample evidence that these workers contributed significantly to the economic growth and rising affluence of the host countries. At the same time, this influx has brought with it a host of major social frictions and costs, including the emergence of new immigrant ghettos, growing racial and ethnic frictions, and increased crime problems, in some communities.[10]

On balance, we must conclude that reliance upon increased immigration of low-skilled workers is one of the least desirable of the options available, and that measures to more effectively control illegal immigration should be adopted. However, any legislation designed to impose sanctions upon employment of illegal aliens already residing here should be tempered with an appropriate amnesty clause, designed to legalize the status of those workers who have been employed here for some period of time and whose only illegal act was their original entry. This is desirable both on humanitarian grounds and to reduce the potentials for their exploitation, thus undermining labor standards of other workers.

Educational Policies

The prototype of educational success for most young persons has, until now, been considered as synonymous with uninterrupted school enrollment through high school, immediately followed by full-time enrollment in a four-year academic program and, increasingly, in further continuous study leading towards advanced academic or professional degrees. Although higher education has many intrinsic values, both for the individual and society, the major expected rewards for most who have entered on this educational path has been the prospect of obtaining a high-level job, with high pay and correspondingly high social status. It has, in fact, produced such rewards for many students who successfully followed this educational routine in past generations.

Yet, increasing numbers of thoughtful educators, as well as students, have come to question the desirability of following this rigid educational routine. Some of the major criticisms of the conventional educational model have been that (1) it does not conform to the real needs and interests of significant numbers of students, many of whom attend college simply because of parental or other social pressures; (2) it is inherently wasteful, as reflected in the high dropout rates, of 40-50 percent, between college entry and completion; (3) it provides little opportunity for contact with the world of work, and therefore does not offer an adequate knowledge base for making career choices; and (4) as a result, there is a further major personal and social cost, reflected in the large proportion of graduates who do not utilize their specialized training in subsequent employment.

The prospective labor market squeeze for future college graduates will, in the absence of corrective measures, intensify these problems in the 1980s. This outlook was one of the central concerns addressed by the Carnegie Commission on Higher Education in its comprehensive assessment in 1973 of major issues facing our nation's higher education system. The following recommendations, adapted from the commission's reports, are particularly relevant in the present context.[11]

First, manpower considerations should not be used as a rationale for slowing down the momentum achieved in moving towards an open-access system of higher education, and in removing remaining inequalities in educational opportunity due to race, sex, level of family income, or geographical location. This implies continued vigorous support of measures to increase the number of low-cost or no-cost community colleges, related financial aid programs, and special consideration in admissions policies for disadvantaged students, including remedial assistance.

Second, to cope with prospective occupational imbalances, what is needed is a systematic broadening of educational options to young people, generally, including either acceptable alternatives to formal college or options to defer college entry, to step out from college in order to get service and work experience (including more opportunities for part-time enrollment), and to change directions while in college.

The NPA report strongly endorsed the first of these recommendations, that is, that manpower considerations not be used as a rationale for encouraging some individuals to tailor their education to the needs of the labor force. It did not directly address the second recommendation, providing for acceptable alternatives to the conventional four-year college routine, but, by implication, rejected it on grounds that these alternatives "run counter to the democratic principle of providing maximum opportunity to all members of society, and they fail to recognize the noneconomic benefits of education as preparation for full participation in our complex society."[12]

The issue here, in our judgment, focuses on a critical assessment of the benefits both to the individual and to society of alternative forms of postsecondary education. There is little doubt that a substantial proportion of college entrants enroll in college because of their expectations that a college education is a necessary condition for entry into higher-paying and higher-status careers. This is particularly true of many students coming from low-income family backgrounds, whose opportunity costs, in terms of foregone earnings, are proportionately greater than for those from more affluent backgrounds. Inevitably, as the relative earnings advantage of a four-year college education declines, many such students—if not otherwise academically motivated—will reassess the balance of educational costs and benefits for them. Their perceptions of these costs and benefits are likely to be based primarily on their own observations of actual labor market developments, including advice from families and peers, rather than on formal counseling or on manpower projections. The perceived choice for many in this dilemma may be viewed as enrolling in a conventional college program or abandoning postsecondary education or training entirely.

If this assessment is valid, strengthening of acceptable alternatives to formal college can, in fact, be an integral part of a comprehensive program for readapting existing educational institutions in the light of both individual and social needs. A necessary condition for the acceptability of those alternatives, however, is reduced emphasis on the part of employers upon conventional educational certification, such as a four-year college diploma, and increased reliance upon alternative criteria for selection and promotion, such as specialized training, experience, and performance.

CONCLUDING OBSERVATIONS

The above discussion of policy issues which have some relevance to the findings of this study will serve to illustrate that those concerned with policy planning, whether in government or in the private sector, rarely arrive at their judgments—and should not—based upon any simple set of criteria, such as labor market trends or manpower projections. To the extent that these projected trends materialize, or are given credence, it is reasonable, however, that they be included as parameters in assessing courses of action.

It is appropriate, too, that we note some of the major limitations of available data and research relevant to this subject area. Comprehensive data on occupational labor supply and on occupational employment trends are only available—in the needed disaggregate form—from the decennial censuses of population. These suffer from serious limitations, particularly in view of noncomparability of data in successive censuses. Very limited periodical information is available, too, on the flows of workers into and among occupations, on unemployment and job vacancies by occupation, and on occupational wage rates.

The amount of analytical research on occupational supply is also quite limited. For example, a comprehensive bibliography of occupational labor supply studies lists 62 analytical studies of individual occupations and occupational groups.[13] These are almost entirely focused on professional and technical occupations. With the exception of the present study, only that by Mattila—a contributor to the present study—also focuses on lower-level occupations. It is our hope that the many unresolved technical problems addressed in the current study will be the subject of more intensive research by future investigators.

NOTES

1. U.S. Department of Labor, Manpower Challenge of the 1960's (Washington, D.C.: U.S. Government Printing Office, 1970.)

2. University of Michigan, Survey Research Center, Survey of Working Conditions (Ann Arbor: Survey Research Center, November 1970), pp. 407-09.

3. Economic Report of the President, 1974-1975 (Washington, D.C.: U.S. Government Printing Office, 1975), pp. 88-89.

4. National Planning Association, Upgrading Low-Level Employment: A Major National Challenge, Report no. 141 (Washington, D.C.: National Planning Association, February 1975).

5. Ibid., chap. 5, p. 13.

6. Ibid.

7. For a description of these impacts, see William Chapman, "Mexican Illegals Now Seek U.S. Cities," Washington Post, December 9, 1973.

8. Wall Street Journal, February 26, 1975.

9. Ibid. See also, Bernard Kayser, Manpower Movements and Labor Markets (Paris: Organization for Economic Cooperation and Development, 1971), pp. 178-79.

10. For a description of the social tensions accompanying increased immigration of North African workers to France, see Edward R.F. Sheehan, "Europe's Hired Poor," New York Times Magazine, December 9, 1973. On the other hand, W.R. Bohning has noted that demands for "social capital" are very low initially, for immigrant workers, as compared to domestic workers, but increase as adult male immigrants are joined by their families. W.R. Bohning and D. Maillat, The Effects of the Employment of Foreign Workers (Paris: Organization for Economic Cooperation and Development, 1974), pp. 103-04.

11. See, particularly, Carnegie Commission on Higher Education, Priorities for Action: Final Report of the Carnegie Commission on Higher Education (New York: McGraw-Hill, 1973).

12. National Planning Association, op. cit., p. 12.

13. U.S. Department of Labor, Bureau of Labor Statistics, Occupational Supply: Concepts and Sources of Data for Manpower Analysis, BLS Bulletin 1816 (Washington, D.C.: U.S. Government Printing Office, 1974), pp. 62-69.

APPENDIX: REVISIONS IN CENSUS OCCUPATIONAL CLASSIFICATIONS AND PROCEDURES

As noted in this study, the 1970 decennial census of population introduced major changes in occupational classification, enumeration, and data processing procedures, whose combined effect was to cause a serious discontinuity in the published occupational statistics as compared to 1960 and preceding censuses. Although a statistical bridge with the 1960 occupational statistics was published by the Census Bureau in the form of a retabulation of the 1960 census occupational data in accordance with 1970 census classifications, the revised 1960 statistics did not provide any detail on the characteristics of the labor force in each 1970-comparable occupation, other than by sex, and therefore were inadequate for use in the present study. Moreover, full comparability with the published 1970 data was not achieved by the Census Bureau, because the procedure followed did not allow for the effects of the concurrent changes in enumeration and processing procedures upon the number of workers reported in each occupation in 1970 as compared to 1960.

This appendix examines evidence concerning the effects of these revisions on intercensal comparability and describes the procedures followed to adjust for the resulting biases in development of the occupational labor supply matrices for 1960 and 1970, presented in Chapter 3 of this study.

The following major revisions affecting occupational statistics were introduced in the 1970 decennial census:

1. The number of detailed occupations was expanded from 297 in 1960 to 441 in 1970, with concurrent revisions in the definition of many of the existing (1960) occupations. A new major occupational group, "transport equipment operatives"—previously included among "operatives and kindred workers"—was established.

2. To obtain more complete and accurate responses on occupations, two additional occupation-related questions were included on the 1970 census questionnaire. In 1960 and preceding censuses, a worker's occupation had been classified based on responses to a single question concerning "the kind of work the person was doing" during the census reference week, if then employed, or in that person's last previous job, if unemployed. The 1970 census schedule, in addition, requested a description of "his most important activities or duties" and his job title, with appropriate examples given.

3. A number of computer-based allocation and editing procedures were introduced. In 1960, persons for whom insufficient information

was provided to prevent their classification in a specific occupation had been tabulated in a "not reported" category. In 1970, such persons were allocated to a major (one-digit) occupation group based on their residence, age, income, industry of employment, and similar characteristics. Other 1970 processing innovations included computer editing of clerically assigned codes and the use of tabulation categories to regroup certain workers, such as apprentices.

4. Another revision, not directly related to occupational classification, was the addition of the category "own business incorporated" to the class-of-worker item, on the 1970 census questionnaire, which resulted in decreasing the number of self-employed and increasing the number of wage and salary workers. This change may also have affected intercensal comparability of classification of persons in the 1960 occupation group, "managers, officials and proprietors, except farm"—which was redesignated as "managers and administrators, except farm" in the 1970 Census.

EFFECTS OF CENSUS REVISIONS ON INTERCENSAL OCCUPATIONAL COMPARABILITY

In order to provide measures of occupational trends between 1960 and 1970, a 100,000 card sample of the 1960 census experienced civilian labor force, containing the occupation, industry, and class-of-worker entries from the 1960 census schedules, was recoded in terms of the revised 1970 occupational classifications. This has provided the basis for published estimates of the 1960 distribution of the experienced civilian labor force comparable to 1970 occupational data. The results of this cross-tabulation of 1960 census occupational data, showing the derivations of workers classified under each 1970 occupational title, in terms of their original 1960 occupational classifications, have been published in a Census Bureau technical report.[1] Since these revised statistics provided no detail on characteristics of workers classified under the revised 1970 titles, other than sex, they could not be directly incorporated into the present study. This dictated (1) an initial grouping and matching of the relevant 1960 and 1970 census occupational titles in such a manner as to minimize incomparabilities resulting from definitional changes; and (2) development of adjustment procedures to minimize the effects of all of the concurrent changes in census occupational data editing and processing upon comparisons of labor force trends by occupation.

Initial inspection of the effects of definitional changes, alone, upon 1960-70 census comparability indicated that these revisions had been very extensive, affecting many occupational titles which

appeared in both the 1960 and 1970 classifications, as well—obviously—
as those which had been further disaggregated in 1970 or otherwise
changed in their defined scope. Even though most of the changes were,
by design, limited to revisions and reallocation within the major
census occupational groups, the effects on net comparability of the
latter groups were still substantial as illustrated by an increase of
over 50 percent in the relatively small group of women classified as
nonfarm laborers and by increases in the number of men classified
as service workers (7 percent) and as operatives (5 percent).[2] The
effects of the definitional changes were particularly severe in the
case of many of the specified occupations in the operatives group,
other than transportation equipment operatives, as a direct result of
the efforts of census staff to reduce the large numbers previously
shown in the category, "operatives, not elsewhere classified," which
had accounted for 4.6 million or nearly two-fifths of all workers included in the 1960 operatives group. Thus, although the occupational
title "assemblers" appears both in the 1960 and 1970 classifications,
the number of workers in the 1960 census classified as assemblers
increased from 685,000 to 786,000 or by 15 percent, mainly due to
reclassifications of workers previously identified as "operatives,
not elsewhere classified."

Much less direct information is available on the effects of the
other procedural changes introduced in 1970 upon intercensal comparability of occupational data. One of the most significant of these
changes was the addition of two questions to the 1970 census schedule
designed to provide more precise information on occupational duties
and job titles. Between July and October 1971, the Census Bureau
conducted a reinterview survey of 4,500 individuals included in its
Current Population Survey (CPS) sample, who had been originally
classified based on the single question appearing in the 1960 schedule.
It was found that, for all occupations, the addition of the two new
questions in the 1970 census schedule resulted in an increase of 2.2
percent in the number of workers who could be assigned a specific
occupational code. However, the small size of the sample did not
permit disaggregation of these relationships below the major census
occupational group level. Moreover, interactions between occupational reclassifications due to definitional changes and those due to
changes in census schedules could not be estimated from this data
base.

In the absence of a more definitive measure of the combined
effect of all of the revisions in census occupational classification,
enumeration, and processing procedures, we relied upon an indirect
measure of the resulting biases, based on data from the Census
Bureau's CPS. The CPS, unlike the 1970 decennial census, had retained the original (1960) census classifications as well as the single

question used in the 1960 census to describe an individual's occupation until January 1971. It was, therefore, possible to use comparisons of the trend of the experienced civilian labor force, by occupation, between the decennial survey months (March 1960 and March 1970, respectively) as shown by the CPS, and as shown by the decennial census data, as a measure of the probable bias in the latter data resulting from definitional and procedural changes. These comparisons are shown in Table A.1, for the experienced civilian labor force, by sex, classified by the eleven major occupational groups and the 22 subgroups for which CPS distributions were available on both dates. The adjustment factor shown in this table represents the ratio of the 1960-70 percentage changes (or ratios), by occupation, based on the CPS, to the corresponding 1960-70 changes, based on decennial census data. Despite the greater sampling error inherent in the CPS data, the trends based upon these data were considered more reliable measures of 1960-70 occupational trends for 1960-comparable occupations.

The comparisons (or adjustment factors) shown in Table A.1 were found to be large and statistically significant for a substantial number of occupational groups, including farmers and farm laborers, service workers, private household workers, and nonfarm laborers, in contrast to smaller differences for most of the white-collar and craftsmen occupational groups or subgroups.

Derivation of Matched 1960-70 Occupational Titles and Subgroups

Although the CPS data provided a reasonable basis for estimating overall trends in the labor force by occupation between 1960 and 1970, it was still necessary to rely upon the decennial census data for detail on trends in the demographic composition of the labor force in each occupation, as well as for more detailed occupational breakdowns than available in the CPS. As an initial step, all relevant occupations in the 1960 census were tentatively ranked in status order based on an average of three criteria: the Duncan SES scale, the Siegel prestige scale, and the percentage of nonwhites in each occupation in 1960. This served as a guide in combinations of related occupations where needed, to provide a minimum 1960 total of at least 250,000 workers in each occupation, since this was considered the minimum feasible base number for analysis of 1960-70 changes in major demographic characteristics—such as sex, race, and broad educational-level groups—by occupation, using the 1/1,000 census samples.

TABLE A.1

Comparison of Relative Changes in Experienced Civilian Labor Force, 16 Years and Over, by Occupation, March 1960–March 1970: Current Population Survey (CPS) Versus Census of Population

Occupation	Both Sexes			Males			Females		
	CPS	Census	CPS/Census	CPS	Census	CPS/Census	CPS	Census	CPS/Census
Experienced civilian labor force, total	1.177	1.194	.9857	1.1010	1.0809	1.0186	1.3708	1.3591	1.0086
Professional, technical and kindred, total	1.4975	1.5067	.9939	1.4285	1.4612	.9776	1.6172	1.5807	1.0231
Farmers, farm managers, unpaid family workers, total	.6384	.5719	1.1163	.6185	.5756	1.0746	.7775	.5327	1.4595
Nonfarm managers, officials and kindred, total	1.1852	1.1343	1.0449	1.1707	1.1056	1.0588	1.2719	1.3035	.9758
Clerical and kindred, total	1.4381	1.3996	1.0275				1.5892	1.5302	1.0386
Secretaries, typists, stenographers	1.4896	1.6946	.8790	1.1270	1.1292	.9981	1.5150	1.6970	.8928
All other clerical workers	1.4216	1.3062	1.0884				1.4540	1.4427	1.0078
Salesmen and sales workers, total	1.1178	1.1015	1.0148	1.0220	1.0487	.9745	1.2778	1.1940	1.0702

Craftsmen and kindred workers, total	1.1681	1.1295	1.0341	1.1577	1.1051	1.0476			
Carpenters	1.0000	.9924	1.0077	.9934	.9837	1.0098			
Foremen, not elsewhere classified	1.2701	1.3514	.9398	1.2535	1.3312	.9416			
Mechanics, auto	1.2405	1.3278	.9343	1.2377	1.3110	.9441			
Mechanics, excluding auto	} 1.3012	} 1.0488	} 1.2407	} 1.2940	} .9442	} 1.3705	1.6068	1.9442	.8265
Machinists, job setters									
Construction, craftsmen, excluding carpenters	1.1605	1.0913	1.0634	1.1634	1.0807	1.0765			
All other craftsmen	1.0557	1.1964	.8824	1.0316	1.1467	.8996			
Operatives and kindred workers, total	1.1326	1.0704	1.0581	1.0820	.9917	1.0911			
Drivers, deliverymen	1.0720	1.0150	1.0562	1.0332	.9777	1.0568	1.2585	1.2721	.9893
All other operatives	1.1462	1.0835	1.0579	1.0986	.9966	1.1023			

(continued)

TABLE A.1 (continued)

Occupation	Both Sexes			Males			Females		
	CPS	Census	CPS/Census	CPS	Census	CPS/Census	CPS	Census	CPS/Census
Service workers, excluding private household, not elsewhere classified	1.3093	1.4446	.9063	1.0873	1.3551	.8024	1.5070	1.5257	.9877
Waiters, cooks, bartenders	1.3236	1.2893	1.0266	1.0611	1.2198	.8699	1.4329	1.3185	1.0868
Protective services	1.2240	1.3635	.8976	1.2003	1.3333	.9002	} 1.5499	} 1.6815	} .9170
Other service workers	1.3196	1.5514	.8506	} 1.0405	} 1.3789	} .7546			
Private household workers, total	.7672	.6612	1.1603	.7386	.5912	1.2493	.7668	.6648	1.1534
Farm laborers and foremen, excluding family workers, total	.7376	.5987	1.2320	.7386	.5912	1.2493	} 1.0796	} 1.4244	} .7579
Nonfarm laborers, total	.9932	.9804	1.0130	.9780	.9310	1.0505			

360

Notes to Table A.1

Note: The relative changes in this table have been expressed in ratio form. Thus the 1970/60 relative change for the total experienced civilian labor force, of 1.177, corresponds to a percentage increase of 17.7 percent. CPS/Census is the ratio of the CPS change, 1960-70, to the census change, 1960-70. Thus the adjustment factor for male professional, technical, and kindred workers, of .9776, indicates that the growth of this group between 1960 and 1970 as reported by CPS (1.4285) was less than that reported by the census (1.4612). Occupational detail not shown where base numbers were less than 50,000.

Sources: CPS – Unpublished BLS Table 24, "Employed and unemployed Persons by Detailed Occupation Group and Sex," March, 1960 and March, 1970; Census – 1960 data from U.S. Census of Population, 1960, PC(2)7A – Occupation Characteristics, Table 4; 1970 data from U.S. Census of Population, PC(2)7C, Occupation by Industry, Tables 7 and 8. Both Census and CPS data for 1960 adjusted to exclude the labor force ages 14-15 years, based on their occupational distribution in the 1960 Census (from PC(2)7A, Table 4).

Estimates of net occupational comparability were computed for
these occupations or occupational clusters based on data from the
census occupational matching study. As a general rule, an attempt
was made to limit 1960-70-comparable occupations or groupings to
those which met a criterion of 90 percent or greater net definitional
comparability under the 1960-70 recoding study. This criterion was
adopted on the premise that within a ±10 percent range, we could
expect limited distortion in comparability of the distribution of workers in each occupation by such characteristics as race, age, and
educational level. (To illustrate, even though the major 1960 group
of "service workers, excluding private household" was increased by
5.6 percent under the 1970 classification criteria, the percentage of
women in this occupational group changed by only 0.8 percent, from
52.4 percent to 51.6 percent.) The only significant deviation from
this criterion was made in the case of service workers in the "cleaning
and building services" subgroup, such as janitors, cleaners, charwomen, and chambermaids. An examination of the detailed changes
in occupational definitions for these groups suggested that the definitional changes had probably resulted in reclassification into these
groups of individuals with characteristics similar to those previously
classified in these groups, and, therefore, should not appreciably
affect the resulting distributions. (The largest of these changes consisted of a reclassification of about 134,000 male building maintenance
workers or handymen, who had been previously classified as craftsmen in 1960, and were reclassified into the janitorial group in 1970.)

The results of this analysis are shown in Table A.2, which
identifies the specific 1960-70-comparable occupations or occupational subgroups developed under these criteria. It will be noted that
only limited detail is provided for high-level groups such as professional and technical workers and managerial workers, in view of our
primary interest in lower-level occupational groups. As indicated,
the net comparability index for each of the selected groups falls within
the 90-110 range, with the exception of the "cleaning and building
services" occupational group.

One consequence of the criteria established was the combining
of many specific occupations into large groupings, such as "all other
operatives" and "nonfarm laborers." These large groups were,
however, disaggregated by a total of seven broad industry groupings
for operatives, not elsewhere classified, and five groupings for nonfarm laborers, as shown in Table 1.3. The industrial combinations
used for this purpose were established after inspection of available
data on interindustry differences in (1) full-time earnings; (2) prestige ratings; and (3) training requirements, as well as on sample
size considerations.

The adjustment factors, by sex, based on the comparison of CPS and census trends for matched occupational subgroups (Table A.2) were, in turn, used to adjust the 1970 experienced civilian labor force totals and the sociodemographic components of these subgroups, as derived from tabulations of the 1970 census public use tapes. The final step in this adjustment was a statistical balancing procedure to force resulting totals for each sociodemographic subgroup, (for example, nonwhite males, aged 16–24 years, with 12 years of education) to correspond to the total number of experienced civilian workers in this category as derived from our tabulations of the 1970 decennial census tapes.

The approximate standard errors of percentages derived from the tabulations of the census 1/1,000 public use samples for 1960 and 1970 are shown in Table A.3.

TABLE A.2

Net Comparability of 1960 and 1970 Census Occupational Definitions for Major Occupational Groups and Specified Occupations, Based on 1960 Census Data

Occupational Group	Experienced Civilian Labor Force (ECLF), 1960, (000)			Net Comparability[a]	Sources of Major Change (000)[b]	
	1960 Definition	1970 Definition	Change		Gains from	Losses to
Professional, technical, and kindred workers, total	7,336	7,090	-246	97	service occupations (42), clerical occupations (31), craft occupations (18)	managerial occupations (178), service occupations (81), clerical occupations (50)
Engineers	872	870	- 2	100	—	—
Medical personnel	1,326	1,283	- 40	97	—	service workers (58)
Teachers, not elsewhere classified	1,682	1,765	+ 83	105	craftsmen (13), professional (90)	—
All other professional and technical workers	3,456	3,172	-284	92	—	—
Nonfarm managers, officials, and proprietors, total	5,490	5,708	+218	104	professional (178), clerical (64)	professional (11), service (9)
Farmers and farm managers, total	2,528	2,528	—	100	—	—
Clerical and kindred workers, total	9,618	9,431	-187	98	professional (50)	service workers (71), managers (64), operatives (64), sales (40)
Bookkeepers	936	951	+ 15	102	clerical (15)	—

364

Secretaries, typists, stenographers	2,313	2,316	+ 3	100	—	—
Office machine operators	318	322	+ 4	101	clerical (4)	—
Telephone operators	372	372	—	100	—	—
Cashiers	492	510	+ 18	104	clerical (17), sales (6)	clerical (6)
Mail carriers and postal clerks	420	440	+ 20	105	clerical (22)	operatives (3)
Shipping and receiving clerks, messengers, and office boys	361	388	+ 27	108	clerical (31)	clerical (5)
All other clerical workers	4,406	4,132	-274	94	—	—
Sales workers, total	4,801	4,799	- 2	100	clerical (40), professional (18)	laborers (55), clerical (7)
Craftsmen and kindred workers, total	9,241	9,465	+224	102	operatives (395), professional (20)	service workers (142), operatives (44)
Foremen, not elsewhere classified	1,199	1,186	- 13	99	—	professional (13)
Mechanics and repairmen, excluding auto	357	381	+ 24	107	—	craftsmen (23)
Metalworking crafts, excluding machinists, mechanics	611	601	- 10	98	craftsmen (9)	craftsmen (22)
Electricians, brickmasons, excavating machine operators[c]	1,181	1,158	- 23	98	craftsmen (12), laborers (13)	operatives (50)

(continued)

(Table A. 2 continued)

Occupational Group	Experienced Civilian Labor Force (ECLF), 1960, (000)			Net Comparability[a]	Sources of Major Change (000)[b]	
	1960 Definition	1970 Definition	Change		Gains from	Losses to
Machinists	516	511	– 5	99	—	—
Carpenters	921	930	+ 9	101	operatives (17), craftsmen (2)	craftsmen (12)
Auto mechanics	705	682	– 23	97	—	craftsmen (23)
Construction painters, plasterers, cement and concrete finishers, roofers, paperhangers	589	568	– 21	96	craftsmen (17)	craftsmen (37)
All other craftsmen	3,162	3,448	+286	109	—	—
Operatives and kindred workers, total	12,846	12,254	–592	95	laborers (68), craftsmen (44), clerical (43)	craftsmen (395), laborers (295)
Deliverymen, routemen	441	462	+ 21	105	operatives (25), craftsmen (2)	laborers (7)
Checkers, examiners	518	554	+ 36	107	clerical (32), operatives (8)	—
Taxi drivers, bus drivers[d]	552	550	– 2	100	—	—
Auto service workers and parking attendants	379	393	+ 14	104	laborers (39), operatives (6)	operatives (31)
Truck and tractor drivers	1,663	1,550	–113	93	operatives (1), clerical (3)	operatives (118)
Packers	497	458	– 39	92	operatives (11), clerical (4)	operatives (35), laborers (13)

Occupation						
Welders and flame-cutters	359	359	—	100	—	—
Laundry and dry cleaning operatives	410	433	+ 23	106	operatives (79)	operatives (19), laborers (32)
All other operatives	8,027	7,495	-532	93	—	—
Nonfarm laborers, total	3,530	3,755	+225	106	operatives (251), sales (56)	operatives (68), service (30), craftsmen (14)
Farm laborers and farm foremen, total	1,560	1,604	+ 44	103	operatives (41)	—
Paid farm workers (and self-employed)	1,247	1,294	+ 47	104	operatives (41)	—
Service workers, total	7,590	7,902	+312	140	craftsmen (142), professionals (81), clerical (70), operatives (38)	managers (42), laborers (12)
Protective services: policemen, firemen	424	431	- 7	102	clerical (6)	—
Guards and watchmen, crossing watchmen, and bridge tenders	282	288	+ 6	102	operatives (8), clerical (2)	services (6)
Health services: hospital attendants	408	420	+ 12	103	professional (8), services (8)	services (4)
Food services	1,999	2,023	+ 24	101	services (36)	services (12)
Cooks, except private household	599	603	+ 4	101	services (3), operatives (3)	—

(continued)

Occupational Group	Experienced Civilian Labor Force (ECLF), 1960, (000)			Net Compa- rability[a]	Sources of Major Change (000)[b]	
	1960 Definition	1970 Definition	Change		Gains from	Losses to
Waiters and counter and fountain workers	1,063	1,067	+ 4	100	services (4)	—
Kitchen workers	337	353	+ 16	105	services (29)	services (12), laborers (1)
Private household workers	1,813	1,776	– 37	98	services (28)	services (64)
Housekeepers and babysitters	502	529	– 27	105	services (28)	—
Private household, not elsewhere classified, including laundresses	1,311	1,247	– 64	95	—	services (64)
Cleaning and building services	1,231	1,467	+236	119	craftsmen (134), services (70), operatives (24)	—
Janitors and sextons	621	785	+164	126	craftsmen (134), laborers (13)	—
Cleaners, char- women, chamber- maids, porters, elevator operators	610	682	+ 72	112	services (50), opera- tives (24), laborers (15), services (20)	services (22), laborers (15)
All other service workers	1,374	1,438	+ 64	105	—	—

Notes to Table A.2

aNet comparability measures the net effect of 1970 changes in definition of detailed occupations upon the 1960 ECLF in these occupations, expressed as a ratio of the original 1960 estimates (multiplied by 100).

bThe major gains and losses itemized add up to approximately 85 percent of the net definitional change (in column 4) and 95 percent of the gross change.

cIncludes electricians; brickmasons; excavating, grading; and road machinery operators; plumbers and pipefitters; structural metalworkers.

dIncludes railroad conductors; subway motormen, railroad brakemen, railroad switchmen, mine motormen, sailors and deck hands, boatmen and canalmen.

Sources: Adapted from unpublished Census Bureau tabulations and from John Priebe, Jean Heinkel, and Stanley Greene, 1970 Occupation and Industry Classification Systems in Terms of Their 1960 Occupation and Industry Elements, U.S. Department of Commerce, Bureau of the Census, Technical Paper 26 (Washington, D.C.: U.S. Government Printing Office, 1972).

TABLE A.3

Approximate Standard Error of Estimated Percentage—1/1,000 Sample

Estimated Percentage	Estimated Number of Persons or Households in Base of Percentage (in thousands)											
	25	50	100	250	500	1,000	2,500	5,000	10,000	25,000	50,000	100,000
1 or 99	—	1.4	1.0	0.6	0.4	0.31	0.20	0.14	0.10	0.06	0.04	0.03
2 or 98	2.8	2.0	1.4	0.9	0.6	0.44	0.28	0.20	0.14	0.09	0.06	0.04
5 or 95	4.4	3.1	2.2	1.4	1.0	0.69	0.44	0.31	0.22	0.14	0.10	0.07
10 or 90	6.0	4.2	3.0	1.9	1.3	0.95	0.60	0.42	0.30	0.19	0.13	0.10
15 or 85	7.1	5.0	3.6	2.3	1.6	1.13	0.71	0.51	0.36	0.23	0.16	0.11
20 or 80	8.0	5.7	4.0	2.5	1.8	1.26	0.80	0.57	0.40	0.25	0.18	0.13
25 or 75	8.7	6.1	4.3	2.7	1.9	1.37	0.87	0.61	0.43	0.27	0.19	0.14
35 or 65	9.5	6.7	4.8	3.0	2.1	1.51	0.95	0.67	0.48	0.30	0.21	0.15
50	10.0	7.1	5.0	3.2	2.2	1.58	1.00	0.71	0.50	0.32	0.22	0.16

Source: U.S. Department of Commerce, Bureau of the Census, Public Use Samples of Basic Records from the 1970 Census: Description and Technical Documentation (Washington, D.C.: U.S. Government Printing Office, 1972), p. 187.

NOTES

1. John A. Priebe, Jean Heinkel, and Stanley Greene, <u>1970 Occupation and Industry Classification Systems in Terms of Their 1960 Occupation and Industry Elements</u>, U.S. Department of Commerce, Bureau of the Census, Technical Paper 26 (Washington, D. C. : U.S. Government Printing Office, 1972).

2. Ibid. , table A.

BOOKS

Bennett, Marion T. American Immigration Policies. Washington, D.C.: Public Affairs Press, 1963.

Berg, Ivar. Education and Jobs: The Great Training Robbery. New York: Praeger, 1970.

Blau, Peter M., and Otis D. Duncan. The American Occupational Structure. New York: John Wiley, 1967.

Blauner, Robert. "Work Satisfaction and Industrial Trends in Modern Society." In Labor and Trade Unionism: An Interdisciplinary Reader, edited by Walter Galenson and Seymour M. Lipset. New York: John Wiley and Sons, 1960.

Bohning, W.R. and D. Maillat. The Effects of Employment on Foreign Workers. Paris: Organization for Economic Cooperation and Development, 1974.

Brecher, Charles. Upgrading Blue Collar and Service Workers. Policy Studies in Employment and Welfare. Baltimore: Johns Hopkins Press, 1972.

Cairnes, John E. Some Leading Principles of Political Economy, Newly Expounded. New York: Hargward Brothers, 1874.

Carnegie Commission on Higher Education. Priorities for Action: Final Report of the Carnegie Commission on Higher Education. New York: McGraw-Hill, 1973.

Commons, John R. et al. History of Labor in the United States. New York: Macmillan, 1935.

Davies, A.F. "Prestige of Occupations." In Man, Work and Society, edited by Sigmund Nosow and William H. Form. New York: Basic Books, 1962.

Doeringer, Peter B., and Michael J. Piore. Internal Labor Markets and Manpower Analysis. Lexington, Mass.: D. C. Heath, 1971.

Douglas, Paul. Real Wages in the United States, 1890–1926. 1930. Reprint. Clifton, N. J.: Augusta M. Kelley.

Drake, St. Clair, and Horace R. Cayton. Black Metropolis. New York: Harcourt, Brace, 1945.

Fine, Sidney A. The 1965 Third Edition of the Dictionary of Occupational Titles—Contents, Contrasts, and Critique. Kalamazoo: W. E. Upjohn Institute for Employment Research, 1968.

Fishel, Leslie H., Jr., and Benjamin Quarles. The Black American: A Documentary History. New York: William Morrow and Co., 1970.

Fuchs, Victor R. Changes in the Location of Manufacturing in the United States Since 1929. New Haven: Yale University Press, 1962.

Ginzberg, Eli, and Douglas W. Bray. The Uneducated. New York: Columbia University Press, 1953.

Glazer, Nathan, and Daniel P. Moynihan. Beyond the Melting Pot: The Negroes, Puerto Ricans, Jews, Italians and Irish of New York City. Cambridge, Mass.: MIT Press, 1963.

Gordon, David M. Economic Theories of Poverty and Underemployment. Lexington, Mass.: Lexington Books, 1972.

Haber, D., and H. Levinson. Production and Productivity in the Building Trades. Ann Arbor: University of Michigan Press, 1956.

Hatt, Paul K., and C. C. North. "Prestige Ratings of Occupations." In Man, Work and Society, edited by Sigmund Nosow and William H. Form. New York: Basic Books, 1962.

Hiestand, Dale L. Economic Growth and Employment Opportunities for Minorities. New York: Columbia University Press, 1964.

Hutchinson, Edward P. Immigrants and Their Children: 1850–1950. Census Monograph Series. New York: John Wiley, 1956.

Kahn, Robert. "The Meaning of Work: Interpretation and Proposals for Measurement." In Human Meaning of Social Change, edited by Angus Campbell and Philip E. Converse. New York: Russell Sage Foundation, 1972.

Kayser, Bernard. Manpower Movements and Labor Markets. Paris: Organization for Economic Cooperation and Development, 1971.

Kendrick, John W. Productivity Trends in the United States. Princeton: Princeton University Press, 1961.

Lebergott, Stanley. Manpower in Economic Growth: The American Record Since 1800. New York: McGraw-Hill, 1964.

Levine, Louis. The Women's Garment Workers. New York: B.W. Huebisch, 1927.

Marshall, Alfred. Principles of Economics. 8th ed. London: Macmillan, 1961.

Marshall, F. Ray, and Vernon M. Briggs, Jr. The Negro and Apprenticeship. Baltimore: Johns Hopkins Press, 1967.

National Planning Association, Upgrading Low-Level Employment: A Major National Challenge. Report no. 141. Washington, D.C.: National Planning Association, 1975.

North, David S. and William G. Weissert. Immigrants and the American Labor Market. Washington, D.C.: Trans Century, 1973.

Okun, Arthur M. "Upward Mobility in a High-Pressure Economy." In Brookings Papers on Economic Activity, no. 1. Washington, D.C.: Brookings Institution, 1973.

Organization for Economic Cooperation and Development, Wages and Labor Mobility. Paris: Organization for Economic Cooperation and Development, 1965.

Quinn, Robert P., and Thomas W. Mangione. The 1969-1970 Survey of Working Conditions: Chronicles of an Unfinished Enterprise. Ann Arbor: University of Michigan Press, 1973.

Reynolds, Lloyd G., and Cynthia H. Taft. The Evolution of Wage Structure. New Haven: Yale University Press, 1956.

Scoville, James G. The Job Content of the American Economy, 1940–1970. New York: McGraw-Hill, 1969.

Smith, Adam. The Wealth of Nations. Bk. 1. New York: Random House, 1937.

Stephenson, George M. A History of American Immigration, 1820–1924. Boston: Ginn, 1926.

Stigler, George T. Domestic Servants in the United States, 1900–1940. Occasional Paper 24. New York: National Bureau of Economic Research, 1946.

Terkel, Studs. Working. New York: Pantheon Books, 1972.

Vernon, Raymond. Metropolis 1985: An Interpretation of the Findings of the New York Metropolitan Regional Study. Cambridge, Mass.: Harvard University Press, 1960.

Ware, Caroline T. The Early New England Cotton Manufacture: A Study in Industrial Beginnings. Boston: Houghton Mifflin, 1931.

Wool, Harold. The Military Specialist: Skilled Manpower for the Armed Forces. Baltimore: Johns Hopkins Press, 1968.

Work in America. Report of a Special Task Force to the Secretary of Health, Education and Welfare. Cambridge, Mass.: MIT Press, 1973.

Wrong, Elaine. The Negro in the Apparel Industry. Philadelphia: University of Pennsylvania Press, 1974.

Journal Articles

Akers, Donald S. "Immigration Data and National Population Estimates for the United States." Demography 4 (1967): 262–72.

Alterman, Jack. "The United States Economy in 1985: An Overview of BLS Projections." Monthly Labor Review 96 (December 1973): 3–7.

Ball, Robert and Larry Ludwig. "Labor Requirements for Construction of Single Family Housing." Monthly Labor Review 94 (September 1971): 12-14.

Bowen, Howard R. "Manpower Management and Higher Education." Educational Record 54 (1973): 5-14.

Construction Review, December 1969.

Foley, Eugene P. "The Negro Businessman." Daedalus 2 (1966): 107-44.

Gustman, Alan L., and Martin Segal. "The Skilled-Unskilled Wage Differential in Construction." Industrial and Labor Relations Review 27 (January 1974): 261-75.

Hayes, Marion. "A Century of Change: Negroes in the U.S. Economy, 1860-1960." Monthly Labor Review 85 (December 1962): 1359-65.

Johnston, Denis F. "Education of Workers: Projections to 1990." Monthly Labor Review 96 (November 1973): 22-31.

_____. "The U.S. Labor Force: Projections to 1990." Monthly Labor Review 96 (July 1973): 3-13.

Kutscher, Ronald E. "The United States Economy in 1985." Monthly Labor Review 96 (December 1973): 27-42.

Mattila, J. Peter. "The Effect of Extending Minimum Wages to Cover Household Maids." Journal of Human Resources 8 (1973): 365-82.

Personnel and Guidance Journal. Selected issues, 1946-75.

Reder, M.W. "The Theory of Occupational Wage Differentials." American Economic Review 45 (1955): 833-52.

Sackley, Arthur and Thomas W. Gavett. "Blue-Collar/White-Collar Pay Trends: Analysis of Occupational Wage Differences." Monthly Labor Review 94 (June 1971): 9-13.

Sheehan, Edward R.F. "Europe's Hired Poor." New York Times Magazine, December 9, 1973.

Swerdloff, Sol. "How Good Were Manpower Projections for the 1960's." Monthly Labor Review 88 (November 1969): 17-22.

U.S. Department of Commerce. Construction Review. Selected
    issues.

U.S. Department of Labor. Monthly Labor Review. Selected issues.

Public Documents

Diamond, Daniel E., and Hrach Bedrosian. Hiring Standards and
    Job Performance. Manpower Research Monograph no. 18 (U.S.
    Department of Labor). Washington, D.C.: U.S. Government
    Printing Office, 1970.

Economic Report of the President, 1973-1975. Washington, D.C.:
    U.S. Government Printing Office, 1975.

Edwards, Alba M. Comparative Occupational Statistics for the United
    States, 1870 to 1940. Washington, D.C.: U.S. Government
    Printing Office, 1943.

Kaplan, David L., and M. Claire Casey. Occupational Trends in the
    United States: 1890 to 1950. Census Working Paper no. 5.
    Washington, D.C.: U.S. Government Printing Office, 1958.

Keely, Charles B. "Immigration: Consideration of Trends, Prospects
    and Policy." In Demographic and Social Aspects of Population
    Growth. Commission on Population Growth and the American
    Future. Research Reports. Washington, D.C.: U.S. Govern-
    ment Printing Office, 1973.

Manpower Report of the President. Washington, D.C.: U.S. Govern-
    ment Printing Office. Annual issues, 1971-75.

Miller, Ann R. Occupations of the Labor Force According to the
    Dictionary of Occupational Titles. Statistical Evaluation Report
    no. 9. Office of Management and Budget. Washington, D.C.:
    U.S. Government Printing Office, 1971.

National Committee on Household Employment. National Pilot Pro-
    gram of Household Employment: Final Report of the Experimental
    and Demonstration Projects. Washington, D.C.: U.S. Govern-
    ment Printing Office, 1971.

Parnes, Herbert S. et al. Career Thresholds: A Longitudinal Study of the Educational and Labor Market Experience of Male Youth. Vol. 1. Manpower Research Monograph no. 16. U.S. Department of Labor. Washington, D.C.: U.S. Government Printing Office, 1971.

_____. The Pre-Retirement Years: A Longitudinal Study of the Labor Market Experience of Men. Vol. 1. Manpower Research Monograph no. 15. U.S. Department of Labor. Washington, D.C.: U.S. Government Printing Office, 1970.

_____. Years for Decision: A Longitudinal Study of the Educational and Labor Market Experience of Young Women. Vol. 1. Manpower Research Monograph no. 24. U.S. Department of Labor. Washington, D.C.: U.S. Government Printing Office, 1971.

Priebe, John A. et al. 1970 Occupation and Industry Classification Systems in Terms of Their 1960 Occupation and Industry Elements. U.S. Department of Commerce. Bureau of the Census. Washington, D.C.: U.S. Government Printing Office, 1972.

Report of the Select Commission on Western Hemisphere Immigration. Washington, D.C.: U.S. Government Printing Office, 1968.

Rosenthal, Neal, and Dixie Sommers. The Labor Supply for Lower-Level Occupations. Supplementary Reports, prepared for the U.S. Department of Labor under Grant No. 21-11-73-02. Washington, D.C.: June 1975. Mimeographed.

Statement by Leonard F. Chapman, Jr., Commissioner, Immigration and Naturalization Service, before the House Subcommittee on Immigration, Citizenship and International Law, Washington, D.C., February 4, 1975.

Taeuber, Irene B. "Growth of the Population of the United States in the Twentieth Century." In Demographic and Social Aspects of Population Growth. Vol. 1. Commission on Population Growth and the American Future. Research Reports. Washington, D.C.: U.S. Government Printing Office, 1973.

Testimony before the Commission on Population Growth and the American Future, by Manuel Aragon, Jr., Los Angeles, May 3, 1971.

U.S. Congress, House. Committee on the Judiciary. Amending the
    Immigration and Nationality Act, and for Other Purposes, Report
    to Accompany H.R. 16188. 92d Cong., 2d sess., 1973., H.
    Rept. 92-13-6.

_____. Committee on the Judiciary. Illegal Aliens. Hearings, 92d
    Cong. 2d sess., 1972, pp. 1255-1528.

U.S. Department of Agriculture. Farm Population Estimates, 1910-
    70. Statistical Bulletin no. 523. Washington, D.C.: U.S. Govern-
    ment Printing Office, 1973.

U.S. Department of Commerce. U.S. Industrial Outlook, 1974: With
    Projections to 1980. Washington, D.C.: U.S. Government
    Printing Office, 1973.

U.S. Department of Commerce, Bureau of the Census. Detailed
    Characteristics of the Population, Census of Population: 1950,
    1960, 1970. Washington, D.C., U.S. Government Printing
    Office, 1971.

_____. Census of Population, 1950. Special Report. "Occupational
    Characteristics." Final Report 1B. Washington, D.C.: U.S.
    Government Printing Office, 1956.

_____. Census of Population, 1950. Special Report. "Population
    Mobility—Farm-Nonfarm Movers." Final Report 4C. Washing-
    ton, D.C.: U.S. Government Printing Office, 1957.

_____. Census of Population, 1950. Special Report. "Education."
    Washington, D.C.: U.S. Government Printing Office, 1953.

_____. Census of Population, 1960. Subject Report. "Educational
    Attainment." Final Report PC(2)-5B. Washington, D.C.: U.S.
    Government Printing Office, 1963.

_____. Census of Population, 1960. Subject Report. "Occupational
    Characteristics." Final Report PC(2)-7A. Washington, D.C.:
    U.S. Government Printing Office, 1963.

_____. Census of Population, 1960. Subject Report. "Puerto Ricans
    in the United States." Final Report PC(2)-1D. Washington,
    D.C.: U.S. Government Printing Office, 1973.

_____. Census of Population, 1970. Subject Report. "Occupation by Industry." PC(2)-7C. Washington, D.C.: U.S. Government Printing Office, 1972.

_____. Census of Population, 1970. Subject Report. "Occupational Characteristics 1970." PC(2)-7A. Washington, D.C.: U.S. Government Printing Office, 1972.

_____. County Business Patterns, 1969. Washington, D.C.: U.S. Government Printing Office, 1970.

_____. Current Population Report. Series P-23, no. 38. "The Social and Economic Status of Negroes in the United States, 1970." Washington, D.C.: U.S. Government Printing Office, 1971.

_____. Current Population Reports. Series P-60, no. 39. "Income of Families and Persons in the United States: 1961." Washington, D.C.: U.S. Government Printing Office, 1963.

_____. Current Population Reports. Series P-60, no. 75. "Income in 1969 of Families and Persons in the United States." Washington, D.C.: U.S. Government Printing Office, 1970.

_____. Historial Statistics of the United States, Colonial Times to 1957. Washington, D.C.: U.S. Government Printing Office, 1960.

_____. Methodology and Scores of Socioeconomic Status. Working Paper no. 15. Washington, D.C.: U.S. Government Printing Office, 1963.

_____. Public Use Samples of Basic Records from the 1970 Census: Description and Technical Documentation. Washington, D.C.: U.S. Government Printing Office, 1972.

_____. Statistical Abstract of the United States, 1971. 92d ed. Washington, D.C.: U.S. Government Printing Office, 1971.

_____. U.S. Industrial Outlook, 1971. Washington, D.C.: U.S. Government Printing Office, 1970.

U.S. Department of Justice, Immigration and Naturalization Service. 1971 Annual Report. Washington, D.C.: U.S. Government Printing Office, 1972.

U.S. Department of Labor. Manpower Administration. Dictionary of Occupational Titles. vol. 1 3d ed. Washington, D.C.: U.S. Government Printing Office, 1965.

U.S. Department of Labor, Bureau of Labor Statistics. Educational Attainment of Workers, March 1969, 1970. Special Labor Force Report 125. Washington, D.C.: U.S. Government Printing Office 1971. Reprint. Monthly Labor Review, October 1970, pp. 9-16, supplementary tables.

_____. Employment and Earnings, United States, 1909-1970. BLS Bulletin 1312-7. Washington, D.C.: U.S. Government Printing Office, 1970.

_____. Employment and Earnings. Annual supp. (November 1961). Washington, D.C.: U.S. Government Printing Office, 1961.

_____. Employment and Earnings. Annual averages. January 1972, January 1973, January 1974. Washington, D.C.: U.S. Government Printing Office, 1972, 1973, 1974.

_____. Formal Occupational Training of Adult Workers: Its Extent, Nature, and Use. Manpower Automation Research Monograph no. 2. Washington, D.C.: U.S. Government Printing Office, 1964.

_____. Handbook of Labor Statistics, 1973. BLS Bulletin 1970. Washington, D.C.: U.S. Government Printing Office, 1974.

_____. Labor and Material Requirements for College Housing Construction. BLS Bulletin no. 1441. Washington, D.C.: U.S. Government Printing Office, 1965.

_____. Labor and Material Requirements for Hospital and Nursing Home Construction. BLS Bulletin 1661. Washington, D.C.: Government Printing Office, 1971.

_____. Labor and Material Requirements for Public Housing Construction. BLS Bulletin 1402. Washington, D.C.: U.S. Government Printing Office, 1964.

_____. Occupational Supply: Concepts and Sources of Data for Manpower Analysis. BLS Bulletin 1816. Washington, D.C.: U.S. Government Printing Office, 1974.

_____. Manpower Challenge of the 1960's. Washington, D.C.: U.S. Government Printing Office, 1970.

_____. Selected Earnings and Demographic Characteristics of Union Members, 1970. Report 417. Washington, D.C.: U.S. Government Printing Office, 1972.

_____. Survey of Consumer Expenditures 1960-61. Consumer Expenditures and Income: Urban United States, 1961. Supplement 3-Part C to BLS Report 237-38. Washington, D.C.: U.S. Government Printing Office, 1964.

U.S. Department of Labor, Employment Standards Administration. Private Household Workers. Washington, D.C.: U.S. Government Printing Office, 1974.

Newspaper Articles and Other Material

Chapman, William. "Mexican Illegals Now Seek U.S. Cities." Washington Post, December 9, 1973.

Duncan, Otis Dudley. "Socio-Economic Status Scores for Detailed Occupations." Mimeographed. Chicago: University of Chicago, Population Research and Training Center, 1961.

International Ladies Garment Workers Union. Report of the General Executive Board to the 35th Convention, New York, May 31, 1974. Mimeographed.

Laborers' International Union of North America. Laborers' Education and Training Pamphlet No. 27. Laborers' International Union of North America, 1972.

Northrup, Bowen. "Foreign Workers Still Flock to West Europe Despite Current Slump." Wall Street Journal. February 26, 1975. p. 1.

Siegal, Jacob S. "Estimates of Coverage of the Population by Sex, Race and Age in the 1970 Census." Paper presented at the annual meeting of the Population Association of America, New Orleans, April 26, 1973. Mimeographed.

Siegel, Paul M. "Prestige in the American Occupational Structure." Ph.D. dissertation, University of Chicago, 1971.

Survey Research Center, University of Michigan. Survey of Working Conditions. Ann Arbor: Survey Research Center, November 1970.

HAROLD WOOL is Associate Director of the Research Center of the National Planning Association in Washington, D. C., where he has been directing major studies in the human resources field since 1972. Dr. Wool retired from the federal civil service in 1972 after a 34-year career during which he held top manpower policy planning and research positions in the Departments of Labor and Defense. He is the author of one previous book, The Military Specialist, contributor to several other books, and has published numerous articles and monographs on both civilian and military manpower issues. Other professional activities have included affiliation with the National Bureau of Economic Research on a study of the Soviet Economy, and part-time lectureships at various universities in the Washington, D. C. area. He was born in New York City, received his undergraduate training at Brooklyn College and his doctoral degree in economics from the American University.

BRUCE D. PHILLIPS is Senior Regional Economist and Project Leader in Demographic Projections at the Bureau of Economic Analysis, Department of Commerce. He holds degrees from the University of Maryland and Queens College. Following graduate school, he participated in various government sponsored and foundation studies for the National Planning Association including a demand forecast of supersonic air travel and authored monographs on population distribution and regional projections. He has published articles in the American Economist, the Journal of Regional Science, The Urban Lawyer, and Projections Highlights; the last, a publication of the National Planning Association.

POLITICIZING THE POOR: The Legacy of the War
on Poverty in a Mexican American Community
                        Biliana C. S. Ambrecht

THE SCOPE OF BARGAINING IN PUBLIC
EMPLOYMENT
                        Joan Weitzman

A SURVEY OF PUERTO RICANS ON THE U.S.
MAINLAND IN THE 1970s
                        Kal Wagenheim

WORKER MILITANCY AND ITS CONSEQUENCES,
1965-75: New Directions in Western Industrial
Relations
                        edited by Solomon Barkin